ROUTLEDGE LIBRARY EDITIONS:
SOCIOLINGUISTICS

Volume 6

LANGUAGE IN INDENTURE

LANGUAGE IN INDENTURE

A Sociolinguistic History of Bhojpuri–Hindi in South Africa

RAJEND MESTHRIE

Routledge
Taylor & Francis Group
LONDON AND NEW YORK

First published in 1991 by Witwatersrand University Press and 1992 by Routledge

This edition first published in 2019
by Routledge
2 Park Square, Milton Park, Abingdon, Oxon OX14 4RN

and by Routledge
52 Vanderbilt Avenue, New York, NY 10017

Routledge is an imprint of the Taylor & Francis Group, an informa business

British Library Cataloguing in Publication Data
A catalogue record for this book is available from the British Library

ISBN: 978-1-138-34952-0 (Set)
ISBN: 978-0-429-43466-2 (Set) (ebk)
ISBN: 978-1-138-35255-1 (Volume 6) (hbk)
ISBN: 978-1-138-35289-6 (Volume 6) (pbk)
ISBN: 978-0-429-43470-9 (Volume 6) (ebk)

Publisher's Note
The publisher has gone to great lengths to ensure the quality of this reprint but points out that some imperfections in the original copies may be apparent.

Disclaimer
The publisher has made every effort to trace copyright holders and would welcome correspondence from those they have been unable to trace.

Language in Indenture

A Sociolinguistic History of Bhojpuri–Hindi in South Africa

Rajend Mesthrie

ROUTLEDGE

London and New York

First published in 1991 by
Witwatersrand University Press
1 Jan Smuts Avenue, Johannesburg, 2001 South Africa

First published 1992 in Great Britain by
Routledge
11 New Fetter Lane, London EC4P 4EE

Simultaneously published in the USA and Canada by
Routledge
A division of Routledge, Chapman and Hall, Inc.
29 West 35th Street, New York, NY 10001

British Library Cataloguing in Publication Data
Mesthrie, Rajend, *1954–*
Language in indenture
I. Title
494.8

Library of Congress Cataloging in Publication Data
A catalog record for this book is available on request
ISBN 0 415 06404 X

Cover design by Jeffrey Lok

Cover reproduction by Industrial Graphics, Johannesburg

Printed in the Republic of South Africa by The Natal Witness Printing and Publishing Company (Pty) Ltd, Pietermaritzburg

To my mother and the memory of my late father

CONTENTS

Acknowledgements ix

Abbreviations xi

Symbols xiv

Prologue xvii

Chapter One
The Historical Background 1

Chapter Two
Dialects in Contact 41

Chapter Three
The Socio-Historical Setting of Language Shift 106

Chapter Four
Language Contact and Language Change 140

Chapter Five
Language Obsolescence 201

Appendix A
A Skeleton Grammar of Indian Bhojpuri 241

Appendix B 282

Appendix C 304

Notes 308

Bibliography 313

Index 323

MAPS

1. Present-day India 4
2. The languages of India 9
3. Areas of origin of North Indian immigrants to Natal 20
4. Distribution of Bhojpuri speakers in South Africa – 1936 33
5. Distribution of Bhojpuri speakers in Natal – 1936 35
6. First and second person future endings in Natal 43
7. Third person future endings in Natal 44
8. Variants in the third person singular past transitive morpheme in Natal 46
9. Variants in the third person singular past intransitive morpheme 47
10. Variants in the first and second persons past tense 49
11. Distribution of past plural verb endings 50
12. Distribution of four lexical items 54

FIGURES

1. The relationship between Sanskrit and some modern Indic languages 12
2. Classification of the Indic languages 16
3. A comparison of six features in overseas varieties of Bhojpuri 76
4. Retention of SB in the family domain, according to gender and age-grouping 126

The author and the Witwatersrand University Press wish to thank the copyright holders for permission to use the following material:

Maps 1 and 2 from *The Indianisation of English: The English Language in India* by B.B. Kachru; Oxford University Press. Map 3 from Girmitiyas by Brij Lal; *Journal of Pacific History*. Figure 2 from *Languages in South Asia* by G.A. Zograph; Routledge. Table 1 from *Documents of Indentured Labour* by Y.S. Meer; The Institute for Black Research. Table 5 from *Gandhi: The South African Experience* by M. Swan; Ravan Press. Tables 22 and 30 from The East Indian Speech Community in Guyana: A Sociolinguistic Study with special reference to Koine Formation by M. Gambhir; the Author. Table 35 from The Social Stratification and Linguistic Diversity in the Bhojpuri Speech Community by R.B. Misra; the Author.

ACKNOWLEDGEMENTS

I am truly grateful to all those who served as informants for this study, for responding to my intrusions and queries with patience and interest, for sharing with me the story of their lives, and for the warm hospitality which always included at least a cup of tea. I regret that it is not possible to name each one individually (for there are too many of them).

Among the many friends and relatives who offered me sustenance and accommodation during field-trips all over Natal, I must thank Ramesh and Premilla Mungal of Pietermaritzburg, Mr and Mrs Badal of Stanger, Mr J. Pandit, also of Stanger, Mr and Mrs B. Maharaj of Ladysmith, Mr and Mrs H. Durgadin, Mr and Mrs B.C. Maharaj, and Mrs G.R. Maharaj, all of Newcastle, and the Mistrey families in Dannhauser.

Thanks are due to Mrs Bhaw and Mrs H.M. Singh of Durban for assistance in interviewing the more elderly informants, and to my former students who assisted in gathering valuable data: 'Bubbles' Juggan, Reena Singh, and Shakila Maharaj. To this list I must add Radhika Chowthee for data from remoter parts of Natal.

In Patna, Bihar I profited from discussions with Professors K.M. Tiwari and B. Varma, who also assisted me with organising some field-trips. I also thank their families for their hospitality. Professor R.N. Srivastava of Delhi University gave me the benefit of his knowledge of Indian sociolinguistics. Communication with scholars working on Bhojpuri in other parts of the world have proved stimulating — I thank Surendra Gambhir, Peggy Mohan, Sita Kishna, Kunti Ramdat, Richard Barz and Theo Damsteegt in this regard. For specific comments on the manuscript at various stages I am most grateful to Roger Lass and Dr R. Sitaram (the co-supervisors of the original thesis), Susan Wright and various readers. Above all, I have benefited from constructive suggestions by Jeff Siegel and Philip Baker.

A work like this invariably depends on others for its very existence: my reliance on Gambhir's work (in Chapter 2), on Dorian (in Chapter 5), on U.N. Tiwari (in Appendix A), and Sir George Grierson (throughout) will be apparent. In addition, I have found Peggy Mohan's thesis on Trinidad Bhojpuri and Jeff Siegel's sociolinguistic history of Fiji valuable, as well as Dominque's study in Mauritius, which first brought Bhojpuri to my attention.

The staff at the Don Africana and Killie Campbell libraries in Durban deserve special mention for their efficient services, as do those at the Natal Archives, Pietermaritzburg, and the African Studies Library, University of Cape Town.

The original research on which this book is based was facilitated by a grant from the Human Sciences Research Council. I also benefited from a travel grant from the Anglo American and De Beers Chairman's Fund, which enabled me to attend a conference at the University of the West Indies. Thanks are also due to Mr M. Keerath for his efforts on my behalf. Publication has been made possible thanks to generous grants from the University of Cape Town and the Human Sciences Research Council. Opinions expressed in this work are my own and are not to be attributed to any of the above sponsors.

My gratitude to Eve Horwitz of the Witwatersrand University Press, Jonathan Price of Routledge and Dr Rose Morris of the Human Sciences Research Council for their confidence in the manuscript at various stages of its development is immense.

Finally, my thanks go to my wife Uma, and my family in Durban and Umkomaas for their solid support at all times.

Author's Note

The Bhojpuri-Hindi of the title is a compromise to link the unfamiliar term *Bhojpuri* with the better-known *Hindi* for the prospective reader. I will not use the term again.

ABBREVIATIONS

ABL	ablative
ACC	accusative
AD	adessive
adj	adjective
affric	affricate
approx	approximant
asp	aspirate
aux	auxiliary
Awad	Awadhi
B	Bhojpuri
BPL	*Bihar Peasant Life*
CAUS	causative
CBH	Calcutta Bazaar Hindustani
Cent	central
CF	counter-factual
CLASS	classifier
COM	comitative
Comp	complement
Conj	conjunctive
CORR	correlative
DAT	dative
DEF	definite
DET	determiner
E	Eastern
EB	Eastern Bhojpuri
E. Hn	Eastern Hindi
Eng	English
F	Fanagalo
fem	feminine
FH	Fiji Hindi
fut	future
fric	fricative
GB	Guyanese Bhojpuri
GEN	genitive

H	High
HAB	habitual
Hn	Hindi
IB	Indian Bhojpuri
IMP	imperative
INCL	inclusive
INF	infinitive
INTERROG	interrogative
intrans	intransitive
IPA	International Phonetic Alphabet
L	Low
L1	first language
lit	literally
LOC	locative
LSI	*Linguistic Survey of India*
Maga	Magahi
Maith	Maithili
masc	masculine
MB	Mauritian Bhojpuri
MIA	Middle Indic
N	noun
NIA	New Indic
No	number
NOM	nominative
NP	noun phrase
O	object
OBL	oblique
OFS	older fluent speaker
OIA	Old Indic
Past P	past participle
pl.	plural
Pn	pronoun
PP	present participle
pres.	present
PURP	purposive
+R	honorific
−R	non-honorific
REFLEX	reflexive
REL	relative
RP	Received Pronunciation
S	subject

SA	South Africa
SB	South African Bhojpuri
SAE	South African English
SAIE	South African Indian English
sg	singular
SH	Sarnami Hindustani
Skt	Sanskrit
SS	semi-speaker
Std Eng	Standard English
Std Hn	Standard Hindi
SUBJ	subjunctive
TB	Trinidad Bhojpuri
trans.	transitive
V	verb
VN	verbal noun
VP	verb phrase
W	Western
WB	Western Bhojpuri
W. Hn	Western Hindi
YFS	young fluent speaker

SYMBOLS

In this text IPA symbols are used for phonetic descriptions, but a slightly different system of transliteration, based on western descriptions of Sanskrit and modern Indic languages, is used otherwise. The following is a list of the symbols and letters used in transliteration, their IPA equivalents, and a brief description of their values. (Symbols like (b), (e), and (s) whose IPA and transliterated values coincide are excluded.)

Trans-liter-ation	*IPA equi-valent*	*Description*	*Example from SB*
t	[t̪]	voiceless dental stop	*t*ār 'wire'
d	[d̪]	voiced dental stop	*d*ānā 'grain'
ś	[ʃ]	voiceless palatal fric.	*ś*eṭ 'shirt'
c	[tʃ]	voiceless alveopalatal affric.	*c*ār 'four'
ch	[tʃʰ]	voiceless alveopalatal *aspirated* affric.	*ch*ū- 'to touch'
j	[dʒ]	voiced alveopalatal affric.	*j*uttā 'shoe'
jh	[dʒʰ]	voiced alveopalatal *aspirated* affric.	*jh*ār- 'to sweep'
f	[ʋ̥]	voiceless labiodental approximant	sa*f*ā 'clean'
v	[ʋ]	voiced labiodental approximant	*V*ed (a proper name)
y	[j]	palatal semi-vowel	mai*y*ā 'mother'
h	[h]	voiceless glottal approx. (at end of syllables)	pato*h* 'daughter-in-law'
	[ɦ]	murmured glottal approx. (elsewhere)	*h*aṇḍī 'pot'

ph	[pʰ]	voiceless bilabial *aspirated* stop	*ph*ūl 'flower'
kh (etc)	[kʰ] (etc)	voiceless velar *aspirated* stop (etc)	*kh*ūn 'blood'
bh	[bʱ]	*murmured* bilabial stop	*bh*āī 'brother'
gh (etc)	[gʱ] (etc)	*murmured* velar stop (etc)	*gh*āū 'a sore'
ṭ	[ʈ]	*retroflex* voiceless stop	*ṭ*āngī 'axe'
ḍ	[ɖ]	*retroflex* voiced stop	*ḍ*ar 'fear'
ṛ (etc)	[ɽ] (etc)	retroflex voiced flap (etc)	ba*ṛ*ā 'big'
ṇ	[ɳ]	retroflex voiced nasal	tha*ṇḍ*ā 'cold'
ñ	[ɲ]	palatal nasal	pa*ñ*c 'public'
ī	[iː]	long high front vowel	t*ī*n 'three'
ā	[aː]	long low back vowel	kh*ā*- 'eat'
ã	[ã]	nasal low back vowel	h*ã*s- 'laugh'
ā̃ (etc)	[ãː] (etc)	long nasal low back vowel (etc)	gh*ā̃*s 'grass'

The following symbols also occur in the text:

ɬ	voiceless alveolar lateral fric.	Zulu *hl*akula 'to hoe'
ɫ	velarised lateral	English ca*ll*
θ	voiceless dental fricative	English *th*igh
ð	voiced dental fricative	English *th*y
ʒ	voiceless alveopalatal affric.	English plea*s*ure
ɾ	voiced alveolar flap	RP ve*r*y
ɝ̫	mid central rounded vowel	(IB dekh*á*- 'see')
ə	unstressed mid central vowel	English *a*go
æ	low front vowel	RP c*a*t
ɔː	rounded mid back vowel	RP ha*ll*
ɒ	rounded low back vowel	RP h*o*t
ï	centralised /i/	SAE b*i*t
a̤	murmured /a/ (etc)	SB bhāī 'brother'
i̥	voiceless /i/ (etc)	IB ā̃kh*i̥* 'eye'

PROLOGUE

This is not a study of the direct theoretical relationship between language and political activity. Rather it is one which examines the linguistic consequences of a political act within world capitalism: the export of human labour from one continent to another in a colonial plantation context. The study of the decline of the languages of African slaves in such a context, and the concomitant rise of pidgins and creoles in their stead, is one of the many high points of the discipline of sociolinguistics. As Sankoff (1979:24) has emphasised, the plantation system created a catastrophic break in linguistic tradition:

> It is difficult to conceive of another situation where people arrived with such a variety of native languages; where they were so cut off from their native language groups; where the size of no one language group was enough to insure its survival; where no second language was shared by enough people to serve as a useful vehicle of communication; and where the legitimate language was inaccessible to almost everyone.

Whilst African languages no longer survive in the New World, it is still possible to examine the evolution and obsolescence of the languages brought by indentured workers to those same plantations in the aftermath of abolition. This study focuses on a group of Indic languages and dialects transplanted to South Africa under indenture (1860–1911]. It treats of the formation of a distinct koine, and the events leading to its current demise.

CHAPTER ONE

THE HISTORICAL BACKGROUND

1.1 *INTRODUCTION*

Bhojpuri in South Africa is (like Tamil and Telugu, and possibly Urdu and Gujarati) a dying language: parents have for some time failed to ensure that it is transmitted to their children, most of whom are now growing up as English monolinguals, with some passive knowledge of Bhojpuri.

Regarding the history and structure of Bhojpuri nothing has been recorded – a statement which holds for all the 'transplanted' Indian languages of South Africa. Ignorance regarding its place of origin, grammar, evolution in South Africa, and its very name has been Bhojpuri's fate for most of the twentieth century (for it has always been misnamed *Hindi* in official notices, and by its latter-day speakers). The following sentiments expressed by Revd. French (1908:150) regarding the development of the language in Natal, are typical of this ignorance:

> The Hindustani which many of the Indians here speak is corrupted by Dutch, English, and Kaffir. The original indentured coolies were to a man illiterate, and early began to forget not only the grammatical construction of their tongue, but even the very words, with the result that the present race have a vocabulary of most limited dimensions, with no grammar or idioms.

The missionary's assumption that it was Hindustani[1] (which he had been exposed to in his service in Lahore) that was current in plantation fields of Natal led to his belief that it was a 'corrupted' language with no grammar and idioms. This attitude is all too readily expressed by priests, educated people captivated by Standard Hindi, and youngsters understandably eager for any explanation to rationalise their lack of competence in Bhojpuri. It is one of the tasks of this work to establish that it was Bhojpuri that was (and still is) spoken in Natal, and that the grammar of the language in Natal approximates fairly closely to the speech forms of rural north-east India of the nineteenth century. Once this has been done (and it will take two chapters, plus a lengthy appendix), a fair point of departure will have been established for an evaluation of its history in Natal, and of its eventual decline.

Far from being unworthy of serious study (as its detractors believe), South African Bhojpuri presents a partial history of its speakers, who are otherwise silent in the history of colonial Natal. Furthermore, it provides a linguistic and historical link between communities as far off as Trinidad, Guyana, Suriname, Mauritius, Fiji and Natal. Regarding its linguistic orientation, this is a case study in socio-historical linguistics, examining dialects and languages in contact, the nature of 'transported' subordinate languages, and the process of language obsolescence.

1.2 *THE MIGRATION TO NATAL*

Organisation of a system of indentured immigration of Indians began in the 1830s, after the abolition of slavery in the British Empire (1834) had brought about a shortage of manual labour in many colonies. The Indian government, entirely British-administered at that time, permitted the recruiting of Indian labourers by the sugar-planting colonies under certain conditions. Five-year contracts between the labourers and the colonial powers had to be drawn up; a Protector of Emigrants had to be appointed in each colony to supervise the terms of indenture; and recruitment of labourers had to be performed by natives of India, under the control of agents appointed by the colonies. Emigration was permitted from three ports only – Calcutta, Bombay and Madras. Colonies more distant than Mauritius had to guarantee a free return passage to workers who had served there for at least ten years (Thompson 1952:11). Under these conditions, thousands of Indians were shipped first to Mauritius (1834), then British Guyana (1838), Jamaica and Trinidad (1844), and later to St Lucia (1856) and Grenada (1858). In 1860 there were shipments to Réunion, Martinique and French Guyana (all French colonies), St Croix (a Danish colony), and Natal (a British colony). Immigration to Suriname and Fiji followed in the 1870s.

By the end of the 1850s planters in Natal, growing a variety of crops, faced a shortage of labour. The most obvious source, given the economics of colonisation, the indigenous, mainly Zulu-speaking population, had earlier been consigned to 'reserves' not readily accessible to the planters. Furthermore, agricultural work was not the prerogative of males in Zulu economic organisation at the time, and planters did not apparently think of employing the females, who were more accustomed to agricultural toil. Basuto workers and Amatonga labourers from Mozambique were recruited on some farms, but there was still a shortage of labour during peak season (Bhana and Brain 1984:12–13). Many Natal planters looked to India for the supply of cheap – and what they presumed to be – transient labour.

The first ship, *Truro*, carrying 330 Indian immigrants from Madras and its environs arrived on 16 November 1860 (Meer 1980:67). It was followed a few days later by the *Belvedere* from Calcutta. The departure of these, and subsequent emigrants, was not always voluntary. Revd C.F. Andrews, an associate of Mahatma Gandhi and himself very much involved in the welfare of the early Indians in Natal, said this of the indentured immigration system:

> . . . it was promoted and controlled by Government . . . Professional recruiters, who were paid a high price for each recruit, were licensed by the Government to go in and out among the village people in order to induce them to leave their homes and be sent abroad for the purpose of labour. This kind of immigration was all too frequently accompanied by deception on a large scale . . . It cannot be stated too clearly that such immigration is artificial in the

extreme. It must never be mistaken for the natural flow of the Indian People to foreign lands. Had it not been for the eagerness of the British Colonies to obtain cheap labour for their plantations, it would never have taken place at all. Indians would have stayed at home. It was Natal, Mauritius, Fiji, etc which wanted the government of India to send Indian labour, and not *vice-versa*. (Sannyasi and Chaturvedi 1931:28)

Map 1 — Present-day India

At the same time, it must be conceded that for many of the migrants employment in Natal held some flickering hope of escape from debt, failing crops, unemployment, problems with the law or within the family (so-called 'push factors').

The period of migration to Natal stretched from 1860 to 1911, with a temporary halt between 1866 and 1874. During this period 152 184 indentured workers had made the journey to a new life, the peak period of migration being between 1874 and 1885 (Meer 1980:311–2). Table 1 indicates the

TABLE 1
NUMBER OF INDENTURED INDIAN WORKERS ENTERING SOUTH AFRICA, 1860–1886

YEAR	CALCUTTA	MADRAS	TOTAL
1860	312	601	913
61	240	359	599
62	0	0	0
63	0	668	668
64	384	1 857	2 241
65	0	984	984
66	0	864	864
67–73	0	0	0
74	4 310	0	4 310
75	2 057	0	2 057
76	754	0	754
77	1 089	1 173	2 262
78	1 722	3 576	5 298
79	0	1 116	1 116
80	505	1 168	1 673
81	1 703	909	2 612
82	872	753	1 625
83	1 457	947	2 404
84	1 337	1 626	2 963
85	389	850	1 239
86	0	227	227
	17 131	17 678	34 809

Source: Meer 1980:311–312.

number of indentured workers arriving in Natal from Calcutta and Madras from 1860 to 1886.

The 1911 Census reports 149 791 Indians resident in South Africa in that year — 93 886 of whom were male; 63 776 of the total Indian population had been born on South African soil.

The bonded labourers soon found out that the new land was not the worker's paradise that many recruiters had made it out to be. Conditions of work in the early years were most unsatisfactory, as the high suicide rate bears out. Long working hours, inequitable male-female recruitment patterns, flogging, overcrowding in barracks, and poor pay have led more than one historian to remark that the main difference between the conditions of slavery and indentureship was that the latter was not for life (see, for example, Swan 1985:25–26; Palmer 1957:44).

Intitially this class of indentured labourers occupied the lowest rungs of Natal's socio-economic ladder – the word *coolie* denoting, at once, 'Indian' and 'indentured worker'. After the initial period of indenture was over (five years, later extended to ten), labourers were theoretically free to seek employment elsewhere, to re-indenture, to return to India (which many did),[2] or to take up farming on small plots of land allotted to those who had served for ten years. This last offer was withdrawn by 1891 (Kuper 1960:2). Imposition of taxes on 'free' Indians forced many to re-indenture. Unlike many other British colonies, Natal did offer opportunities for independent economic advancement: immigrants found small-scale vegetable and fruit production more profitable than labouring in the cane fields. As early as 1866 many Indians were being employed on the railways in various menial positions. By the end of the nineteenth century there were 1 317 Indian workers in the coal mines of Northern Natal, and thousands employed in jobs that were more rewarding than that of field-labourer – as waiters, hawkers, fishermen, domestics and so on (Bhana and Brain 1984:28).

Another group of Indian migrants came mainly via Bombay to Natal, from 1875 onwards. The group comprised Hindu and Muslim merchants, who arrived voluntarily with the intention of setting up small businesses in various parts of the province. These were the so-called 'passenger Indians', whose relative wealth and trading interests kept them apart socially, and sometimes politically, from the indentured Indian.

The earliest of these passenger Indians came from Mauritius, rather than directly from India (Palmer 1957:42–3). Links between Mauritius and Natal began in 1849 when Rathbone experimented with cane in Natal, bringing over four Indo-Mauritians, 'apparently the first Asiatics to work among cane in Natal' (Hattersley 1950:119). Rathbone subsequently brought over twenty-five Franco-Mauritian settlers wishing to cultivate sugar.

The Mauritian influence was extended considerably by the recruitment of about a thousand indentured Indians in the 1870s and '80s. The Protector's Report for 1876 mentions 'two to three hundred of such recruits who were chiefly employed in the construction of railway lines'. In the following year 316 Indo-Mauritian recruits arrived in Natal, while for 1878 the figure was 186. The final element in the Indo-Mauritian connection in Natal concerns a few teachers specially recruited in the 1880s to fill the gap for suitable teachers in the schools of the Indian Immigration School Board (Kannemeyer 1943:93).

The subsequent history of Indians in South Africa records the enormous influence of Mahatma Gandhi in their early politics, the fight for a less degrading status and greater economic rewards, as well as the fight against the threat of repatriation. Only in 1961 was permanent citizenship unambiguously guaranteed to Indian South Africans. Problems stemming from inequalities in a segregated society continue today, as they do for the majority of the populace.

Today very few Indians are still to be found in the canelands, and the descendants of the original settlers hold diverse positions, ranging from manual labourers to white-collar workers and entrepreneurs (some of whom themselves own small sugar estates). The financial outlook has improved over the last few decades, together with the level of education, the scale ranging from very poor illiterates, mainly in country districts, to the affluent in a few 'select' suburbs. Most traders were able to maintain close ties with India, both economic and social, to the extent of encouraging marriage between their offspring and natives of India, until this was banned by South African law in 1956. The descendants of indentured labourers on the other hand have virtually no contact with the villages their forefathers left behind. A visit to India is for most of them a fairly recent experience, made possible by an improved economic position. Those who have recently holidayed in India express mixed emotions about the experience – typically mixing awe at the grandeur of certain aspects of Indian religious life and culture with feelings of alienation from India's crowded cities and rural poverty.

The many families who chose to return to India in the 1930s and '40s did not find it easy to re-assimilate into village life, with its fine caste gradations and other restrictions (Sannyasi and Chaturvedi 1931). The original workers who had migrated to Natal had not all been of the same caste. There were members of all four caste groupings: *Brahman* (priests), *Kshatriya* (warriors), *Vaishya* (merchants), *Sudra* (workers), though the majority tended to be of a relatively 'low' caste. Kuper (1960:7) estimates the latter to be 60 per cent.[3] The new economic situation that the indentured labourer and his family found themselves in necessitated great changes in the caste structure.

Caste rules in India determined whom one socialised with, married, ate with, where one ate, what one ate, to whom one offered food, how one prayed, dressed and spoke. In Natal, however, people of all castes were expected to labour together, live in close proximity to each other, and share common facilities. Upon serving his contract the ex-indentured labourer could not simply return to his traditional caste-occupation, because that occupation presupposed a well-defined village system in which the role of one inhabitant complemented that of the others in a fine economic network. In addition, some caste-occupations were rendered obsolete in the new land – the oil-maker, popcorn-maker, and shepherd all had to look for more viable means of livelihood. Today caste lingers on as a memory, and there has been a levelling out of caste distinctions for all practical purposes (in terms of work opportunities, place of residence etc.). Caste does manifest itself, however, in the occasional ban on marriage by parents, between a so-called (and vaguely defined), 'high-caste' and 'low-caste' couple (usually by the 'high-caste' family).

1.3 *THE LANGUAGES OF INDIA*

A broad classification of the language families of India follows as a prelude to the discussion of the linguistic affiliations of the South Africa-bound migrants.

In present-day India there are, according to the 1961 census, 723 Indian languages, divided into 1 652 dialects. The

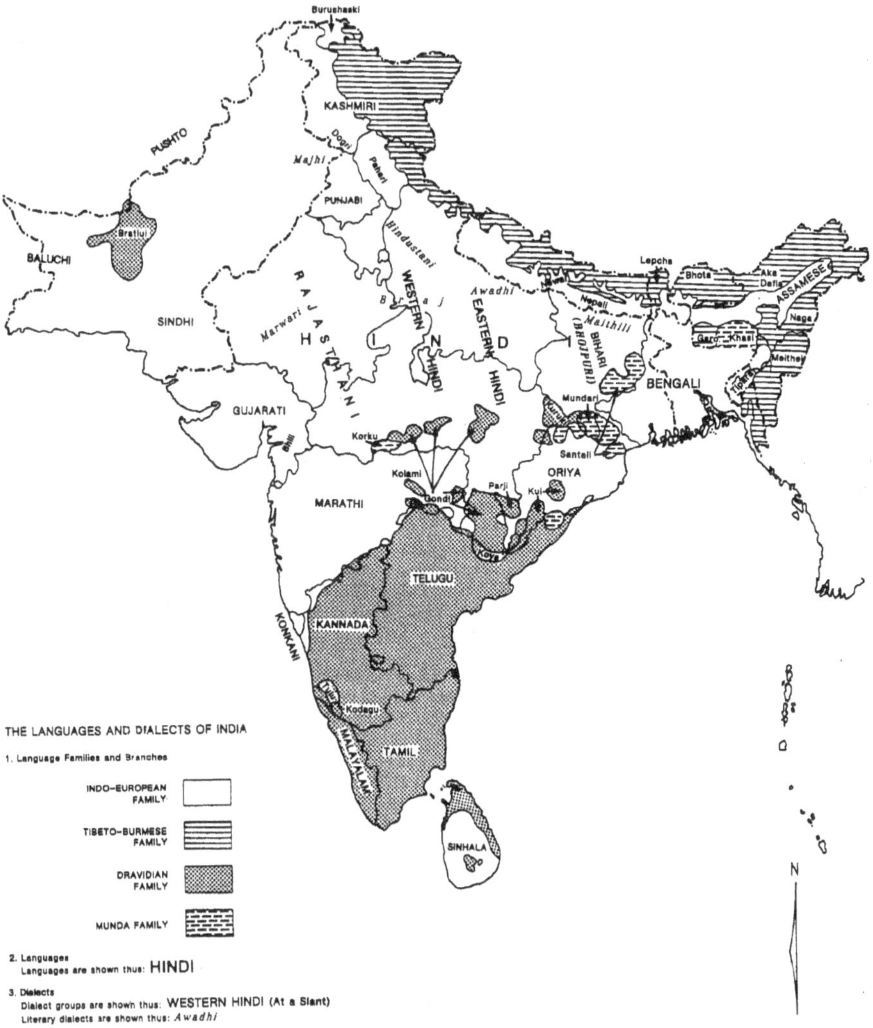

Source: KACHRU. 1983

Map 2—The languages of India

census also lists 103 'Non-Indian' languages, including important ones like English and Arabic. However only 50 of the Indian languages have over a hundred thousand speakers, 14 of which have more than ten million speakers each.[4] These languages (excluding immigrant languages of the recent past) can be divided into four major families:

(a) *The Indic family*, which covers most of north and central India, and includes Hindi–Urdu, Bengali, Panjabi, Kashmiri, Gujarati, Marathi etc., all of which are traceable eventually to Sanskrit – that Indo-European language brought to India around 1500 BC, or to related dialects – the Prakrits.

(b) *The Dravidian family*, which is today restricted mainly to the south, comprising Tamil, Telugu, Kannada, and Malayalam (all written languages), and many unwritten languages such as Toda, Kota, Tulu etc., some of which are in danger of extinction today. These languages all descend from a common ancestor language, dubbed *Proto-Dravidian*.

(c) *The Munda family*, which is perhaps the oldest language family in India, and includes languages like Santali, Mundari and Ho – spoken by so-called 'tribals' – and Nicobarese, spoken on the Andaman Islands. It is thought to be related to the Austro-Asiatic languages outside India – to Khmer, Malay, etc.

(d) *The Tibeto-Burman family*, which exists in the Himalayan region and areas bordering on Burma, comprising languages like Bhote, Khasi, and Ladhaki. In terms of the number of languages it contains, this is the most prolific family in India, though in terms of the total number of its speakers it is only third, almost fourth. It is generally accepted as belonging to a larger Sino-Tibetan family outside India.

Though historically unrelated and quite dissimilar in structure and vocabulary three thousand years ago, these languages have over time converged on account of their mutual influence over each other (Emeneau 1956).[5]

A simple example of convergence relates to the use of a set of retroflex consonants in most Indian languages, irrespective of the family they belong to. These are pronounced with the tip of the tongue curled back to strike hard against the back of the alveolar ridge, in contrast to a dental series, involving the tongue against the upper teeth. The retroflex series is usually cited as an example of the Dravidian family's influence on the sub-continent (for example, Burrow 1955:96–7). Some linguists believe it to be a Munda contribution, or a spontaneous development within certain branches of Indo-Iranian.

1.3.1 *The Indic languages*

As our concern in this study is with some languages belonging to the Indic family, a brief outline of the history of this group of languages might be useful. Although a detailed (paleo-historical) background is unnecessary in a socio-linguistic history of this sort, some knowledge of the place of the languages and dialects brought to Natal within the overall evolution of the Indic family is desirable, especially for those who believe South African Bhojpuri to be lacking in grammatical pedigree. Linguists outline three stages in the history of Indic (also known as *Indo-Aryan*): *Old Indic*, *Middle Indic*, and *New Indic* (often abbreviated to OIA, MIA, and NIA).[6]

Old Indic: This is the term for the aggregate of dialects spoken by those Indo-Europeans who came to India in several groups and over many generations around 1500 BC, which appear in literary form in ancient religious texts, the *Vedas*. Although the *Vedas* show signs of later editing by priests, they retain many archaic features uncharacteristic of later texts. The term *Vedic Sanskrit* (or just *Vedic*) is used to differentiate this literary language from its ensuing Sanskritic phase.

Sanskrit represents a literary development of some Old Indic dialects, and came to be the standard norm for writing, especially after Pāṇini's grammar, the *Aṣṭādhyāyī*, of the fourth century BC, completely specified its rules of usage. Literature in Sanskrit stretches from about the beginning of the first millenium BC (Epic Sanskrit of the *Rāmāyaṇa* and *Mahābhārata*) till well into the Middle Indic phase, Classical Sanskrit being a major written medium up to about AD 1000.

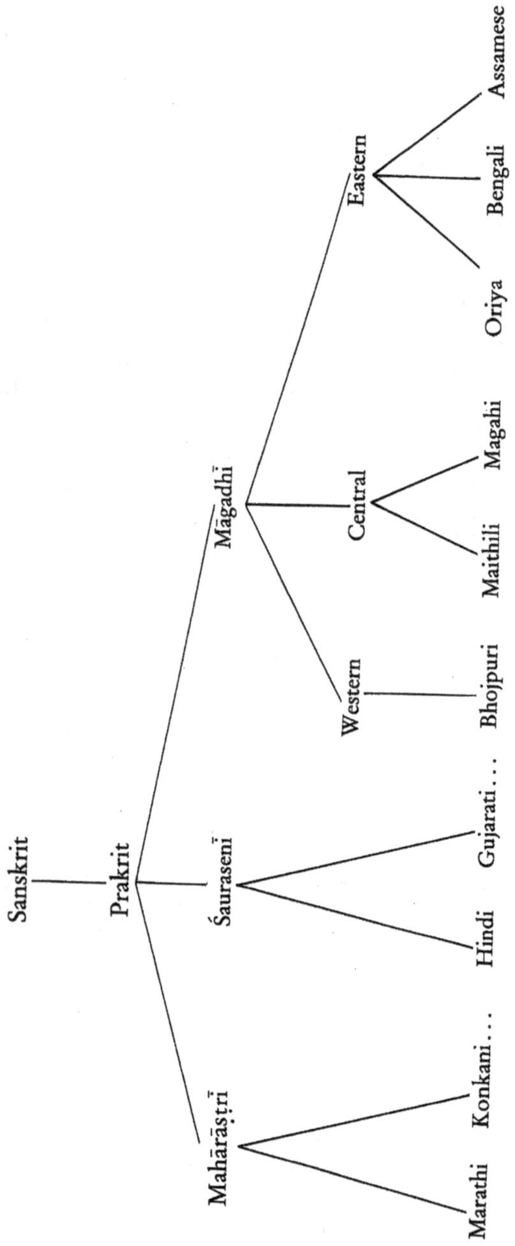

Figure 1 – The relationship between Sanskrit and some modern Indic languages.

Middle Indic: While Sanskrit remained perfected and unchanging as a literary medium for centuries, the spoken varieties of Old Indic continued changing, until by the middle of the first millenium BC we can speak of a new stage of the language – Middle Indic. Early in this period arose the Prakrits, developments of the spoken Old Indic dialects, with phonetic changes and variation in grammar that marked them off as being clearly different from Old Indic. These Prakrits were favoured by reform movements like Buddhism and Jainism because they were closer to the living speech of the majority than was Sanskrit, the language of orthodox Brahmanism. Prakrit is divided into three branches: i. Śaurasenī (or Central Prakrit) which was spoken in the central area between the Ganges and the Jumna; ii. Māgadhī (or Eastern Prakrit) spoken in Magadha (today's South Bihar); iii. Mahārāṣṭrī (Western Prakrit). Religious Prakrits based on these vernacular forms were favoured by the great reform movements. Ardha-Māgadhi is one such Prakrit, which was used in the Jain canonical literature, and Pālī the other, used in the Buddhist canon.

The Prakrits were still synthetic languages, like Sanskrit, but they show assimilation of conjunct consonants, and a great reduction in the number of case forms, noun classes, and verb forms. Towards the latter half of the Middle Indic period *c.* AD 500 the Prakrits themselves had become primarily associated with literature, and in ordinary speech the Apabhraṁśas took shape. (Etymologically *Apabhraṁśa* means 'corrupted or decayed speech', as opposed to *Samskrta* 'perfected' or 'polished', and *Prakrta* 'natural' or 'ordinary'.) They represent a spoken development of the Prakrits, but eventually came to be used for literary purposes as well, though to a lesser extent than Sanskrit. These Apabhraṁśas represent a transitional stage between the Prakrits and the modern languages of India.

New Indic: After AD 1000 differences between the various Apabhraṁśas intensified, resulting in the rise of many new vernaculars. These, too, came to be used as media for poetry and some prose: around 1200 Prithvi Raj Rasan was written in a form of Western Hindi; Narsimha Mehta's works, in an early form of Gujarati, are dated between 1415 and 1418;

while Tulasi Das's version of the *Rāmāyaṇa* in Early Awadhi dates to the sixteenth century. The New Indic phase is characterised by languages which are more analytic than their predecessors, which have fewer case forms, use a great number of postpositions, develop a system of compound verbs, and have an ergative or ergative-like construction in the past (see 2.9.1). In terms of lexis they contain a large core of items from non-Sanskritic sources: chiefly from Persian (which in many instances had itself borrowed them from Arabic) after the Muslim Conquest of India, and from indigenous languages of Dravidian and Munda origin (though loans from these two families are also to be found in Sanskrit, albeit to a lesser extent).

1.3.2 *Classification of the modern Indic languages*

Grierson's (1927) categorisation of the present-day vernaculars into three groups, based on historical origins as well as synchronic differences can be seen in Table 2.

TABLE 2
CLASSIFICATION OF THE INDIC LANGUAGES

A. OUTER SUB-BRANCH	C. INNER SUB-BRANCH
I. North-western Group	V. Central Group
1. Lahnda (or Western Panjabi)	9. Western Hindi (i.e. Hindi, Dakhini Hindi, Braj, Bangaru, Kanaujī, Bundeli)
2. Sindhi	10. Panjabi
II. Southern Group	11. Gujarati
3. Marathi	12. Bhili
III. Eastern Group	13. Khandesi
4. Oriya	14. Rajasthani
5. Bihari	VI. Pahari Group
6. Bengali	15. Eastern Pahari (or Nepali)
7. Assamese	16. Central Pahari
B. MEDIATE SUB-BRANCH	17. Western Pahari
IV. Mediate Group	
8. Eastern Hindi (i.e. Awadhi, Bagheli, Chatisgarhi)	

After Grierson 1927

The Inner languages descend from Śaurasenī Prakrit, and the Apabhraṁśas that arose from it. They differ from the Outer languages in having a less synthetic morphology; in their treatment of /s/ (which remains as [s], whereas it is changed to [ɦ] or [ʃ] in the Outer languages); in the absence of /l/ in the past participle suffix (with the exception of Gujarati); in the use of a passive construction with the past form of transitive verbs, and others (see Grierson 1927).

The Outer languages descend from various sources: The Eastern group from Magadhi Prakrit, Marathi from Mahārāṣṭrī Prakrit (which was a sub-division of Ardha-Māgadhī Prakrit, leaning more towards Māgadhī than Śaurasenī), while Sindhi and Lahnda, whose early histories are not entirely clear, seem to be derived from Apabhraṁśas which show Śaurasenī influence.

The Mediate group, comprising various dialects of Eastern Hindi, is descended from Ardha-Māgadhī. It shares some features with the Inner languages such as the absence of /l/ in the past participle suffix; and others with the Outer branch such as the treatment of transitive verbs via a passive construction in the past.

Grierson's classification, enormously influential, but not without its problems, tied as it is to a *Stammbaum* model of language evolution, and inconsistent in its criteria for the distinctions language/dialect and what he occasionally terms 'corrupt' or 'mixed speech' as against 'true' dialects, has been partially modified by a few scholars. Zograph's (1982) adaptation of Chatterji's (1926) refinement of Grierson is worthy of note. He discards the notion of an Inner and Outer core of languages, and repositions problematic cases like Gujarati and Bihari, as set out in Figure 2.

1.4 *THE LINGUISTIC SITUATION IN NATAL*

Migrants to Natal spoke languages belonging to either the Dravidian or Indic families; there are no traces of Munda or Tibeto-Burman languages ever being used locally. From the south, via Madras, came the Dravidian languages Tamil, Telugu, and Malayalam, the last having only a few score speakers. From the north, via Calcutta, came Bhojpuri, Hindi, Awadhi, Bengali, Panjabi and a few other languages. From the west, via Bombay, came Gujarati (in particular the Surti and Kathiawadi dialects) and Meman (a dialect of

I NORTHERN NIA LANGUAGES			
'WESTERN' TYPE		'EASTERN' TYPE	
WESTERN	CENTRAL	TRANSITIONAL	EASTERN
Sindhi Lahnda	Panjabi Hindi (with its western dialects)	Eastern dialects of Hindi Bihari languages	Oriya Bengali
Marathi Konkani	/Pahari/ Rajasthani	Nepali	Assamese
← Gujarati →			

III ROMANY	II SINHALESE

Figure 2. Classification of the Indic languages (after Zograph 1982)

Sindhi). In addition there was Urdu, the language mainly of indentured Muslims, and Konkani, a language historically related to Marathi. The earliest census reports (1911) are, unfortunately, quite unreliable for estimating the numbers of speakers of these languages.[7] By 1936 the only languages with a sizeable number of speakers were, in descending order: Tamil, 'Hindi', Gujarati, Telugu, and Urdu. Some figures for Indian languages, taken from various Population Census records, are set out in Table 3.

TABLE 3
NUMBER OF SPEAKERS OF INDIAN LANGUAGES IN SOUTH AFRICA, 1936–1980

	1936	1951	1960	1970	1980
Tamil	83 731	120 181	141 977	153 645	24 720
'Hindi'	60 276	89 145	126 067	116 485	25 900
Gujarati	25 408	39 495	53 910	46 039	25 120
Telugu	25 077	30 210	34 483	30 690	4 000
Urdu	13 842	25 455	35 789	–	13 280
Other	2 737	26 090	2 053	71 070	–

At the outset, these various groups (South Indian, North-east Indian, Gujarati, Urdu-speaking Muslim and others) were quite distinct culturally and linguistically. The Bhojpuri-speakers of the north knew no Tamil and vice versa. Gujarati-speaking traders quite often had some knowledge of Hindi. English, the official language of Natal, was unknown to the majority of indentured migrants. The Protectors' Reports of the nineteenth century frequently mention translation difficulties in both court and cane-field, since few interpreters had been brought over from India, and even fewer were competent in English as well as Tamil and Hindi.

Contact between indentured families on the fields and in the barracks resulted in some bilingualism amongst their children, especially in Bhojpuri and Tamil. In addition, Fanagalo – a pidginised form of Zulu, with a lexicon that drew from English, Afrikaans, and Zulu – was learned by the whole Indian community, for communication with Zulus and occasionally with employers (see 3.3). The acquisition of English was slower and less perfect. Women were slower than men in taking to English, lacking contact with native speakers of that language. Today in isolated communities one still finds one or two Indians (usually women), who are able to converse in Bhojpuri, Tamil and Fanagalo, but not English. There are also a few cases where the only common language between two elderly Indians, usually female, is not Tamil, Bhojpuri, or English (say), but Fanagalo. (Further discussion of the early socio-linguistic situation will be found in Chapter 3.)

Up to the last fifteen years, the various Indian linguistic groups have tended to keep apart socially as far as possible. In particular, marriages between persons of different language groups were rare, and generally met with disapproval from the respective communities. In spite of this, the outlook on life of most Indians growing up in South Africa in the twentieth century has been quite uniform. Education acted as a leveller, overriding linguistic and cultural differences to some extent, since it was conducted almost entirely in English and from a Western point of view.

The first fifty years of Indian education in South Africa was characterised by a lack of system (Kannemeyer 1943). In the early years English missionaries ran a few schools which admitted Indian pupils; subsequent progress in education was instigated by the Indians themselves, with some teachers being recruited from Mauritius and India. The medium of instruction in these schools was English, with no Indian languages featuring at all. Education was not always effective because of the high drop-out rate at an early age in favour of full-time jobs, the lack of well-educated teachers and the often tenuous relationship between subject matter emphasised in syllabuses and the life-style of the pupils. Reading, writing and arithmetic predominated, with a little grammar, geography and history in the larger schools (Kannemeyer 1943:108).

Vernacular education was in the beginning largely oral, with traditional wisdom and knowledge being passed on by elders. Religious and epic poetry was often learnt by heart and vernacular plays (especially in Tamil) were staged frequently. Vernacular classes were eventually introduced by various religious bodies each concerned with fostering the values and literature of a particular linguistic group, but these met with several difficulties pertaining to staffing, the establishment of suitable classrooms and attendance. The first Tamil school, for example, was established in Durban in 1899 (Kuppusami 1946:70). Such private schools were never numerous at any time. Kichlu (1928:31) records fifty private (vernacular) schools in Natal, maintained by the Indian community, a figure which includes both full-time and part-time schools. Many of these (about forty, according to Kichlu) were attached to mosques, using Gujarati as the medium of instruction, and in some cases Urdu. The full-time sectarian schools were eventually closed down on the recommendation of Indian educationists, and vernacular classes have since the 1930s been offered on a part-time basis in those areas where numbers warranted it (see further 3.5.4).

The increase in the use of English at school was accompanied by a decline in the use of the Indian languages, even in the home. There were only a few linguistically homogeneous neighbourhoods (for example, Indians residing in the inner city of Durban are still mainly Gujarati-speaking.) Some neighbourhoods inhabited by linguistically homogeneous groups of Indians were uprooted by the notorious Group Areas Act of 1950. Since then, for the most part, a Tamil-speaking household could be flanked by a Bhojpuri-speaking neighbour on one side and a Telugu-speaking family on the other.

Bughwan's survey (1970:39–99) suggests that the decline in use of Indian languages is part of a language shift towards the dominant language of the country. There have been a few attempts to stem the tide. After a trial period of a few years, Indian languages were introduced in about a hundred primary schools as an optional subject in 1984 (see 3.5). Prior to that Urdu and Arabic had been offered at a few schools catering for mainly Islamic students. The motivation for introducing Indian languages has been cultural rather than purely linguistic: the use of these languages is encouraged as a gateway to Hindu and Muslim culture which many perceive to be on the decline under Western influence. With regard to colloquial speech the effort is probably too late: it is not uncommon for attempts to be made to bolster an obsolescent language only after it has been eroded by another.

1.5 *NORTH INDIAN DIALECTS IN NATAL*

We now turn specifically to Bhojpuri – the Indian language with the second largest number of speakers in South Africa. Like the other languages, it is markedly on the decline – a fact reflected in Table 4, based on the census reports.

TABLE 4
NUMBER OF BHOJPURI SPEAKERS IN SOUTH AFRICA, 1936–1980

1936	1951	1960	1970	1980
60 276	89 145	126 067	116 485	25 900

The figure for 1980 shows a dramatic decrease from 1970; and if the census figures are reliable, the language would have lost 100 000 speakers in a decade. This is not the case, however. The figure for 1970 is the main cause of confusion, and would need to be halved. That is, the real decline had set in by the 1960s, and by 1970 less than half the members of a household claiming to be 'Hindi-speaking' actually used the language to any significant degree.

The 1980 figures are a fair reflection of mother-tongue usage, though one ought to bear in mind that there are almost as many speakers having Bhojpuri as a second language who are not included in the census count.

North Indian immigrants came from a vast geographical area, as Map 3 shows. The provinces that provided the most indentured workers were (in decreasing order): Bihar, Uttar Pradesh (formerly Agra and Oudh), Madhya Pradesh, Orissa and West Bengal. A few immigrants originated from further afield (Delhi, Kashmir, Panjab, Rajasthan, etc.) Table 5 gives the district of origin of a random sample of 1 384 immigrants,

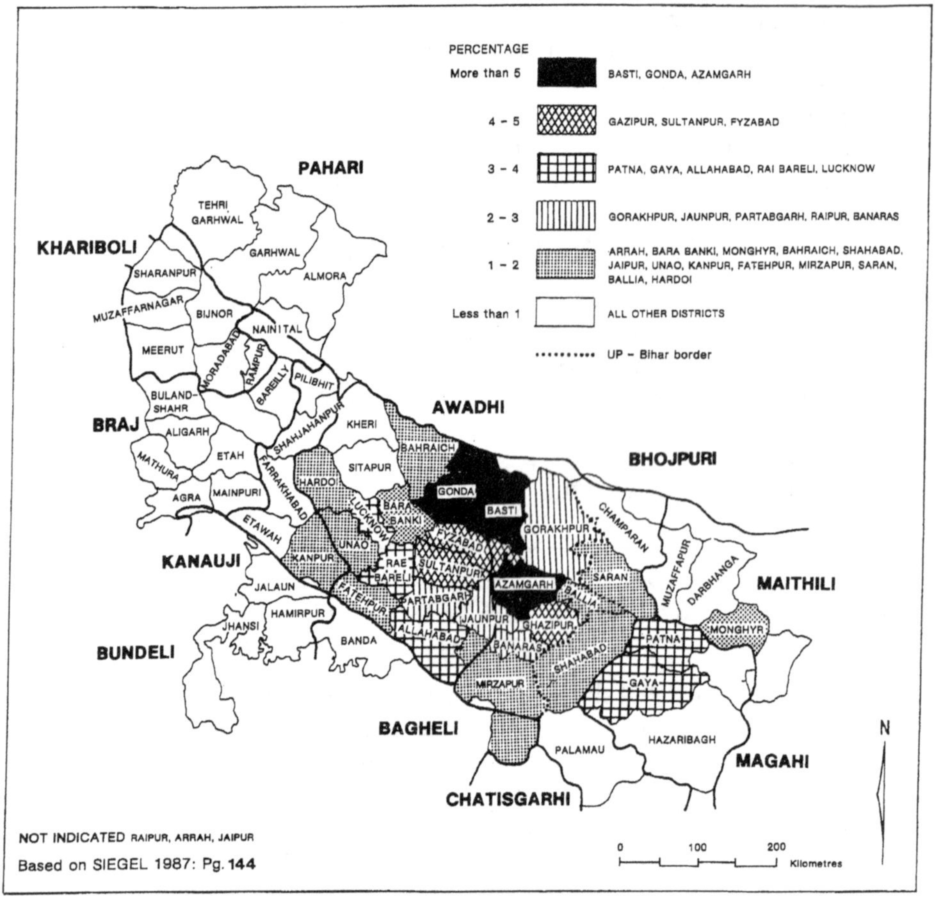

Map 3 — Areas of origin of North Indian immigrants to Natal and principal dialects

adapted from Swan (1985:284). The geographical locality of these districts is shown in Map 3.

Before discussing the languages brought to Natal from these areas, some comments about general language trends over North India are necessary. It would be a brave scholar who attempted to sort out all the terminological and taxonomic problems concerning Indian village dialects. Villagers themselves are sometimes vague about the name of their language, as emphasised by Grierson (1927:19):

> Just as M. Jourdain did not know that he had been speaking prose all his life, so the average Indian villager does not know that he has been speaking anything with a name attached to it. He can always put a name to the dialect spoken by somebody fifty miles off, but, – as for his own dialect, – 'O, that has no name. It is simply correct language.' It thus happens that most dialect names are not those given by the speakers, but those given by their neighbours, and are not always complimentary. For instance there is a well-known form of speech in the south of the Punjab called 'Jangali', from its being spoken in the 'Jungle' or unirrigated country bordering on Bikaner. But 'Jangali' also means 'boorish' and local inquiries failed to find a single person who admitted that he spoke that language. 'O yes, we know Jangali very well, – you will find it a little further on, – not here.' You go a little further on and get the same reply, and pursue your will-o'-wisp till he lands you in the Rajputana desert, where there is no one to speak any language at all.

Gumperz and Naim (1960) describe the relationship between village speech and regional languages rather well. They suggest that at the level of village speech there is a chain of mutually intelligible Indic varieties in North India, extending from the west coast to the east. Superposed above this chain are a variety of sub-regional dialects, which avoid the extreme localisms to be found in village speech, and are consequently understood over much wider areas. They are the native languages of the castes which traditionally engage in trade in

TABLE 5
PLACES OF ORIGIN OF A RANDOM SAMPLE OF 1 384 NORTH INDIAN IMMIGRANTS

Basti	98	Cawnpur	18	Sitapur	4	Lodhiana	2	Ganjam	1
Gonda	83	Fatehpur	18	Etah(?)	4	Jodhpur	2	Indore	1
Azamgarh	69	Mirzapur	16	Bhagalpur	4	Orai	2	Lahore	1
Gazipur	66	Saran	16	Chota Nagpur	4	Surat	2	Moradabad	1
Sultanpur	62	Ballia	15	Nawabgunj	3	Tikamgarh	2	Panipat	1
Fyzabad	55	Hardoi	15	Jhansi	3	Chittagong	1	Rohtak	1
Patna	52	Purulia	13	Mathura	3	Haripur	1	Darbhanga	1
Gaya	48	Farrukhabad	11	Meerut	3	Karauli	1	Midnapur	1
Allahabad	48	Muzaffarpur	11	Ajmere	3	Patiala	1	Bhopal	1
Rai Bareilly	46	Alwar	10	Gurgaon	3	Deoghar	1	Batia	1
Lucknow	45	Bareilly	9	Manipur	3	Bhumihar State(?)	1	Dinapur	1
Gorakpur	38	Chapra	9	Rewa	3	Delhi	1	Hoogly	1
Jaunpur	37	Hazaribagh	9	Pilibhit	3	Girdaspur	1	Kishangarh	1
Partabgarh	37	Hamirpur	8	Ayodhya	2	Kheri	1	Maksudabad	1
Raipur	37	Dholepur State(?)	7	Dattia	2	Kasbah	1	Purnea	1
Banaras	28	Nepal	7	Mymansing	2	Muzaffarnagar	1	Rampur	1
Arrah	25	Tirhut	7	Ambala	2	Ranchi	1	Sowuth	1
Barabanki	25	Agra	6	Badaun	2	Sirauhi	1	Dumka	1
Monghyr	24	Aligarh	6	Bankura	2	Cuttack	1	Samtar	1
Bahraich	23	Etawah	6	Bulandsahar	2	Jabbalpur	1	Songhat	1
Shahabad	23	Bharatpur	5	Hoshiarpur	2	Bardwan	1	Other	6
Jaipur	20	Shahjehanpur	5	Kalpi	2	Bundelkhand	1	Illegible	28
Unao	19	Gwalior	4	Banda	2	Dulamow	1		

Source: Swan 1985: 284

the small bazaar towns and larger city centres, catering for the needs of the rural population. These rural dwellers themselves employ such sub-regional dialects as a second speech style for trade and inter-group communication.

Superimposed on these regional dialects are the regional languages, which have been standardised with their own distinct scripts and literatures. The chief regional languages in North India are Panjabi, Hindi, Bengali, Gujarati, Marathi, Assamese and Oriya. There is some correspondence between state and language boundaries today. As the national language, Hindi is used more widely than the other languages. Native speakers of standard Hindi (or *Khaṛī Bolī*, as it is known) represent an educated urban minority, though a growing one. They are scattered over cities like New Delhi, Bombay, Calcutta, Hyderabad, but the heartland of Hindi comprises cities from Uttar Pradesh (Lucknow, Allahabad, Agra), Patna from Bihar, Jaipur from Rajasthan, and Bhopal from Madhya Pradesh. The presence of standard Hindi can be felt throughout India in newspapers, schools and universities, and on the radio.

In ascertaining which of these speech forms are relevant to the experience of indentureship in Natal, we must bear in mind the places of origin of the migrants. Swan's record (1985:284) of the places of origin of a random sample of 1 384 (of a total of about 60 000) workers who had embarked at Calcutta proves extremely useful in this regard (see Table 5). Her work suggests that it is to the village dialects of eastern Uttar Pradesh and western Bihar that we must look for the roots of South African Bhojpuri.

While the ships' lists record details like place of origin, age and identification marks of each migrant, no mention is made of home language. We are in the fortunate position of being able to work out the languages spoken by the indentured workers, by using the detailed linguistic maps of late nineteenth-century India provided by Grierson's *Linguistic Survey of India* (1903–1928, chiefly Vols V, VI, and IX). Assuming that the home language of an individual coincides with the predominant language of his home village, we arrive at the figures presented in Table 6.

In terms of Grierson's classification of the Indic languages by historical criteria four language groupings can be

TABLE 6
NUMBER OF SPEAKERS OF INDIVIDUAL DIALECTS AMONG THE ORIGINAL MIGRANTS (BASED ON A RANDOM SAMPLE)

DIALECT	NO. OF SPEAKERS
Bhojpuri	500
Awadhi	447
Magahi	97
Kanauji	69
Bengali	47
Standard Hindi	43
Chatisgarhi	39
Maithili	36
Rajasthani	17
Braj	14
Bundeli	13
Nepali	7
Bagheli	6
Oriya	3
Panjabi	3
Other (indeterminate)	43
	1 384

discerned here: Bihari, Eastern Hindi, Western Hindi, and 'other languages'. Although some points of Grierson's classification are in dispute today, his framework still provides a useful way of categorising the Natal-bound North Indian languages and dialects, as can be seen in Table 7.

The figures in Table 7 can only be regarded as approximate, since there are a number of problems involved in making such a calculation. The accuracy of the district of origin stated by a migrant wishing to escape his past might be called into question, and the assumption of one language per district is not always a safe one. (For example, did all the people who claimed Patna as their home district speak Magahi, the usual variety of the area, or were there some Bhojpuri speakers among them, as in present day India?) The position is not a hopeless one, however, since Grierson does give figures for different varieties within the same district, if there were

TABLE 7
LANGUAGE AFFILIATIONS OF THE ORIGINAL NORTH INDIAN MIGRANTS ACCORDING TO GRIERSON'S GROUPINGS (n = 1 384)

LANGUAGE	BREAKDOWN BY DIALECT		
Bihari	Bhojpuri	500	
	Magahi	97	
	Maithili	36	
		633	(46 %)
Eastern Hindi	Awadhi	447	
	Chatisgarhi	39	
	Bagheli	6	
		492	(36 %)
Western Hindi	Kanauji	69	
	Std Hn (Khari Boli)	43	
	Braj	14	
	Bundeli	13	
		139	(10 %)

OTHER LANGUAGES		
Bengali	47	(3 %)
Rajasthani	17	(1 %)
Nepali	7	(0,5 %)
Oriya	3	(0,2 %)
Panjabi	3	(0,2 %)
Indeterminate	43	(3 %)
	120	(8 %)

substantial numbers of these. The existence of a small proportion of Muslims (approximately 10 per cent) is a further complication, as a decision has to be made whether their first language was Urdu, Awadhi or the usual language of their district of origin. For convenience I have chosen the last option. Barz (1980) argues that what passes as Urdu in Mauritius has its roots in Bhojpuri. Likewise the Urdu of South Africans of indentured origins seems to be based on Bhojpuri, Awadhi and Dakhini Urdu. Finally, the figures do not include the thousand or so Indo-Mauritians who arrived as indentured workers in the 1870s and '80s. The majority of these were speakers of a variety of Bhojpuri (judging from present day Indo-Mauritian linguistic trends), and would also have had a command of Mauritian Creole.

Despite these caveats, it is clear that the Bihari group of dialects is the most important numerically in the shaping of a new South African brand of North Indian speech. In particular, the Bhojpuri dialect was the most important representative of the group, with the Awadhi dialect of Eastern Hindi being next in importance.

Not even the oldest speakers in South Africa use the terms *Bhojpuri* or *Awadhi*, however. The choice of label for the speech variety that is the subject of this book has, accordingly, not been easy. Any of the following could have been used: *Kalkatiyā bāt* (the term that older speakers use, based on the port of embarkation, Calcutta); *Hindi* (used by many speakers and in official sources); *Natali Hindi* (used by some commentators, such as Bughwan 1979) and Bhojpuri (since it is the base for the language used in Natal, as we shall see in Chapter 2). My choice of 'South African Bhojpuri' has been influenced by the terms used by linguists working with similar groups in ex-colonies elsewhere: *Mauritian Bhojpuri* (Domingue 1971), *Trinidad Bhojpuri* (Mohan 1978), and *Guyanese Bhojpuri* (Gambhir 1981).[8] Because the earliest recruitment of workers (to Mauritius, to British Guyana and to the other West Indian islands) had taken place in Bihar and eastern Uttar Pradesh, the heartland of the Bhojpuri language, the language spoken by these North Indians and their descendants in those new colonies is clearly Bhojpuri, albeit a mixture of related dialects. By the late nineteenth century recruiters, no longer finding it easy to attract enough people from Bihar, had to go further inland into western Uttar Pradesh, the domain of Awadhi and related Eastern Hindi dialects (Saha 1970:28–9). The transplanted languages in South Africa and Fiji (to which recruitment began in 1860 and 1879 respectively) therefore show greater influence from languages other than Bhojpuri. Moag (1977:v), discussing the Fijian situation, claims that this influence makes the language quite unlike any particular regional Indian language or dialect, and accordingly prefers the term *Fiji Hindi*. I have settled on *South African Bhojpuri* (hereafter SB), because, although the Awadhi influence is strong in some parts of the country, there is some justification for considering Bhojpuri to be the base, as I will show in Chapter 2. It would be incorrect, though, to think of SB as an offshoot of Indian Bhojpuri alone.

Although Table 7 suggests that speakers of Awadhi came a close second to speakers of Bhojpuri in terms of their numerical input in Natal, Bhojpuri seems to have played a more important role in the formation of the speech variety that evolved in Natal. One of the reasons for this is that the earlier years of immigration, crucial to the new speech form, involved greater proportions of Bhojpuri speakers. This can be gauged from a scrutiny of the computerised records of the ships' lists made by the History Department of the University of Durban-Westville. In 1860, the first year, the home district claimed by 27 per cent of the 341 people who had embarked ship at Calcutta was Purulia, making Bengali the most spoken North Indian language in Natal for a brief and insignificant period. Tables 8 and 9 give the breakdown for the first three, and twenty-one years respectively. (The first twenty-one years include a period of nine consecutive years and three other years when there were no shipments from Calcutta.).

The input into SB can be compared with the other variety for which a similar calculation has been made, Fiji Hindi (Siegel 1987:141). Siegel's estimates of 35,4 per cent for Bhojpuri and 32,9 per cent for Awadhi are virtually identical to the South African figures. His figures for the other Bihari dialects are lower (6 per cent as opposed to 10 per cent in South Africa), and for the Western Hindi contribution are higher (15 per cent, as opposed to 10 per cent in South Africa). In Chapter 2 we shall see that the South African speech form does not stray significantly from a Bhojpuri base, whereas Fiji Hindi does. Why this should be so must remain a question for future study, though a partial answer will be provided in 2.5.

TABLE 8
PROPORTIONS OF NORTH INDIAN LANGUAGES BROUGHT TO NATAL, 1860–1862
(Percentages to the nearest whole number; n = 970)

LANGUAGE GROUP	BREAKDOWN BY DIALECT		
Bihari	Bhojpuri	43	
	Magahi	20	
	Maithili	4	68
Eastern Hindi	Awadhi	13	13
Western Hindi	Std Hindi (Khari Boli)	1	1
Other Languages			
Bengali	14		
Indeterminate and minor contributors	4	18	

A brief characterisation of some of the varieties mentioned in Tables 7–9 is necessary here, since the majority of them are unknown outside India. *Bihari* is a cover term for three varieties spoken chiefly in the state of Bihar (Bhojpuri, Maithili and Magahi). The term is really a linguist's construct, since people claim one of its sub-varieties as their home language, and do not use *Bihari* as a linguistic term. According to the 1970 census of India there were 16 805 691 native speakers of 'Bihari', making it the tenth most widely spoken 'language' in the country. This figure probably needs to be increased by several millions to gain a truer picture, since many who receive their education in Standard Hindi claim that language as mother tongue instead of Bihari. Writing in 1903, Grierson indicates the number of Bhojpuri speakers alone to be twenty million, while Shukla (1968:ix) states that Bhojpuri had thirty million speakers in 1968. Tiwari (1960:xxv) characterises the function of Bhojpuri as follows:

> Bhojpuri is a language which is very much alive. Although the primary and secondary education in the Bhojpuri area is imparted through the medium of the Standard Hindi and Urdu and the literary language is Hindi and Urdu, yet Bhojpuri occupies a place of honour and prestige in the hearts of its speakers. The oral explanation of difficult portions in Hindi and Urdu is frequently made in class in Bhojpuri when teachers and students both are Bhojpuri speakers. The students, both in their classrooms and outside, talk to each other in Bhojpuri and they would even address the teacher in the mother tongue in the lower classes.

The name *Bhojpuri* is derived from *Bhojpūr*, once an important old town in western Bihar. *Bhoj* denotes the warrior clan of rulers of the city in earlier times – the Ujjaini Bhojas, while *pūr* is the word for 'town', common

TABLE 9
PROPORTION OF NORTH INDIAN LANGUAGES BROUGHT TO NATAL 1860–1880
(Percentages to the nearest whole number; n = 10 957)

LANGUAGE GROUP	BREAKDOWN BY DIALECT		
Bihari	Bhojpuri	40	
	Magahi	13	
	Maithili	3	57
Eastern Hindi	Awadhi	20	
	Bagheli	1	
	Other	1	22
Western Hindi	Kanauji	3	
	Other	1	4
Other Languages			
Nepali	1		
Indeterminate and minor contributors	15	16	

throughout the country. In time, when the fame of this clan spread, the entire area to the south took its name from the town, while the term *Bhojpuri* gradually came to refer to the people as well as the speech of the surrounding areas, on account of the fame of the Bhojpur *Rajputs* (or warrior-rulers) in Mughal times (Tiwari 1960:xxiii). The Bhojpuri area today covers most of north Bihar as well as eastern Uttar Pradesh.

Bhojpuri does not have a great literary tradition, unlike its sister dialects, Maithili, which has an established literature, and Magahi, once prestigious as the language variety favoured by the Buddha and his followers. However, many folk-songs, poems, short stories, and folk-dramas are often written down and are becoming increasingly popular in print. The script employed in recording Bhojpuri is the *Kaithi*, an adaptation of the *Devanāgarī*, also used extensively in the state of Gujarat, though more recently writers and printers are making greater use of the *Devanāgarī* script, to bring their literature in line with Hindi.

The other dialect featuring prominently in the language history of Natal, Awadhi, is grouped by Grierson together with Bagheli and Chatisgarhi under the cover term 'Eastern Hindi', an intermediate variety between Western Hindi and the Eastern group of Bihari, Bengali, Oriya etc. The term *Awadhi* denotes the language of Awadh (or Oudh), one of the old provinces of the north, which together with the former province of Agra is today known as *Uttar Pradesh* ('North Province'). Awadhi is spoken throughout central Uttar Pradesh, with the exception of a few districts in which Bhojpuri prevails. In addition, Awadhi is the vernacular language of many Muslims living in areas where a Bihari dialect predominates. Oudh is famous for its ancient capital, Ayodhya – birthplace of the hero Rama, whose exploits are celebrated in epic literature and folk-song, much of which was composed in the language of the area. Tulasi Das wrote his verson of the *Rāmāyaṇa* in Awadhi in the late sixteenth century. Although Awadhi is not an official state language today, it is still looked upon as a natural vehicle of epic verse, including – among others – the standard vernacular translation of the Sanskrit *Mahābhārata*.

We must clarify the nature of Bhojpuri and the other

varieties like Awadhi. Is Bhojpuri a language or a dialect, and, if the latter, is it a dialect of Hindi or some abstract language we have termed 'Bihari'? The concepts of *language* and *dialect* have always been troublesome ones for linguists, since they are often dependent upon extra-linguistic factors, chiefly political ones. It is a linguistic commonplace to point out that what count as separate languages in one area may be treated as dialects of the same language elsewhere (see Trudgill 1980:5–13). Hudson (1980:37) goes so far as to despair of using the terms dialect and language in a scientific manner. On linguistic grounds alone, Bhojpuri may be said to be independent of Hindi, since they derive from different branches of Middle Indic. We have seen in Table 2 that Bhojpuri belongs to a set of languages (Grierson's *Bihari*) which may be grouped with Bengali rather than Hindi. Social and political facts, however, suggest otherwise, for Bhojpuri exists in an area which has long been under the influence of Hindi as formal and literary language. Tiwari (1960:xvii) writes, 'At the present moment Hindi is overshadowing Bhojpuri as the language of education and public life'.

Co-existence with Hindi has made Bhojpuri seem to its speakers to be a kind of Hindi. Zograph (1982:31) is thus able to say, 'Understood in a wide sense, Hindi is often taken to include the dialects of Bihar – Bhojpuri, Maithili and Magahi – which also lie in the effective sphere of Literary Hindi'. In Chambers and Trudgill's terms (1980:10–11) Bhojpuri is heteronomous with standard Hindi, even though scientific classification may tell another story. Grierson himself was aware of the discrepancy between his classification and the socio-geographical realities. All family ties and traditions, he wrote (1903:1) pointed to the west (the domain of Hindi) rather than the east where Bengal lay. Siegel (1987:138) handles the problematic Hindi–Bhojpuri relationship by considering the latter to belong to a sub-system of Hindi. Barz (1980:3–4) differentiates between standard Hindi in a narrow sense and the more general 'Hindi language family' (which would include varieties like Bhojpuri and Rajasthani). 'Language family' in this sense clashes with the more established usage of the term in historical linguistics, showing up the tension once again between historical and functional classifications of language.

Like Barz, I would argue that Bhojpuri may at a pinch be considered a kind of Hindi, possibly a dialect of Hindi, provided that we are quite clear that we are here referring to Hindi in a very general sense, and that the characterisation should not lead to viewing Bhojpuri as some kind of substandard version of (standard) Hindi.

1.6 *LOCATION OF SOUTH AFRICAN BHOJPURI*

The indentured Indian of nineteenth-century Natal, initially restricted to working on sugar and sometimes coffee plantations, found on completion of his contract that there was some scope for individual economic development. There were ready markets for small-scale farmers planting fruits and vegetables (Ginwala 1974:77). Others resumed their traditional village occupations as tailors, cobblers, cooks, launderers and artisans. Some forms of employment which took them further into the interior were railway work (as early as 1866), and coal-mining in northern Natal. By the end of the nineteenth century there were as many as 1 317 Indian workers on the mines, the earliest of whom had been recruited directly from India (Bhana and Brain 1984:28). Some left the British colony of Natal in search of employment in the gold and diamond fields of the Transvaal and Orange Free State, until the free movement of Indians was restricted at the turn of the century. By 1911 there were 3 121 male and 1 055 female Indian wage workers in the Transvaal, a minority of whom were SB speakers. Their numbers were sufficiently large, however, for Swami Bhawani Dayal to open a Hindi school in Germiston on a part-time basis in 1914 (Rambiritch 1960:68). Residence in the Orange Free State has been barred since 1891 and Indians living there in the twentieth century have been a mere handful. In the Cape the Indian population is still a small one. The earliest of these had been sent there directly from India, while others followed early (in the 1880s) to such jobs as catering and running retail stores after completing their indentureship in Natal.

Map 4 illustrates the distribution of SB speakers for 1936. It shows that the Cape is negligible as a linguistic area for SB, with only two centres having more than a hundred speakers

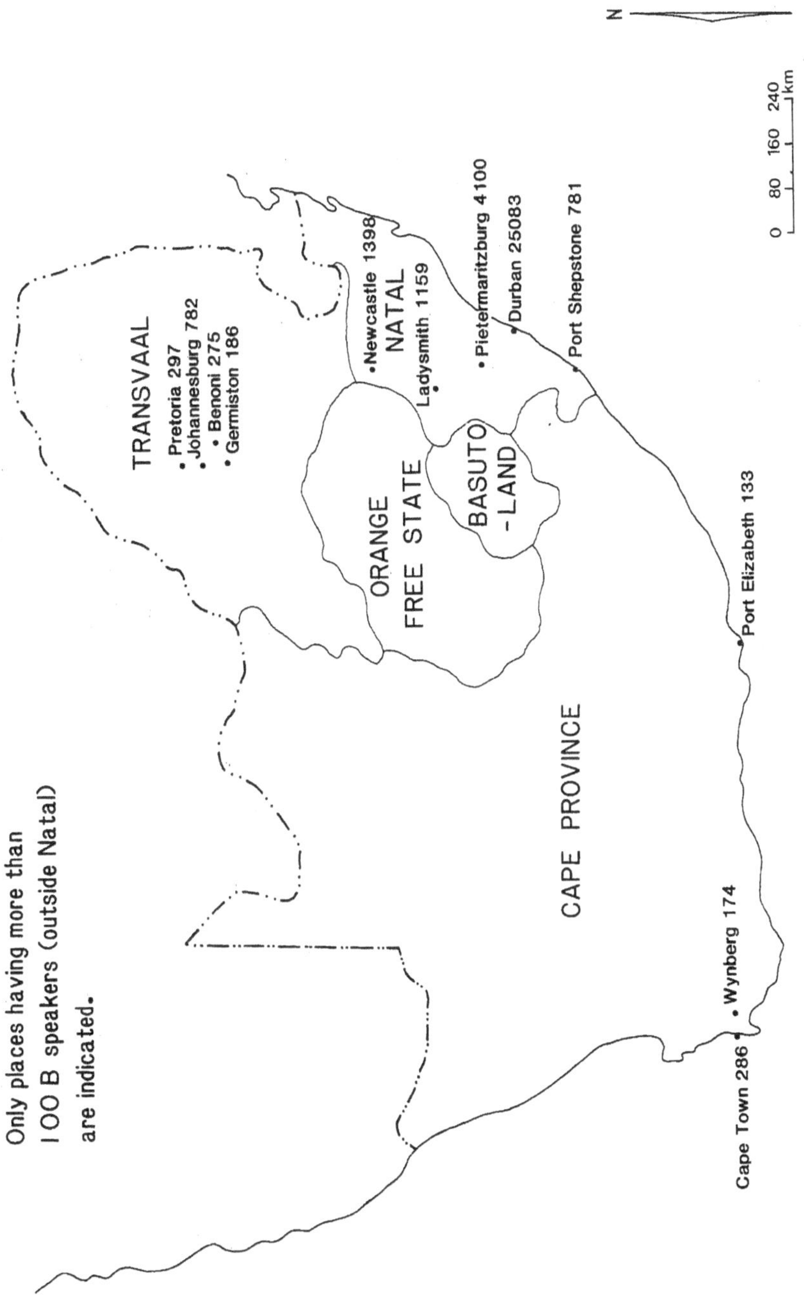

Map 4—Distribution of Bhojpuri speakers in South Africa, 1936

in 1936 – Cape Town and Port Elizabeth – and that only a few urban centres in the Transvaal need be considered. The 1970 figures in Table 10 reflect ethnic identity (descendants of Bhojpuri-speaking settlers), rather than linguistic reality, since they include a number of people, mainly children, who do not actively use the language. The increased figures for 1960 in the Cape and Transvaal are a result of the movements of younger people filling vacancies in both governmental jobs – especially teaching – and private industry. They are often resident for short periods only (less than a decade), and very seldom use an Indian language in the new environment.

TABLE 10
PROVINCIAL DISTRIBUTION OF SOUTH AFRICAN BHOJPURI SPEAKERS, 1936–1970

	1936	1951	1960	1970
Natal	56 489	86 588	116 566	114 584
Transvaal	2 228	2 091	7 043	1 730
Cape Province	1 533	460	2 458	171
Orange Free State	6	6	0	0
Total	60 256*	89 145	126 067	116 485

* The census records give 60 276 here.

In the Transvaal and Cape, Bhojpuri has come into contact with chiefly English and Afrikaans. In Natal it exists side by side with English, other Indian languages, Fanagalo and Zulu. The language was, until recently, equally distributed between farm and city. In 1936, for example, the census records that there were 24 564 'Hindi' speakers in rural areas, as compared to 35 712 in urban dwellings. This ratio of 5:7 for rural to urban speakers was the highest for a local Indian language. The other ratios were: Tamil 3:5; Telugu 3:5; Gujarati 1:5; Urdu 1:11. The 1970 ratios demonstrate a shift to urban areas: Bhojpuri 1:3; Tamil 1:4; Telugu 1:5; Gujarati 1:22.[8]

In most areas of Natal, SB tends to be the second most widely spoken Indian language after Tamil. In the Transvaal and Cape it trails behind Gujarati and Tamil. Notable

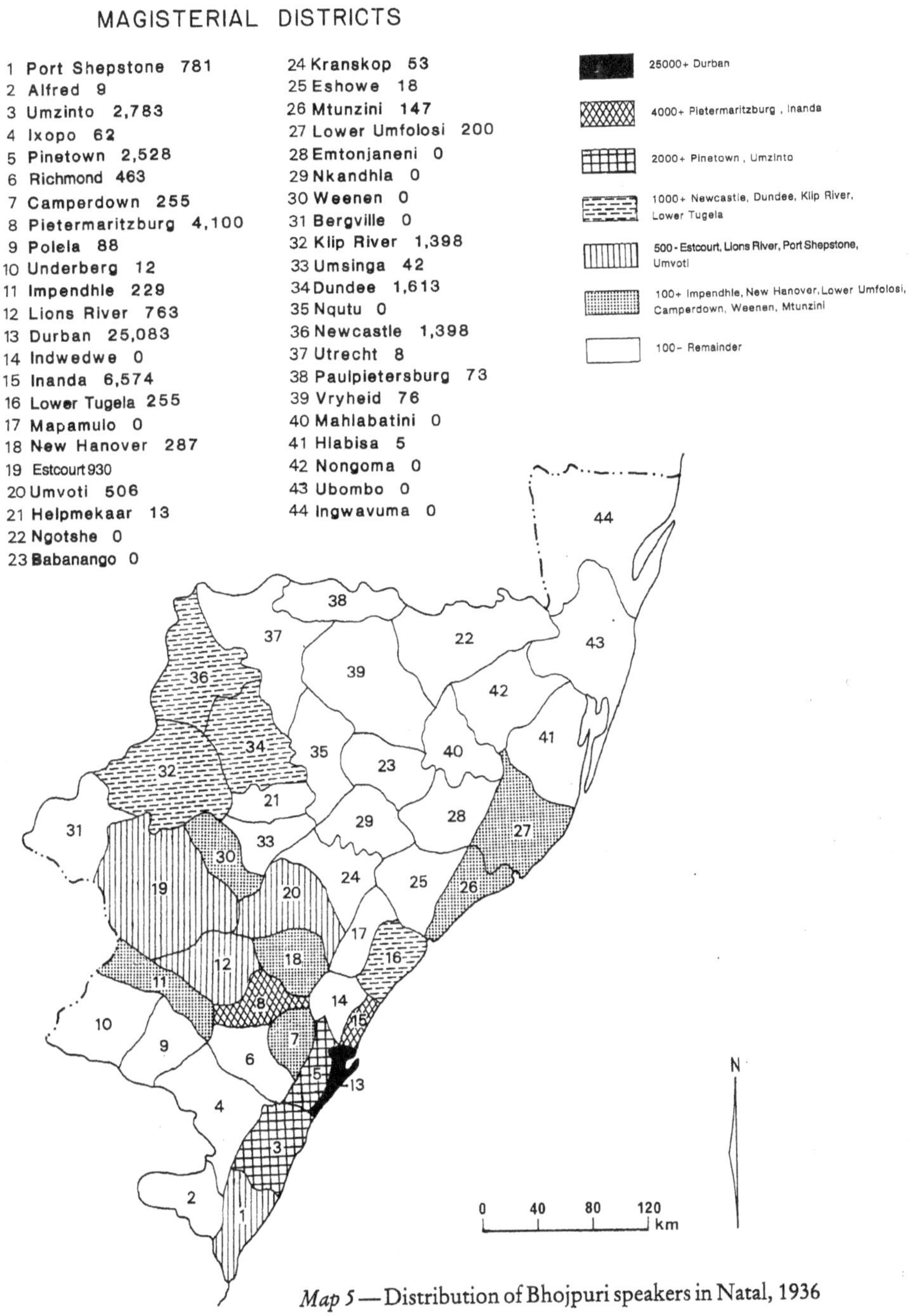
MAGISTERIAL DISTRICTS
1 Port Shepstone 781
2 Alfred 9
3 Umzinto 2,783
4 Ixopo 62
5 Pinetown 2,528
6 Richmond 463
7 Camperdown 255
8 Pietermaritzburg 4,100
9 Polela 88
10 Underberg 12
11 Impendhle 229
12 Lions River 763
13 Durban 25,083
14 Indwedwe 0
15 Inanda 6,574
16 Lower Tugela 255
17 Mapamulo 0
18 New Hanover 287
19 Estcourt 930
20 Umvoti 506
21 Helpmekaar 13
22 Ngotshe 0
23 Babanango 0
24 Kranskop 53
25 Eshowe 18
26 Mtunzini 147
27 Lower Umfolosi 200
28 Emtonjaneni 0
29 Nkandhla 0
30 Weenen 0
31 Bergville 0
32 Klip River 1,398
33 Umsinga 42
34 Dundee 1,613
35 Nqutu 0
36 Newcastle 1,398
37 Utrecht 8
38 Paulpietersburg 73
39 Vryheid 76
40 Mahlabatini 0
41 Hlabisa 5
42 Nongoma 0
43 Ubombo 0
44 Ingwavuma 0
25000+ Durban
4000+ Pietermaritzburg, Inanda
2000+ Pinetown, Umzinto
1000+ Newcastle, Dundee, Klip River, Lower Tugela
500- Estcourt, Lions River, Port Shepstone, Umvoti
100+ Impendhle, New Hanover, Lower Umfolosi, Camperdown, Weenen, Mtunzini
100- Remainder
0 40 80 120 km
N

Map 5 — Distribution of Bhojpuri speakers in Natal, 1936

exceptions are in northern Natal, KwaZulu, and a few rural areas in southern Natal (for example, Louisiana in Port Shepstone). In the northern Natal city of Newcastle, for example, the 1970 census records 2 391 'Hindi' (Bhojpuri) speakers, 605 Gujarati, 415 Tamil, and 13 Telugu speakers. Bhojpuri is, according to that census, the most spoken Indian language in the following areas: KwaZulu, Camperdown, Richmond, Pietermaritzburg, Dannhauser, Dundee, Glencoe, Newcastle, Ladysmith, Weenen, Lions River, Mooi River, and Estcourt. The 1970 figures for Pietermaritzburg, for example, are: 6 753 for 'Hindi', 4 510 for Tamil, 1 368 for Gujarati, 324 for Telugu and 3 318 for other Indian languages.

1.7 GATHERING OF DATA

Descriptions of SB in this study are based primarily on fieldwork undertaken in Natal from January 1982 to September 1984. During this period I interviewed 182 fluent speakers from most parts of Natal, wherever there were sizeable Bhojpuri-speaking communities. The interviews were as informal as possible, and spontaneous in so far as very few were conducted by prior arrangement. There were very few refusals, and most families were eager to assist in a project related to language and culture, despite some initial shyness about disclosing aspects of their lives and speech habits. Two factors facilitated the gathering of reliable data at the informal end of the speech spectrum: firstly, the interviewer was governed by the same speech norms as most of the interviewees – colloquial (Indian) English and colloquial 'kitchen Hindi' (Bhojpuri), rather than formal English and standard Hindi; secondly at the time of the interviews a fair amount of publicity had been given to the possibility of introducing Indian languages into the curriculum of full-time schools. This made the interview situation seem less of a novelty than it might otherwise have been.

In each town I visited a minimum of fifteen homes, and many more in the larger cities. I took care to interview people from newer suburbs as well as from poorer 'housing schemes'. In addition, in places unfamiliar to me I was often directed by residents to feeder rural areas, where older, more settled communities exist. Interviews were initiated in colloquial (Indian) English (the natural medium of communication in this speech community between a young outsider and a person under fifty), unless the person who answered the door appeared to be well over fifty. For such older informants I used Bhojpuri, and enlisted the aid of other family members in setting up an informal interview. In this way I was able to neutralise any significant influence from my own (Coastal) dialect. Older informants were encouraged to talk about their family histories, present and past occupations, and any other topic that took their fancy. This proved quite successful in eliciting natural speech, with apparently very few interviewees inhibited by the presence of a tape-recorder. Those who were naturally reticent were asked to narrate a *khīsā* ('folk-tale'), which yielded longer pieces of continuous data.

Informants under fifty, generally more fluent in English than Bhojpuri, were asked to orally translate a word list and a series of sentences from English into 'Hindi' (SB). This proved useful in eliciting morphological data (especially for dialect study) and phonological information in a short space of time. No inferences concerning syntax were made from these, since some speakers showed the influence of the English phraseology in their translations. All observations of a syntactic nature in this study are drawn from spontaneous conversation or from non-translated narratives.

From channel cues (which included crying in two interviews and laughter in many others) it was obvious that most interviews were sociolinguistically successful. Younger speakers, however, sometimes treated the translation section as something of a test to be passed, and were often determined not to be tripped up. One problematic area, which led to some interviews having to be disregarded, was that a few speakers preferred to answer in standard Hindi (however difficult and unnatural for them), rather than the Bhojpuri they actually used at home. It was obvious that they were not responding in their vernacular (as the term is used by Labov 1972:208), from the erratic forms they used, and the hesitations and false starts. On the other hand, there were a few who had a command of standard Hindi derived from prolonged trips to India, from formal study of the language, or in their capacities as priests. Their speech samples also had to be discarded for the purpose of this study.

In another ten instances students and friends of mine made tape recordings of conversations in their homes when there were mainly elders about, ensuring that Bhojpuri, not English, would predominantly be used. Since this was often done covertly, it provided more informal data than the interviews I had conducted – and useful information on code-switching.

The ethics of such covert recording could be called into question (see, for example, Milroy 1987:87–93). My assumption was (and still is) that the families of students and friends of mine would not object to being used as unwitting subjects, if the data were treated in confidence and if the project were of some use to the community being studied.

These figures exclude fifteen younger (and less fluent) speakers, for whom a slightly different interview procedure and questionnaire were used (see 5.5). Finally, by taking advantage of my own speech networks and privately noting down patterns of usage in the homes of relatives and other acquaintances, I was able to gather much information regarding all aspects of SB, especially semantic change and the use of loanwords. This proved the best way of circumventing what Labov (1972:209) has described as the Observer's Paradox: that the linguist wishes to observe the kind of speech that people use when they are not being observed.

The size and structure of the sample is given in Table 11. Certain imbalances in the sample were unavoidable. Women (especially housewives) were more easily available for interviews than men. Men in outside employment by day often proved reluctant interviewees. As SB is more often spoken in the home, and by women (see 3.5 where a detailed analysis of speech networks within twenty families is presented), the male-female ratio in the sample might not be an unrealistic one.

Although the figures indicate many more urban interviewees than rural ones, one should take into account that many of the former had been brought up in a rural environment. The low percentage of informants under the age of thirty reflects the rarity of fluent speakers in this age-group (see Chapter 5). The level of education in English of

TABLE 11
SIZE AND STRUCTURE OF THE SAMPLE

TOTAL NUMBER INTERVIEWED	
Detailed informal conversation	28
By participant observation	8
Quick questionnaire interview	146
n =	182
	%*
PLACE OF RESIDENCE	
Upland Natal	25
Midland Natal	37
Coastal Natal	37
Rural Natal	26
Urban Natal	74
GENDER	
Female	70
Male	30
AGE	
Over 70	7
60–69	19
50–59	34
40–49	19
30–39	17
Under 30	4
No information	1
OCCUPATION	
Housewives	61
Blue collar jobs	15
Clerks	5
Private businesses	5
Farming	4
Priests	4
Teachers (in English schools)	3
Unemployed	3
HINDI EDUCATION (PART-TIME)	
4 years or more	16
1–3 years	17
No education	65
No information	2

* To the nearest whole number.

the informants was not fully analysed; the majority, however, had only four to six years of full-time schooling, while many older interviewees had had no formal education. Only a few of the younger ones had had a high school or college education.

CHAPTER TWO

DIALECTS IN CONTACT

2.1 *INTRODUCTION*

In this chapter I shall delineate the characteristic features of South African Bhojpuri before its decline, emphasising grammatical choices arising from contact between speakers of related North Indian dialects and languages. One of my aims is to demonstrate that SB is structurally continuous with Indian Bhojpuri (IB henceforth). For ease of reference I have appended a skeleton grammar of IB, containing items discussed in this chapter (Appendix A). Core structures of IB are also listed there, to convince sceptics that SB really does have a grammatical basis, and is not some degenerate form of standard Hindi (Std Hn). I will also examine the contribution of non-Bhojpurian varieties to SB, and in this way place SB within the spectrum of overseas varieties of Bhojpuri (B).

2.2 *DIALECTS OF BHOJPURI IN NATAL*

SB is today fairly uniform, considering the great diversity of regional forms initially brought in by indentured immigrants. Some morphological and lexical variation exists along regional lines in present-day Natal, however. There are two distinct dialect areas – Coastal Natal and the Uplands of Natal, with a third intermediate area in the Natal Midlands. Such regional variation has not been reported for the other transplanted Bhojpuris.[1]

2.2.1 *Variation in the future tense of the verb*

There are two sets of future endings for the verb in SB, one involving *-ab* (1st person), *-be* (2nd person), and *-ī* (3rd person); the other involving *-egā* (all persons), with an alternative in *ī* for the third person. Thus the SB form for 'I will see' is either *ham dekhab* or *ham dekhegā*; and for 'you (sg) will see' is either *tū dekhbe* or *tū dekhegā*. The future in *-b* is most often heard in the Durban–Pinetown area, and all along the Natal coast wherever SB is spoken. In this area only a handful who are influenced by Std Hn norms use the *-egā* future. Furthest inland and in northern Natal (the 'Uplands') the characteristic future ending for the first and second persons is *-egā*, an ending which alternates with *-ī* in the 3rd person.

In the Midlands of Natal both *-b* and *-egā* futures are used by roughly the same number of speakers, with a speaker generally using one form and not the other in casual conversation. In the 3rd person *-ī* forms predominate over *-egā*, though the latter occurs with greater frequency in the Midlands than on the Coast.

Tables 12 and 13 show that the preference for one form over the other is not categorical in any area. The distribution

TABLE 12
REGIONAL VARIATION IN THE USE OF FIRST AND SECOND PERSON FUTURE ENDINGS (Percentages)

ENDING	COASTAL NATAL	MIDLANDS	UPLANDS
-b	87	56	10
-egā	13	44	90
n =	60	45	42

TABLE 13
REGIONAL VARIATION IN THE USE OF THIRD PERSON FUTURE ENDINGS (Percentages)

ENDING	COASTAL NATAL	MIDLANDS	UPLANDS
-ī	91	84	50
-egā	9	16	50
n =	46	32	28

of forms, is wave-like, rather than discrete. The 10 per cent who used the *-b* future (1st and 2nd person) in the Uplands, for example, were either recent arrivals from Coastal Natal, or people living close to the Midlands. Thus Estcourt and Mooi River had noticeably more *-b* endings than cities furthest north like Newcastle and Ladysmith. Note that two maps are required to characterise the geo-linguistic distribution of first and second person endings on the one hand and third person on the other. The full paradigms and their derivations are given in 2.4.3, while the social connotations of using one set of endings rather than the other are discussed in 3.6.2.

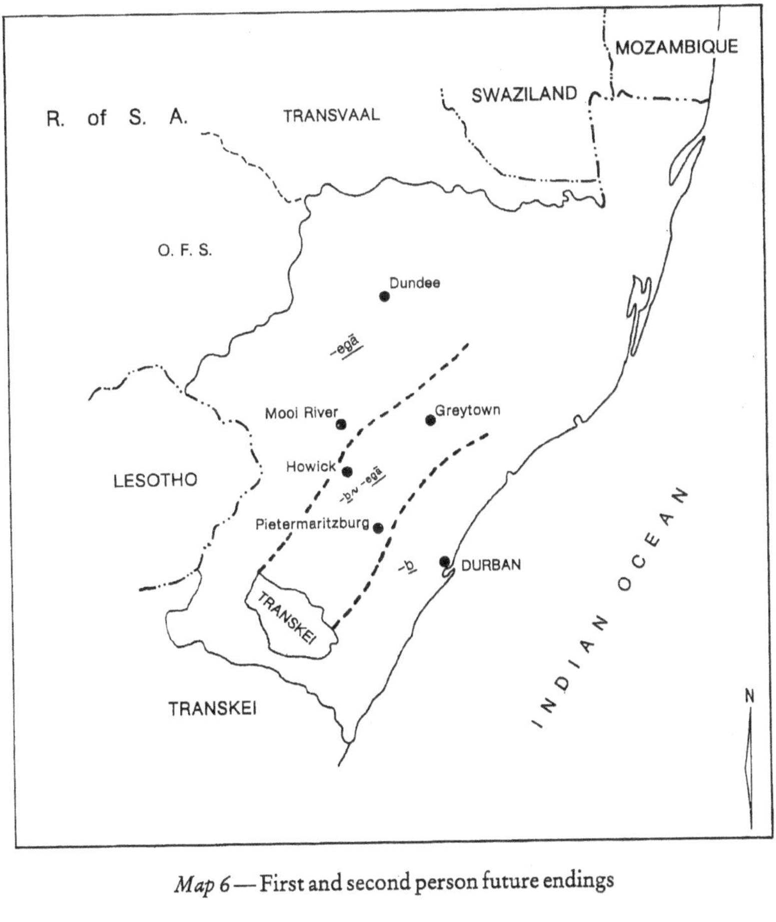

Map 6—First and second person future endings

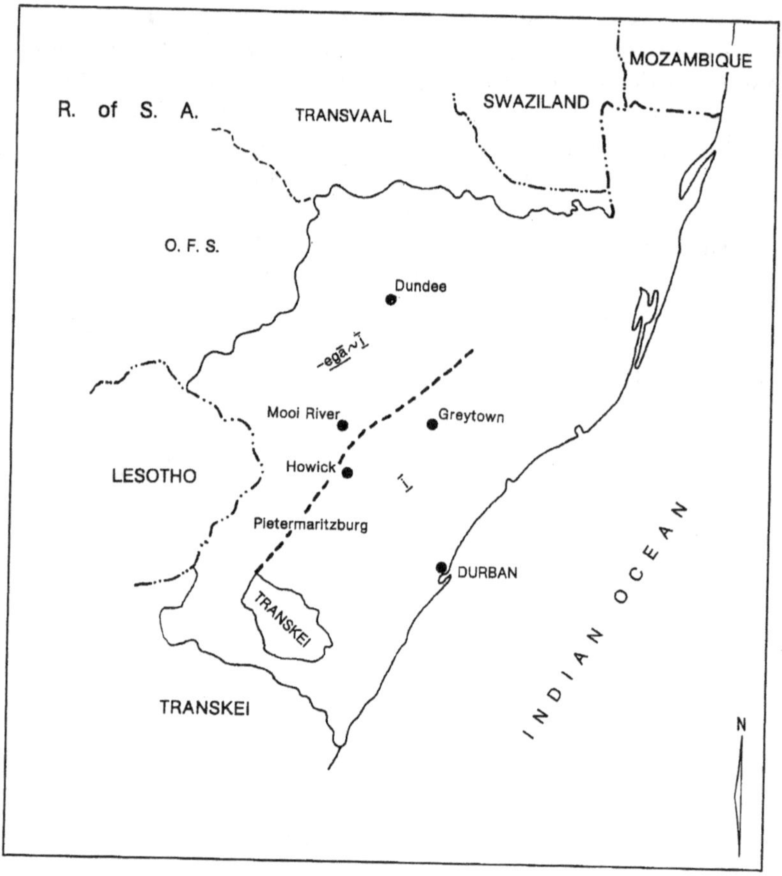

Map 7—Third person future endings

2.2.2 *Variation in the past tense of transitive verbs*

In the modern Indic languages the difference between transitive and intransitive verbs is manifested in the past tense, whereas the other tense-paradigms do not overtly distinguish between these two categories.

Some Indic languages (for example, Std Hn) have an ergative construction in the past (see further 2.9.1). While IB and other 'Outer' languages do not have an ergative syntax, the difference between transitive and intransitive verbs is nevertheless shown by an *-l* ending in the third singular for past intransitives, as opposed to some other ending for transitives. Three main transitive endings occur in SB:

(a) The Durban–Pinetown area as well as coastal Natal excluding the southernmost part (Port Shepstone and districts), use the ending *-lak*.

1. ū bаccā ke marlak.
   he baby ACC hit.3sg.past

   'He hit the baby.'

(b) The rest of Natal tends to use the ending *-is*:

2. ū bаccā ke māris.
   he baby ACC hit.3sg.past

(c) The third major variant used by a minority in all parts of Natal is the ending *-ā*, but only in and around Ladysmith is it as widely used as the *-is* transitive.

3. ū bаccā ke mārā.
   he baby ACC hit.3sg.past

A major variant of *-lak* is *-las*, which occurs mainly in Coastal Natal in roughly the same proportion. It is not perceived as being any different from *-lak* by native speakers; indeed very few are aware of the difference and can accurately say whether their neighbours use the *-las* or *-lak* ending. Many speakers use both forms in free variation. Another form *-lis* is used by a few of the oldest speakers.

The above statements imply that the variation for the third

TABLE 14
REGIONAL VARIATION IN THE USE OF THE THIRD PERSON SINGULAR PAST TRANSITIVE ENDING (Percentages)

ENDING	COASTAL NATAL	PORT SHEPSTONE	MIDLANDS	UPLANDS
-lak	41	23	0	1
-las	28	0	5	4
-is	9	59	70	64
-ā	21	18	25	31
-lis	1	0	0	0
n =	51	11	44	40

singular transitive verbal endings is not as simple as Map 8 suggests. However *-lak* tends not to be used outside the coastal area, whereas *-is* does sometimes occur in the *-lak* areas.

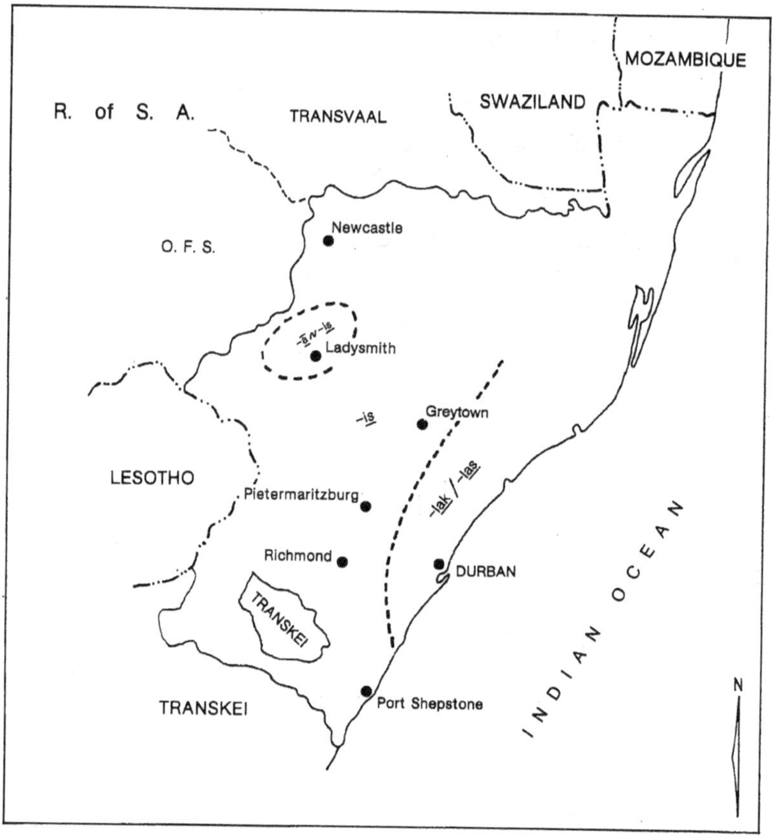

Map 8—Variants in the third person singular past transitive morpheme

2.2.3 *Variation in the third person singular past tense of intransitive verbs*

There are three main dialectal forms here: *-l*, *-ā*, *-is*, whose isoglosses do not resemble those of the transitive variants. Map 9 depicts the situation, which is as follows:

(a) the *-l* ending occurs over the major part of Natal, on the coastlands, and further inland as far as Greytown

(Midlands) and Dundee (Uplands). Furthermore, in places like Pietermaritzburg, Ladysmith and Newcastle it occurs with roughly the same frequency as the ending *-is*. For example *ū ail* 'she came', *ū bhāgal* 'he ran', *ū pahucal* 'he reached'.

(b) Pietermaritzburg serves as an intermediate area between the coastal variants in *-l* and the *-ā* endings (*āyā, bhāgā, pahucā*) found inland.

(c) the *-is* ending (*āhis* or *ais, bhāgis, pahucis*) occurs frequently inland beyond Pietermaritzburg, but only in Mooi River and Newcastle is it predominant. In Lions River, Greytown, and Ladysmith it is used almost as frequently as the *-l* and *-ā* endings.

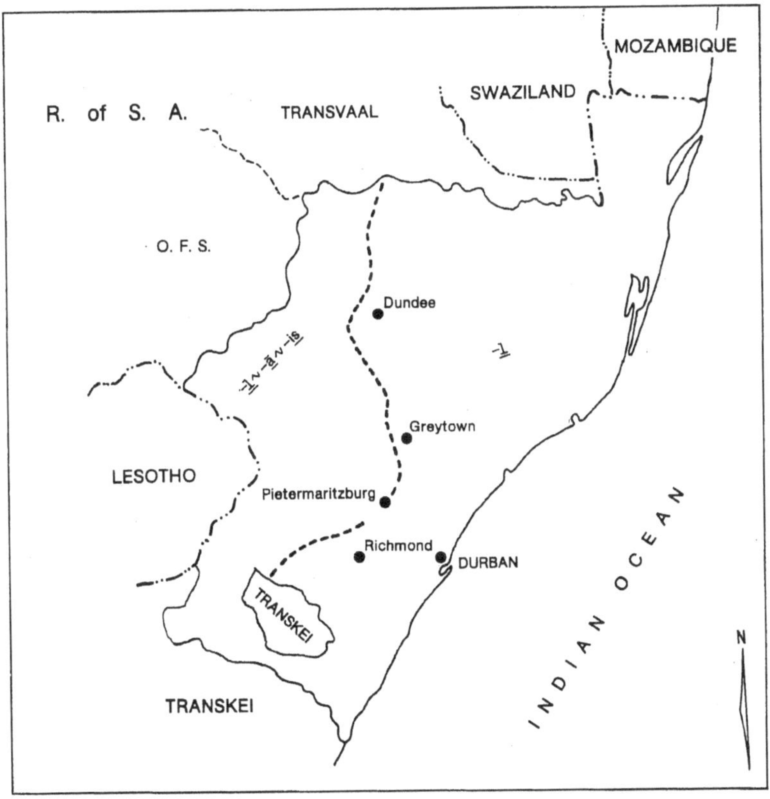

Map 9—Variants in the third person singular past intransitive morpheme

Still other variants, which are largely idiolectal, occur. The forms *āi* and *gī* or *gei* are sometimes heard in place of *ail* and *geil*. These seem to have originated by assimilation of *-l* to a following *-r*, in the frequently occurring past-perfect phrase *ail rahā* 'she had come' and *geil rahā* 'he had gone', and subsequent loss of *-l* in these contexts. The process has been carried out for some speakers in all, or almost all, occurrences of these two words. Some rural speakers use the forms *āwā* and *gāwā*.

TABLE 15
REGIONAL VARIATION IN THE USE OF THE THIRD PERSON SINGULAR PAST INTRANSITIVE ENDING (Percentages)

VARIANT	COASTAL NATAL	MIDLANDS	UPLANDS
-l	84	51	34
-a	6	31	27
-is	10	18	23
other	1	0	16
n =	64	44	46

2.2.4 *Variation of the use of verb forms for the first and second persons past tense*
In addition to the above variants for the third person singular, there are dialectal forms for the first and second persons in the past tense, irrespective of verb type, which differentiate Coastal SB from the rest of the areas in which it is spoken. The ending characteristic of the Coastal variety is *-l*, whereas *-ā* is the usual suffix in the Uplands of Natal. Some examples follow:

Coastal B	Uplands B	
ham dēkh-lī	*ham dēkh-ā*	'I saw' (trans)
ham āi-lī	*ham āy-ā*	'I came' (intrans)
tū dēkh-lē	*tū dekh-ā*	'You saw'
tū āi-lē	*tū āy-ā*	'You came'

A few speakers in the Uplands used *-n* or *-is* endings where one expected an ending in *-ā*. This was probably due to analogic paradigm levelling *vis à vis* the third singular *-is* ending and the third plural ending in *-n* (see also 2.2.5). The verb endings for the first and second persons plural are the same as for the singular, the difference in number being conveyed by pronominal marking. Table 16 and Map 10 set out the situation, and show that though there is some variation in Midlands usage, this time it accords more with Upland patterns.

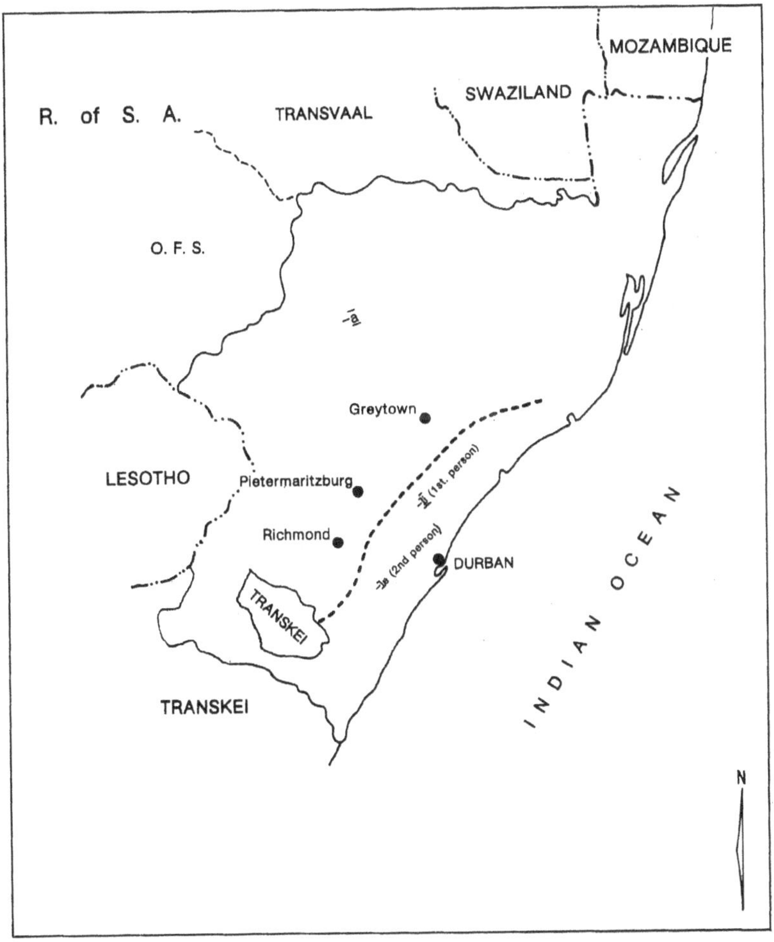

Map 10—Variants in the first and second persons past tense

TABLE 16
REGIONAL VARIATION IN THE USE OF FIRST AND THIRD PERSON PAST ENDINGS FOR ALL VERBS (Percentages)

ENDING	COASTAL NATAL	MIDLANDS	UPLANDS
-lī (1st) and *-le* (2nd)	82	20	10
-ā (1st and 2nd)	18	75	90
other	0	5	0
n =	58	44	42

2.2.5 *Variation in the third person plural past verb forms*
While SB does not generally distinguish between singular and plural in its verbal endings, Ladysmith and areas to the north

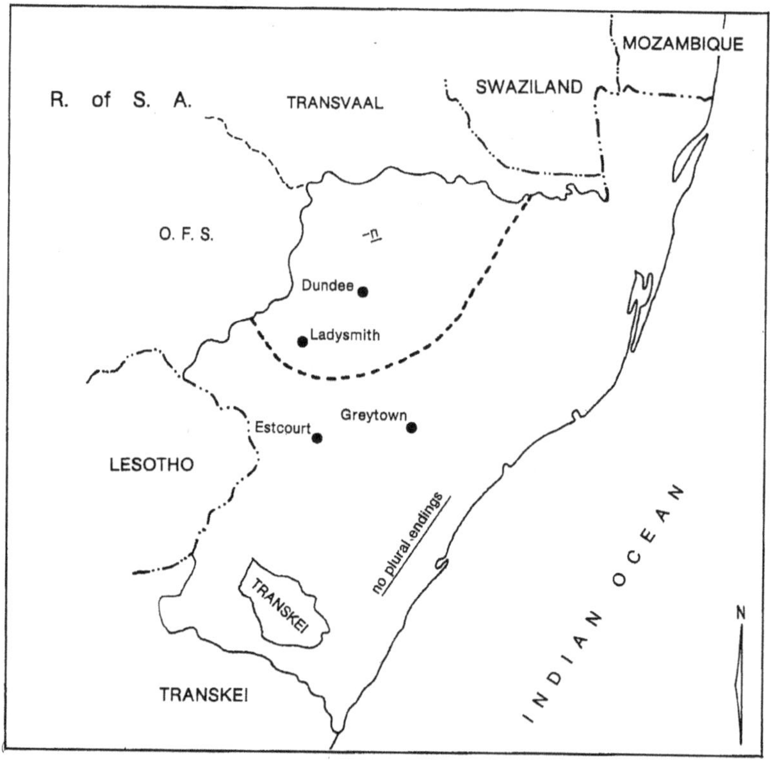

Map 11—Distribution of past plural verb endings

of it are unusual, in so far as they use a separate ending in *-n* to differentiate third person plural from the third person singular in *-ā* or *-is*, in both the transitive and intransitive past paradigms. Thus *ū geyā* or *ū geis* 'he went' contrast with *ū lōg gein* 'they went'; whereas *ham geyā* 'I went', and *ham lōg geyā* 'we went' show no change in the verb morphology, for first (and second) persons.

TABLE 17
REGIONAL VARIATION IN THE USE OF PAST PLURAL ENDINGS FOR ALL VERBS (Percentages)

ENDING	LADYSMITH AND AREAS TO THE NORTH	NATAL, SOUTH OF LADYSMITH
-n plurals	83	5
no pl. endings	17	95
n =	43	102

2.2.6 *Variation in the second person present copula/auxiliary verb*

In Coastal Natal the auxiliary and copula verb form for the second person, present tense is *hawe*, the equivalent form further inland being *he*. Thus Coastal Natal uses *tū husiār hawe* 'you are clever', whereas in the Uplands one most often hears *tū husiār he*. Likewise the equivalent of a Coastal Natal expression like *(tū) hamke cirhāwat hawe* 'You are teasing me', would be *(tū) hamke cirhāwat he*. Statistics for the relevant regions are provided in Table 18; but as the isogloss coincides with that in Map 10, it is not reproduced here.

TABLE 18
REGIONAL VARIATION IN THE USE OF THE SECOND PERSON COPULA/AUXILIARY (Percentages)

VARIANT	COASTAL NATAL	MIDLANDS	UPLANDS
hawe	75	9	4
he	25	91	96
n =	38	32	26

I have so far treated morphological diversity only. Since inter-regional differences in syntax and phonology are not discernible, I conclude with a discussion of the minor lexical variations that occur.[2]

2.2.7 *le versus kīn- 'to buy'*

The verb root *le-* has the basic meaning 'to take' in SB. This root is used additionally in the Uplands to mean 'to buy', a meaning not generally associated with it in Coastal Natal, where the latter meaning is supplied by the verb root *kīn-*. There are a few exceptions to this rule, as shown in Table 19. A handful of people in the '*le-* area' actually use *kīn-* 'to buy' or other verb roots like *mol le-* or *kharīd-*; while in Coastal Natal the root *le-* may carry the additional sense of 'to buy'.

TABLE 19
REGIONAL VARIATION IN THE USE OF THE VERBS *LE-* AND *KĪN-* 'TO BUY' (Percentages)

VARIANT	COASTAL NATAL	MIDLANDS	UPLANDS
kīn-	90	58	24
le-	10	42	76
n =	31	26	29

TABLE 20
REGIONAL VARIATION IN THE USE OF *KAL* AND *BIHĀN* 'TOMORROW' (Percentages)

VARIANT	COASTAL NATAL	MIDLANDS	UPLANDS
bihān	70	13	4
kal	30	87	96
n =	40	31	25

2.2.8 *kal versus bihān 'tomorrow'*

In many Indic languages, Std Hn included, the same word is used for both 'yesterday' and 'tomorrow' (usually a variant of the root *kal*), the tense marker on the verb usually clarifying any potential semantic confusion. In IB *bihān* refers solely to 'tomorrow morning'. *Kal* may be used for both 'tomorrow' and 'yesterday', though it most often refers to the latter. In South Africa both *kal* and *bihān* are recognised by all B speakers, though there is a tendency for Coastal Natal speakers to use *bihān* for 'tomorrow', thus reserving *kal* for 'yesterday'; while in the Uplands *kal* is used in both senses, to the exclusion of *bihān*. Some speakers claim to use *kalyā̃* for 'yesterday' and *kal* for 'tomorrow'.

2.2.9 *Use of the lexical item lejī*

In the English of most elderly Indian South Africans the word *lazy*, in addition to describing a laggard, has the connotation of 'not intelligent'. In Uplands B *lazy* is borrowed as *lejī* (showing the usual loanword change of [z] to [dʒ], and [eɪ] to [e:]). The primary meaning of *lejī* is 'not intelligent', though it might also be used for 'indolent'. In Coastal Natal *lejī* is rarely used, preference being given to the original form *bhaddā* 'not intelligent, physically sluggish', or *jāngar-cor* 'shirker'. The loanword *lazy*, if used in this area, occurs in totally unassimilated form – that is, with the English fricative [z] and the diphthong [eɪ]. This marks it off as being an English rather than a SB word.

TABLE 21
REGIONAL VARIATION IN THE USE OF THE LEXICAL ITEM *LEJĪ*
(Percentages)

VARIANT	COASTAL NATAL	MIDLANDS	UPLANDS
lejī	14	20	70
other (*bhaddā*, etc.)	86	80	30
n =	28	25	23

We can, on the basis of these near-systematic differences, posit two main dialect areas for SB – Coastal Natal and the Uplands, with a third intermediary zone – the Midlands. The difference between these dialects lies mainly in the verb

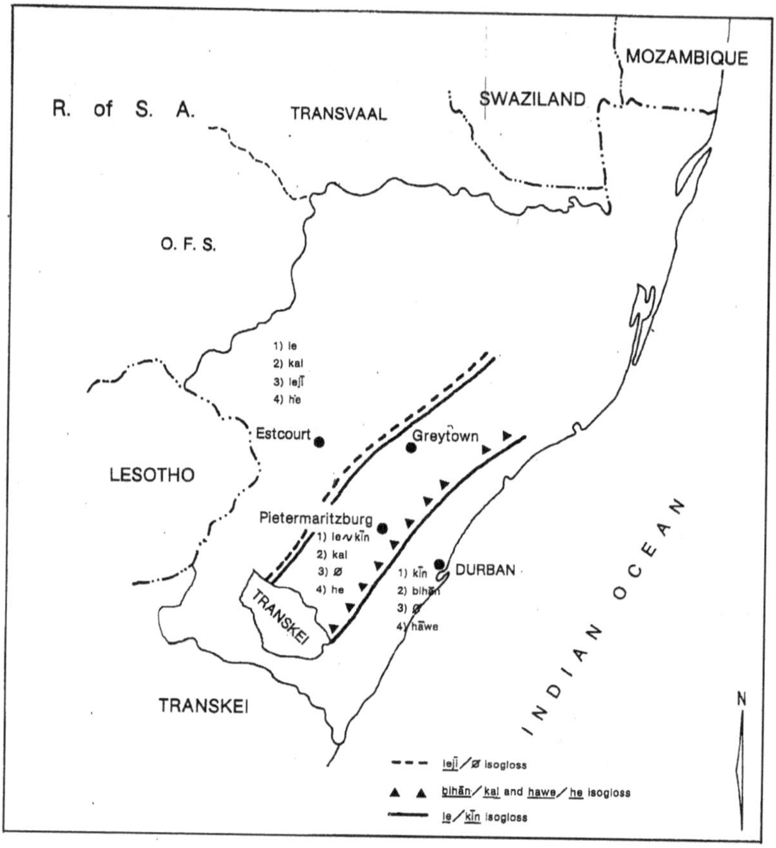

Map 12—Distribution of four lexical items

morphology, with a few lexical variants, and virtually no phonetic or syntactic differences. Accordingly, there is perfect intelligibility between the dialects, though one can easily gauge whether a speaker is from one or other of these areas.

Women who moved from one dialect area to another after marriage tend to show the influence of the new environment, whilst retaining some of the characteristic features of their childhood dialect. For example, one sixty-year-old woman, who had moved from the Midlands to the Uplands after her marriage, retained the following non-Upland features in her speech: third person past transitives in *-las*; and second person present copula/auxiliary *hawe*. She showed the influence of the Uplands in sometimes using third person past plural endings in *-n*; third person singular transitive endings in *-is*; and in the use of the words *lejī* 'lazy', and *le-* 'to buy'. Her speech thus wavered between forms like *dekhis* 'she saw', (with the Uplands *-is* ending) and *delas* 'she gave' (with the Midlands *-las* ending); and between *ahis he* 'he has come' (with an Uplands ending) and *geil he* 'he has gone' (with the *-l* more typical of the Midlands).

Another fifty-year-old who had made a similar move in her youth showed vacillation between *-n* past plural verb forms typical of the Uplands, and the *-l* forms of the Midlands; and between future endings in *-egā* (probably acquired during her stay in the Uplands), and those in *-b* (not typical of the Uplands). Her lexical repertoire was, likewise, mixed – containing the item *kīn-* 'to buy', atypical of her new environment, whilst including new ones like *kamārī* 'door' (as against *kũarī* the more usual Midlands form), and *kal* in the sense of 'tomorrow'. The rest of her household were not aware of these differences in her speech: indeed, it was a source of some surprise to them to discover that the two daughters-in-law of the house, originally from different dialect areas, had been using different verb forms all these years, unnoticed by them or the rest of the household.

An historical perspective on dialect variation in SB is offered in 2.5.

2.3 *KOINE FORMATION*

In this section the extent to which the various dialects and languages of the first generation of migrants interacted with each other is estimated, as well as the degree of coalescence involved in the formation of SB. The process will be shown to involve koineization. The term *koine* originated from the Greek *koinē* 'common', with reference to a particular variety of Greek – the one used as a lingua franca in the Roman and Hellenistic periods. Siegel's definition (1985:375–6) of koines and koineization is the most comprehensive:

> Koineization is the process which leads to mixing of linguistic subsystems, that is, of language varieties which either are mutually intelligible or share the same

> genetically related superposed language. It occurs in the context of increased interaction or integration among speakers of these varieties. A koine is the stabilized composite variety which results from this process. Formally, a koine is characterized by a mixture of features from the contributing varieties, and at an early stage of development, it is often reduced or simplified in comparison to any of these varieties. Functionally, a koine serves as a lingua franca among speakers of the different varieties. It also may become the primary language of amalgamated communities of these speakers.

Siegel distinguishes further between regional and immigrant koines. The former remain in the region where the contributory dialects are spoken (for example, the original Greek koine, and colloquial koineized Arabic described by Ferguson 1959b), whereas immigrant koines develop in an extraterritorial environment. Modern Hebrew belongs to the latter category, as do all the transplanted varieties of B.

In clarifying the notion of koineization Siegel distinguishes it from the following processes, with which it shares some similarity:

(a) Pidginisation – in which contact is accelerated, different languages are involved, and there is no integration between substrate and superstrate speakers involved in the pidginisation process.
(b) Dialect mixing – in which dialects influence each other without bringing about a new (and additional) variety.
(c) Convergence and large-scale borrowing – where two languages become structurally similar in time via a process of bilingualism.

The parallels between pidginisation and koineization of the sort giving rise to the colonial varieties of B are quite striking. 'Classic' pidginisation involves three or more languages in rapid contact, under imperfect migratory conditions (often slavery). It gives rise to a new variety which is structurally discontinuous with the contributing languages. The koineization that resulted in the formation of new varieties of

B (which we might term 'classic' koineization) involved three or more dialects or related languages (that is, those having a shared superposed language) in rapid contact, under imperfect migratory conditions and indenture. It gave rise to a new variety which was structurally continuous with the contributory dialects.

In describing the koineization process for SB, I shall examine the individual contributions of the various contributory languages and dialects. I shall also describe the idiolectal differences that persist, and that cannot be correlated with social factors, regional variations, or differences of register.

I shall use Grierson's grouping: Bihari dialects (B, Magahi, Maithili), Eastern Hindi dialects (Awadhi, Bagheli, Chatisgarhi), Western Hindi dialects (Braj, Kanauji, Bundeli) and Std Hn. In Grierson's classification Std Hn is a form of Western Hn, but it is separated here because of its importance as the prestigious norm of formal discourse and writing (Siegel's 'superposed variety'). I have omitted minor contributing languages which do not fall into these groups (Panjabi, Oriya, Nepali, Bengali, and Rajasthani), since they total only 5 per cent, and show no influence on the formation of SB. The features common to each of these language groups and to SB are listed systematically in Table 22 below:
(+) signals the presence of the feature under discussion;
(−) signals its absence in the language under consideration;
(+•) denotes a feature used by some sub-dialects in the language/dialect under question; and
(+••) denotes a form used by some speakers of SB that cannot be tied down to one of its three dialects.

In this way we can isolate the features of SB which are attributable to one Indian language only, to all the above languages, or to intermediate groupings. (My presentation here owes a great deal to Gambhir 1981:188–200.)

2.3.1 *Some observations based on Table 22*

(a) Items I to V range over the core features of SB which, with the possible exception of one item – V (feature 32) – are all found in IB and the other Bihari dialects. The 16 features under 'I' are those which are common to SB and all the languages under consideration here. In terms of their basic structures these languages are all quite similar, as is suggested by such broad categories as 'phonological system', 'tense and aspect system', 'semantic structure' etc. This similarity was to lead to koine development, rather than, say, pidginisation.

Item II shows 3 significant ways in which Std Hn differs from the other languages, including SB, while features common to SB, Bihari, and E. Hn that are not found in Std and W. Hn are listed under III. Item IV shows that in terms of linguistic structures, SB is closest to Bihari (in particular to B).

(b) Items V to IX cover features absent in Bihari, but present in SB which we can attribute to another of the above sources. These items show that the exclusive contribution of W. Hn is nil. The number of items from W. Hn and Std Hn is small, but these are frequently occurring forms (future and past endings) of dialectal and stylistic significance in SB. The future endings in *-egā* may not be entirely due to early koineization. I shall argue in 3.6.4 that they are possibly the result of Std Hn teaching in the twentieth century. An alternative origin from Calcutta Bazaar Hindustani is considered in 2.6.

(c) Item X lists features which are peculiar to SB, differentiating it from Indian languages as well as from other varieties of B throughout the world. Feature 39, 'English loanwords' should not be taken to imply that these are absent in the other languages in Table 22. What is being claimed is that the English loanwords in SB differ partly from those in the other languages (see Chapter 4).[3]

(d) Items XI and XII list four important features of Std and W. Hn which are not found in SB. Locals who wish to dissociate their speech from SB (for example, priests in their public – and sometimes private – capacities, public speakers, and a few socially upward-mobile people who have had close contact with the priesthood or with speakers of Std Hn from India), use these shibboleths of Std Hn. (See further 3.5.2.)

TABLE 22
LINGUISTIC FEATURES OF SOUTH AFRICAN BHOJPURI AND THEIR ROOTS IN INDIC LANGUAGES AND DIALECTS

ITEM	STD HN	W. HN DIALECTS	E. HN DIALECTS	BIHARI DIALECTS	SB	LINGUISTIC FEATURES
I	+	+	+	+	+	1. Phonological system (see A.1) 2. Word order (A.3) 3. Impersonal constructions/Dative subjects (A.6.7) 4. Common reflexive pronoun for all persons (A.4.6) 5. Distinction between trans and intrans verb (A.4.2) 6. Tense and aspect system (A.5.2) 7. Compound verbs (A.5.4) 8. Passives (A.6.1) 9. Relative clauses (A.6.2) 10. Conjunctive construction (A.6.3) 11. Imperatives with stem + Ø (A.6.6) 12. Deletion rules (e.g. subject deletion) (A.6.8) 13. Reduplication rules (A.5.2c; A.2.3c) 14. Semantic structure (A.2) 15. Basic vocabulary (A.2) 16. Echo construction (A.2.3b)
II	–	+	+	+	+	17. Third person future < *h(i)* (2.4.2) 18. Imperfect in stem + *-t* (A.5.2) 19. Verbal noun in *-b* (A.5.6)
IIIa	–	–	+	+	+	20. Genitive pronoun *hamār* 'my' (A.4.6) 21. Past copula *rah-* (A.5.2) 22. Classifiers *ṭho/ṭhe/go* (A.4.8)
IIIb	–	–	+•	+	+	23. Long form of nouns (A.4.1) 24. First and second person future in *-b* (A.5.2)
IIIc	–	–	+	+	+••	25. Imperative in stem + *-ā* (A.6.6)

ITEM	STD HN	W. HN DIALECTS	E. HN DIALECTS	BIHARI DIALECTS	SB	LINGUISTIC FEATURES
IV	–	–	–	+	+	26. Noun and adjective inflections (A.4.1 and A.4.5) 27. Past tense in *-ī* (A.5.2) 28. Invariant modifiers (e.g. for plurals) (A.4.3) 29. Plural marker *-jā* for verbs (2.11.5a) 30. Obligation construction with agent + inf + *ke* + aux (A.6.4) 31. Emphatic construction with agent + VN in *-be* + aux (2.9.5)
V	–	+	+	–	+	32. Stem + *-e* verb forms (2.4.1)
VI	+	+	+	–	+••	33. Imperative verb ending *-o* (2.9.7)
VIIa	+	+	–	–	+	34. Future imperative ending *-nā* (2.9.6)
VIIb	+	+	–	–	+•	35. Trans past ending *-ā* (2.4.4)
VIIIa	–	–	+	–	+•	36. Intrans 3rd sg ending *-is* (2.4.5)
VIIIb	–	–	+	–	+••	37. Suffixes *au* 'also' and *ai* 'only' (2.12)
IX	+	–	–	–	+•	38. Future ending *-egā* (2.4.3)
X	–	–	–	–	+	39. English loanwords (4.2) 40. Tamil and Fanagalo loanwords (4.2.2; 4.2.3) 41. The verb *honā* 'to want' (2.9.8) 42. The phrasal verb *khalās kar-* 'to complete' (2.9.9)
XI	+	–	–	–	–	43. Pronouns *mæ̃*, *tum*, and *āp* 44. Past copula/aux *thā*
XII	+	+	–	–	–	45. Ergative constr in the past (2.9.1) 46. Progressive aspect with verb stem + *rah-* + *ho-*

ITEM	STD HN	W. HN DIALECTS	E. HN DIALECTS	BIHARI DIALECTS	SB	LINGUISTIC FEATURES
XIIIa	–	–	–	+	–	47. Aux/copula *bā/bāṭī̃/bānī̃* (A.5.2)
						48. Habitual ending *-lā* in 2nd and 3rd person (2.4)
						49. The verb *hokh-* 'to become' (2.11.3)
						50. Second person pronoun *tē̃* (2.11.1)
						51. Third person pronouns *huā̃ka, ihā̃ka* (2.11.1)
						52. 1st person endings used as 2nd/3rd honorifics (2.11.5)
XIIIb	–	–	–	+•	–	53. Negative copula *naikhī̃* (2.11.2)
						54. Honorific pronoun *rauwā̃* (A.4.6)
XIV	–	–	+	–	–	55. Reduplication, with only first vowel changed (2.12)
						56. Plural marker *panc* for pronouns (2.12)
						57. Postpositions *badi, ḍagar*, and *tanā* (2.12)
						58. Future imperative endings *-e* and *-eu* (2.12)
XV	+	+	+	+	–	59. Stylistic range (3.2)
						60. Social Variation (3.2)
						61. Honorific forms of verbs and pronouns (2.11.5; A.5.2)
						62. Feminine verb forms (A.5.2; 2.10.1)

Adapted from Gambhir 1981 : 196–8.

(e) Item XIII lists a few striking features of IB which have not survived in South Africa. The loss of features 47, 48 and 53 particularly contributes to the weakening of the Bhojpurian flavour of the language, since these are characteristic features which are to be heard in the streets and villages of Bihar and Eastern Uttar Pradesh, but nowhere else in India. It is only with features 26 to 31, especially the past tense in *-l* and the future in *-b*, plus some characteristic vocabulary, that the Bhojpurian character of the language remains. Similarly, item XIV outlines characteristic features of Awadhi which have not survived in South Africa. These are discussed further in 2.12.

(f) Items XV and partly XIII indicate language simplification concomitant with the process of koineization, as well as the restriction of the new koine to certain domains of usage only.

While Table 22 gives an overall view of the relative contribution of each of the languages concerned to SB, it does not reveal the dialect-mixing in verbal and nominal paradigms. In the following section I present the main verb paradigms of SB, with an outline of their origin.

2.4 *VERB PARADIGMS*

2.4.1 *The present habitual*

(*dekh*- 'to see')

Sg 1.	ham dekhi-lā	'I see'	Pl 1.	ham lõg dekhi-lā	'We see'
2.	tū dekhe he	'You see'	2.	tū lõg dekhe he	'You see'
3.	ū dekhe he	'He/she/it sees'	3.	ū lõg dekhe he	'They see'

This paradigm conveys the sense of 'to be in the habit of seeing', or 'to usually see'. It may occasionally convey the present progressive sense to 'to be seeing'.

The first person forms in *-l* here are characteristic of IB, though the vowel following the *l* varies from dialect to dialect. They do not occur in the other Bihari dialects, nor in dialects of E. or W. Hn.

The second and third person forms, on the other hand, are not used in contemporary IB, which has an *-l* form throughout the paradigm (2nd sg *dekha-lā*, pl *dekha-le*; 3rd sg *dekhe-le*, pl *dekhe-lā*). Grierson (1903:52) does cite verb stem + *e* forms as second and third conditional forms ('if you see'), but, unfortunately, does not illustrate their use. The stem + *-e* forms are often used by uneducated speakers of W. and E. Hn, but less so today than in the past. Instead, periphrastic forms with present participle + auxiliary *he* are on the increase (Gambhir 1981:236).

It is nevertheless quite a puzzle that a mixed paradigm should prevail in SB, when one might have expected a 'levelled-out' paradigm with only *-l* forms to occur (as in modern IB and Trinidad Bhojpuri (TB)), or with only stem + *-e* forms. Only two speakers in South Africa, of hundreds interviewed, showed levelling – both were females living in semi-isolated surroundings, aged 50 and 31 respectively, using *-l* throughout. In all other instances, this paradigm was exceptional in showing no idiolectal or regional variation, leading one to question whether it is really a mixed paradigm or whether this system was not present all along in IB for some strata of the population, but somehow managed to elude the attentions of grammarians of the period like Grierson and Hoernlé. This doubt is enhanced by comparisons between S and other overseas varieties of B. In the B of both Suriname (Huiskamp 1978:173) and Guyana (Gambhir 1981:226), the situation is identical with stem + *-e* forms reported only in the second and third persons. In TB *-l* forms are used throughout the paradigm by most speakers, but an alternative to the second and third persons is the use of stem + *-e* forms, with the auxiliary sometimes deleted (Mohan 1978:142, 146). Damsteegt (1988:104) notes that the *-e* form for second and third persons is found in Magahi and some B literature.

2.4.2 *The present continuous*

Sg 1.	ham dekh-at hai/he	'I am seeing'	Pl As for sg, with plural pronoun forms
2.	tū dekh-at hawe/he	'You are seeing;	
3.	ū dekh-at he	'He/she/it is seeing'	

This paradigm, comprising the present participle in *-at*, plus the auxiliary *he* 'to be', resembles that of WB as described by Grierson (1903:251), and has some similarity to the present continuous system of Awadhi. In particular the auxiliary forms *hãĩ* (1st person), *hawe* (2nd person), and *he* (3rd person) are limited to WB. Awadhi is somewhat similar in having *hãĩ* (sometimes *ahai*) in all persons, except the second plural in *hau*, and the third plural in *hãĩ*. EB uses the auxiliary *bāṭi* 'to be', instead of *hai* throughout this paradigm, as do some varieties of Awadhi. The W. Hn dialects, excluding Std Hn, also use a present participle in *-t* together with *hai* throughout this paradigm, though the pronouns associated with the verb forms are quite distinct from that of SB.

The paradigm thus retains the most typical characteristics of the contributing languages, avoiding the extremes of the EB forms with *bāṭi*, and the irregular auxiliary forms used in Std Hn.

2.4.3 *The future tense*

(a) Coastal Natal

Sg	1. ham dekh-ab	'I will see'	Pl As for sg, with usual change of pronouns
	2. tū dekh-be	'You will see'	
	3. ū dekh-ī	'He/she/it will see'	

(b) The Uplands

Sg	1. ham dekh-egā	Pl As for sg
	2. tū dekh-egā	
	3. ū dekh-egā/dekhī	

The Uplands paradigm has two possible sources:

(i) A levelling off of the Std Hn endings, which are: *masc. sg.*: 1st *-ũgā*, 2nd/3rd *-egā*; pl: 2nd *-oge*, 1st/3rd *-ẽge* *fem. sg.*: 1st *-ũgī*, 2nd/3rd *-egī*; pl: 2nd *-ogī*, 1st/3rd *-ẽgī*.

(ii) Bazaar Hn which has an invariant ending *-egā* (Chatterji 1960:258. See further 2.6).

The W. Hn dialects usually have futures in *-h* (for example, Braj *marihai* 'he will strike'), but also have an alternative in -g (for example, Braj *marigau* 'he will strike').

The Coastal paradigm is similar to that of EB, except that the latter has a separate *-h* ending in the third person plural, whereas in SB the singular and plural endings are identical. Table 23 lists the endings employed by the relevant dialects. For this paradigm we need to differentiate three varieties of Awadhi, since there are regional variables here – E. Awadhi, which is influenced by B; W. Awadhi which is influenced by W. Hn; and Central Awadhi.

Table 23 shows the close similarity between SB and IB for this paradigm. The +/− for the third plural under IB indicates the use of an *-i* ending in some areas, and an *-h* in others. Likewise, the +/− under Central Awadhi indicates the use of *-b* endings in the second person in some districts and an *-h* in others.

TABLE 23
ORIGIN OF COASTAL SOUTH AFRICAN BHOJPURI FUTURE ENDINGS

STD HN	W HN	W AWADHI	CENTRAL AWADHI	E AWADHI	IB	MAG-AHI	MAI-THILI	COASTAL SB
–	–	–	+	+	+	+	+	*-b* (1 sg)
–	–	–	+	+	+	+	+	*-b* (1 pl)
–	–	–	+/–	+	+	+	+	*-b* (2 sg)
–	–	–	+/–	+	+	+	+	*-b* (2 pl)
–	–	+	+	+	+	+/–	+	*-ī* (3 sg)
–	–	–	–	–	+/–	–	–	*-ī* (3 pl)

2.4.4 *The past tense of transitive verbs*

(a) Coastal Natal

Sg 1. ham dekh-lī̃ 'I saw' Pl As for sg
2. tū dekh-le 'You saw'
3. ū dekh-las/lak 'He/she/it saw'

(b) The Uplands

Sg 1. ham dekh-ā
2. tū dekh-ā
3. ū- dekh-ā/is

Pl 1. ham lōg dekh-ā
2. tū lōg dekh-ā
3. ū lōg dekh-ā/in

The first paradigm is very similar to that of all the Bihari dialects, though they all differentiate plural from singular forms. The two variants in the third person, which for Coastal Natal speakers are unpredictable and sometimes interchangeable, show the influence of the different Bihari dialects: *-lak* is from Magahi, Maithili, and a few B varieties bordering on them (for example, the B of the district of Champaran); while the ending *-las* is typical of most B dialects. (From Grierson's survey it seems that *-l* endings here are not found in the other non-Bihari dialects, except as a variant in some Bagheli-speaking villages.)

The Upland Natal paradigm is again a conflation of W. Hn and E. Hn. Table 24 presents the contribution of these dialects to Uplands SB. (For a discussion of Calcutta Bazaar Hn – CBH – see 2.6.)

The minuses under W. Hn might be misleading since they represent endings which are closely related to the *-ā* of the Std (for example, most of these dialects have historically related

TABLE 24
ORIGIN OF UPLAND SOUTH AFRICAN BHOJPURI PAST TRANSITIVE ENDINGS

CBH	STD HN	W. HN DIA-LECTS	E. HN DIALECTS AWA-DHI	BAG-HELI	CHAT-ISGARHI	BI-HARI	UPLAND SB
+	+	–	+/–	–	–	–	-*ā* (1 sg)
+	+	–	+/–	–	–	–	*ā* (2 sg)
+	+	–	–	–	–	–	-*ā* (3 sg)
+	–	–	+	+	+	–	-*is* (3 sg)
+	+	–	+	–	–	–	-*ā* (1 pl)
+	+	–	+	–	–	–	-*ā* (2 pl)
+	+	–	–	–	–	–	-*ā* (3 pl)
+	–	–	+	+	+	–	-*in* (3 pl)

-*o* or *(y)au* endings). It should also be noted that while the Std Hn of the literary type has separate plural endings in -*e*, the colloquial variety has -*ā* plural endings. The +/– for the first and second persons denotes the use of -*ā* endings in some sub-dialects of Awadhi, and -*eu* in others (Saksena 1971:260).

2.4.5 *The past intransitive*

(a) Coastal Natal

Sg 1. ham gei-lī̃	'I went'	Pl As for sg
2. tū̃ gei-le	'You went'	
3. ū̃ gei-l	'He/she/it went'	

(b) Upland Natal

Sg 1. ham gey-ā	Pl 1. ham lōg gey-ā
2. tū̃ gey-ā	2. tū̃ lōg gey-ā
3. ū̃ gey-ā/gei-l/gei-s	3. ū̃ lōg gey-ā/gei-l/gei-n

The Coastal Natal paradigm closely resembles those of the different varieties of IB, except, once again, for the latter's differentiating the third person plural from the third person singular. The first person endings in -*lī̃* are characteristic of WB; the other dialects having -*lī̃* instead. The third person in -*l*, on the other hand, is from EB; WB has the ending -*lai* here (Grierson 1903:43). The other Bihari dialects, Maithili and

Magahi, while sharing *-l* endings with B, have different vowels following the *-l*.

Possible sources for the mixed Upland SB paradigm can be gauged from Table 25.

TABLE 25
ORIGIN OF UPLAND SOUTH AFRICAN BHOJPURI PAST INTRANSITIVE ENDINGS

CBH	STD HN	W.HN DIALECTS	E.HN DIALECTS	BIHARI DIALECTS	UPLANDS SB
+	+	–	+/–	–	*-ā* (1 sg)
+	+	–	+/–	–	*-ā* (2 sg)
+	+	–	+/–	–	*-ā* (3 sg)
+	–	–	+	–	*-is* (3 sg)
–	–	–	–	+	*-l* (3 sg)
+	+	–	+/–	–	*-ā* (1 pl)
+	+	–	+/–	–	*-ā* (2 pl)
+	+	–	+/–	–	*-ā* (3 pl)
–	–	–	+	–	*-in* (3 pl)
–	–	–	–	+	*-l* (3 pl)

Once again, the W.Hn endings are not as disparate from the other dialects as the list of minuses suggests: they are quite close to the Std Hn forms – phonetically and historically.

2.4.6 *Counter-factual conditional*

This category refers to suppositions concerning past events and to events that could have taken place in the past, but which did not. The paradigm closely resembles that of the past, with a *-t* replacing the *-l* characteristic of the past.

Sg	1. ham dekh-tī̃	'If I had seen'	Pl As for sg
	2. tū dekh-te	'If you had seen'	
	3. ū dekh-at	'If he/she/it had seen'	

Some illustrations from SB follow:

4. ham sĩk raha-tī̃ tab dakṭar
I sick be.past-CF.1sg then doctor
kane jātī̃.
GOAL go-CF.1sg
'If I were sick, I would have gone to the doctor.'

5. sāṛī nahī liaw-te, ghare
   sari not bring-CF.2sg house.LOC
   nei aw-te.
   not come-CF.2sg
   'If you hadn't had to bring the sari, you wouldn't have come to my house.'

6. jo barkā moṭar rah-at
   If big.DEF car was-CF.3sg
   tā ham lõg mar jā-tī.
   then we pl die go-CF.1pl.
   'If it had been the big car, we would have died.'

This paradigm resembles that of IB more closely than that of any other Indic language. The first person ending is from WB (EB has the ending *-tī* here), while the second person ending is found in all the sub-dialects of B. The third person ending is found in both B and Awadhi.

2.4.7 *Subjunctives*

This category refers to suppositions concerning the future, to events that used to take place, but which no longer occur at the time of speaking, and to habitual optatives. The paradigm is as follows:

Sg 1.	ham dekh-ī	'If I see'	Pl As for sg
2.	tū dekh-e	'If you see'	
3.	ū dekh-ī	'If he/she/it sees'	

Some examples are given below:

7. ham lõg gīt-ūt beiṭh ke
   we PL song-ECHO sit CONJ
   sūn-ī, ham log sīkh-ī.
   listen-SUBJ.1pl we PL learn-SUBJ.1pl
   'We would sit and listen to the songs and tunes, and would learn them.'

8. kuch kām nei kar-ī, khalli
   any work not do-SUBJ.3sg only
   dīn-bhar beiṭhal rahī,
   day-full sit.PAST P be.past-SUBJ.3sg

khalli	khāī̃	ke	ṭem	khāī̃.
only	eat.INF	DAT	time	eat-SUBJ.3sg

'He will not do any work, he remains seated all day; except for eating at meal-times.'

In 7 the use of subjunctive rather than habitual endings carries overtones of volition on the part of the subject. There is some overlap between this paradigm and the ordinary future indicative, with the third person future identical in form to the third person subjunctive. This gives some support for the idea of *irrealis* marking. Sentence 9 shows the difficulty in deciding which is which:

9.

jab	baccā	lõg	baṛā	ho
when	child	PL	big	become

jāī̃	ta	ū	lõg	bhej-e.
go.3sg.fut	then	he	PL	send-HAB

'When the children are grown up, then they send them (away).'

The main verb *bheje* in 9 is a present habitual form (with the auxiliary *he* deleted), while the verb *jāī̃* in the first clause could be construed as either subjunctive or future indicative (the speaker seems to have intended the latter).

First person subjunctives in *-ī̃* are from WB and Awadhi (EB has *-ī̃* here). The second person form is found in all dialects of B; whereas Awadhi has *ø* or *-as*. The third person ending in *-ī̃* is not reported by Grierson, though both present-day B and Awadhi have it.

2.4.8 *Other minor variations in verb forms*

In addition to the verb forms characteristic of SB given above, there are some idiosyncratic forms used by a few older speakers, which are not generally dependent on their place of birth (in South Africa). These forms are relics of the dialect input into SB, hinting at the great variety of forms prior to koineisation. Significantly, they occur in the speech of a few rural speakers, leading isolated lives. In almost all instances these speakers had learnt the forms from a parent born in India. We must conclude that most immigrants probably continued using their own dialects in the home, and that nativisation of the koine took place with the first generation of Natal-born speakers. There are two sets of exceptions:

(i) These few isolated Natal-born individuals who use some pre-koine morphology (though their syntax and vocabulary is clearly that of SB);

(ii) A few speakers interviewed, who had been born in India and brought to Natal as children and used a variety that was essentially Coastal SB. It is likely that they had accommodated to SB norms early in their lives.

The main pre-koine forms still in existence today, but uncharacteristic of SB, are listed below:

(a) *Present participle in -it, not -at*: For example, *ham jā-it hai.* 'I am going', *u dēkh-it hē* 'he is watching'. Such forms are reported in some villages in the E. Hn area (Grierson 1904).

(b) *Second person futures in -bā, not be*: For example *ai-bā* 'will you come', *cal-bā* 'will you move'. This ending occurs regularly in Maithili, is an alternate form in Magahi, and is also reported in a few neighbouring B-speaking villages. In Natal it is used to connote respect for the addressee, but is not used by more than a handful of (rural) speakers.

(c) *Third singular intransitive past in -wa*: For example, *ā-wā* 'he came', *ga-wā* 'he went'. This irregular past formation for these two verbs (only) is fairly widespread in Awadhi; in South Africa these forms are used by a handful of older speakers, mostly from rural districts in northern Natal.

(d) *First person intransitive ending in -n, not -a*: For example, *ai-n* 'I came', *rah-in* 'we stayed'. Whereas these are associated in most dialects of Awadhi with the third person plural, there are a handful of villages which use them in the first person as well. This should warn one against attributing all variation in SB to the mingling of people originally from different areas – there must have been some variation in each contributing dialect in India to start off with.

(e) *Third person transitive forms in -le, not -las*: For example, *ū de-le* 'she gave', *ū mār-le* 'she hit'. In some dialects of IB this is an alternative form to *-las*.

(f) *Third person transitive forms in -lis*: A few speakers in the Natal coastlands use *-lis* as an occasional variant of *-las* or *-lak*. The *-lis* ending occurs in a few sub-dialects of IB, notably in Basti – the district which had the highest number of South Africa-bound immigrants.

2.4.9 *Internal morphological variation*

Despite the wide range of alternative morphological forms existing in an area, there is little individual variation in SB. That is, most speakers consistently use the same set of endings. For example, one who uses past transitives in *-l* usually does not use the variants in *-a* or *-is*. There are, however, a few exceptions:

(a) For some coastal speakers *-las* and *-lak* (trans. 3 sg) occur in free variation.

(b) Some speakers attempt to produce Std Hn endings in speaking to priests and others educated in Hn – usually *-egā* future endings and *-a* past endings.

(c) A few third-generation speakers in Coastal Natal fluctuate between *-is* and *-ā* (especially when speaking to priests), and the more usual *-l* endings of the third person singular past. Most speakers, however, retain their vernacular *-l* forms, irrespective of the status of the addressee.

(d) Some older speakers seem to command an array of past tense endings on account of the influence of their (first-generation) elders early in life, but do not seem to attach social values to these endings. An example of such internal morphological diversity is exhibited in the folk-tale set out in Appendix B–3c, narrated by a sixty-year-old female residing in Durban.

2.5 *THE PLACE OF SB AMONG OTHER OVERSEAS VARIETIES*

My characterisation of SB has so far been in terms of its historical antecedents in India. Another illuminating dimension concerns the comparison of the new varieties of B that developed in the different colonies. In terms of their morphological features, especially verb endings, the overseas varieties of B preserve the historical record pertaining to recruitment patterns and the times of emigration.

The periods of indentured emigration to the different colonies are listed in Table 26.

TABLE 26
PERIODS OF EMIGRATION OF INDENTURED WORKERS TO DIFFERENT COLONIES

Mauritius	1834–1917
Guyana	1839–1916
Trinidad	1845–1917
South Africa	1860–1911
Suriname	1873–1915
Fiji	1879–1946

Recruitment was at first concentrated in more easterly areas – Bengal Presidency and Bihar (Tinker 1974:46–53; Saha 1970:28–9), and moved in a westerly direction further into the interior. It thus happens that MB shows the most influence from eastern dialects, and that colonies listed below Mauritius in Table 26 show progressively fewer features of these eastern dialects, culminating in FH, which is certainly the least Bhojpurian of all the varieties (see Moag 1977:v). In support of these assertions the usual verb forms and the classifier (see A.4.8) in each overseas variety are presented in Table 27.

SB occupies a mid-position in the scale of overseas varieties, both temporally and linguistically. Its Uplands dialect shares many similarities with SH and FH, while Coastal B shows close accord with the varieties in Guyana and Trinidad. Table 27 shows the following patterns:

(a) *Present habitual*: There is a broad division here between FH, which uses verb stem + *-tā* plus the copula *hai*, and the other overseas varieties, which have stem + *-lā* (all persons), or stem + *-lā* (first person) and stem + *-e*, plus the copula *hai*. The FH forms may be attributed to Std

Hn teaching in Fiji (Moag 1979:119) or to Bazaar Hn usage in Calcutta (Siegel 1987:196). The origin of the forms current in the other varieties has been noted in 2.4.1.

(b) *Present continuous*: Once again the main division is between FH (which has the same form for the present habitual and progressive (Moag 1977:232) and the other varieties having participle in *-at* + auxiliary (*hai/bāṭī*). GB is exceptional in that *-at* + *hai* forms are rare and replaced by present habitual forms (Gambhir 1981:116). (The origins of the *-at* + *aux* present are discussed in 2.4.2)

(c) *Future*: Taking a broad division between endings in *-b* (and *-ī* in the third person) versus *-egā* endings we have two main groups: MB, GB, TB and Coastal SB for the former and Upland SB, FH for the latter. SH is intermediate between the two types, having both *-ī* and *-igā* for third person.[4]

(d) *Past transitive*: The distribution of endings in *-l* as against *-ā* (with *-is* in the third singular) yields the same grouping as for the future: MB, GB, TB and Coastal SB have the *-l* form (from IB) while Uplands SB and FH take the other option (from Awadhi). SH once again is intermediate between the two groups.

(e) *Auxiliary/Copula*: The broad patterns established so far are operative over the use of *bā/bāṭī* (from IB) and *hai* (from E. and W.Hn), except for GB. Furthermore there is no differentiation between Upland and Coastal SB in this regard. The division is *bā/bāṭī*: MB, TB versus *hai*: GB, SB, FH. SH once again has both *hai* and *bāṭī*.

(f) *Classifiers*: Eastern B uses the classifier *go* (see A.4.8) while Western B and Awadhi have *ṭho*. Once again the division is between MB, GB, TB for the former and SB and FH for the latter, with SH having both forms. (There is no differentiation between Uplands and Coastal SB here.)

This information is presented in graphic form in Figure 3, in which Uplands SB has been moved between SH and FH, in order to illustrate the similarities between these three.

TABLE 27
A COMPARISON OF SOME MORPHOLOGICAL FEATURES OF TRANSPLANTED VARIETIES OF BHOJPURI

VERB ENDINGS	MAURITIUS	GUYANA	TRINIDAD	S. AFRICA	SURINAME	FIJI
(a) *Present Habitual*						
Sg 1	*-lā*	*-lā*	*-lā*	*-lā*	*-lā*	*-tā+hai*
2	*-lā*	*-e+he*	*-lā*	*-e+he*	*-e+hai*	*-tā+hai*
3	*-lā*	*-e+he*	*-lā*	*-e+he*	*-e+hai*	*-tā+hai*
Pl 1	*-lā+sa*	(as for sg)	(as for sg)	(as for sg)	(as for sg)	(as for sg)
2	*-lā+sa*					
3	*-lan+sa*					
(b) *Present Continuous:*	*-at*+aux	*-lā* forms	*-at*+aux	*-at*+aux	*-at*+aux	*-tā*+aux
(c) *Future*						
Sg 1	*-b*	*-b*	*-b*	*-b* (or *-egā*)	*-b*	*-egā*
2	*-be*	*-iho*	*-be*	*-be* (or *-egā*)	*-iye*	*-egā*
3	*-ī*	*-ī*	*-ī*	*-ī* (or *-egā*)	*-i/igā*	*-ī*
Pl 1	*-b+sa*	(as for sg)	(as for sg)	(as for sg)	(as for sg)	(as for sg)
2	*-bā+sa*	(as for sg)	(as for sg)	(as for sg)	(as for sg)	(as for sg)
3	*-ihan+sa*	*-ihe*	(as for sg)	(as for sg)	(as for sg)	(as for sg)

(d) *Past Transitive*						
Sg 1	*-lī/nī*	*-lī*	*-lī*	*-lī* (or *-ā*)	*-lī*	*-ā*
2	*-le*	*-le*	*-le*	*-le* (or *-ā*)	*-le*	*-ā*
3	*-lak*	*-le*	*-al*	*-lak/las/-is*	*-is*	*-ā/-is*
Pl 1	*-lī/nī+sa*	(as for sg)	(as for sg)	*-li* (or *-ā*)	(as for sg)	*-ā*
2	*-la+sa*	(as for sg)	(as for sg)	*-le* (or *-ā*)		*-ā*
3	*-la+sa*	(as for sg)	(as for sg)	*-lak/las/-in*		*-ā/in*
(e) *Aux/ Copula*	*bā* (less commonly: *hai*)	*hai*	*bā*	*he/hai*	*hai/bā*	*hai*
(f) *Classifiers*	*go*	*go*	*go*	*ṭho*	*go/ṭho*	*ṭho*

Notes: Information based on Moag 1977; Mohan 1978; Gambhir 1981; Domingue 1971; Baker and Ramnah 1985; Damsteegt and Narain 1987. Forms in brackets are systematic dialectal differences in South Africa. Minor alternative forms in each country are excluded.

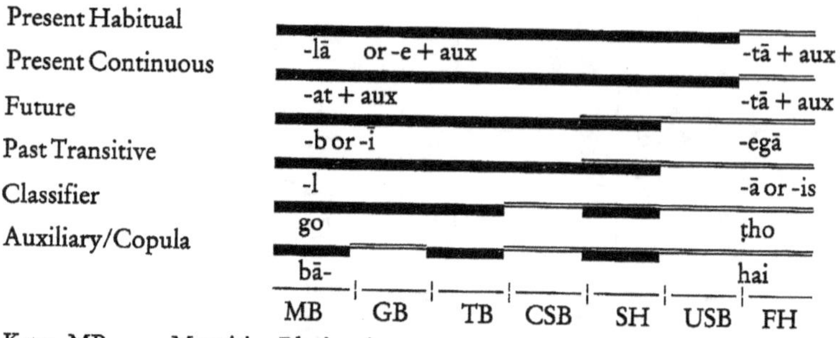

Key: MB — Mauritian Bhojpuri
GB — Guyanese Bhojpuri
TB — Trinidad Bhojpuri
CSB — Coastal South African Bhojpuri
SH — Sarnami Hindi
USB — Uplands South African Bhojpuri
FH — Fiji Hindi

Figure 3 – Six selected features in overseas Bhojpuri.

Recruiting patterns over space and time in India account quite neatly for the particular features of overseas varieties of B. The same historical factors are responsible for shaping the three dialects of SB that developed. Just as recruiters in India began in more easterly areas and gradually moved into the interior, employment of indentured labour in Natal began along the coast and gradually spread into the Uplands. Bhana and Brain (1984:26) note that:

> In the first decade of the indenture system . . . the coastal planters were the largest employers of Indian labour and there was still considerable opposition from the inland agriculturists and pastoralists to the whole idea of bringing in Indians while Black labour was present in such large numbers.

By the 1890s, however, thirty years after the first immigrations to Natal, employment patterns were less restrictive. The Protector noted in his report for 1892 that Indians were spread 'almost throughout the length and breadth of the colony'.

Coastal SB thus shows a more easterly character (and similarities with MB, GB and TB), while Uplands SB accords more with the varieties that were formed in the 1870s – SH and FH.

2.6 CALCUTTA BAZAAR HINDUSTANI AND OVERSEAS BHOJPURI

A possible complication to the theory that links the characteristics of overseas B with recruitment patterns is the contribution of CBH. CBH is the reduced variety of Hn that developed in Calcutta, where it was the native language of some, but not many, of the first inhabitants of the city. Chatterji (1972[1931]) claims CBH to be the lingua franca of all non-Bengali and Oriya speakers in the city. Siegel (1987:193) quotes a pertinent section from Chatterji (1972[1931]:218):

> Groups of people are growing up, whose home language and sometimes whose only language is this jargon or Bāzār Hindustani – in the *bustee* slums of Calcutta, in the coolie lines in our jute mill areas, in the Andaman Islands, and among Indian emigrants in Fiji, Trinidad and British Guiana and elsewhere.

That Chatterji has overstated the case for Fiji is pointed out by Moag (1979: 118–19), and for Guyana by Gambhir (1981:276–86). Both iterate Chatterji's claim that CBH is based on Std and W. Hn, while showing in their work that FH and GB have their roots in E. Hn and Bihari dialects. Siegel (1987: 276–86), however, maintains that CBH played a significant role in the development of overseas B, especially in FH. He believes that the following forms in overseas B reflect the influence of CBH:

māng	'want'	*khalās*	'finished'
is/us māfik	'like this/that'	*nagīj*	'near'
muluk	'place of origin'	*kauncī*	'what'

(Four of these items occur in SB, the two exceptions being *is/us māfik* and *kauncī*. *Muluk* means simply 'India', while the usual form in SB is *nagīc* not *nagīj*.)

In addition he claims the following morphological items to have been reinforced by CBH usage:

ham log	'we'	*tum log*	'you' (pl)
-is	(3rd sg past)	*-in*	(3rd pl. past)
rah-	(aux/copula)	*hai*	(invariant aux copula)
-tā	(perfective)	*-egā*	(invariant future)

TABLE 28
COMPARISON OF BASIC VOCABULARY BETWEEN SOUTH AFRICAN BHOJPURI AND OTHER INDIC LANGUAGES/DIALECTS
(Figures are also percentages since n = 100)

STD HN	W. HN DIALECTS	E. HN DIALECTS	B	MAGAHI	MAITHILI	SB	NO. OF ITEMS	LEXICAL ITEMS (SB form given)
+	+	+	+	+	+	+	60	(see below)
−	+	+	+	+	+	+	5	*bār* 'hair', *āge* 'in front', *kākā* 'uncle', *biah* 'marriage', *dām* 'price'
+	+	+	+	+	−	+	2	*sau* 'hundred', *beiṭh* 'sit'
+	+	−	+	+	+	+	4	*seitān* 'devil', *nām* 'name', *cānd* 'moon', *picche* 'behind'
−	−	+	+	+	+	+	5	*ham* 'I', *tor* 'your', *ū* 'he/she/it', *ke* 'who', *ū̃ch* 'high'
−	+	+	+	+	−	+	2	*kā* 'what', *kāhe* 'why'
+	+	+	+	−	−	+	1	*jo* 'if'
+	+	−	+	+	−	+	2	*admī* 'man', *kutta* 'dog'
+	−	−	+	+	+	+	2	*beṭī* 'daughter'
−	−	−	+	+	+	+	3	*dū* 'two', *harin* 'deer', *kīn-* 'buy'
−	−	+	+	+	−	+	1	*goṛ* 'foot'
−	+	+	+	−	−	+	1	*nagic* 'near'
+	−	−	+	+	−	+	1	*kharāb* 'bad'
+	−	−	−	+	+	+	1	*baccā* 'baby'
−	−	+	+	−	−	+	1	*suruj* 'sun'
+	−	−	−	+	−	+	1	*aurat* 'woman'
−	−	−	+	−	−	+	2	*baki* 'but', *peṛ* 'tree'
+	−	−	−	−	−	+	1	*che* 'six'
−	−	−	−	−	−	+	1	*muṇḍī* 'head' (from Dakhini Urdu)
							4	not classifiable ('shepherd', 'slave', 'saddle', 'cultivator')

Although I would not want to exclude CBH as one of the dialectal inputs to SB, I would doubt the extent of its influence. As Siegel concedes (1987:195–6), it is not possible to decide conclusively whether a form like *ham log* is from CBH or from one of the village dialects (in this case Magahi), or both. The number of immigrants to Natal from Calcutta itself was insignificant (it does not feature in Table 5); and appeals to the influence of CBH must therefore rest on its possible use as a lingua franca. Tinker (1974:52), however, calls Hindustani the lingua franca of the emigration traffic, without referring to CBH specifically. If the forms posited by Siegel are really from CBH, we would have no systematic way of accounting for their presence in certain colonies, but not others. Nor would we be able to explain the dialectal differences between Upland and Coastal SB. For the CBH origins to be viable, we would need to determine why its influence should be particularly felt in areas receiving indentured workers last (Upland Natal, Suriname, Fiji). The temporal and regional recruitment perspective would appear to offer a better explanation. It shows that the descriptions of regional dialects in Grierson's LSI are sufficient to characterise overseas B, without being complicated by CBH, except in a tiny role.

2.7 *VOCABULARY*

In order to gauge the lexical contribution of the various languages to SB I will compare one hundred items taken from the word-lists given by Grierson in the appendices to his linguistic surveys of India (1903, 1904, 1916). For each language and major dialect of India he provides lists of the most common words in everyday use, based on fieldwork in representative districts. In Table 28 a comparison is made between SB and the relevant North Indian languages. The column on the extreme right indicates the number of items in SB (out of the hundred selected) which are traceable to all the contributing languages, to some of them, or none at all. This procedure of assigning pluses and minuses is not foolproof: it is possible that where a minus has been recorded for a language/dialect, there might still exist village dialects which do use the SB form under consideration, but which have not been noted by Grierson.[5] Furthermore dialects are rarely as discrete lexically as an 'either-or' characterisation suggests.

The sixty words of the hundred in Grierson's lists common to all the languages are as follows (SB form cited):

ek 'one'	*tīn* 'three'	*cār* 'four'	*pā̃c* 'five'
sāt 'seven'	*āṭh* 'eight'	*nau* 'nine'	*das* 'ten'
bīs 'twenty'	*pacchās* 'fifty'	*tū̃* 'you'	*hāth* 'hand'
nāk 'nose'	*ā̃kh(i)* 'eye'	*mū̃h* 'mouth'	*dā̃t* 'tooth'
kān 'ear'	*jībh* 'tongue'	*peṭ* 'stomach'	*pīṭh(i)* 'back'
lohā 'iron' (n)	*sonā* 'gold'	*chāni* 'silver'	*bāp* 'father'
māī 'mother'	*bhāī* 'brother'	*beṭā* 'son'	*bahin(i)* 'sister'
bhagwān 'God'	*tāra(i)* 'star'	*ghoṛā* 'horse'	*gāī* 'cow'
pānī 'water'	*ghar* 'house'	*murgā* 'rooster'	*battak* 'duck'
gadahā 'ass'	*ū̃t* 'camel'	*cirai* 'bird'	*jā* 'to go'
khā- 'to eat'	*ā-* 'to come'	*mār-* 'to hit'	*mar-* 'to die'
de- 'to give'	*upar* 'above'	*nīche* 'below'	*dūr* 'far'
au(r) 'and'	*hā̃* 'yes'	*sā̃ṛ* 'bull'	*carāw* 'to graze'
nahi 'no'	*rah-* 'to live'	*bāndh-* 'to tie'	*pahāṛ* 'hill, mountain'
ujjar 'white'	*āg(i)* 'fire'		

(Two others are discussed below – 'to run', and 'to stand')

The various words for 'shepherd', 'cultivator', 'saddle', and 'slave' in all these Indic dialects were unknown to SB speakers interviewed, English loans or paraphrases being used instead.[6] For two of the items in Grierson's lists ('run', and 'stand'), both the Std Hn and B/Awadhi words are in use, with preference being given by younger speakers to the Std Hn form. Thus *bhāg* 'to run', and *khar-* 'to stand' are more frequently used than *dhaur* and *ṭhar-* respectively, the latter two words from Awadhi and B being restricted mainly to older speakers.

The percentage of basic vocabulary that SB has in common with each of the Indic languages/dialects above can be estimated from Table 29, in which the percentage contribution of each language/major dialect is given for the hundred words. It must be emphasised that these should be read as relative rather than absolute values, on account of the small sample, and the restriction of Grierson's lists to a few villages per dialect.

TABLE 29
PERCENTAGE OF BASIC VOCABULARY COMMON TO SOUTH AFRICAN BHOJPURI AND VARIOUS INDIC VARIETIES

INDIC DIALECT	PERCENTAGE
Bhojpuri	92
Magahi	89
Maithili	80
Eastern Hindi	78
Western Hindi	77
Standard Hindi	75

These figures are not representative of the total situation, since there is a large number of other vocabulary items which are typical of SB, IB and to a lesser extent Awadhi, but not of Std and W. Hn. A sampling of these items is given below.

WORDS COMMON TO SB AND IB	GLOSS	STD HN EQUIVALENT
(a) Kinship Terms		
bhaujī	'elder brother's wife'	*bhābī*
bahnoi	'sister's husband'	*jījā*
barkī	'eldest son's wife'	*baṛī bahu*
choṭkī	'younger son's wife'	*choṭī bahu*
phūā	'father's sister'	*fūa/būa/phūphī/fūfī*
phuppā	'father's sister's husband'	*fūfā*
ājī	'paternal grandmother'	*dādī*
ājā	'paternal grandfather'	*dādā*
(b) Food Terms		
nīmak	'salt'	*namak*
lāsun	'garlic'	*lahsun*
sarso	'mustard'	*sarson*
kohaṛā	'pumpkin'	*kumharā* ~ *konrā*
chān	'strain with a sieve'	*chān*
bhū̃j	'to roast'	*bhun*

(c) Matrimonial Terms

biah	'marriage'	*biah ~ vivah*
baryāt	'marriage procession'	*bārāt*

(d) Temporal Terms

bihān	'tomorrow'	*kal*
phajire	'in the morning'	*sabere*
sanjhā	'evening'	*śām*
jūn	'time, period of day'	*belā*
bīphe	'Thursday'	*guruvār ~ brihaspativār*
suk	'Friday'	*śukravār*

(e) Miscellaneous Terms

gaṭai	'neck'	*galā ~ gardan*
rakkam ~ kisim	'type, sort' (n)	*tarah*
bīya	'seed'	*bīj*
pahunā	'guest'	*mahman*
jangar ~ jor	'strength'	*saktī ~ jor*
khalli	'only'	*kewal ~ sirf*
bhittar	'inside'	*andar ~ bhītar*
ke lage	'near'	*ke pās*
ujjar	'white'	*ujlā ~ safed*
ḍher	'plenty, much'	*kāfī ~ zyādā*
agor-	'to wait for'	*intazār kar-*
pauṛ-	'to swim'	*tairnā-*
chā̄ṭ	'to vomit'	*oknā-*
bār de-	'to set fire to'	*jalā denā-*
pirā-	'to hurt' (intrans.)	*darad lagnā- ~ dukhnā-*
cīnh-	'to recognise'	*pahcānnā-*

There is far less lexical variation in SB than morphological variation. For example, although there were several dialectal alternates for the word 'goat' in the relevant Indic dialects: *khassi, chageri* and *bakrā*, only one is in constant use in SB – namely, *bakrā*.[7] Likewise, given the following dialectal options for the word *but* in the relevant Indic languages: *lekin, magar, mula, par, muda, lagiṇ, bakī, bakir*, we find only one in wide currency in SB – *bakī*. However, *lekin* might be used as a conscious Std Hn form, while a few of the oldest speakers use *lagin*. It would be of some interest to check whether this phenomenon – less lexical than morphological variation – is a general characteristic of all koines. We nevertheless do find the following lexical variants in SB, traceable to different source languages and dialects.[8]

baccā ~ *laikā*	'child'	*kuā̃ri* ~ *kamārī* ~ *darwājā*	'door'
pustak ~ *pothī*	'book'	*chappar* ~ *chaprā* ~ *chānī*	'roof'
dhapna ~ *dhakna*	'lid'	*bhikmangā* ~ *bigārī* ~ *bhikārī*	'beggar'
dū ~ *dui*	'two'	*kuttā* ~ *kukkur*	'dog'
āg(i) ~ *angār*	'fire'		

2.8 *PHONOLOGICAL FEATURES*

The phonological differences between the main contributory languages/dialects and SB are minimal. SB is especially close to IB in its phonology, as might be expected, except for the treatment of loanwords. Some of its typically IB features are given below, together with their better known Std Hn counterparts. Std Hn forms are given here, as throughout this study, as reference points: they should not, of course, be construed as being the only 'correct' forms.

(a) [s] where W. Hn and Std Hn have [ʃ]: for example, SB and IB have *sahar* 'town', *muskil* 'difficult', and *saram* 'shame' where Std Hn has *śeher*, *muśkil*, and *śaram* respectively.

(b) Lack of a labiodental approximant [ʋ], having in its place [w] intervocalically (sometimes [b]); the stop [b] before vowels; and [o] elsewhere (that is, between a vowel and a consonant, or at the end of words). Thus for Std Hn *Divāli* 'Divali festival', *Pārvatī* (name of a Goddess), *van* 'forest', and *devrānī* 'husband's younger brother's wife', B has *Diwāli*, *Pārbati*, *ban* and *deorānī* respectively. Occasionally Std Hn [ʋ] has as its counterpart a rounded back vowel [o:] or [u:] in B, for example, Std Hn *vo* 'he/she/it/that' versus B *ū* or *o*.

(c) [r] in place of Std Hn [l] in some words – an alternation that dates back to Vedic Sanskrit, and even Indo-European (for example, Latin *lupus*, Skt *vṛkah*- 'wolf'; Latin *linquit*, Skt *rinakti* 'he left'). SB, in keeping with the Bihari dialects, maintains an [r] in the following words: *kherā* 'banana', *karejā* 'heart', *ujjar* 'white', *dubrā* 'thin', *phar* 'to bear fruit', *hardī* 'turmeric powder', *bār* 'hair', whereas Std Hn has *khelā, kalejā, ujal, dublā, phal, haldī* and *bāl* respectively. To add to this notorious '*r/l* confusion', there are Std Hn forms with [r], where B has [l], for example, Std Hn *parivar* 'family', B *palwar*. There is at least one form in SB which corresponds to Std Hn rather than B: *nālā* 'drain' as against IB *nārā*. Doublets like *phagile* ~ *phagire* 'morning', *bil* ~ *bir* 'hole', *phal* ~ *phar* 'fruit' are still found in SB.

(d) Diphthongs [ai] for Std Hn [æ:], and [ou] (and sometimes [au]) for Std Hn [ɔ:] Thus SB, like its Indian counterpart, has [paisa] 'money', [baiṭh] 'to sit', and [kaise] 'how' in contrast to Std Hn [pæ:sa], [bæ:ṭhna], [kæ:sa], and [dʒoun] 'who (rel.)', [mousi] 'maternal aunt', for Std Hn [dʒɔ:n], and [mɔ:si].[9]

(e) Retention of MIA short vowel plus double consonant in some words where Hn shows reduction of consonant clusters and compensatory vowel lengthening: IB and SB *uppar, nicce, picche, dusrā, maṭṭī*, and *acchā* correspond to Std Hn *ūpar* 'above', *nīcē* 'below', *pīche* 'behind', *dūsar* 'another', *māṭī* 'sand', and *āccha* 'fine, nice' respectively.

2.8.1 *Phonetic selection*

SB differs from IB in a few details, notably in the non-occurrence of three highly marked sounds:

(a) There is one significant phonological feature of IB which is not found in South Africa, not even among the very oldest speakers – the vowel which Grierson denotes as *â*, calling it a 'long drawled vowel . . . which is pronounced like the *aw* in *awl* . . . [and] is of such frequent occurrence that it gives a tone to the whole language which is recognised at once' (1903:41–42). Tiwari (1960:xli) calls it 'a developed long sound [ɔ:]', transliterating it as *á*. This vowel, best transcribed by IPA [ɜ̫:] is a long, partially rounded mid, central vowel, having sub-phonemic status, since it is a morphologically conditioned allophone of /e:/, occurring in verb paradigms usually in the second person non-honorific usage. In B verb paradigms listed in the *LSI*, it also occurs between [l] and [w]. That there is no trace of this vowel in SB is less surprising in view of Grierson's note (1903:52) to the effect that some SB speakers use [ɑ:] instead of [ɝ̫:] in words like *hâ* 'he is', and [ɑ̃:] for [ɝ̫̃:] in *hẫ* 'they are'.

(b) I have found no trace of final voiceless [i̥] and [u̥] of the sort described in Appendix 1.3, which are characteristic of EB. Instead, SB usually agrees with WB, which has dropped these final vowels altogether. Thus SB *rahab* 'I will be', *jāt* 'caste', *khaib* I will eat', *bhabhut* 'ashes' all show the absence of final voiceless [i̥]. In some instances, however, SB seems to have retained the EB form, with the final vowel becoming fully voiced: *bahinī* 'sister', *rākhī* 'ashes', *murtī* 'image'.

2.9 *SOME SYNTACTIC FEATURES*

The syntax of SB of the oldest speakers today is closer to IB than to any other dialect, with virtually no features exclusive to W. Hn or E. Hn to be found in it. Table 30 shows the distribution of some significant morpho-syntactic variables in the relevant Indic dialects, and their presence or absence in

TABLE 30
ORIGIN OF SOME SOUTH AFRICAN BHOJPURI SYNTACTIC FEATURES

STD HN	W. HN DIALECTS	AWADHI	B	MAGAHI/ MAITH.	SB	SYNTACTIC FEATURE
+	+	–	–	–	–	Ergative constr with *-ne*
–	–	–/+	–/+	+	+	Invariant noun modifiers
–	–	–	+	+	+	Obligative constr: *-e* + *ke*
–	–	+	+	+	+	Classifiers
–	–	–	+	+	+	Emphatic constr: *-be* + *kar-*
+	+	–	–	–	+	Future imperative in *-nā*
–	–	–	–	–	+	Indirect imperatives
–	–	–	–	–	+	Desiderative constr with *honā*
–	–	–	–	–	+	Completion denoted by *khalās kar-*

Adapted from Gambhir 1981:209

SB. (−/+ indicates that some sub-varieties of Awadhi and B have the construction concerned.)

2.9.1 *The ergative construction*

This involves the use of the agentive particle *ne* after the subject of transitive verbs, and concord between the verb and the direct object; whereas for intransitive verbs the usual concord between verb and subject holds. This construction, which is a characteristic of W. Hn, is absent in SB; though it does occur in the Hn spoken by a few priests on formal occasions. It is noticeably absent in all the overseas varieties of B.

2.9.2 *Noun modifiers*

All dialects of W. Hn have separate masculine and feminine forms for noun modifiers. The Std Hn qualifier *kais-*, for example, takes an *-ī* ending with feminine nouns (*kaisī nadī* 'what sort of river') and an *-ā* ending with masculine nouns (*kaisā ām* 'what sort of mango'). This concord holds for adjectives as well. Maithili, Magahi, and most dialects of both B and Awadhi, on the other hand, have invariant modifiers. Although WB and some varieties of Awadhi do show adj-noun agreement, SB and other overseas B generally do not. Thus the SB equivalents of the Hn phrases above are *kaisan naddī* 'what sort of river', and *kaisan ām* 'what sort of mango'.

2.9.3 *Obligative construction*

SB retains the obligative construction characteristic of the Bihari dialects, involving the use of the dative particle *ke* after the subject, the main verb in stem + *-e* (infinitive) form followed by *ke* again, plus an auxiliary verb expressing obligation.[10]

10. chokrī ke cāī banāwe ke
girl DAT tea make-CAUS-INF DAT
paṛī
'fall' 3sg.fut.

'The girl will have to make tea.'

The construction has also been reported for GB (Gambhir 1981:197) and FH (Moag 1977:267). I have no information on

TB, SH and MB, though it would be surprising if these varieties did not have a similar construction.

In Std Hn the equivalent sentence has the agent followed by the particle *ko*, and the main verb in infinitive form (inflected to agree in gender with the object noun), but without a following particle like *ko/ke*:

11. larkī ko cay banānī
girl DAT tea.fem make.CAUS.INF.fem
paṛegī.
'fall'.3sg.fut.fem.

'The girl will have to make tea.'

2.9.4 *Classifiers*

The use of these bound morphemes denoting 'units of' (see A.4.8) in SB shows, once again, the eastern character of the language, since these are generally not found in dialects of W. Hn. The classifier most often used in SB is *ṭho*, the WB form. *Ṭhe*, found in WB and Awadhi, does sometimes occur as an alternant in SB. The classifiers *ṭhai* and *ṭhī*, which are characteristic of Awadhi (Saksena 1971:151), do not occur in SB. *Go*, widely used in EB, turns up in SB in two instances: the fossilised sandhi form *ekko* 'one only, one type of only' and its negative form *jarko* '(not) even one'. For the classifiers favoured in overseas B see 2.5 (f).

2.9.5 *Emphatic construction*

There is a construction peculiar to the Bihari dialects using the verbal noun in *-be* (its oblique form) plus the verb *kar* 'to do'. It places more emphasis on the agent's intention than the usual future indicative forms do, and stresses the action expressed by the verbal noun. This emphatic construction has been retained in SB, though it is not frequently used. Two SB examples are given in 12 and 13.

12. tab ham bollī nei– ham jai-be
then I say.1sg.past no I go-VN
karab.
'do'2sg.fut

'Then I said, "No, I will *go*".'

13.	ab	ḳhai-be	nei	karī	na	ṭī
	now	eat-VN	not	'do'3sg.SUBJ	nor	tea
	pī.					
	drink. 3sg. SUBJ					

'He won't eat, nor will he drink . . . (no matter what you do).'

As these sentences suggest, the construction co-occurs more frequently with negative items, though it is used affirmatively as well, in the future or the past:

14.	ū	puchabe	kailas.
	he	ask.VN	do.3sg.past

'He did ask.'

Gambhir (1981:173) and Siegel (1987:192) report that the construction is limited to negative emphatic sentences in GB and FH respectively. It is also reported to be in use in SH (Damsteegt 1988).

2.9.6 *The future imperative*
SB has a future imperative formed by adding *-nā* to the verb stem, identical to that of Std and W. Hn. Like its Std Hn counterpart, this construction is used mainly in the second person, singular or plural, with the pronoun often deleted.

15.	bol	delas,	tū	jā . . .	kām
	say	'give'3sg.past	you	go PRES IMP.	work(n)
	khoj	lenā.			
	find	'take'FUT IMP.			

'He said, "You must go and look for work".'

In sentence 15 the verb *jā* is the ordinary (present) imperative ('go now'), while *lenā* is a future imperative ('look for work when you get there'). The use of future imperatives is not reported in grammars of IB. Awadhi uses future imperative endings *-e* (sg) and *-eu* (pl), which are not found in SB. This construction also occurs in FH (Moag 1977:240), where it appears to be a polite imperative, rather than future imperative.

2.9.7 *Indirect imperatives in -o*

The usual imperative form in SB is a bare verb-stem, a construction found in all its contributory dialects/languages. These imperatives have none of the overtones of familiarity, or lack of respect for the addressee, associated with them in Std and W. Hn.

16. wahā rakh.
    there place.IMP
    'Place it there.'

Another imperative form, the use of a stem + *-ā* ending (originally from IB alone) is extant in South Africa, but restricted to a few of the oldest speakers:

17. tū dekh-ā.
    you see-IMP
    'Take a look.'

While this usage has become archaic, another imperative formed by a verb-stem plus an *-o* ending (found in W., E. and Std Hn) is slightly on the increase in SB.

18. kām kar-o.
    work(n) do-IMP
    'Work!'

In the Indic dialects in which it occurs, this usage is honorifically neutral, in contrast to stem + Ø imperatives. In SB, however, the imperative in *-o* carries overtones of formality, and is consequently little used in domestic settings.

A construction which, to my knowledge, does not have analogues in the Indic source languages or dialects is one which uses imperative verb forms in an emphatic, past, obligative context.

19. . . . kām kar-o, pakāw-o,
    work(n) do-IMP cook.CAUS-IMP

    khāw-o, baccan samhār-o
    eat.CAUS-IMP child.PL look after-IMP

. . . aur kuch nei.
and else not

'We had to work, cook, feed and feed the children . . . and nothing else.'

20. phagire phīn ūṭh-o . . . phīn
morning LOC again awaken-IMP again
bhāg-o markaṭ kane.
run-IMP market GOAL

'Every morning we had to awaken, and then make haste to the market.'

This construction is used by the oldest speakers (most of whom are second generation South Africans) and is uncommon among succeeding generations. It seems to be a stylistic rule, quoting the direct commands of overseers on the plantations. It is characterised by a string of verbs, without a co-ordinator or conjunctive particle. The more usual IB construction involving an impersonal construction with the infinitive in *-e* + particle *ke* and the modal verb *par* (literally 'to fall'), or the auxiliary *hai* 'is', or *rahā* 'was', in their third person form, however, prevails in less emphatic instances of obligation:

21. ham lõg ke bahut kām kare
we PL DAT much work do.INF
ke paral.
DAT 'fall'.3sg.past

'We had to do a lot of work.'

Siegel (1987:197) exemplifies a similar use of the *-o* suffix to mark verbs used as infinitives in FH:

22. hamār kām lakrī lā-o kūā me
my work wood bring-INF well LOC
se pānī bhar-o.
ABL water fill-INF

'My work is to bring firewood, get water from the well.'

Siegel (1987:198) also attributes the origin of the construction to its plantation context:

> The history of this *-o* imperative suffix, then, is an interesting one. The imperative verb-form was the most frequently heard in plantation Hindustani; subsequently this form, rather than an infinitive, was over-generalized as the general verb-form in PH [= Pidgin Hindustani, formed in Fiji under impetus of European overseers and South Indian labourers]. Now it has come full circle by being reanalyzed as the neutral infinitive form in Fiji Hindustani.

2.9.8 *Desiderative constructions with honā*

This verb, uninflected for person, number, and even tense, is used with dative subjects as follows:

23. chokrā ke nahai ke honā.
    boy DAT bathe.INF DAT want

    'The boy wishes to bathe.'

24. nātī lõg ke pũche ke
    grandchild PL DAT ask.INF DAT

    honā rahāl.
    want be. 3sg.past

    'He wanted to ask about the grandchildren.'

It has ousted the usual IB verb *cāh-* 'to wish, want', and such expressions as *ū jae cāhatā* 'he wishes to go' would not be accepted in ordinary SB today. There is no parallel use of *honā* in any language of North India; in Std Hn the word *honā* is the infinitive form of the verb 'to be', and functions quite differently from SB *honā*. It seemed to me at one time that this construction might be an example of the influence of Fanagalo on SB, where a phonetically and syntactically parallel word *funa* occurs.

25. yena funa lo muhle muti.
    he want DEF good medicine

    'He wants strong medicine.'

26. mina funa hamba lapa lo ndawo
I want go there DEF place
ga doktela.
GEN doctor

'I want to go to the doctor's surgery.'

Funa, like *honā*, is an invariant verb that functions as both main verb and auxiliary. However, it is not used with dative subjects. The similarity between the two forms is, however, accidental, as I have since encountered *honā* in two southern Indic sources. The first is Dakhini Urdu of India (Schmidt 1981:43):

27. use ek naī sāṛī honā kate.
she.DAT a new sari want say. 3sg.pres

'She says she wants a new sari.'

The second source is Bombay Hindi–Urdu (Apte 1974:30):

28. apne ku ek kap cāy honā.
I DAT one cup tea want

'I want a cup of tea.'

Both sources are operative in South Africa: Dakhini Urdu as one of the varieties brought to Natal by indentured workers from Hyderabad and its environs, and Bombay Bazaar Hindi as a trade lingua franca used by some Gujarati merchants. The *honā* construction exists in South African Urdu (a composite of various dialects: the Urdu of north-east India, Dakhini Urdu, Awadhi and IB). It must have entered the SB koine at an early stage, since it is used by all speakers to the exclusion of the original form *cāh*.

A related verb *māng* overlaps semantically with *honā* in SB, having as its main meaning 'to ask for', with 'to want' as a secondary connotation. In the other varieties of overseas B 'to want' is usually supplied by *māng*, and *honā* does not feature at all in this sense. Although Siegel (1987:195) is of the opinion that the main impetus for *māng* comes from CBH, both *māng* and the more commonly used IB verb *cāh-* are given in Tiwari's historical grammar of IB. He glosses *māng-*

as 'to seek, to ask for' (1960:37), and *cāh-* as 'to wish' (1960:195). Note that *māng-* also occurs in Bombay Bazaar Hn (Apte 1974:30).

2.9.9 *Khalās as completive marker*

Another modal-like verb *cuk-* 'to finish' has become obsolete, being replaced by an invariant form *khalās*, plus some form of the verb *kar-* 'to do', or the copula *he-* /*rah-*/ *bheil*.

29. āpan kām nei khalās kailas.
    REFLEX work not finish do.3sg.past

    'She did not complete her work.'

30. jab pūjā sabh khalās bheil,
    when prayer all finish happen.3sg.past

    tab ham lōg ghare lauṭailī.
    then we PL house return 1pl.past

    'After the prayers were completed, we returned home'.

Khalās also occurs in FH (Siegel 1987:195), and is probably from CBH where it is a typical form (Chatterji 1972 [1931]). A secondary influence in South Africa might be the Bombay Bazaar Hindi used by Gujarati merchants. (The form occurs in colloquial Natal Gujarati, though it is not listed in Apte's (1974) account of Bombay Bazaar Hn.) It is noteworthy that *cuk-* is replaced in both TB (Mohan 1978:191) and GB (Gambhir 1981:54) by the Creole English particle *don*, denoting completion of action (from English *done*).

2.10 *CONTINUATION OF LANGUAGE-CHANGE PROCESSES STARTED IN INDIA*

In general, overseas varieties of B are characterised by having fewer grammatical categories, and less social and regional variation, than one encounters in IB. Much of the simplification found in the transplanted varieties is attributable to the process of dialect levelling, especially on the part of the first generation of colonial-born speakers, though some of it is due to the diminishing use of the language by succeeding generations.

The term 'simplification' is not an unproblematic one, as Mühlhäusler (1974:67–75) shows. I will use it here to indicate both reduction in the number of categories (for example, non-use of plural verb endings), as well as an increase in regularity in certain paradigms (for example, the use of periphrastic plural forms for pronouns).

Some simplification is due to processes that had already begun in some varieties of IB, prior to migration. Before describing the overall simplifications in SB that have no parallels in IB, I describe two such instances of the completion of processes of change begun in India.

2.10.1 *Changes in gender distinctions for verbs*

The grammars of Grierson (1903) and Kellogg (1875) record separate masculine and feminine forms in most verb paradigms (present progressive, present habitual, future, and past). We take as an example the simple past paradigms of EB and central Awadi (Tables 31A and B).

TABLE 31A
THE SIMPLE PAST IN BHOJPURI

SIMPLE PAST – BHOJPURI			
MASC SG	FEM SG	MASC PL	FEM PL
1. (dekh^{a}lõ)	–	1. <u>dekh^{a}lī̄</u>	dekh^{a}lyū
2. <u>dekh^{a}le</u> dekh^{a}las	dekh^{a}lī dekh^{a}lis	2. dekh^{a}lâ(h)	dekh^{a}lū
3. dekh^{a}le <u>dekh^{a}las</u> dekh^{a}lasi	dekh^{a}lī	3. dekh^{a}lan dekh^{a}lani	dekh^{a}lin

From Grierson 1903:52

(^{a}) is Grierson's symbol for a schwa-like voiceless vowel (a reduced form of /a/; and (â) represents a mid-central, rounded vowel (see 2.8.1). The variants for each person are mainly sub-regional ones. Grierson notes that 'it is quite common to use masculine forms instead of the feminine' (1903:51). His silence with respect to Awadhi suggests that feminine forms were still being used by its speakers.

TABLE 31B
THE SIMPLE PAST IN AWADHI

SIMPLE PAST – AWADHI			
MASC SG	FEM SG	MASC PL	FEM PL
1. dekheũ	dekhiũ	1. dekhā	dekhī̃
		dekhan	
		dekhen	
2. dekhes	dekhis	2. dekheu	dekhī̃
dekhis	dekhisi	dekhā	
3. dekhes	dekhī	3. dekhen	dekhī̃
dekhis(i)	dekhisi	dekhin	dekhini
dēkhai		dekhē	
		dekhaī̃	

From Grierson 1904:16

The underlined forms in Tables 31A and B are those which are in use in SB. It can be seen that for the simple past the feminine verb forms have all been lost; and since this is true of all verb paradigms, it means that gender concord on the verb no longer exists in SB. While this paradigmatic simplification is partly due to the great diversity of forms accruing from the various contributory dialects (the above lists show but two dialects which account for less than 70 per cent of the speakers), it is equally a completion of a process begun in IB in the late nineteenth century.

The trend towards levelling of verbs has been reversed in IB, with Tiwari (1960) citing separate feminine forms for all paradigms, including most of the irregular verbs. Gambhir (1981: 249–54) is of the opinion that Grierson (1903) may have overstated the case for gender simplification.

2.10.2 *Changes in number distinctions for verbs*

The grammars of Kellogg and Grierson also suggest that the distinction between singular and plural was becoming unstable at about the turn of the century. Grierson (1903:51) states:

> In all verbs, the first person singular is hardly ever used, except in poetry. The plural is used instead. The use of the second person singular is vulgar. The plural is here also used instead. The first person plural is

> commonly used instead of the second person when it is desired to show respect. The syllable *sâ* may be added to the second or third person to show the plural number or respect.

Modern B has a tendency to use the same endings for the singular and the plural. Shukla's data (1981) suggest that only in the third person are singular endings distinguished from the plural,[11] while Gambhir (1981:247) claims that merger of singular and plural 'is emerging as a very strong phenomenon'.

SB has no separate plural endings, except for the Uplands variety, in which many speakers make a distinction between singular and plural, but only in the past tense. They use *-is* for the singular and *-in* for the plural – a distinction characteristic of Awadhi (in which separate singular and plural forms still exist). The first person ending of all verbs in all tenses in SB is historically a reflex of the first person plural B form, as Grierson leads us to expect. In the second and third persons, it is the singular form which persists, not the plural – a reflection, perhaps, of the lowly status of the original migrants.

2.11 *SIMPLIFICATION ACCOMPANYING THE FORMATION OF THE KOINE*

2.11.1 *Changes in the pronominal system*

There has been a tendency to use more analytic forms in SB for the plural and oblique cases of pronouns, and to obliterate the distinction between honorific and unmarked forms. The following paradigms show the typical forms of IB and Awadhi from which the SB forms had been derived. The paradigms in Tables 32 and 33 are slightly adapted from Grierson (1903:50 and 1904:16) in view of certain omissions in his text. (The underlined forms are those still used in South Africa.)

The pronominal paradigms of SB are not nearly as elaborate, as can be seen from Table 33. From the SB paradigm it can be seen that there are no special honorific pronominal forms. The plural endings of Indian dialects are not in use, preference being given to periphrastic plurals

TABLE 32
THE PRONOUNS OF INDIAN BHOJPURI AND AWADHI

FIRST PERSON PRONOUN

		Indian Bhojpuri 'Ordinary' form	Indian Bhojpuri 'Respectful' form	Awadhi (no distinctions of 'respect')
Sg	Nom.	mẽ	ham	mai
	Obl.	mo/mohi	hamarā̃	mo
	Gen.	mor/more	hamār/hamāre	mor
Pl	Nom.	hamani	hamaran	ham
	Obl.	hamani	hamaran	ham/hamare
	Gen.	hamani	hamaran	hamār

SECOND PERSON PRONOUN

		Indian Bhojpuri 'Ordinary' form	Indian Bhojpuri 'Respectful' form	Awadhi (no distinctions of 'respect')
Sg	Nom.	tū̃/tẽ	tū̃/tẽ	taī̃/tū̃
	Obl.	to/tohi	toharā̃	to
	Gen.	tor/tore	tohar/tohare	tor
Pl	Nom.	tohani	toharan	tum
	Obl.	tohani	toharan	tum/tumār/tumare
	Gen.	tohani	toharan	tohār

THIRD PERSON PRONOUN

		Indian Bhojpuri Proximal	Indian Bhojpuri Distal	Awadhi Proximal	Awadhi Distal
Sg	Nom.	ī/īhe/ihā̃	ū/o	ī/yā	ū/wai
	Obl.	e/ehī̃/ihā̃	o/ohi/uhā̃	e/ehi	o/ohi
	Gen.	ehke/ekar	ohke/okar	ekar/ekare	okar/okare
Pl	Nom.	inh	unh	e/in	o/on/un
	Obl.	inh	unh	in	on/un
	Gen.	inkar	unkar	inkar/inkare	unkar/unkare

TABLE 33
THE PRONOUNS OF SOUTH AFRICAN BHOJPURI

		1st Person	2nd Person	3rd Person (Proximal)	3rd Person (Distal)
Sg	Nom.	ham	tū̃	ī̃	ū
	Obl.	ham	to	e	o
	Gen.	hamār/hamāre	tor/tore	ekar/ekare	okar/okare
Pl		ham lõg	tū̃ lõg	ī̃ lõg	ū lõg

involving the use of the singular pronoun forms, together with the free morphemes *lōg* (literally 'people') or less frequently *sab(h)* (literally 'all'). From Grierson's data in the *LSI* it seems that these periphrastic plurals were alternate means of expression in the late nineteenth century, which became the norm in South Africa.

2.11.2 *Non-use of the present negative copula*

A striking feature of EB is a negative copula *nahĩkhī̃* or *naikhī̃* (sometimes *naikhe*). It is a defective verb which, though conjugated regularly in the present, has no past or future equivalents.

    31.   ab   ham   rāur   larikā
         now   I   you.GEN.HON son
         kahāwe   jog   naikhī̃
         call.CAUS.INF worthy not-am

'Now I am unworthy of being called your son.'
                                             (from Grierson 1903:208)

Naikhe may, in addition, be used as an auxiliary verb with the present (progressive) and past (perfective) participles. It is, however, not generally used in WB, where a more analytic construction using the ordinary negative *nahi* 'not' and the present copula *bā* or *hai* occurs.[12] No trace of *naikhī̃* or its variants exist in SB today. Only a few people recall its use by some of the oldest speakes a generation ago, and consider it to be extremely 'old-fashioned' and amusing. It therefore seems likely that *naikhī̃* was used in South Africa only by those arriving from EB districts, and was not passed on to the first generation of South African-born children. It has not survived in any other overseas B (Gambhir 1981:271).

2.11.3 *Non-use of the auxiliary hokh-*

Like *naikhī̃*, this is a defective verb in IB, having present tense forms only, and used solely in a subjunctive sense of 'to become' as follows:

    32.   jo   tū   dekhale   hokh-ā,   ta
         if   you   see.PP   may be-2sg.pres then

hamarā se kahā.
I-OBL ABL tell.IMP

'If you have seen (it), tell me.'

33. je hamār bakharā hokh-e
which I.GEN share(n) may be-3sg.pres

se hamarā ke de dâ
that.CORR. I.OBL DAT give 'give'.IMP

'Give me whatever my share might be.'
(from Grierson 1903:207)

This verb does not occur in South Africa, and even fewer people recall their parents or grandparents ever using it. In its place SB uses the verb *ho-* 'to be/become' which is actually a lesser used alternate in IB and Awadhi.[13] Sentence 34 illustrates the use of this (defective) verb in SB.

34. tū wahā jaibe, tā kabhi ghar
you there go.2sg.fut then perhaps house

me ho-ī
LOC be-3sg.SUBJ

'If you go there, he might be in the house.'

Among overseas Bhojpuris only MB retains the form *hokh-* (Gambhir 1981:271).

2.11.4 *Non-use of the copula bā/bāṭe/bāṛe*
IB has two copulae – *hai* and *bā*. The basic paradigms for these are: Sg 1. *hai/bāni*; 2. *haua/bāṛa*; 3. *haue/bāṛe*; Pl 1. *hai/bāni*; 2. *haua/bāṛa*; 3. *hauē/bā*, with many social and regional variables (see Tiwari 1960:177, 181). According to Verma and Hill, cited by Gambhir (1981:163), the *hai* paradigm has an equational function, while *bāṭe* and its variants serve a locative – existential function.

Tiwari (1960:177) notes that the *hai* paradigm had become archaic in some dialects of EB. In WB the situation is reversed with *haw* or *hai* being used in the first person (but not *bā-*), while in the second and third persons *bā-* alternates with *haw-* (Misra 1980:212). In SB the *bā-* form is in disuse, with one isolated rural informant using *bā* as a third person copula form – only as the less frequent alternate to *he*. A small number of older informants were able to recall the use of this now-lost form by their parents who had been born in India. *Bā* is extant in a few riddles cited by older informants – see Appendix B-5b.

2.11.5 *Loss of the grammatical feature 'respect'*

The use of verbal and pronominal endings with connotations of respect (and sometimes lack of deference, or disrespect) for the addressee is typical of many languages, including those of the Indian sub-continent. They occur widely in verb paradigms (especially in, but not restricted to, the second person), in pronouns and nominal forms. In addition there are some phonological differences between the speech of a person addressing one of a significantly higher caste, and the same individual's speech to one of his own caste group (see, for example, Gumperz 1958).

An indication of the manifestations of the feature 'respect' (+R) can be found in 2.11.1 and A.4.6 for pronouns, and A.5.2 for verb forms in IB. A more detailed treatment is given in Gambhir (1981:260–9). It seems that this feature did not survive in the koine formation process in Natal, no doubt because of the levelling of social distinctions among SB speakers (see 1.4). There is no systematic way of demarcating respect in SB, in verb, pronoun or any other paradigm. Present-day speakers are nevertheless able to 'soften' their speech when addressing priests or strangers of high status in non-systematic ways. These attempts fall into categories: (a) internal SB resources; (b) relics from IB and (c) borrowings from Std Hn.

(a) *Using internal SB resources*

(i) One would try to avoid direct commands when addressing people of higher status: the future imperative in *-nā* is accordingly more appropriate than the ordinary imperative involving just the verb stem.

(ii) Likewise the use of the local auxiliaries *le-* and *de-* (literally 'take' and 'give' respectively – see A.5.4) after the verb stem is construed as a more respectful

> imperative. Intransitive verbs in this construction, are followed by the auxiliary verb *jā* (literally 'to go'), also in stem form. Thus whereas *rakh* 'keep' is an unmarked imperative, a slightly more respectful form is *rakh le* 'keep it (for yourself)' or *rakh de* 'keep it (for someone else).[14] Similarly, the unmarked imperative form and the respectful form for the intransitive verb 'to sit' are *baiṭh* and *baiṭh jā* respectively.

An even more deferential usage would be one which combines the above two – that is, the use of a verb stem + auxiliary (*le, de, jā*) + future imperative ending *-nā*. For example:

35.	wahā	rakh	de-nā.
	there	keep	'give'-FUT IMP

'You must keep it there' or 'Please keep it there.'

(iii) The use of the optional first person plural suffix *-jā* carries in addition overtones of politeness. Thus *ham lõg dekhlī* is unmarked, while *ham lõg dekhlī-jā* is marked as slightly respectful.

(iv) Respect for one's addressee may sometimes be signalled by avoidance of the second person pronoun as in Sentence 36.

36.	khānā	khaibe?
	food	eat.2sg.fut

'Will you eat?'

(v) For the genitive form of the second person pronoun there is an alternative honorific item – the reflexive pronoun *āpan* 'your own'. The pronoun in 37 is unmarked, while its equivalent in 38 is in some contexts slightly more respectful.

37.	tor	ghar	kahā	he?
	you.GEN	house	where	be.3sg.pres

'Where is your house?'

38. āpan ghar kahā he?
REFLEX house where be.3sg.pres

'Where is your (+R) house?' or 'Where is your own house?'

(b) *Relics from IB*
The use of *-ā* endings by a few rural speakers for second person, future has been noted in 2.4.8b They appear to retain these relic endings from IB in order to draw a distinction between forms like *aibā* 'you will come (+R)' and *aibe* 'you will come (unmarked)'. The distinction would be unfamiliar to most SB speakers, however.

(c) *Borrowings from Std Hn*
(i) Some speakers use the honorific *āp* as pronoun of address to convey politeness or formality, a borrowing from Std Hn cognate with *āpan*.[15] It is not a mandatory form in SB, however: I have heard some people address priests in the neutral pronoun *tū̃*, unaware of any connotations of lack of respect. The pronoun *rauwā̃*, characteristic of EB, has long disappeared in South Africa, with very few older speakers being able to recall its being used by their parents.
(ii) In Uplands SB a handful of speakers, on the analogy of Std Hn, use plural *-e* endings in place of the usual past endings (in *-ā*) to denote respect. Sentence 39 contains such a plural ending on the verb, even though the context in which it was uttered makes it clear that the subject is feminine singular.

39. khāna-ona sob banā dīye.
food-ECHO all make.CAUS 'give'-3pl.past

'She made all the food and things.'

Adopting features from an influential superposed standard language much later after the koineization phase is analogous to the process of decreolisation in a post-creole continuum. In this sense Siegel (1985:208) is able to speak of a post-koine continuum for FH, where the superposed variety (Std Hn) appears to have played an even greater role than in SB.

2.12 *A NOTE ON AWADHI*

For the sake of completeness I list some characteristic features of Awadhi (based on Saksena 1971) which were not retained in SB.

(a) *Reduplication:* In Awadhi reduplication of words with the initial consonant unchanged, but the first vowel changed is characteristic. For example, *bāndh* 'to tie' has a reduplicated equivalent *bāndh-būndh* 'to tie up completely'. This type of reduplication does not occur in SB, which employs the usual B echo construction only: thus *bāndh-ondh* 'to tie up' (see A.2.3b).

(b) *Plural morpheme panc:* Whereas Awadhi uses both *log* and *panc* as plural markers for pronouns, SB uses only the former. The usual sense of *panc* (like *log*) is 'people', etymologically from OIA *pañca* 'five'.

(c) Certain postpositions widely used in Awadhi do not occur in SB, for example, *badi* 'for', *ḍagar* 'through', and *tanā* 'like, as' – though the last survives in fossilised form as in *etanā* 'this much, so much', and *otanā* 'that much' (deictics that occur in SB, Awadhi and IB).

(d) *Future imperatives*: The Awadhi endings for these are *-e* (sg) and *-eu* (pl), as in *dekhe* 'you must see'. There is no trace of their use in SB.

(e) The past forms *āwā* and *gawā* for 'come' and 'go' (3rd sg past), highly typical of Awadhi, are of idiolectal occurrence only in SB, and even then used as occasional alternatives to *ayā/gayā* (the Std Hn forms) or *ail/gail* (the IB equivalents).

(f) *The suffixes -au* and *-ai:* These particles are suffixed to nouns and adjectives in Awadhi, for emphatic effect, with the meanings 'also', and 'only' respectively. For example, *ek* 'one' versus *ekau* 'one also'; *kitāb* 'book' versus *kitabau* 'the book too'; *ghar se gā* 'she went from the house', versus *gharai se gā* 'she went from the house itself'. The particle *-au*, may also be used with verbs: *mai dekhat haū̃* 'I am seeing' versus *mai dekhatau haū̃* 'I am also seeing'. In SB the lexical items *khalli* 'only' and *phīn* 'again' are preferred to these synthetic forms, though some older speakers do use *-au* 'also, even', restricting it as a qualifier of nouns and some numerals.

2.13 CONCLUSIONS

In this chapter I have tried to correlate features of SB with those of various Indic dialects. Since its speakers came from a very wide area, it is not surprising that SB does not accord with any single language or dialect of North India, displaying – rather – a blend of features from several sources. Although there is a small amount of structural simplification, there is no evidence of pidginisation or creolisation – certainly not in the classic sense of pidginisation being a result of contact between three or more mutually unintelligible languages under the colonial plantation pattern, and producing a new variety structurally and semantically discontinuous with its 'parents'. The structural continuity between SB and its Indian counterparts is apparent in the close resemblance of verb paradigms, including the subjunctive and counter-factual, in the major syntactic constructions, and in the phonological system remaining intact (including such highly marked sounds as murmured sonorants surviving into the third generation – see 4.3). The main difference between SB and nineteenth-century IB lies in the loss of specialised features like the negative copula and honorifics, (though even these were of limited geographical occurrence in India), and the loss of specialised vocabulary (illustrated in 4.5).

I have also shown that it was IB which contributed the most features to SB, though Awadhi proved an influential component language. Table 34 shows that SB is closer to the Western dialect of IB than to EB (or any other sub-dialect).

WB agrees with SB in eight of the ten features; EB in only two. This is a reflection of the slight numerical superiority of people emigrating from the WB area, and of the intermediate position that WB holds between EB on the one hand and Awadhi on the other.

Table 34 may also be used to characterise the other overseas B. MB, for example, would qualify as closer to EB than SB, since it has at least three more features of EB (– copula *bāṭī*; classifier *go*; honorific *rauwā* – Domingue 1971).[16]

TABLE 34
COMPARISON BETWEEN SOUTH AFRICAN BHOJPURI, EASTERN BHOJPURI AND WESTERN BHOJPURI

SB	EB	WB
1. Copula *hai* (Absence of *bāṭī*)	× (copula *bāṭī*)	√ (*hai* ~ *bāṭī*)
2. Pronoun *rauwā̃* absent	× (*rauwā̃* widely used)	√ (absent)
3. Neg. copula *naikhe* absent	× (*naikhe* widely used)	√ (absent)
4. 1st person past ending *-lī*	× (*-lī̃*, *not* *-lī* used)	√ (*lī* used)
5. Classifier *ṭho*	× (classifier *go*)	√ (*ṭho*)
6. Genitive pronouns *ekar* and *okar* used	× (not in use)	√ (used)
7. 3rd sg past ending *las*/*lak*	√ (used)	× (not used)
8. 3rd intrans past ending *-l*	√ (used)	× (*-lai*, not *-l* used)
9. Doubling of consonants common	× (not common)	√ (common, e.g., *maṭṭi* 'sand' (not *māṭi*))
10. Final voiceless vowels absent	× (present (e.g. [khaibi̥] 'I will eat'))	√ (absent)

Key: √ similar to SB
× different from SB

CHAPTER THREE

THE SOCIO-HISTORICAL SETTING OF LANGUAGE SHIFT

3.1 *INTRODUCTION*

In this chapter I shall discuss South African Bhojpuri in its socio-cultural setting, examining in the process the range of functions it has fulfilled in the past, and its current status.

3.2 *THE LINGUISTIC SITUATION PRIOR TO MIGRATION*

Detailed information on the sociolinguistic situation in the villages during the period of migration is lacking, but we can get a fair idea of the use of language at that time from current practice in Bihar and Uttar Pradesh. Although I shall be discussing Bhojpuri in the following commentary, much of what is said could also apply to Awadhi and other dialects brought to South Africa.

Bhojpuri, spoken in ten districts of Bihar wholly, and four partially, in nine districts of Uttar Pradesh and two of Madhya Pradesh (Misra 1980), exists today in a diglossic relationship with Std Hn (or more often, a colloquial form of Std Hn heavily influenced by B). B is used as a language of intimacy within the family, and of solidarity between local friends and neighbours. It is inappropriate for a son – even a highly educated one – to use Std Hn (or a colloquial variant) to his parents, as this would be construed as impertinence or anger on his part. Priests and professors, likewise, use B at home. The use of B is, however, not appropriate in certain formal domains and in talking to strangers whose home language is not the same as the local B of the speaker. In this case it is usually regional Hindi (much coloured by B) which is employed.

In his evaluation of communication at the village level in Roopadhamna, Mauranipur (in Jhansi, Uttar Pradesh) Srivastava (1978:30–31) comments on the present-day interface between the village dialect (Bundeli) and Hn:

> Our study reveals that there is a gradual shift towards the assimilation of higher codes (codes above the village dialect) and that it is correlatable with age and education. Furthermore, this competence in acquiring higher codes is becoming slowly definable in terms of the domains of usages, e.g. in informal and intimate situations children are retaining the use of the village dialect, while they are shifting to the use of Hindi in speech situations characterized by non-intimate and formal situations.
>
> This switchover is inversely proportional in age, e.g. old villagers (36 years old) prefer to use the village dialect in most situations.

He points out further that people in this village have no productive control over Std Hn (which he terms 'High Hindi'), and only marginally control receptive skills in it. If this is true of present day relations between a dialect of W. Hn and Std Hn, then we can assume that competence in colloquial and formal Hn was even less among the predominantly adult migrants from villages in the E. Hn and Bihari areas in the nineteenth century.

Table 35 sets out the relationship between B and the other languages employed by its speakers in Bihar and Uttar Pradesh, with (+) signalling predominant use of language in the relevant domain, and (*) signalling partial use.

Although B plays a subordinate role to Hn, attitudes of its native speakers to it are quite positive. Professors whose native language is B may use it in informal conversation at work; while someone who has been to a big city like Delhi and who returns to Bihar or Uttar Pradesh speaking Std Hn is not necessarily an object of admiration.[1] Likewise, migrant workers in distant cities like Bombay and Calcutta have pride in keeping up their native speech form.

In addition, folk-attitudes of speakers of neighbouring languages to B are not negative. Outsiders claim that the language is a 'rough' one (see, for example, Grierson 1903:5), in keeping with the stereotype of the robust Bhojpurian. Many of the swear-words that can be heard in the Indian army are of B origin, and so is the 'tough talk' of policemen in some cities of north-east India – even policemen whose native language is not B adopt it to sound more authoritative on the streets (K. M. Tiwary: personal communication, December 1983). Social variation in language use between high castes and the lower ones is not as great for B as has been reported for Hn and other languages (see Gumperz 1971: 25–47). Educated people and higher castes (the two often go hand in hand), tend to be influenced by Std Hn and English in the pronunciation of loanwords, and use more learned *tatsama* (or Sanskritic) vocabulary. In order to be truly formal or to give evidence of one's high social standing one switches to 'refined' Hn. The so-called formal B of Brahmans is so much

TABLE 35
HINDI-BHOJPURI DIGLOSSIA IN NORTH-EAST INDIA

DOMAIN	HN	B	ENG
Family and friends		+	
Work (in rural areas)		+	
Business and urban work	+	+	
School	+		
University and college	+		*
Religion (prayer)	+		
Political or public speech	+		*
Personal letter	+	+	
Radio broadcasts	+		
Folk songs, tales, dramas, etc.		+	
Film and song	+	*	
Newspapers	+		
Books (prose and poetry)	+	*	
Courts	+		*
Dreams		+	

Adapted from Misra 1980:263

influenced by Std Hn and Sanskrit as to be virtually non-Bhojpurian.[2]

As a 'folk' language B, not surprisingly, has a large store of songs (for births, marriages, historic occasions, deaths, and so forth), folk-tales, proverbs, riddles and witticisms. Worthy of note, too, is its vast array of formulaic phrases and terms of abuse and insult (see 4.7).

3.3 *THE EARLY LINGUISTIC SITUATION IN NATAL*

The migrants from north-east India brought with them this diglossic situation – the large majority knew B but had only a passive competence in colloquial Hn. The languages of Natal – Zulu and English – were unknown to them. The English of Natal at this time was quite close to Southern British English (Lanham 1978:19), devoid of Afrikaans influence, apart from some lexis. (Afrikaans was not an influential language in Natal after the British annexation of 1845, when many of the Afrikaner Trekkers left the republic of Natalia that they had earlier established.)

Zulu, a Bantu language of the Nguni group, is one of the major languages of South Africa in terms of numbers using it as a mother tongue (6 million in 1980, most of whom reside in Natal). However, communication between Zulus and other non-African groups (Afrikaner, English, Indian) has often taken place via another language – Fanagalo. This is a pidgin language comprising elements of English (=Eng), Afrikaans and, principally, Zulu.

Cole (1953) suggested that Fanagalo (=F) might have originated on account of contact between Indians (both traders and indentured workers), Zulus and the English, with the Indians providing the impetus for its early development and diffusion. It was Trapp (1908) who pointed to the possible significance of the name *Isikula* used by Zulus around the turn of the century in connection with this simplified speech form. The word is based on the Zulu class 7 noun prefix, *-isi* denoting, *inter alia*, language names, and the English *coolie*.

Explaining the non-occurrence of words from Indian languages in F, Cole says (1953:3):

> . . . it must be remembered that his own language was of no economic value to the Indian at that time. He had perforce to make himself understood to the Englishman and the Zulu, neither of whom spoke his language, or was even remotely interested therein. It follows therefore that the Indian having acquired limited vocabularies of both English and Zulu, would have mixed the two in attempting to make himself understood . . .

Attractive as this theory is, it is incorrect, as I show in Mesthrie (1989). An unpublished manuscript (Lister *c.*1905) written by an English settler gives a clear indication of pidginogenesis in Natal at least ten years before the first arrival of immigrant labourers from India. F nevertheless did play an important role in colonial Natal, and Indians were probably responsible for its stabilisation. The Protector of Indian Immigrants commented in his report for 1878 on the acquisition of the new languages of the colony (*Kafir* most certainly refers to F here):

> Very often when Indians are employed in out of the way places, there exists a great difficulty in explaining themselves there being very few who can speak their language. Fortunately, the Indians themselves are very quick in most instances in picking up both English and Kafir, *but chiefly the latter* (emphasis mine).

The value of F for Indian immigrants must have been that it was easy to learn, and that it could be used for communication not only with Zulus (though Zulu and F are quite distinct entities – see Cole 1953), but with others with whom one did not share a common language (the English, Afrikaners and Indians from a different geographical territory – in effect the Indic-Dravidian divide). The use of F by a few elderly women as a lingua franca for communication with other women with whom one had no other common language continues today. The practice was, however, never widespread because some bilingualism developed in the plantation barracks. Furthermore, Indians who received an English education favoured the use of Eng as lingua franca.

There is a little archival evidence pointing to the use of F between the English and Indians in the period of indentureship. One English settler wrote a letter of complaint to the Protector in 1880, regarding what he considered to be the insolence of two of his house-servants. Concerning one who had been rude to his wife, he writes, 'He constantly turns around to my wife when she gives him an order and says it is "luto" '.[3] (*Luto* or *lutho* is the word for 'nothing' in F.) More conclusive evidence can be found concerning the use of F in this way in the post-indentureship period.

How important were B and Hn in the period of indenture for inter-group communication? Siegel (1987:150–83) notes the widespread knowledge of Hindustani (colloquial Hn) among overseers and planters in Fiji, and the development of a plantation pidgin Hindustani used first by European overseers, and probably stabilised by South Indians who arrived in large numbers almost twenty-five years after the first North Indians.

Some people of European descent in Natal had a knowledge of Hindustani from previous experience in India (as civil servants, missionaries or soldiers). Others had acquaintance with Hn or B from prior residence in a colony that had indentured labour: these were chiefly Franco-Mauritian planters.

There does not appear to have been a general plantation Hindi learnt by white employers, however. The large number of people of South Indian descent on the plantations made Hindi less useful in this regard than in the other overseas colonies. Letters written by planters to the Protector frequently allude to communication problems and ask for his intervention in an Indian language. The want of good interpreters is an annual theme in the Protector's reports of the 1880s. The Report of the Indian Immigrants Commission (1885–87) makes the following point:

> Complaints were made to us concerning the defective interpretation in the Courts of Resident Magistrates, in cases wherein Indians are parties or witnesses. The Magistrates themselves are not satisfied with such interpretation, and, having no knowledge of any of the Indian languages, they feel uncomfortable and

> uneasy when deciding Indian cases burdened with a conflict of testimony.

In 1880 the Medical Officer of Howick complained about the problems in administering medical care to indentured workers, one of which was the lack of an interpreter. Regarding the post of Protector itself, the desideratum of fluency in Indian language was often, but not always, met. Major-General Lloyd was described as a 'specialist' who was able to converse with immigrants without the aid of an interpreter, thanks to his experience in India. His immediate successors were not so lucky, however. The comment on interpretation in the Report of the Indian Immigrants Commission (1885–87:37) indicated that the Protector had had to rely on two interpreters since 1877 and that 'Protectors have been as helpless with respect to Indian languages, as the Resident Magistrates of the Colony'.

With regard to the North-South language division the Report is equally explicit:

> In some instances, the Interpreter, attached to a Resident Magistrate's Court, is familiar with one or more of the dialects of northern India, but is quite ignorant of, or very imperfectly acquainted with Tamil, which is the language spoken by the immigrants from southern India. Thus, as often happens, in cases wherein some witnesses came from northern India and some from its great Southern division, the interpretation becomes broken, disjointed and unreliable.

Notices of importance to indentured workers and their families had to be printed in Hn, Tamil and Telugu and read out to groups on the plantations by sirdars (overseers) in the nineteenth century. In Durban Dunning (1901) compiled a vocabulary of Hindi, Tamil and Telugu using Roman characters. In the introduction he states that, 'In publishing this Vocabulary, the compiler has done so in the hope of supplying planters and other employers of Indians with a guide to the three languages dealt with'. It is unlikely that his book was widely used, since problems in communication eased off somewhat after 1900, with the development of Tamil-B bilingualism among children born in Natal, and/or some knowledge of Eng among children of the indentured. The Protectors' reports are less vociferous in their complaints in this regard during this period.

Most Gujarati-speaking traders, coming from a different social and educational milieu, were knowledgeable in Hn (either a variety close to Std Hn or more likely, Bombay Bazaar Hn), and could consequently converse with SB speakers easily enough, with some accommodation on both sides.

Communication between SB speakers and Urdu speakers in Natal has never been a problem, given that the variety of Urdu spoken by many indentured migrants (Dakhini) and B are similar in structure and lexicon. Although SB and Urdu in South Africa are considered different languages, they are quite similar, except for verb and participle endings. The Natal Urdu system is closer to Upland B (and Awadhi) than to Coastal SB. Common experiences in the period of indentureship must have drawn B and Urdu closer together than they had been in India. There is evidence that Dakhini Urdu participated in the koineization process, contributing an important desiderative construction in *honā* (see 2.9.8), and the lexical item *muṇḍī* (see Table 28).

The linguistic situation of the first generation born on South African soil is not much clearer. It seems reasonable to hypothesise that the adult migrants born in India had to rid themselves of the extreme features of their dialects when speaking to others in public, but retained these features in their homes. They had, in this view, taken the first, incomplete step towards koine-formation. Their children, although accustomed to their parents' idiolects from birth, must have begun to use the SB of the larger neighbourhood – the koine. In this way the koine must have been modified and stabilised.

Of course, this process did not occur in discrete stages, since at all times the age-range of the first generation South African-born children must have been considerable – with an upper limit formed by those few who were born on board the ship to Durban. Succeeding shiploads of North Indians (especially the younger ones) must have gradually learnt the new koine for ease of communication with the South African-born indentured workers. Incorporated into the koine were some words from Eng, Zulu and Tamil, which were quickly learnt by the incoming north Indians.

What evidence is there in support of this hypothesis concerning the time and place of koineization? Firstly the speech of the oldest users of SB is very much like that of younger speakers, and differs considerably from IB. Even the speech of three of the oldest speakers interviewed – all born in India and brought to South Africa before 1900 at a very young age – was almost identical to that of younger South African-born speakers. This argues for the early existence of the koine. (Exceptions to this rule are a very small number of rural dwellers brought up in isolation, whose speech retains some of the archaisms used by their Indian-born parents – see 2.4.8). In addition I could find very little correlation between the speech of the few older persons who knew one or both of their parents' districts of origin in India, and the data presented for those districts by Grierson in the *LSI*.

That the original migrants did adjust their language to some extent to be maximally comprehensible is suggested by the fact that as many older speakers interviewed claimed that they could not perceive any difference between their own speech and that of their parents, as those who vehemently proclaimed the difference of their parents 'India speech' from their own. This points to at least some of the migrants commanding two styles – their native dialect and the SB koine. This koine generally lacks a broad stylistic range, except for differences in verb endings which signify degrees of formality. Even today, formal transactions are conducted in Hn or Eng. To appreciate the uniform character of SB we need compare the variation according to social grouping that is found in IB. Misra (1980:50, n) isolates two social varieties of B in India: that of high castes (Brahmans and Kshatriyas) (henceforth 'H'), and that of the middle and low castes (henceforth 'L'), on the following grounds:

(a) Middle and low castes use comparatively simpler and shorter sentences in terms of syntactic complexity and total number of words per sentence. (This Bernsteinian claim is not demonstrated in his work, however.)

(b) Higher castes use more synonyms and semi-synonyms and have a greater range of appropriate forms to choose from.

(c) H speech is characterised by a larger number of loanwords from Skt, Eng, Perso-Arabic and Hn.

(d) Loanwords in L show a greater degree of metathesis, cluster simplification and spontaneous aspiration, whereas H speech shows knowledge of the original loanwords and often retains some sounds and sound sequences which are not characteristic of B – like [v] and [ʃ]. Among Misra's illustrative examples are: H *notis*, L *lotis* from Eng 'notice' (where H is closer to the original pronunciation), H *ṭrekṭar*, L *ṭeṭar* 'tractor' (where L shows cluster simplification), H *invarsiṭi*, L *nausiṭī* 'university' (where H retains an Eng [v]).

(e) H shows gender agreement between adjective and noun, while L does not.[4]

In all these respects SB resembles L, and there is no equivalent to H usage. Anecdotal evidence suggests that in the first generation there was such an H used by a minority, but that it was not influential enough to be transmitted to the next generation. Phrases cited by older speakers to support the occasional assertion that some India-born parents 'spoke better than us' (for example, *bhojan pā-* 'to take food' as against L *khāna khā-* 'to eat') do correspond to Misra's 'high-caste speech'. In the following list of words used in H speech and their L equivalents (from Misra 1980:133), I have underlined the form that exists in SB today. As is to be expected, most of these are from the L variety, with a few exceptions.

H word	*L equivalent*	*Gloss*
kalyā̃ṛ/kalyān	bhalā	'good, auspicious'
jal	pānī̃	'water'
asnan	nahān	'bath'
bhojan	khaykā	'food'
sāg	bhājī̃	'leafy vegetables'
bidhawa	rā̃ṛ(i)	'widow'

H word	*L equivalent*	*Gloss*
santusṭ	tirpit	'satisfied'
dusṭ	badmas	'mischievous'
haluā	lapsī	(a sweetmeat)
tarkārī	tiyanā	'curried vegetables'
nasṭ	jiyān	'spoiled'
kasṭ	taklīph	'sorrow'
pranām/praṛām	goṛ lāgī	(a greeting)
ānand/prasann	khus	'happy'

Some of these H forms are known in SB, but are not in general use: for example, *kalyān* 'good, auspicious, *jal* 'water' (used in specialised sense of 'holy water'), and *pranām* (a greeting). Both forms of the word 'widow' occur but the L form *rāṛ* is stigmatised as being especially vulgar. Of the two forms *haluā* and *lapsī* (a sweetmeat), the first (H) is more often used.

B-speaking children growing up in Natal acquired F, and some, especially in Northern Natal, commanded a variety that was closer to Zulu than the pidgin. In some areas where it was the predominant language of the barracks or neighbourhood, Tamil was learnt. However, when bilingualism in B and Tamil existed, it was more often on the part of the native speaker of Tamil (Kuppusami 1946:74). The acquisition of Eng was slower, with Eng education in the early phase (1860–1900) being very slight indeed.

Men learnt some Eng at work, especially if the completion of their indenture took them to jobs that demanded some use of Eng. Women, who were more home-bound, had less exposure to Eng.

A summary of the linguistic situation for B speakers around the turn of the century follows:

(a) *Emigrants born in India*

(i) Indian language – usually B or Awadhi (or one of the others given in Chapter 1). Stylistic range including passive knowledge of Std Hn (for some), and competence in regionalised colloquial Hn (much coloured by the native B or Awadhi). At the other end of the scale, some speakers occasionally simplified their speech when it was not maximally communicative.

(ii) Sanskrit and Std Hn: used by priests at religious gatherings, weddings and other ceremonial occasions.

(iii) A little F acquired at work.

(b) *South African born*

(i) The SB koine.

(ii) Some knowledge of colloquial and/or formal Hn on the part of a few.

(iii) F (widespread) and Zulu (for some).

(iv) Tamil – a small proportion of speakers.

(v) Eng – a small proportion; mainly men.

(vi) Sanskrit and Std Hn: as for (a) (ii) above.

3.4 *SOUTH AFRICAN BHOJPURI IN THE 1930s*

By the 1930s most Indians had moved out of the indentured situation to run small farms or to work in the towns. With respect to language use, the main target for the majority was to acquire fluency in Eng for educational and economic reasons. By 1925 only 27,6 per cent of Indian children of school-going age were at school (Kannemeyer 1943:203), and these were destined to stay on for only two or three years on average, long enough to pick up only the rudiments of the three Rs in Eng.

In rural areas, especially, Eng was often foreign to children, who were brought up on B and gained familiarity with F and Tamil. Interviews with several people who went to schools run by English Christian missionaries in this period reveal the problems of communication in the early years. In the first days of school communication between these children and their mission-school sister-tutors was in F. One informant, speaking of the 1930s, vividly recalled her mother's being invited to the school on the last day of the school year. Having been born in India, her Eng was non-existent, and her F not sufficiently advanced for much communication. When asked by the head of the school in F how many children were still at home, who might be educated in the following years, she could only gesture with her fingers – 'five'.

It is little wonder then that during this period efforts were directed at promoting the use of Eng, rather than planning long-term survival strategies for the vernacular. Yet for 'Hindi' in South Africa there were early warning sirens. There was, for example, one public occasion where no one confident enough in Hn or B could be found on short notice to make an important speech. At this gathering at Clairwood, Durban in 1929, organised in honour of the arrival of the new Indian agent-general, Sir Kurma Reddi, in South Africa, there were speeches of welcome made in Tamil, Telugu and Gujarati, but on short notice no one was willing to make a formal speech in Hn (Rambiritch 1960:69). Table 36 sets out the changing patterns of language use in this period.

TABLE 36
LANGUAGES USED BY SOUTH AFRICAN BHOJPURI SPEAKERS AROUND 1940

DOMAIN	HN	B	ENG	F
Family and friends		+		
Work (in rural areas)		+		*
Business and urban work			*	*
School			+	
University and college			+	
Religion (prayer)	+			
Political or public speech	*		+	
Personal letter	+	*		
Radio broadcasts			+	
Folk songs, tales, dramas, etc.		+		
Film and song	+			
Newspapers[5]			+	
Books (prose and poetry)	*		+	
Courts			+	
Dreams		+		

A Table like 36, using Ferguson's (1959a) scheme, does not represent with total accuracy the situation in a community whose speakers are illiterate in any language and economically under-privileged. In such instances radios, newspapers, written poetry books and colleges are of peripheral interest in the short term, though the prestige attached to the language predominant in them (Eng in this case) does filter through, making that language a target of eventual language shift by the community, at least for some functions.

The diglossic relationship that originally obtained between B and Std Hn is clearly disrupted at this time, by the association of many H contexts with Eng. The use of Eng by learned persons in the fields of education, law and politics rendered large portions of B and Std Hn vocabulary redundant. For the generation that was growing up then, such native vocabulary – unstudied and unused – gradually became unknown.

Men were quicker in acquiring Eng, being exposed to it at work, but the language of the home remained solely B up to at least the 1950s. The Eng acquired in the early period was, of course, makeshift, because of limited exposure, and with much influence from Indian languages. Educationists writing in the 1930s and '40s often comment on the imperfect command of Eng by school teachers, many of whom had only six years of schooling themselves – but there were exceptions. One of the more famous was Sastri, an Indian-born diplomat working in the late 1920s in South Africa, whose powers of rhetoric, admired even in Britain, must have set the standard for aspiring leaders.

Although Eng was already being used in certain spheres as early as the turn of the century, it did not seriously challenge the vernaculars in the home until the 1950s. Whereas it is a matter of conjecture that children stabilised the SB koine, it is certain that Eng gained a foothold in the home and thence all but took over, via their influence. The 1950s and '60s saw the spread of education and the increasing use of Eng in the playgrounds of schools and neighbourhoods. It was the child who unconsciously accustomed his parents to the use of Eng in the home in this period.

A brief language history of one family will illustrate the process: At the end of 1954, the Biharis, living in a rural environment, were a family of six – with Mr Bihari aged forty, Mrs Bihari twenty-four, two daughters aged five and four, a son aged two and another newly arrived baby boy. At this time no Eng was used in the home, even though Mr Bihari had a good command of it, through various forms of employment in the past, and Mrs Bihari had had three years of Eng schooling. The eldest children had some knowledge of Eng, however, through contact with others in the neighbourhood who did not speak B. The eldest child, like all in her class, went to school not well-equipped to cope with the medium of instruction, Eng.

It was not long before she began using Eng at home, first to new playmates from school and then to her sister and brothers. Consequently the second child knew slightly more Eng when it was her turn, the following year, to attend school – though B for a time continued to be her main language, as family anecdotes concerning her quick repartee in B to elders testify. With two children at school who regularly brought home their primers, Mrs Bihari was motivated to begin reading books again, first to the children, then for her own amusement, after fourteen years away from the written word.

The third child arrived at school two years later, having B and Eng as equal first languages. His first classroom utterance, a standing joke in his family, was a macaronic answer to a teacher who had asked him to verbalise the situation in a picture showing a dog drinking milk from a bowl: *Dog cāṭo* 'The dog is licking (it)'. Significantly neither the Eng nor the B sections of his sentence are well-formed; the Eng noun phrase lacks an article, and instead of the imperative *-o* ending on the verb *caṭ-* 'to lick' there should have been a present participle ending in *-t*, plus auxiliary *he-*. (The intonation patterns that his family claim he had used suggest a declarative rather than an imperative sentence.)

The fourth child, by now aged four, heard so much Eng from his siblings that it was firmly established as his first language, with B being pushed back as a language he had a good passive knowledge of, but which he only occasionally used. Although he sometimes coined mixed phrases like *Mālik, mālik . . . so big* 'Oh God, God . . . (the river is) . . . so big', it was never at school, where he did well in Eng.

By 1964, when a fifth child (born in 1958) entered school, Mr and Mrs Bihari had become accustomed to using both languages to all the children but continued speaking only B to each other.

3.5 *SOUTH AFRICAN BHOJPURI TODAY*

We now move forty years on to the present day to note the diminishing use of B. In virtually no domain does the language have unopposed sovereignty, not even at religious gatherings, where in some cases the priest conducts *kathās* (prayer meetings characterised by recitals of religious tales) usually in Hn (often, Hn with an SB colouring), but in deference to younger members of his audience, repeats some of the material in Eng. The same is true of weddings where only the most orthodox priest refuses to use any explanatory Eng in addition to the ritualised Sanskrit and Hn. Even when an audience is composed largely of comprehending elders, priests, in my observation, find it difficult not to code-switch from Hn to a more common or popular Eng proverb or other expression for the benefit of the audience.

Table 37, which was devised for the description of a diglossic situation, is not precise enough for our purposes – since there is a great deal of variation according to age-groupings and sex. To take one example, we will have to differentiate between the two pluses assigned under 'dreams' to B and Eng, since most people over fifty report dreams in B only, while those under thirty state that they only dream in Eng.

Similarly, special considerations govern the choice between B and Eng in conversations between family members and friends. The use of B in public has gradually diminished and the language is literally becoming a restricted 'kitchen' language, used mainly by women to each other, to their elders, and – to a lesser extent – unilaterally to their children. Men below the age of fifty, in general, find little use for the language, except to elders in domestic settings. It is rare for men to converse in B to each other, except if they are both elderly and the setting is a predominantly Bhojpurian one. Thus the likelihood of SB being used is heightened at weddings, prayer meetings, family gatherings, and funerals,

TABLE 37
LANGUAGES USED BY SOUTH AFRICAN BHOJPURI SPEAKERS AROUND 1980[6]

DOMAIN	HN	B	ENG	F
Family and friends		+	+	
Work (in rural areas)			+	+
Business and urban work			+	*
School			+	
University and college			+	
Religion (prayer)	+			
Political or public speech			+	
Personal letter			+	
Radio broadcasts			+	
Folk songs, tales, dramas, etc.	*	*	*	
Film and song	*		*	
Newspapers			+	
Books (prose and poetry)			+	
Courts			+	
Dreams		*	+	

where a large contingent of elderly individuals might be found.

In the early 1980s a forty-year-old male was more likely to speak mainly SB and some Eng to his mother or mother-in-law, but almost only Eng to his father or father-in-law. In such a case most mothers/mothers-in-law usually reply in B, while the fathers/fathers-in-law switch between the two languages. It is not uncommon, when married couples between the ages of forty-five and fifty-five visit each other, that, whilst the women speak to each other in B with occasional code-switching to Eng the men use Eng only. When a man and woman of this age-group converse with each other, other factors come into play – like seniority of the female (in which case B is more likely to be used), seniority of the male (in which case the reverse is more likely), degree of respect (to be respectful to an elder person, or even a younger priest, one uses B if possible), and so on.

Such interactions between SB interlocutors can best be reflected in tables of dyadic relationships. In Figure 4 M1 denotes 'male over 50', M2, 'male between 35 and 50'; F1, 'female over 50'; F2, 'female between 35 and 50'. The speech of a male over 50 to a female over 50 is designated M1 F1, while her reply to him is designated F1 M1 etc.

Figure 4 and Table 38 are based on interviews with twenty families, supported by personal observation of the interactions of family members with each other. The families were chosen to represent a cross-section of the B-speaking community: twelve families lived in an urban environment, ten seemed financially secure, with one or both parents having been educated for at least six years; while another six families lived in obvious poverty. In eight of these homes at least one grandparent was still alive and living with the family.

The numbers in Table 38 are based on interactions in the home, chiefly with close relatives and some friends (keeping formality of discourse, and setting as constants). They are percentages of speakers from each age and sex-group using either Eng or B, or some proportion of each. Thus the first row states that 63 per cent of the males over the age of 50 (*M1*) used only B to other males over 50 (*M1*); another 13 per cent used more B than Eng to males over the age of 50; and 25 per cent used both languages in roughly equal proportion to other males over 50. Likewise the second row states that 69 per cent of males over the age of 50 (*M1*) used only B in speaking to females over the age of 50 (*F1*); while another 19 per cent of the males over the age of 50 used both languages equally to women over 50.[7]

In Figure 4 *M1, F1, M2, F2*, etc. each represent only one person per household belonging to that age and sex-group; where more than one family member belonged to the same group an arbitrary choice was made. On the other hand, some families did not have members belonging to each group – as in homes where there was no one over 50 years old, or between the ages of 35 and 50.

The situation involving speakers under the age of 35 (M3 and F3) differs in a crucial way. Whereas competence in SB is constant for speakers over 35, it becomes a significant variable in analysing interactions of under 35s with others. Figure 4 shows the minimal use of B by these speakers, whose competence is discussed in Chapter 5. Whereas most speakers between the ages of 15 and 35 have a passive knowledge of the language, for most children under the age of 10 even such a passive competence is altogether lacking.

TABLE 38
RENTENTION OF SOUTH AFRICAN BHOJPURI IN THE FAMILY DOMAIN BY GENDER AND AGE-GROUP *(Percentages)*

		B ONLY	MORE B THAN ENG	BOTH EQUALLY	MORE ENG THAN B	ENG ONLY
Over 50s	*n*					
M1 M1	(16)	63	13	25	00	00
M1 F1	(16)	69	13	19	00	00
F1 M1	(16)	75	13	13	00	00
F1 F1	(18)	89	11	00	00	00
Over 50s and 35–50s						
M1 M2	(12)	50	00	17	33	00
M2 M1	(12)	00	50	25	25	00
M1 F2	(14)	43	14	00	43	00
F2 M1	(14)	29	29	14	14	14
F1 M2	(16)	75	00	13	13	00
M2 F1	(12)	17	33	17	17	17
F1 F2	(16)	75	13	00	13	00
F2 F1	(18)	44	22	11	22	00
Over 50s and under 35s						
M1 M3	(14)	29	14	00	14	43
M3 M1	(18)	00	33	00	17	50
M1 F3	(14)	29	14	00	14	43
F3 M1	(14)	00	43	00	14	43
F1 M3	(16)	38	25	13	25	00
M3 F1	(16)	00	25	13	25	38
F1 F3	(18)	44	22	11	22	00
F3 F1	(18)	00	33	11	22	33
35–50s						
M2 M2	(16)	00	00	00	25	75
M2 F2	(16)	00	00	00	25	75
F2 M2	(16)	00	00	25	13	63
F2 F2	(16)	00	14	14	14	57

		B ONLY	MORE B THAN ENG	BOTH EQUALLY	MORE ENG THAN B	ENG ONLY
35–50 and under 35s						
M2 M3	(9)	00	00	11	11	78
M3 M2	(10)	00	00	00	10	90
M2 F3	(9)	00	00	11	00	89
F3 M2	(9)	00	00	11	00	89
F2 M3	(9)	00	11	00	44	44
M3 F2	(14)	00	00	14	00	86
F2 F3	(9)	00	11	00	44	44
F3 F2	(10)	00	00	10	00	90
Under 35s						
M3 M3	(14)	00	00	00	00	100
M3 F3	(14)	00	00	00	00	100
F3 M3	(14)	00	00	00	00	100
F3 F3	(16)	00	00	00	00	100

KEY:

M	Male	n (M1) = 16	n (F1) = 18
F	Female	n (M2) = 12	n (F2) = 18
1	Over 50	n (M3) = 18	n (F3) = 18
2	Between 35–50		
3	Under 35		

Figure 4 and Table 38 show a cohesive pattern of clustering, from top-left (representing the over-50 age-group using B almost exclusively amongst themselves) to bottom right (with the shift to Eng amongst the under 35s) with a dominant middle range (using both languages). These are general patterns of language use, with several exceptions, of course. For example, some grandmothers now converse with their grandchildren entirely in Eng. On the other hand, I have come across young teenagers who speak quite fluent B regularly to their grandparents and even parents, in a few rural areas.

While the tables do illustrate the shift from B to Eng, they do not reflect the total linguistic profile for the community in Natal. This can be graded in descending order or frequency of usage as follows:

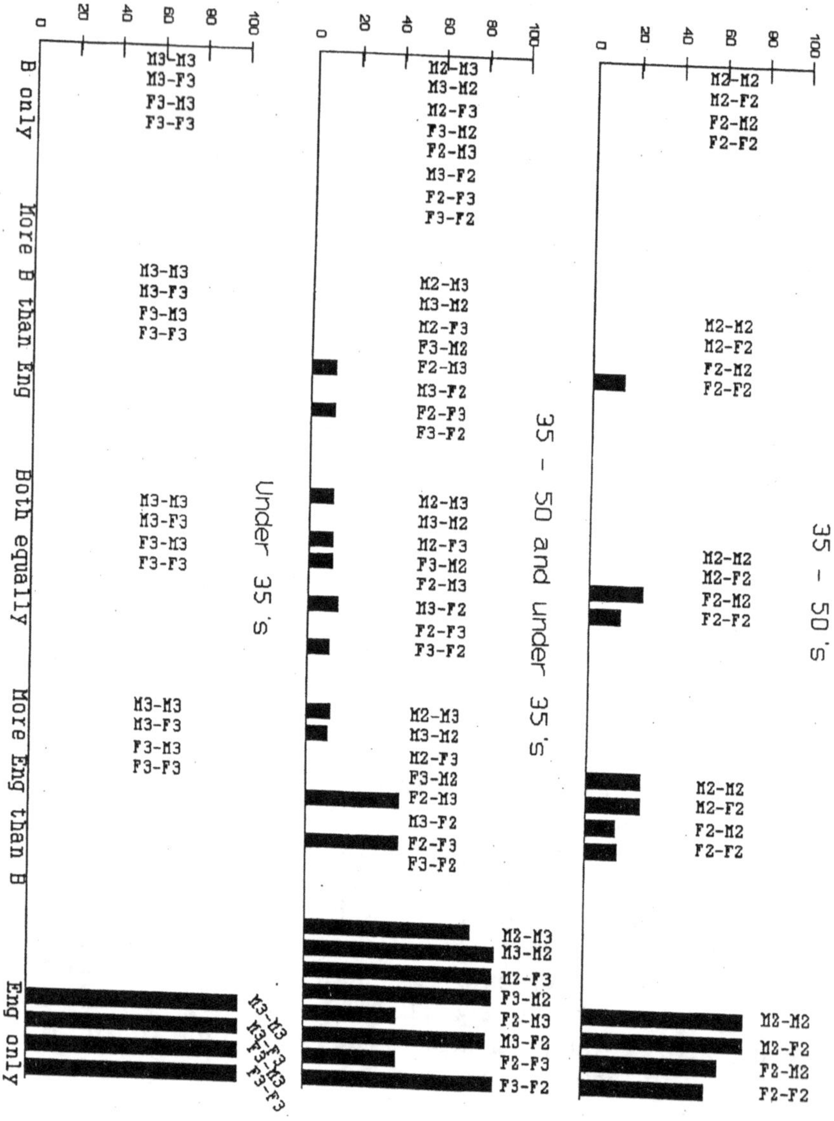

Figure 4 — Retention of SB in the family domain, according to gender and age-grouping

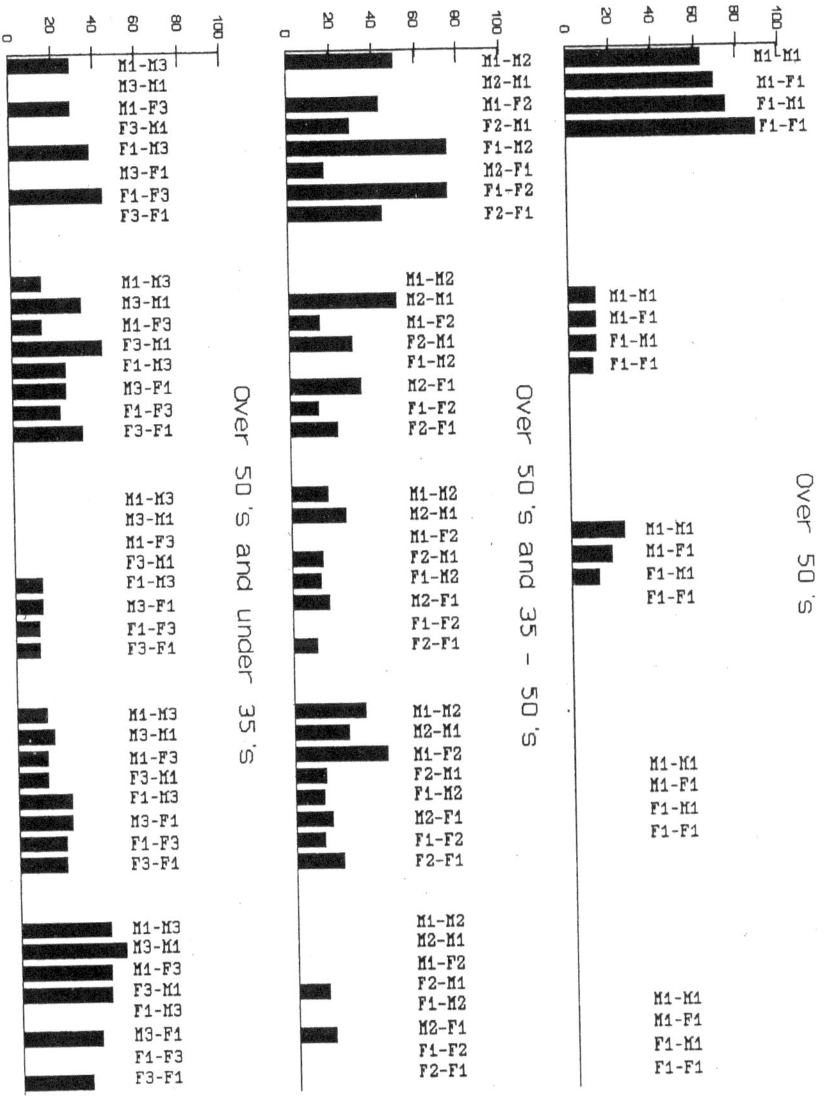
Over 50's
Over 50's and 35 - 50's
Over 50's and under 35's
0
20
40
60
80
100
M1-M1
M1-F1
F1-M1
F1-F1
M1-M2
M2-M1
M1-F2
F2-M1
F1-M2
M2-F1
F1-F2
F2-F1
M1-M3
M3-M1
M1-F3
F3-M1
F1-M3
M3-F1
F1-F3
F3-F1

(a) *The over 50s*
  (i) B (everyone)
  (ii) F (everyone)
  (iii) Eng (all but the oldest, with varying degrees of proficiency)
  (iv) Other Indian language (Std Hn – less than a third of the group; Tamil – less than 5 per cent)

(b) *30- to 50-year-olds*
  (i) Eng (everyone)
  (ii) B (everyone)
  (iii) F (everyone)

(c) *The under 30s*
  (i) Eng (everyone)
  (ii) F?/B?/Afrikaans?

The position of the youngest generation is markedly different from that of the rest – their proficiency in Eng far exceeds that of their elders, but is accompanied by a great decline in the understanding and use of B and F or Zulu, so much so that most children are now being brought up on only one language – Eng.

If Eng has pushed the vernaculars to more and more restricted domains, then the compulsory introduction of Afrikaans by state legislation as a second language subject in Indian schools, from Standard 1 to matriculation (a period of ten years), as from 1973, has rendered any chance of massive revival very remote indeed.

The compulsory use of Afrikaans in schools in callous disregard of the preferences and abilities of African pupils was brought to world attention in a tragic way by the schoolchildren of Soweto in 1976 (see, for example, Hartshorne 1987). No less calculated has been its introduction in Indian schools, though opposition to it tends to remain below the surface. In 1929 the *Cape Times* discusses the sentiments of the Afrikaans newspaper *Die Afrikaner*, a mere four years after Afrikaans was recognised as a language of South Africa (as opposed to Dutch). With regard to the propagation of Afrikaans among the 'non-European' pupils of the (then) Union, *Die Afrikaner* expressed the opinion that it would hasten the desired common South African patriotism.

> 'When a start is made in that direction the Indian section should not be overlooked', says *Die Afrikaner*. '. . . Indian and native children are taught only English . . . Whether the money for the colossal favour for English comes from the purses of the English taxpayers only, would be interesting to know.' (*Cape Times* 28 Dec 1929)

Afrikaans, by and large unimportant for ordinary communication in most of Natal, is furthering the inter-generational linguistic rift. Once an alien language, artificially fostered in Indian schools, it is now gaining a foothold in many homes, on account of compulsory equal time given to it on television on the same channel as Eng. For the new 'television generation', Afrikaans seems destined to fulfil the vacant slot of second language. This can be seen in the 'tip-of-the-tongue' phenomenon for a few young speakers interviewed. Three pre-teenage boys (aged 10, 11 and 12) who understood some B were encouraged to reply to a few simple questions in that language. They were unable to do so, claiming that 'only Afrikaans wanted to come out'. The same test on 20- to 30-year-olds with only a passive competence in B invariably leads to the use of some F words in their attempts at B sentences.

However, the recent introduction in the schools of Indian languages (Tamil, Telugu, Urdu, Gujarati, and Hn) might help stem the tide. In 1984 eighty-two schools offered, for the first time, one or more of these languages (subject to sufficient demand) as an optional subject in the curriculum for Standards 2 to 5 (a pupil's fourth year of schooling to the seventh). Educationists are optimistic that this will have a postive effect in bolstering the declining vernaculars, but it seems too early to anticipate the results of such teaching.

It is Std Hn which is being offered and not B which, as in India, plays no official role in education. The passive knowledge of B that some students bring to school is, according to two teachers interviewed, a stimulus and aid to the study of Std Hn, with students often taking pleasure in comparing what they are taught in class with the forms they hear at home. While it is probably tactically appropriate in such a situation that a language of some prestige be taught, rather than a localised unwritten language, it is probably a herald of the end of SB.

3.6. *THE DECLINE OF BHOJPURI IN SOUTH AFRICA*

If we compare the history of B in South Africa with that of dozens of immigrant languages throughout the world, then its demise seems to have been inevitable from the start. For example, the shift to Eng in the USA by second and third generation descendants of European and Asiatic immigrants in varying degrees is well documented (see, for example, Ferguson and Heath 1981; Fishman 1966). Even though languages like Pennsylvania German have managed to outlive other migrant languages on account of factors like the size of the communities and their relatively isolated location, they seem destined to succumb eventually to the pressures exerted by Eng (see Kloss 1966). What is thought of as an ethnic language (for example, Texas German) becomes eventually functionally limited, overridden by Eng influence in structure and vocabulary, and as Haugen (1973:563) puts it, 'doomed to wither on the vine'.

In the first half of this century the problem to which Indian immigrants in South Africa applied themselves was the mastery of Eng. Their own vernaculars seemed quite secure and education in them was a privilege, if not a luxury. Kuppusami, writing in 1946, mentions the split in opinion regarding the survival of the Indian languages at the time. One school of thought held that they would continue to co-exist with Eng for a long while; the other prophesied that Eng would become the home language in fifty years. Both views, as it turns out, were over-optimistic, with Eng becoming the first language within twenty-five years of 1946 for most of the community.

B has had mixed fortunes in the other overseas colonies. It is obsolescent in Trinidad (Mohan and Zador 1986) and Guyana (Gambhir 1981), but not in Mauritius (Barz 1980), Suriname (Kishna 1984) or Fiji (Moag 1977). Finding the reasons for its decline in three of the territories and its survival in the other three, must surely lie in a careful appraisal of the socio-economic, educational and demographic factors involved. The work of Gal (1979) on the social determinants of language shift in bilingual Austria (from Hungarian to German) is particularly suggestive in this regard. This is a matter for future research; for the present study I list the factors which have retarded the maintenance and spread of B in South Africa.

3.6.1 *The multiplicity of Indian languages*

B is simply one of the several languages spoken by Indian immigrants in South Africa, and even within this small group (approximately three-quarters of a million today), it is not the language of the majority, nor intelligible to the entire group.

Using the 1936 and 1960 population censuses I estimate that 27 per cent of South Africa's Indians belong to the B-speaking sub-group. In only a few areas were there settlements of predominantly B speakers. Elsewhere they were in roughly equal proportion to the number of Tamil speakers (for example, Pietermaritzburg) or in a decided minority (for example, South Coast of Natal).

In the other overseas colonies speakers of Tamil were in a distinct minority, compared to B. The two exceptions are Mauritius, where the number of speakers of Tamil was in the region of 31,9 per cent, and Fiji where the percentage in the first thirty-seven years was 24, rising up to 42 per cent in the rest of the indenture period (Siegel 1987:134–5).

Although a number of Tamil speakers learnt B on South African soil, there was never any question of it (or any other Indian language) becoming the lingua franca of the entire immigrant Indian community. In this regard the situation was different in Fiji, where FH is used by all people of Indian descent (Siegel 1987). In Mauritius, Tamil has given way not to MB so much, as to Creole. Group identification in the case of the first and second generation of migrants to Natal was based on religious and sub-ethnic lines: the cover term 'Indian' had no single linguistic correlate. This relative proliferation of tongues has always posed a problem for educationists willing to contemplate the incorporation of an Indian language into the schools.

Kuppusami (1946) in his Master's dissertation in education speaks with great urgency of the need for such classes. While acknowledging the problem of the diversity of local Indian languages, he tentatively suggests Hn as the one which should be offered at schools, citing its use by non-Hn speakers at the time and its relatively simple structure. Such an enlightened stance (the writer himself being Tamil-speaking) was rare, however, and consequently never brought to fruition. In time, group identification expanded beyond one's linguistic community to rest with one's 'Indian-ness', a consequence of various factors, mainly political and educational. For the younger generation today, group solidarity is largely reflected (unconsciously) by Indian Eng with certain characteristic turns of speech, pronunciation and vocabulary (see Mesthrie 1987, 1988).

3.6.2 *Lack of prestige*
Bhojpuri is a dialect with no great literary tradition, boasting instead, of a 'little tradition' of folk songs and plays. We have noted that in the states of Bihar and Uttar Pradesh, it shares a diglossic relationship with Std Hn, the prestigious language of education, literature and officialdom. Although such functions for Hn are lacking in South Africa, it is still looked up to as the correct 'high' language, the phrase 'High Hindi' being of wide currency locally. The prestige of Hn is enhanced by the exceeding popularity of films and film music in that language, as well as its use by priests at weddings, and at religious and some social gatherings.

While the prestige of Hn is to be expected, the accompanying negative attitude towards SB is surprising in its intensity and pervasiveness. The average native speaker's knowledge of the background to his language is, not surprisingly, nil. Lacking a strong literary tradition and educational associations. B is disparaged by its very own speakers – lay and learned alike – as being not just a poor, second cousin to Std Hn, but a debased form of it, lacking the subtleties of grammar and a sophisticated vocabulary. The attitude adopted by elderly and youthful speakers throughout Natal was a uniformly apologetic one, comments like the following being extremely common:

> 'We speak a broken language . . .'
> 'What we speak is kitchen Hindi – it's not so good . . .'
> 'If you want to hear proper Hindi, go to the Pandit (priest) . . .'
> 'Why waste your time talking to us? . . .'
> 'Our language is mixed and corrupted . . .'
> 'We don't speak so good Hindi (= B) here, but if you go to . . .' (*naming the next town*).
> 'We say this . . . (*citing a basic B word, for example, muṇḍī* 'head', *bhittar* 'inside') but the proper way to say it is . . .' (*giving its Std Hn equivalent, for example sīr* 'head', *andar* 'inside').

Such linguistic insecurity proved disastrous for the transmission of B. There are similar reports in the literature for many other immigrant languages, though the degree of denigration of one's mother tongue seems to be nowhere quite so strong as for SB. For example, in his book on the Norwegian language in America, Haugen (1953) discusses the low status of the various Norwegian dialects and the uncertainty amongst some of the speakers occasioned by the original dialectal diversity, as well as the inroads made by Eng into the language. But others could be found who championed the cause of both Standard Norwegian and the lowly dialects in America – an attitude for which there is no analogue in South Africa: of all the hundreds of people interviewed only a few displayed a positive attitude towards SB; one uneducated old man affectionately claiming it to be *safā* ('clean' or 'pure').

Denigration by its own speakers has been B's fate in all the colonies: In Suriname it is referred to as *tūṭṭi-phūṭṭi bhāsā* 'broken language' (Kishna 1984); in Guyana it is described as *tūṭal* 'broken' or *rekār bolī* 'lowly speech' (Gambhir 1981:31–2); and in Mauritius it is called *motia* 'coarse, boorish' (Domingue 1971:20). Similar attitudes are reported for FH (Moag 1979:113) and TB (Mohan 1978:2).

In South Africa the ones who are the most apologetic are third-generation speakers of SB, even though they are quite fluent and do not use a large number of loanwords from Eng when speaking to each other. The oldest speakers (mainly second generation), with little education and partial knowledge of Eng, are less disparaging about the quality and status of their speech. The inferiority complex that many speakers have towards the language is exacerbated by several factors:

(a) The language in which priests, natural leaders in the maintenance of cultural and religious traditions, conduct their official duties is either Std Hn, or a variety of B that is heavily influenced by Std Hn. These (part-time) duties touch upon the most important events in a family's life – ceremonies at the birth of children, marriage, death, and prayers.

The priest himself unconsciously encourages such linguistic insecurity in his disparagement of the language of the ordinary people. Most priests wish to dissociate themselves from the 'kitchen Hindi' of the people. More than one priest interviewed professed not to be able to speak B or to find it very difficult to do so, yet went ahead and used it minutes after the interview, in (secular) communication with acquaintances, when they were not conscious of being observed. Some priests, however, were more candid in freely acknowledging the use of B in the home, and occasionally at formal gatherings in addressing people who might not understand Std Hn.

Many a comment on the imperfection of B, especially by women, seems to be lip-service to the linguistic preferences of priests and others educated in Std Hn, rather than an expression of deep-seated private convictions.

(b) Many teachers in charge of Hn classes for adults have likewise tended to be patronising towards B, and have encouraged the viewpoint that Hn morphology and lexical items are 'naturally' superior (and not just different). The partial similarity in structure and vocabulary between the two languages has, paradoxically, lent credence to the view that B is a corrupt version of Hn.

The snobbery on the part of those who became literate went unchallenged by those uneducated in Hn. Both parties were convinced that what was written in books

(Hn, not B) must be superior and correct. This situation is common to many societies of course, if not true of all literate ones. There was much amusement among SB speakers that their language was deemed worthy of this study, and even incredulity that it could be written down at all.

(c) The fact that almost all the popular Bombay-based films and songs screened locally are in Hn raises its prestige. It is prestigious to claim that one can understand all the dialogue, which includes a more Persianised lexicon that one might encounter in other Hn discourses. I have heard a few viewers claim, after watching one or two films that included E. Hn dialect extensively in the village scenes, that it sounded inappropriate and that they would have preferred the 'normal dialogue' (colloquial Hn) throughout. B folk-songs, too, are unable to match the prestige of popular film songs, and are becoming increasingly relegated to special occasions only (marriages and births), and associated by and large with ageing grandmothers. Local radio broadcasts have never used B or any other Indian language as medium, this position being reserved for English.

Under this general heading ('lack of prestige') mention must be made of a phenomenon which I term 'the *ailī-gailī* complex'. Two of the words most often used in B are the intransitive verbs *ā* 'to come', and *jā-* 'to go'. In addition to being full verbs they are used as auxiliaries to denote a sense of completion of action, and are sometimes used as markers of the passive construction (see Appendix A.6.1). The past tense forms of the two verbs, which have the usual *-l* endings of B have become greatly stigmatised in South Africa. This is especially true of the first person forms *ham ailī* 'I came', *ham gailī* 'I went', used in Coastal SB and, to a lesser extent, in the Midlands. It has been drummed in by priests and teachers that these forms are particularly vulgar, and that the 'correct' forms are *āyā* and *gayā* (the Std Hn equivalents).

This stigmatisation has had a twofold effect on many speakers: they either avoid using these *-l* forms in the first person (often for these two verbs only), or if they do continue using them, either deny that they do so, or are extremely apologetic about retaining them. Northern Natal speakers look down upon the '*ailī-gailī* language' of Durban and the Coast, claiming that it sounds 'crude' or 'slangy', oblivious to the fact that their speech has its own dialectal pecularities. (Upland B speakers use the socially respectable forms *ham āyā*, *ham gayā* in the first and second person, but *ū ais, u geis* (originally Awadhi verb-forms), or *ū ail, ū gail* (originally IB, and Coastal SB forms) in the third person.) Some speakers use *āyā, gayā* as third person full verb forms, but use *ail, geil* as third person past auxiliaries. A minority use *āyā, gayā* throughout the paradigm, as full and auxiliary verbs.

This topic – the use of *ailī/gailī* – seldom fails to elicit comments from interviewees. One young woman from the Midlands, with a strong religious background said with very polite conviction, 'With the Almighty's help we don't use such words'. Two others, also from the Midlands, ventured, 'No, we never use that kind of language, but they do next door', only to revert to it between themselves when this interviewer's back was turned. In Durban, where these stigmatised forms are the norm, the most common reaction is, 'Yes we use them, but it's not the right way of speaking'.

Kishna (1984) reports the use of the term *ailī-gailī* in connection with Std Hn, while Siegel (1987:146) notes that labourers who spoke B (as opposed to other more westerly dialects) in the period of indentureship in Fiji, were known as *āilī-gailī-walā* 'the ones using *āilī* and *gailī*'.

The other variable which exhibits social evaluation is the future tense ending *egā* (originally Std Hn) in preference to the *-b* endings (originally IB). Though this opposition does not have as much emotional force as the *ailī/gailī* distinction, the use of both *-egā* futures and *-ā* past verb forms carries overtones of refinement, education and formality. This was confirmed by a few speakers from the Midlands who commanded both styles – using *-egā* futures, *-ā* past forms, and a few 'high' lexical items (for example *āp* 'you' (+R)) to the interviewer, but *-b* futures and *-l* past forms in asides to friends in the same room. These speakers would, if asked formally, nevertheless deny that they use the '*ailī-gailī*' form of the language.

Such style-switching from dialect to attempts at the superposed language is rare: a speaker from northern Natal usually uses *-ā* past and *-egā* future endings, while a Coastal speaker uses *-b* futures and *-l* past forms all the time. It is likely that a number of men from the Coast and Midlands who, in the interview situation, used such markers of formality as *-ā* and *-egā* verb endings, and *āp*, the (+R) second person pronoun, might use the more colloquial equivalents in normal conversation, though they vigorously asserted the contrary.

This linguistic insecurity is typical of socially-mobile people dwelling in cities, usually the third generation who happen to be financially better off than their parents, and who use B as a second language. The oldest speakers, for whom B is the first language, are usually quite content to use their language without worrying too much about external norms. Their tolerant attitude to linguistic variation is epitomized by the proverb I have heard more than once: *Jetnā jaghā otnā bāt* 'As many places, so many speeches'. In rural areas there were generally no guilt feelings about linguistic practices, and very few had any idea that the forms they used were in any way disparaged by people elsewhere.

The low prestige attached to SB is reflected in the diminished use of it by men. Figure 4 shows that is is amongst males that Eng has gained ascendancy over B more easily. This conclusion is in a somewhat paradoxical relationship to the fact that at one stage men had a greater stylistic range than women. That is, men had slightly more exposure to formal Hn than women (via contact with educated speakers from India, or via formal study), and could incorporate some salient features of Hn in their repertoire to use when necessary. Clearly the prestige of Hn did not match up to the prestige of Eng in the long term.

3.6.3 *Low socio-economic value*

From the beginning a knowledge of SB alone was of little economic value to its users in Natal. In daily interactions of public life it was vital that the migrants obtain a command over Eng and F. Eng was accordingly readily acceptable as medium of instruction at school, bearing the promise of a better-paying job. There is a line in a traditional B song of India, sung by women before a wedding, that captures this sense of the economic potency of Eng: *hamār bābū paṛhele angarejī, tilak baṛā thor bā* 'my son studies English, why then is the dowry so meagre?' (Misra 1980:255).

Being 'educated' (in Natal) has, since the 1950s, implied a good knowledge of Eng, both oral and written, whereas being knowledgeable only about B/Hn (rare, except for some priests) reflects a movement away from ordinary economic activities. Today most priests are as fluent in Eng as in the vernacular. Whereas there is no stigma attached to older men over fifty speaking B, it is inappropriate for a middle-aged male (35–50) to use B extensively with men of his age, because that would be taken as not being 'progressive', lacking in education (that is, Eng education), and a possible sign of poverty and a rural upbringing. A young person growing up in the sixties was accordingly, more likely to associate B with older folk and the home, rather than with the world of education and work.

3.6.4 *Lack of a systematic vernacular education*

Vernacular Hn education in South Africa has always lagged behind that of other languages – Tamil, Gujarati and Urdu (Kuppusami 1946, Rambiritch 1960). The first vernacular school for Hn was set up in 1914, when Swami Bhawani Dayal, an energetic worker in the cause of indentured Indians in Natal, opened a school in Germiston for Hindi classes. Northern Natal towns like Newcastle, Dannhauser, Hattingspruit, Glencoe, Burnside, Ladysmith and Weenen followed suit, but Durban, although it had some schools, generally lagged behind – if one takes into account the larger population there.

By the 1940s the situation for Hn education had improved with respect to the number of part-time classes held in most towns. In 1933, for example, one of the largest schools for Hn was in Merebank, Durban, with 315 pupils served by four teachers and several 'monitors' (senior pupils), up to the Standard 6 level (Rambiritch 1960:69). Most schools were run by temple committees, welfare societies, the *Hindi Shiksha Sangh* ('Hindi-Teaching Society') and the *Hindu Maha Sabha* ('Great Hindu Society' – a large religious organisation). The curriculum was largely restricted to the three Rs, at an elementary level. After these had been mastered, emphasis was placed on the learning of religious material from the scriptures by heart, rather than on communication in a wide variety of situations.

For all the earnest efforts of such bodies and of individuals, the education imparted was less than comprehensive. It was generally below the standard set by Gujarati and Urdu schools, and much lower than the level attained at full-time Eng schools. To be fair, these schools had longer hours than the Hn classes. Limited finance must be cited as a factor which prevented the acquisition of good classroom and adequate teaching/learning facilities. Hn teachers laboured more for love and duty than for financial reward, and the poor pay kept some of the better qualified people away from the part-time schools. Pupils – and perhaps teachers too – were, understandably not fired with enthusiasm at these part-time classes after a working day elsewhere. Absenteeism seems to have been quite widespread (Rambiritch 1960:72), and the length of stay of the average pupil a mere two to three years.

The influence of these schools on SB is accordingly slight. In Durban the ones who have benefited from vernacular classes are those religiously motivated, especially by the possibility of a career in the priesthood. In northern Natal the widespread use of future endings in *-egā* and past endings in *-ā* are probably attributable to the efforts of Std Hn teaching in the early part of this century, rather than to the koine-formation process described in the previous chapter (see 2.4.3).

Rural northern Natal and Durban speakers seem in their colloquial speech quite unaffected by vernacular classes. Indeed one might question whether the Hn classes were a good thing after all – since most people today who went to vernacular classes for two or three years have forgotten how to read and write, and do not speak Std Hn, yet retain the blind faith in the Std and the accompanying negative attitudes to SB picked up (partly) at these schools.

CHAPTER FOUR

LANGUAGE CONTACT AND LANGUAGE CHANGE

4.1 *INTRODUCTION*

Linguistic change in South African Bhojpuri is the subject of this chapter, whether due to the processes of contact with other languages of South Africa, to changes independent of Indian Bhojpuri but not attributable to language contact, or to changes in social circumstances.

4.2 *THE USE OF LOANWORDS*

As with any group migrating over great distances, the North Indians who arrived in Natal had to make several linguistic adaptations to suit the new situation they found themselves in: a new geography, new climate, different peoples and occupations. As Haugen says (1953), the process of borrowing is also a process of learning. New words were sometimes fashioned from existing native words, but more often from the dominant language of Natal – Eng, through necessity. However, some neologisms were formed even when there were adequate existing B words for certain concepts. In this section I discuss loanwords chronologically, and according to certain themes.

We first need to separate Eng loanwords already incorporated in IB for many decades before the period of emigration, from those first adopted in South Africa. To the former category belong some words pertaining to the British administration of India – for example, *dipṭī* 'deputy'; *kalekṭar* 'tax-collector'; *rel* 'rail'; *rasīd* 'receipt'; *ṭesan* 'station'; *aspatāl* 'hospital' and other domestic terms like *gilās* 'drinking glass'; *bakas* 'box'; *ṭamaṭar* 'tomato'; and *tamākhu* 'tobacco'. Terms like these are, by and large, retained in SB.

4.2.1 *Words connected with the experience of indenture*

Every North Indian soon began using some Eng words, adapted to the B pattern, in connection with their new situation, irrespective of whether they understood Eng or not. The immigrant signed a *girmiṭ* in Calcutta to come to *Naṭāl*, thereby becoming a *Kalkatiā girmiṭyā*. This term *girmiṭ* (from Eng *agreement*) refers to the contract of indentureship, while *girmiṭyā*, which shows the addition of the agent suffix *-yā*, denotes 'one who signed the indentured contract, an indentured worker'. A sentence one often encounters in talking to old people concerning their personal history is *Hamār girmiṭ Birlam mē rahal.* 'My indentureship was in Verulam.' (I have, of course, arbitrarily chosen one place-name for this sentence.) *Kalkatiā*, as we have noted in 1.5, denotes 'one who embarked at Calcutta', not necessarily a native of Calcutta. *Kalkatiā bāt* refers to the language – probably the koine, not the diverse regional dialects and languages. While the ship which transported the migrants needed no special terms, the B word *jahāj* sufficing, a new compound *jahājī bhāī* 'ship-brother' (feminine form *jahajīn* 'ship-sister') was coined to signify the special relationship that sometimes developed between fellow passengers . The term *ḍippū* is still remembered by the oldest SB speakers, used in connection with the depot at which indentured workers were housed until the arrival of the next ship. Many of these terms are not unique to Natal, but can be heard in the other ex-colonies where B is spoken.

Most indentured workers were taken to the canelands of Natal – cane being a crop well known to the migrants, as the retention of a B word for it – *ganna*, confirms. The SB word for 'mill' is *ḍamolā*, whose source is the MB of workers brought to Natal in the nineteenth century. The word is derived from Mauritian Creole *dã mulẽ*, ultimately from French *dans le moulin* 'in the mill'. No other SB loan shows the incorporation of a determiner into a content word, a process characteristic of Mauritian Creole (for example, *lapos* 'post office') and MB (for example, *dāpia* 'well' from Creole *dã pi* 'in the well', ultimately from French *dans le puits*). Another lexical item from the same source, concerned with sugar production, is *lalwā* 'aloe'. Although the word appears to be made of the root *lāl* 'red', plus definite suffix *-wā* (hence 'the red one'), it is most probably from MB *lalwā* 'aloe' (definite form *lalwawā*), based on an identical form in Creole, ultimately from French *aloes* (Philip Baker: personal communication, Jan 1989). (A particular variety of aloe was grown in Mauritius until recently, for the fibre used to make the bags in which sugar was exported.)

The migrants referred to their employers as *Angrejī lõg* 'the English people' or *gorā lõg* 'the fair/white people', though some worked for *gorā lõg* who were *Dec* or *Dacerā* 'Dutch, Afrikaners'. Of these four terms, only the last pair is new to the B lexicon, as terms for the English had originated in IB. The word *Jūlū* was used for the Zulu language, not usually for the people, for whom several terms exist. *Kafri*, or *Kāfar* and *Kaffani* (fem) were known from India, related to – but not sharing the present derogatory overtones of – Eng *kaffir* (ultimately from Arabic). But many referred to the Zulus as *rācas, rākhas* or *rawan lõg*, terms expressive of fear, marvel, and pejoration, since they refer to ancient heroic enemies of mythology (*Ravanna*, the king of Lanka or ancient Ceylon, who, together with his followers, the *rakhśas* waged war against the god *Rama*). Other terms coined for new groups of people encountered in Natal were *Mandrājī* or *Madrājī* for South Indians (both Tamil and Telugu speakers who had come via Madras) and *Baniyā* for Gujarati-speaking traders (the term *baniyā* in IB refers to any merchant or shopkeeper). All these terms have today a slight overlay of pejoration on account of in-group rivalry, but as originally used in SB by older speakers were probably neutral terms arising out of necessity of reference.

Other loans connected with the early experience of indentureship are *barkīs* (from Eng *barracks*), used to describe the communal dwelling-place of many families in their early days on the canelands, though the B term *koṭī* 'large simple dwelling' was also applied here; *raicen, raiśen* or *raisen* (from Eng *ration*) signifying the weekly and monthly supplies of rice, fish, maize meal, cooking oil, and so on, given to workers; *pās* (from Eng *pass*), which refers to the birth-certificate or other document they were obliged to carry; and *mesan-koṭ*, an eponymous term for the Indian Immigration Office, derived from (L.H.) *Mason*, the first 'coolie-agent', who later became Protector (1882–1901), and *koṭī* 'building'. For an interesting parallel from Guyana I quote Tinker (1974:224):

> Finally, there was the Protector, the last 'court of appeal', as it were, for the estate labourer. He would spend most of his time at headquarters, dealing with arrivals and departures, but he would occasionally tour the plantations. Though remote, he was a household name to the Indians. When a mission from India visited Demerara in 1913, they found that the Immigration Office was called *Krasbi* by the indentured Indians: James Crosby was appointed Immigration Agent-General, or Protector, in 1858, and he retired in 1880! Crosby fought a battle with the unsympathetic Governor Hincks, but he survived to make improvements.

The terms *luṭerā* and *ṭhagwā* are still used by older speakers in referring to those who enticed Indians to go overseas as indentured workers, the so-called 'coolie-catchers'. The suspicion with which the recruiters were held can be gauged from the Eng words *loot* and *thug*, which are borrowings based on these terms. The more neutral term *arkhaṭiyā* (from Eng *recruiter*) extant in Hn in India, and in FH (Siegel 1987:129), seems not to have been used by SB speakers. The word *kūlī* 'coolie' can also be listed here. In most Indic languages, including IB, it means 'porter', but acquired the colonial Eng sense of 'indentured labourer, Indian labourer' in SB and other Indian languages of Natal in the nineteenth century. Gandhi (1928:40) observes that the word was used in this way at the time of his arrival in 1893. Although this sense does not survive in SB (due largely to the efforts of Gandhi), the original meaning is almost unknown today. This can be gauged from the objections lodged by locals to the title of a Hn film, *Coolie*, screened in 1983, which they took to be the needless use of a derogatory word, but which was, in fact, a film romanticising the simple, honest porter.

4.2.2 *Loanwords from Fanagalo*

The language that most of the immigrants learnt first was F, a heritage that remains in the form of several loanwords, some of which have been completely assimilated into SB. To this category belong the following words:

basop kar 'to look after, to guard, to herd'. In F *basop* is usually an imperative form 'look out, beware', but may also be used as indicative form 'to watch over' etc. The word is ultimately of Afrikaans origin (from *pas op*). In SB it has been made into a phrasal verb by adding the verb *kar* 'to do'. We thus have an interesting shift from the original Afrikaans exclamatory imperative to a similar use in F, plus an extension to a full verb with similar meaning, to only the latter usage in SB; where the imperative sense of *pas op* is still served by a native construction (SB future imperative *dekhnā* = 'watch out'). An example of the use of *basop* follows:

1.

ek	dusrā	bhāī	rahā...	oke
one	other	brother	be.3sg.past	he.DAT

muṇḍī	nai	rahā...	janāwar	basop
head	not	be.3sg.past	animals	watch

karā.
do.3sg.past

'There was one other brother, who was feeble minded... he grazed animals.'

The B word for 'to graze cattle' (*carāw-*) persists, in free variation with *basop kar*, which is recognised as an unprestigious loanword, but seldom avoided in normal conversation.

bagāśā kar- 'to visit, go on a holiday'. In F *fagash/vagasha/vakasha* as a verb means 'to go for a walk, to visit' (Bold 1974:72), while its nominal equivalent *kufagash* denotes 'holiday'. In SB it usually occurs as a phrasal verb with *kar*, with the basic meaning 'to visit', and occasionally 'to go on holiday', while it may sometimes occur as a noun 'a visit, a holiday'. (On this use of *kar* see 4.6.1 f.)

2. ham lõg āī rahā bagāśā kare
We pl come.PAST P visit do.INF

baki ū moṭar me cal
but he car LOC move

gā rahā.
'go'PAST P be.3sg.past

'We had come to visit him, but he had gone by car.'

3. bagāśā keise rahal?
Visit how be.3sg.past

'How was the trip/visit?'

ḍāgā 'mud', from F 'mud, dirt', itself from Zulu *udaka* 'mud, mortar for building'. In SB it is a noun, which can be used attributively as the first element of a compound, as in *ḍāgā-pānī* 'muddy water' literally 'mud-water'.

dongā 'a drain, a hollow', from F, and South African Eng (henceforth SAE) *donga*, ultimately Zulu *udonga*.

jās 'a raincoat, an overcoat', from F *jāz*, Zulu *ijazi*, ultimately Afrikaans *jas*.

baleṭhā 'a method of carrying a child on one's back' (based on Zulu custom), Zulu *ukubeletha*.

banselā 'small gift' (usually given by shopkeeper to customer), from F *bansela*. The word also occurs in Afrikaans and some styles of SAE, ultimately Zulu *umbanselo*.

gwāi 'snuff', from F *gwaai*, Zulu *ugwayi*.

ḍoś/*ḍośa* 'snuff box', from F *dosh* and Zulu *idosha*.

phūṭū 'cooked mealie-meal, thick porridge', from F *phutu*, Zulu *uphuthu*.

ḍuk 'scarf tied around the head', from F *duk*, Zulu *iduku* ultimately Afrikaans *doek*.

boulā 'a home-made heater; small drum in which coal is burned', from F *boyila*, ultimately Eng *boiler*.

bā̃f 'a bath-tub', from F *baf*, itself from Eng *bath*.

These loanwords occur in the speech of all SB speakers and are used more often than the original B forms like *ghūm* 'to visit, to wander, to turn', *pā̃k* or *kīcar* 'mud' and *carāw* 'to herd'. Several others are used less frequently, usually by a few older rural dwellers:

dūnā 'head of a gang of workers, overseer', from F and Zulu *induna* (IB *sardār* also used.)

pūpū 'mealie-meal', from F *mpupu*, Zulu *impuphu*.

phāliś 'porridge', from F *phalishi*, Zulu *iphalishi*; ultimately Eng *porridge*.

slagulā 'weeding', from F *hlagula* and Zulu *ukuhlakula* 'to weed'; rarely used in SB, but recorded during interviews with elderly rural informants.

nyogā 'snake', from F *nyoga*, Zulu *inyoka*; also very rarely used.

These words are easily perceived as being 'foreign' by most speakers, unlike the previous thirteen. One elderly woman, trying to display her knowledge of formal Hindi, said that it was a sign of a speaker of 'High Hindi' to use expressions such as *Me Deben gayā bagāśā karne* . . . 'I went to Durban for a holiday'. In her attempt to convince the interviewer of her awareness of 'the book language' she showed no intuition that *bagāśa* was a loanword, but took it, with rather comic emphasis, to be a sign of 'very high Hindi'. Another four loans from F will be discussed in section 4.2.5 below under the rubric of 'plant names'.

4.2.3 *Loanwords from Tamil*

SB speakers were always in close contact with Tamil-speaking South Africans – an association which resulted in an exchange of a small number of loanwords, chiefly restricted to the domestic sphere. While SA Tamil borrowed words like *roṭī* 'flat, round bread', *gulgulā* 'small, round cake', *pudīna* 'the mint plant', it contributed the following to SB: *cambu* 'a small can, cup without a handle' (from Tamil *sombu*, or the sandhi form *combu*), *rasso* 'king-soup', and the following names of originally Tamil sweetmeats or savouries or snacks: *saigo, polī, dose, murkū* and *veḍde*, the last ousting the B word *bara* for all but the oldest speakers. Two Tamil words have marginal status in SB, being recognised as loanwords: *karpule* 'curry leaves' and *kauḍī* 'Kavadi religious festival'. These loans differ from the previously cited F loans in that they are not a result of bilingualism, but entered SB via South African Indian Eng (SAIE) which draws upon the vernaculars for culinary and some domestic and religious terms. The class division between indentured workers and merchants from India (who spoke Gujarati and Meman), is perhaps reflected in the non-occurrence of loanwords from these languages.

Although SB speakers lived amidst Tamil and Zulu speakers, the most influential language for them proved to be Eng, on account of its tremendous prestige and economic value. Even in the earliest phases when Eng was not widely known, Eng loanwords tended to outnumber those from other languages, pointing to the importance of the prestige factor in borrowing. In the following sections I will categorise these early loans according to certain semantic themes, and then discuss the use of more recent loans, characteristic of the third and succeeding generations, but not generally used by older speakers.

4.2.4 *Place names*

The new country was to most migrants *Naṭāl*, or simply *deś* (or *des*) 'the country'. India, which was the original referent of this term, is most commonly referred to as *muluk*, and hardly ever by *India* or *Bhārat*. Rarely did the incoming migrants coin new terms for the places they were to inhabit: most usually they took the natural line of least effort in adopting the existing name, usually from Eng and Zulu, and sometimes Afrikaans. As a rare example of a toponymic neologism we can cite the old SB name for the residential area of Clairwood in South Durban – *Lakriban* – literally 'wooded forest'.

Place-names adopted early on, before Eng was acquired, prove extremely interesting in that they capture something of the mental struggle to become familiar with the new land and its linguistic practices. South African place-names proved tongue-twisters to the first generation, who modified them to suit the phonological, and sometimes semantic, structure of their own language. For example, they tended to identify the Afrikaans suffix *burg* with *bāg*, which is B for 'garden'. Hence *Johannesburg* (or more colloquially in SAE *Jo'burg*) became *Jobāg* – 'Joe's garden' to a few perhaps – and the capital of Natal, Pietermaritzburg (or Maritzburg) became for some *Miricbāg*, literally 'garden of chillies'. Whether this folk-etymon is linked to the myth propagated by recruiters in India around 1860, that Natal was a fabled land in which money grew on chilli trees, I am unable to say.[1]

The following place-names, reflecting settlements of Indians in the cane-lands of coastal Natal, would not be recognisable to the ordinary speaker of SAE, but still live on today in SB, and occasionally in some varieties of SAIE): *Maṇḍijkōm* (from Eng *Mount Edgecombe*), *Billam* or *Birlam* (Eng *Verulam*), *Rībesaid* (Eng *Riverside*), *Grenḍel* (Glendale), *Kilāran* (formerly Clarence Estate, now Clare Estate), *Haṭrī* (Hartley Estate) and *Baṭrī* (Bartley Estate). Durban itself was first known as *Ḍarban*; later generations modified this to *Ḍeban or Ḍeben*; while many referred to it simply as *ṭaun* 'town', even though they lived in other magisterial districts. Other residential areas within Durban inhabited by Indians were *Sinnam*, sometimes *Sillam* (Eng *Sydenham*), *Kemanḍiś* (Cavendish), *Ginuḍpak* (Greenwood Park) and *Mebal* (Mayville) while later came adjacent townships like *Meribenk* (Merebank), *Spingo* (Isipingo) and *Ceswet* (Chatsworth). Of other places beyond Durban I present a sampling: *Pocepsṭen* (Port Shepstone), *Grāḍvil* (Groutville), *Wesel-snek* (a re-interpretation of *Wessels Nek*, the Afrikaans *nek* 'col' and the proper name *Wessel* being opaque), *Calisṭaun* (Charlestown), *Nukāsal* (Newcastle), *Kepṭaun* (Cape Town).

4.2.5 *Trees, plants and flowers*

The newcomers made no attempt to find names for all the trees and plants that they encountered in Natal. Even today trees which proliferate in Natal, but have no practical function or do not produce edible fruit, are simply known as *peṛ* 'tree'. For example, no informant could supply me with names for the *Erythrina* tree (or *Kaffirboom* as it is called in South Africa), for the varieties of fig trees found on the coast, for aloes, etc., though a few referred to certain aloes as *lalwā* see 4.2.1). Plants and trees brought over from India or common to both territories retained their names if they were of particular value to households, for example *ām* 'mango', a particularly popular fruit whose leaves could also be used in religious ritual, *tulsī* 'basil plant', whose leaves were of great medicinal and religious importance, *raharī* 'oil-dāl tree' etc. As with place-names, there were virtually no new terms coined for unfamiliar plants, the corresponding Eng or Zulu term being adopted instead. We can cite borrowings like *slingeberī* (from Eng *syringa berry*), in free variation with B *bakain ke per, nācīs* (from SAE and Afrikaans *naartjie*), *gamṭrī* (from Eng *gum tree*) and *ṭebe* 'arum-lily plant' (from Zulu *intebe*).[2]

As market gardening on a small scale was an important source of income for a large section of the ex-indentured population, they had to acquire the Eng terms for fruits and some vegetables quickly. The second generation seems to have had great difficulty in keeping these English names apart from the B equivalent. This resulted in various doublets in SB such as *gājar* and *kāraṭ* 'carrot'; *jāmun* and *plamus* 'plums'; *ghobī/kobī* and *koliflauwe* 'cauliflower'; *kerā* and *banānā* 'banana'; *maṭṭar* and *phīz* 'peas'; *nibbū* and *laman* 'lemon'; *amrūd* and *govā* 'guava'; *seo* and *āpul* 'apple'. In each case above it was the Eng form, given second, that was to eventually become the form more frequently used by third-generation speakers. Interestingly, even the cover terms *pfrūṭ/frūṭ* 'fruit' and *bejiṭebal* 'vegetable' occur side by side with the original B forms *phal* and *tarkārī*. Whereas *frūṭ* is in free variation with, but less commonly used than, *phal*, *bejiṭebal* has taken over some of the semantic space of *tarkārī*, in referring to uncooked vegetables in general. *Tarkārī* is now reserved for cooked vegetables, usually curried. This specialisation of terminology does not occur in IB, where *tarkārī* refers to both categories.

The dominance of Eng loanwords can be seen in the

following list of fruit and vegetables where the original B form has long been ousted, or, if known, is restricted to a small fraction of speakers: *painapal* or *painaphal* 'pineapple' with a possible folk-etymology based on *phal* 'fruit' (*ananas*, the Indian term is not used at all); *popo* 'papaw' (*papaya*, the original term, is unknown to most speakers); *mendrin* 'mandarine'; *līcis* 'lichi'; *picis* 'peach'; *binīs* 'beans'; *laim* 'lime'; *grenḍel* 'granadilla'; *kābij* 'cabbage' and *letīs* 'lettuce'.

The opacity of many of these words to the first and second generation can be seen in unanalysed or folk-etymologised forms like *gamṭrī ke peṛ*, which one might unkindly gloss as 'gumtree tree'; *koṭepē* for 'avocado pear'; and numerous plural Eng items interpreted as singular (*līcīs, ṭamāṭīs, picis, nācis, binīs*), which together with the similar sounding *letīs* almost results in a new morpheme *-īs*, denoting 'fruit or vegetable'.

On the other hand, there is a very high degree of retention of terms for small vegetables, and for small plants used as seasoning, which have no rival Eng form. Thus, loanwords are not generally used for the following: *laukī* 'calabash'; *baingan* 'egg plant'; *ālū* 'potato'; *taroi* (type of gourd); *karailā* 'bitter gourd'; *bhinḍī* 'okra'; *chichindā* (a long gourd); *piyāj* 'onions'; *korhā* 'pumpkin'; *mircā* 'chilli' and many Indian plants like *gwālin, sem, dhania, sarso, pudinā, cansur, caurai ke bhājī, lahsun*, etc. Several reasons may be suggested for this state of affairs. Firstly, unlike the fruits mentioned above, these vegetables were grown for domestic consumption or for sale to Indian rather than Eng-speaking customers, so that Eng equivalents were not necessary. Secondly, the Eng forms are, from the viewpoint of a foreign learner, long and cumbersome, for example, *sauph* 'aniseed', *dhania* 'coriander', *bhinḍī* 'hibiscus esculentus' (or 'okra'), *methī* 'fenugreek', etc. This also applies to some fruit which retained their B names with ease, on account of their unpopularity with other sections of the population, and the difficulty posed by their Eng names: *anār* 'pomegranate', *sītā-phal* 'custard-apple'.

The greater use of loanwords for fruit might be attributable to the fact that men, who were first to acquire Eng and use it actively in the outside world, were responsible for either growing fruits and marketing them, or for purchasing them.

Vegetables of the sort mentioned above, on the other hand, were often cultivated by women as well, for purely domestic use. Vegetables purchased by men in public markets had to be brought home to be cleaned and cooked by non-Eng-speaking women, unlike fruits which could be consumed without the benefit of a linguistic trip to the kitchen. And finally, while most vegetables encountered in Natal were familiar to them, the poorest sections of the population of Bihar and Uttar Pradesh were possibly not acquainted with fruit like pineapples, pears and peaches.

For the sake of completion plant terms from other languages can be added here. From Zulu and F were adopted the following: *maḍūmbī* (a type of yam), which ousted the old B term *arui; paṭāṭā* 'sweet potato' (ultimately from Eng, replacing B *sakarkhand*); *mabelā* 'maize' (used by a few rural speakers in free variation with B *makei*); and the already mentioned plant *ṭebe*. From Tamil, the sole contribution was the word *karpule* 'curry-leaf'.

4.2.6 *Money*

The Indian units of currency are the *rūpī*, further divided into the *annā*, which is itself subdivided into *paisā*, though the *annā* is now in disuse. The general term for money is *rupayā*, the same as the plural from of *rūpī*. First-generation migrants must have had some difficulties in tuning their minds to think in terms of the new units – the *pound, shilling, penny*, as well as of secondary units like the *farthing, halfpenny, guinea*. The solution to this problem in SB was quite ingenious, with both the Indian and British systems being neatly integrated as follows: for the base units the Eng terms were borrowed – *paun, siling* and *penī*, but none of these corresponded to the old Indian base-units. 'Two shillings' carried the right economical and emotional weight and so came to be designated *rupiyā* in SB (though the hybrid form *dū siling*) existed as an alternant). Similarly one and a half pence (or three halfpence) came to be known as an *annā*. The old Eng *crown* (a special coin valued at five shillings), and *half-crown* were sufficiently striking to deserve their own appellations: *āfkaran* 'half-a-crown', and less commonly *ek karan* 'one crown'. All the other coins and sums of money were gauged in terms of these units, for example, ten shillings were *pā̃c rupiyā* 'five rupees', and eighteen pennies (or colloquially 'one-and-six') worked out to be *bārā annā* 'twelve annas'. Some people referred to the penny by an alternate name *diblīś* taken from F.

A summary of this information and of the main terms existing in SB is given in Table 39.

TABLE 39
Units of money in South African Bhojpuri

SB TERM	ENG EQUIVALENT
penī	penny
annā	one and a half pence
dū annā	threepence (or a tickey) (lit. 'two annas')
cār annā	sixpence (lit. 'four annas')
siling	shilling
bārā annā	eighteen pence (lit. 'twelve annas')
rupiyā (or *dū siling*)	two shillings (lit. 'rupee')
āfkaran (or *bīs annā*)	half-a-crown (or 'twenty annas')
pān siling	five shillings
pā̃c rupiyā	ten shillings (lit. 'five rupees')
paun	pound

The switch to a decimalised system in South Africa in 1960 was to change this pattern eventually for most speakers. The new rand, roughly equivalent to the old ten shillings, and its subdivisions into five-cent, ten-cent, twenty-cent and fifty-cent coins were at first still described in the old terms, especially by non-Eng speakers. The twenty-cent piece became the *rupiyā*; the ten-cent piece, the *siling*; twenty-five cents, the *āfkaran*; the fifty-cent piece, *pān siling* (or 'five shillings') and the rand note, *das siling* (or 'ten shillings') etc. Because Eng B bilingualism was at this time quite widespread, it was not long before these incongruous terms were replaced by direct Eng terminology for all but the oldest, non-Eng-speaking rural dwellers: *rān* 'rand', *senṭ* 'cent', *fifṭī sent* 'fifty cents', etc.

4.2.7 *Clothing*

The change from village attire to more Westernised modes of dress, especially on the part of men, necessitated many new vocabulary items.

Men's tailored trousers came to be known as *pajāmā*, which is not, as may seem, a borrowing from Eng; on the contrary it is the Eng term which had been adopted from India by the British. In SB the word was extended to refer to Westernised pants adopted by the younger men, in addition to the loose Indian-style pants. For 'sleeping-clothes' another term, *sutnā* applied, some people later using a hybrid form *sutnā-pens* 'pants for sleeping in'. Only today among monolingual Eng-speaking children is the conflicting usage between the SB sense of *pajāmā* and the Eng sense of any consequence, with children not always certain which sense is intended by a bilingual grandparent or parent.

The word *kamīj* refers to a Western-style shirt, though gradually the loanword *śet* came to be more popular especially with third-generation speakers. The word *kurtā*, on the other hand, was reserved for the long, loose fitting Indian shirt (and for some styles of girls' dresses). Of the two terms for shoes in IB, *panahī* and *juttā*, the former gradually lost out to the latter which was more prestigious, being the term also used in Std Hn. Other Eng loans used in connection with men's clothing are: *sūṭ* 'suit'; *koṭ* 'coat'; *singleṭ* 'vest, singlet'; *belṭ* 'belt'; *sākis* 'socks'; *ṭhai* 'tie'; *askiṭ* 'waistcoat' and the compound *śoṭ-pens* 'short-pants'.

For women's clothes, basic terms like *sāṛī*, *lahangā* 'skirt worn under a sari', and *orhnī* 'veil, head cloth' remained. Some Eng terms were gradually introduced: *blaus* 'blouse', (which is much more frequently used than the older B *benwār*), *dres* 'dress' and *piṭī-kōṭ* 'petticoat' (possibly a folk-etymology based on analogy of B *piṭhī* 'back', and Eng *coat*).

The term *simij* 'slip, women's underskirt' was adopted from Mauritian Bhojpuri — the third SB word from that source — this time showing the influence of women from the island, who are otherwise — to my knowledge — voiceless in the written history of Natal. The term once again comes from French (*chemise* 'petticoat) via Creole *simij*, referring to a shirt today (Philip Baker: personal communication, Jan 1989). Later women began wearing a *bodiz* and a *breizye* (from Eng *bodice* and *brassière*); the [z] sounds show these to be relatively late loans.

For other accessories the rate of borrowing was slightly

higher, especially among third and later-generation speakers. The term *nekles* 'necklace' rendered the older *larchā* obsolete, while *bengel* 'bangle' is today used by all but the oldest speakers in preference to *curiyā* or to the original Hn form *bangrī* (on which Eng *bangle* is ultimately based). Similarly other doublets occurring in the language today on account of Eng influence are *yering* and *kānphūl* 'ear-rings', *henbeg* and *jhorā* 'handbag', *sendel* and *campal* 'sandals'.

4.2.8 *Sickness and disease*

The old word for 'sick' (*bimār*) has been replaced by Eng *sīk*, for all but a handful of old speakers. Also in widespread use are *emblens* 'ambulance', *dokṭar* or *dokṭe* 'doctor', *nes* 'nurse', *stāf-nes* 'staff-nurse', *speslis* 'specialist-doctor', *opreiśen* 'operation' and *dicāj* 'discharge' (n) (from hospital). There are many loanwords denoting illnesses well known to, and often discussed by, families: *cūge* or *śūge* '(sugar) diabetes' (this loanword hardly ever means 'sugar', for which B *cinnī* remains); *hāṭ* 'heart complaint' (again not 'heart', for which the B *karejā* persists); *ṭhī-bī* 'T.B.'; *preśe* 'high blood pressure'; *sṭrok* 'stroke'; *atraiṭes* 'arthritis'; *hemrij* 'brain haemorrhage'. It is noteworthy that for ordinary ailments B terms are still frequently used: *sardī* 'cold', *khokī* 'cough', *bokhār* 'fever', *sir ke darad* 'head ache', as well as for afflictions like lameness (*langaṛā*), blindness (*andhapan*) etc. Data in Misra (1980:274) suggest that a number of hospital and medical loanwords are also used in present-day IB. That the SB loans are independent of these is suggested by the differences in their phonological forms: for example, SB *nes*, IB *nars* 'nurse'; SB *opreiśen*, IB *aparesan* 'operation'.

4.2.9 *Domestic Terms*

Even though this has been the domain in which the vernacular was able to hold sway most effectively against the dominating language, a large number of terms concerning household effects, domestic procedures and so on have filtered through from Eng. There are terms like *rūm* 'room', *kicīn* 'kitchen', *bātrum* 'bathroom', *siṭingrum* 'sitting room', *garāj* 'garage' and *pesij* 'passage'. *Braṇḍā* 'veranda', which I have always taken to be an adoption from the English is actually from IB, corresponding to Hn *varandā*, which was borrowed into Eng in the early days of British rule.[3]

Items of furniture showing the influence of Eng are: *ṭebal* 'table', *wāḍrob* 'wardrobe', *ces-ḍro* 'chest of drawers' and *beḍ*. This last item is used to describe a modern bed one purchased from a store, whereas a simpler bed made of bamboo and cloth (now rare) is designated *khaṭia*. Related loans include *ḍabbal-bed* 'double-bed'; *rolwei-bed* 'roll-away bed'; *meṭres* 'mattress'; *pilo-kes* 'pillow case' (though) the B phrase *takiā ke khol* still survives and is interchangeable with *pilo-kes* in the speech of the older speakers); and *sofā* 'sofa'.

Other loans for household effects are: *sṭov*, which refers to a stove one purchased, not the traditional fireplace on which many families continued to cook – which retained the B name *cūlha; reḍyo* 'radio'; *gremefon* 'gramophone'; *fon* 'telephone'; *bāf* 'bath-tub'; *ḍeṭī-boks* 'dirty-box' (that is, 'dirt-bin'); *keṭal* 'kettle'; *ṭenk* 'water-tank'; *ḍram* 'water-drum'; *baskiṭ* 'basket'; *pleṭ* 'plate' (though the traditional large Indian plate used on ceremonial occasions continues to be called *thariyā*); *kop* or *kopā* 'cup'; *sā̃sar* 'saucer'; *botal* 'bottle'; *thep* 'tap'; *nepkin* 'napkin'; *plesṭik* 'plastic'; and *khāḍboḍ* 'cardboard'.

In addition to the adoption of Eng terms for the main meals of the day (*brekfes, lanc, sape*), we have food terms such as: *breṭ* 'bread', (though for bread prepared at home the traditional term *roṭī* and variants like *pūrī* are still widely used); *baṭe* 'butter'; *jem* 'jam'; *cīz* 'cheese' (the old term *makhān* for cheese and butter is rarely used); *ṭī* 'tea' (in free variation with B *cā/cāī*); *kofī* 'coffee'; *koko* 'cocoa', and *mailo* 'drinking chocolate' (based on a popular brand-name). There is also an interesting compound form *baṭe-bred* 'bread and butter' which comprises two Eng words compounded on the B *dvandva* pattern (see A.2.3).

A few Eng verbs belonging to this domain are used as phrasal verbs, by the addition of the verb *kar* 'to do': *poliś kar* 'to polish'; *śain kar* 'to shine'; *airan kar* 'to iron clothes'; *peint kar* 'to paint'; and, occasionally, *boil kar* 'to boil' (see further 4.6.1f).

The number of loanwords in this sphere might seem large, but is quite small in comparison to the entire B lexicon for domestic items and procedures. A sampling of the latter is given in 5.7.3 in connection with language retention amongst younger speakers.

4.2.10 *Miscellaneous*

Several other domains in which loanwords from Eng proliferate may be identified: transport; work; government and officialdom; schooling; and time and numbers. It is not the place to list them all here. Other loans not easily classifiable are: *weiṭ* 'wait', rendering the B word *sabūr* relatively archaic; *sṭorī* 'story' (used more for tales narrated in Eng, while *kissā* refers to more traditional tales usually); *raiṭ-hen* 'right hand'; *lefṭ-hen* 'left hand'; *ceik-hen* or *śeik-hen* 'shake-hands' (used in the phrasal construction *śeikhan kar*); *sapreṭ* 'separate' (adj); *ges* 'gas'; *hol* 'hall' (usually one in which a wedding is to take place); *ṭaun* 'town'; *frenḍ* 'friend'; *birīj* 'bridge'; *ṭuins* 'twins'; *baiskop* 'bioscope, cinema'; and *laiṭ* 'electric light' (though for 'moonlight' and 'sunlight' the usual terms (*anjoriā* and *ghām*) remain.

4.2.11 *More recent loans*

In contrast to the borrowings described above, which have in varying degrees been assimilated into SB, and are used by all age groups, there are a number of marginal or semi-loans used by younger Eng bilinguals to one another, and not generally to older non-Eng speakers. These are often taken piecemeal from Eng without the adaptations characteristic of earlier loans and can be regarded as manifestations of code-switching (see 4.6.4) rather than loanwords. Older speakers judge these to be unnecessary intrusions of Eng because there are simple and commonly-used B words which would suffice in their stead. These are listed below in their Eng spellings: *photo* (B *chēṛha*); *visit* (B *ghūm-*); *boil* (verb) (B *khaul-*); *enjoy* (B *pāsin lag-*); *satisfy* (B *khus kar-*); *clean* (verb) (B *saphā kar-*); *slice* (verb) (B *kāṭ-*); *worry* (verb) (B *soc-*); *think* (B *soc kar-*); *road* (B *rastā*); *tired* (B *thakkā*); *chair* (B *kursī*); *pillow* (B *takia*); *cheeky* (in the SAIE sense of 'stern', B *badmās*); *farm* (B *khēt*); *bank* (of river) (B *naddi ke kināre*); *dirty* (of inanimates) (B *maila*); *busy* (B *kām me bajal hē*); *battle* (verb, in the sense of 'to struggle') (B *taklīph mē hē*); *all right* (B *acchā, ṭhīk*); and several others like *divorce, surprised, mistake, serious, used* (in the sense of 'accustomed to'), *holiday*, etc.

The use of motor vehicles as a matter of course in the last two decades has led to a spate of words which retain their Eng 'feel' even in the mouths of older female speakers: *battery, plugs, hand-brake, steering wheel*, and terms like *jek kar-* 'to jerk' (intrans); *mis kar-* 'to miss' ('experience engine trouble'); *swic on kar-* 'to switch on'; *swic of kar-* 'to switch off', etc.

The total number of loanwords is very high, but a false impression can be obtained by simply scanning these lists, without considering their actual function. Although no one – not even a priest – is able to avoid the use of Anglicisms in colloquial conversation, there is a hidden check on the number of loanwords in any conversation in that the speaker who employs an excessive amount of them would be an object of some ridicule, tacitly judged to be an imperfect speaker.

To gain an impression of the proportion of loanwords in ordinary speech two counts were taken. The first was from a fifteen-minute stretch of conversation between a seventy-five-year-old woman, who speaks SB and very little Eng, and her daughter-in-law, who conducted the interview. This yielded 6 per cent of loanwords from Eng or F, of a total of 321 words. The second involved an extract from a more spontaneous situation involving two female speakers: one a B-dominant fifty-year-old, whose Eng was fluent; the other a forty-seven-year-old equally proficient in Eng and SB. The percentage of loanwords was also comparatively low: 7,4 per cent out of 445 words. The second conversation, however, had a great deal more code-switching, with 17 out of 67 sentences being entirely or almost entirely in Eng. Code-switching was non-existent in the first interview.

4.3 *PHONOLOGICAL CHANGE*

4.3.1 *The addition of fricatives*

The use of a large number of loanwords resulted in the introduction of certain new phonemes into SB: /f/, /v/, /ʃ/, and /z/. For the oldest speakers these sounds played only a marginal role, occurring in free variation with other sounds of B ([p^h], [b], [s] or [tʃ], and [dʒ] respectively). Where these sounds did occur, it was presumably with some awareness of their 'strangeness' or marginal status. For some second- and most third-generation speakers, the situation is quite different, with these new sounds being used regularly without any awareness of their novelty. This is enhanced by two factors:

(a) Over the last few decades there has been a tendency in South Africa, and in India, to replace traditional, 'village' first names (like *Buddhu* 'the one born on Wednesday', *Jhagarū* 'the quarrelsome one', *Choṭī* 'the short girl') by more prestigious names denoting Sanskritic concepts of righteousness or good-omen, or names taken from popular film stars. In SB the Sanskrit sounds /v/ and /ʃ/are often (though not always) retained, and /ʂ/ occurs as [ʃ]. Names like the following, which have originally non-B sounds, have become the rule, and not the exception, in SB: *Vijay* (which occurs far more frequently than the IB equivalent *Bijay*); *Veena* (again out-rivalling *Beena*); *Vinay; Vidia; Sanjeev; Naveen; Dev Anand; Pravesh; Shanti; Sharma; Rishi; Nishal; Vinesh* etc. (Eng spellings given). /f/ and /z/, which are non-Sanskritic sounds, do not occur in these proper names, and are associated with Islamic names.

(b) In SB medial and final /p^h/ has become [ʋ̥], except for the oldest surviving first and second-generation speakers. Some examples are: [saʋ̥a] 'clean' (IB *sāph* or *sapha*); [daʋ̥a] 'time, occasion' (IB *dapha*); [sauʋ̥] 'aniseed' (IB *sauph*); (bi:ʋ̥e:] 'Thursday' (IB *bīphē*); [bārʋ̥i:] (a type of sweetmeat, which in IB is *barphī*), etc. In one instance [ʋ̥] (or [pf] for some speakers) has replaced [p^h] in initial position – [ʋ̥aida] 'use, avail' and in another occurs as a slightly more prestigious alternate to it – [ʋ̥i:n] ~ [pfi:n] ~ [p^hi:n] 'again.' The non-occurrence of this change among the oldest speakers suggests that the use of [ʋ̥] is attributable to the influence of Eng, reinforced by prestigious Hn forms.

4.3.2 *The treatment of* /ɦ/

Final /ɦ/ is no longer used by third and succeeding generations. These speakers use forms such as [mu:] 'mouth', [ba:ra] 'twelve', [paṭo:] 'daughter-in-law', whereas IB retains a final /ɦ/ in at least some styles. Tiwari (1960:14) notes that 'the current tendency is to make [ɦ] inaudible' in IB. Since final /ɦ/, is in any case, voiceless, not murmured (see A.1.2), this suggests that the SB change might even have had its genesis on Indian soil.

The pronunciation of medial /h/ differs according to the nature of the syllable in which it occurs, and shows age-graded variations. In primarily or secondarily stressed syllables [ɦ] remains unchanged, and is clearly discernible in everyone's speech, for example [de:ɦi] 'body'; [biɦa:n] 'tomorrow'; [baɦuṭ] 'much'; [soɦa:r] 'birth-song', etc. In unstressed syllables or at the end of medial syllables, older non-Eng speakers usually retain /ɦ/, but often in a greatly reduced form in ordinary conversation, discernible only as a murmur on an adjacent segment. For example, /maɦina/ 'month' may be realised by the oldest speakers as three syllables, with the medial unstressed syllable intact. The /ɦ/ would then occur as strong, glottal air-flow which renders the following vowel murmured, and sometimes the whole of the next syllable as well. It may also happen, especially in fast speech, that the three syllables are reduced to two, with the medial /ɦ/ perceivable only as murmur accompanying both segments of the first syllable.

Third- and fourth-generation fluent speakers produce weakly-murmured [ɦ] in unstressed syllables, and show a greater tendency to realise it as a weak murmur accompanying preceding syllables, or to delete it altogether in fast speech. Thus /mahina/ 'month' in their speech, fluctuates between [ma̤ɦina], [m^{ɦ}a̤i̤na], and sometimes [maina.]. That the change is not yet completed can be gauged from the fact that these speakers always pronounce medial [ɦ], and retain medial syllables, in citation forms.

[ɦ] is very often deleted in fast speech in commonly occurring auxiliary verb forms like *rahalī* 'I was' (becoming [rallī]; and the dialectal forms *aihis* 'he gave', *lihis* 'he took' (becoming [d̪is] and [lis] respectively); and *ahis* 'he came' (becoming [aïs], with vowel hiatus for some speakers, though younger speakers tend to use the diphthong [ai]). [ɦ] is always dropped in the frequently occurring negative particle *nahi* (becoming [nei] or [nai]), and sometimes dropped in the interrogative particle *kahe ke* 'why' (becoming [kai ke]).

For the treatment of medial [ɦ] by semi-speakers, in contrast to the older groups, see 5.9.3.

4.3.3 *Murmured sonorants*

The consonants [lʱ], [mʱ], [nʱ], [ŋʱ], and [ɽʱ] still survive into the third generation, despite their relative infrequency in IB, and their restriction to non-initial positions. The only exception is [rʱ] which is not used in SB, because words in which it did occur in IB have become obsolete locally (see below). With the exception of [ɽʱ], the number of words in which the other murmured sonorants occurs is extremely small, again because many lexical items containing them have either been lost, or show internal changes (e.g. [mʱ] > [mbʱ]).

[lʱ]: The following words containing [lʱ] have become obsolete in SB, and are not even passively understood: *cilh* 'kite' (the bird); *kolh* 'creek'; *olha* 'a play'; *telha* 'son'; *mālh* 'string of a spinning wheel'. Of the two forms for 'tomorrow' – *kal* and *kālh* – the latter, characteristic of EB, does not occur in South Africa. The only SB words containing this phoneme are *cūlha* 'fireplace, simple stove'; *melh-* 'to loiter, linger'; and *kolhu* 'a small oil-press', though the last form is an archaism, not used in everyday conversation.

[mʱ]: Words like *gamhāri* (a type of tree); *pāmhī* 'little whisker'; and *bhomhār* 'big hole' have become obsolete. [mʱ] > [mbʱ] and [mb], respectively, in the words *jambhai* 'a yawn', and *khamba* 'post, pole' (IB *jamhai* and *khamha*). [mʱ] does occur in two SB words: *samhār* 'to rear, raise', and *mhendi* (type of paste made from the leaves of the myrtle tree).

[nʱ]; IB *bānh* 'embankment', *kānha* 'christening; and *chonha* 'false anger' are obsolete in SB. The words *kandh* 'shoulder', and *andhār* 'darkness' are the SB equivalents of IB *kanh* and *anhār*.[4] Although [nʱ] has become [nn] or [n] for most SB speakers in many forms of the verb *cinh* 'to recognise', (for example, [tʃinli:] 'I recognised'; [tʃi:ne: ɦe:] 'she recognises'), it does re-surface in other forms (for example, [tʃinʱila:] 'I recognise'; [tʃinʱi:] 'she will recognise').

In view of the fact that [m^{ɦ}] and [n^{ɦ}] in some instances are reflexes of MIA [mb^{ɦ}] and [nd^{ɦ}], it is possible that the SB forms like *kandh* 'shoulder', and *khambā* 'pole', are actually archaisms and not innovations, and that these are dialectal forms which have been neglected by grammarians (see footnote 4).

[r^{ɦ}]: This phoneme seems to be lost entirely in SB, IB forms like *mūrhi* 'fried rice', and *mārh* (a type of grain) being obsolete today.

[ɽ^{ɦ}]: This consonant remains in many words, including *paṛh- 'to read'*, *piṛhā* 'stool', *caṛh-* 'to climb', *bāṛh* 'flood', *loṛhā* 'grinding-stone' etc., though the retroflexion as well as the accompanying murmur tend to be much weaker than in IB.

[ŋ^{ɦ}]: The murmured velar nasal occurs in *sangh* 'a guild', and the proper name *Singh*, though an acceptable alternative in each instance is a plain velar nasal. Other IB terms like *penghā* (a type of bird), *ṭanghan* 'a horse with huge legs', and *lānghani* (a disease) are not to be found in SB.

4.3.4 *Other minor changes*

(a) [ai] > [ei]: This is a change still in progress. For all but the oldest speakers [ei] has replaced earlier [ai] in the following words: *murai* 'radish', *thailī* 'a bag', *gail* 'he went', *bhail* 'it happened', *kaise* 'how', and others. In the following words there is much variation, with second-generation speakers using [ai] more frequently than [ei], while third and later generations tend to use [ei] more frequently: *baiṭh* 'to sit', *paisa* 'money', *aisan* 'such', *kaisan* 'what sort', *saitān* 'devil', etc. In *ainā* 'mirror, window pane', the [ei] pronunciation occurs more often in the interior dialects than on the Natal coast. There are just as many words in which the change of [ai] to [ei] is not permissible, even for the youngest speakers: *māī* 'mother', *ail* 'he came', *khail* 'she ate', *bidāi* 'sending-off', etc. Similar (but fewer) alternations in TB (Mohan 1978:103) suggest that this might have been an incipient change in IB at the time of immigration: *aisan* ~ *eisan* 'of which type', *kaisan* ~

keīsan 'of which type', *jaīsan* ~ *jeīsan* 'of the type which', etc.

(b) In some words a pronunciation limited to a few districts of India has gained currency in South Africa, and become the norm, not the variant. These include (with the usual IB form given in brackets: *kal* 'tomorrow' (*kāl/kālh*); *khatin* 'for the sake of' (*khatir*); *phin* 'again' (*phir*); *Buth* 'Wednesday' (*Budh*); *ghugurī* 'fried grain' (*ghugunī*); *Atwār* 'Sunday' (*Etwār*); *pareṭhā* 'a type of *roṭī*' (*parāṭhā*); and *bandar* 'monkey' (*bānar*).

4.4 *SEMANTIC CHANGE*

SB differs lexically from IB and other overseas varieties of B not only on account of the many loanwords taken from Eng and other South African languages, but also because some items have undergone subtle shifts in meaning. These can be grouped as follows:

(a) *Widening of meaning:*

bihān: The primary meaning of this noun is 'dawn, tomorrow morning' in IB, with a secondary meaning 'tomorrow'. In the Coastal and Midland dialects of SB the word signifies 'tomorrow', with no indication whether it is the morning or afternoon that is being referred to. The word *phajir* is used in SB for both 'morning' and 'dawn'.

ainā: In IB this noun refers almost only to a mirror, whereas in SB it refers to mirrors, windows and glass in general.

(b) *Narrowing of meaning:*

baṛāī: In IB this noun is a neutral term for 'praise'. In SB it more usually denotes negative qualities like boasting about others or self-praise.

naksān: In IB this word denotes a general wastage, as of energy, food or human life. This general meaning is used in SB today, but only by some speakers. For many speakers the principal meaning is 'wastage of food', a consequence of the language being restricted to mainly domestic contexts. The sentence *naksān nei kar* 'don't waste' would, in the absence of a specific context, be construed as referring to food.

bāsī: While the primary meaning of this word is in IB 'food saved from supper for breakfast, left-over food', it may occur as an adjective meaning 'stale, giving off an odour'. In SB only the latter sense prevails, and *bāsi* is not used as a noun; some kind of paraphrase (for example, *baccal khāna* 'left-over food') would be used instead.

tarkārī: This is glossed as 'vegetables' in works dealing with IB (Misra 1980:134; Grierson 1885:254). In SB the word refers to cooked vegetables, especially curried ones. Vegetables in an uncooked state would be referred to by their specific names, by the cover term *tarkāri ke cīj* 'things for cooking', or the loan *bejiṭebal*.

gadrā: In IB this denotes any unripe crop cut for food. In SB it refers specifically to matured bean seeds used as food. Although the hybrid form in SB and SAIE, *gadrā-beans* suggests an earlier stage when *gadrā* might have referred to any crop in general, the word currently does not refer to any other vegetable.

phusilau: In IB this is glossed as 'to tempt, appease, coax', used with adult or child as object. In SB the word has narrowed in meaning, referring to children mainly, and can be characterised as meaning 'to placate, appease, divert the attentions of a child'.

(c) *Semantic shift:*

daliddar: The primary meaning of this word has shifted in SB from 'poor' a century ago to 'greedy'. It is not difficult to guess how such a shift could come about: from being an adjective describing the poor, it might then be associated with other characteristics, notably the habit of eating as much as one could when food was available, especially when provided by others. A sentence like *daliddar eisan khā he* 'He eats like a poor man', can gradually come to be understood as 'He eats ravenously/greedily', or 'He eats like a greedy man'. Although older informants claim that the primary meaning of the word is 'poor' – not 'greedy', actual usage suggests otherwise and the word *garīb* (an alternate IB form) is used for 'poor'. *Daliddar* is most often used as a derogatory epithet – 'that greedy person', and the original adjective *lalcī* 'greedy' may also be used with slightly less invective force. In IB *daliddar* still means 'poor', with 'greedy' only a faint secondary connotation (K. M. Tiwari and B. Verma: personal communications, December 1983).

nahā-: The basic meaning of this verb remains 'to bathe', but it can also be used as a variant of *paur-* 'to swim', a secondary meaning that does not occur in IB. Indeed for some third- and fourth-generation speakers it has ousted the verb *paur* altogether. This semantic shift is understandable for those rural communities in which it might have been easier to have a bath in a nearby stream or river than in a domestic setting. A similar extension of meaning is reported for MB (Baker and Ramnah 1985:236).

ghīn: Whereas this is glossed in works dealing with IB as 'hatred, contempt', a more accurate gloss as far as SB is concerned would be 'distaste, repugnance, repulsion'. *Hamke ghīn lage he, suar ke dekhe*, for example, means 'I experience revulsion, looking at a pig'.

There are some words whose denotations have changed on account of either changes in material circumstances, or on account of interference from loanwords taken from Eng. These include:

sẽwai: This refers in IB to a dessert comprising tiny coiled strips of flour and milk. In South Africa even though this preparation is no longer made at home, the name persists for a close equivalent – *vermicelli* purchased from stores, but prepared in the old style.

piyalī: IB retains the distinction between *piyalā* 'a big cup' and *piyalī* 'a little cup', whereas this morphological distinction has proved unnecessary in SB, where *piyalā* refers to a large bowl and *piyalī* refers to a bowl out of which one eats or drinks. The loanword *kop* denotes 'cup', irrespective of size.

pajāmā: In India this term (from which Eng *pyjama* originates) refers to 'men's drawers', though once again a change in habits in South Africa resulted in the eventual change of denotation, with *pajāmā* referring to both long trousers, and to shorts (though the loanword *short-pants* could also be used specifically for the latter).

lahangā: In IB this refers to a long skirt worn by women, usually decorated, and donned at weddings and festivals. Since this outer garment was rarely used in South Africa, the word came to refer solely to the long, skirt-like undergarment worn under a sari (replacing IB *sāya*).

(d) *Changes in caste terminology*:
Of greater interest is the semantic change contingent upon social changes in the new colony. The shortage of people belonging to one's exact sub-caste, and the new economic organisation away from an agricultural, village-economy conspired to break down the old caste barriers quite rapidly. In addition many traditional caste-occupations like oil-pressing, rope-making, toddy-tapping, salt-working, were no longer viable in the new economy. These changes in social circumstances are partially mirrored in the language itself. The loss of scores of caste-terms is recorded in 4.5.2. I shall restrict myself here to discussions of changes in meaning.

caṇḍāl: In IB this is the name for an out-caste, one of the lowest, which, according to Hutton (1963:279), originally contained offspring of the union of a Brahman woman and Sudra man. The word survives in SB, but not as a caste term. Instead it refers to stereotypic characteristics associated with those who might have belonged to such a group. In local parlance the term *caṇḍāl* is a term of abuse, branding its referent as good-for-nothing, troublesome, harsh, etc. (female equivalent: *caṇḍālī*n).

doglā: This is another term for an out-caste of people originating from unions across caste-divisions. Like *caṇḍāl*, this term is opaque to most South Africans, but retained as a term of contempt, equivalent to Eng *bastard*.

camār: This refers to an out-caste of people engaging in skinning animals, tanning or working with leather. The word is still used in the stigmatisation of those of this ancestry in SB, though the exact meaning of the term has obviously changed with the dissolution of a recognisable caste system. Equally often, *camār* is used as a term of abuse for anyone one is displeased with, devoid of strict caste association.

noniyā: Although this term denoting a low caste of labourers and salt workers is known to the oldest speakers, a few third-generation SB speakers said that they had always taken it to be a term of insult, stripped of strict caste connotation.

malicchā: This is a derogatory term used in many Indian languages for a foreigner, or any outsider to one's caste-group. In SB it has become a contemptuous term signifying 'a dirty or despicable person', not necessarily an outsider (female equivalent: *malicchīn*).

jāt: The very word for 'caste', *jāt* seems to have undergone a subtle semantic shift. The sentence *Okar jāt weise he* rarely means what it literally says 'That's the way of his caste/that's characteristic of his caste'. Instead it could equally well be interpreted, especially by third and later generations, as 'That's his way/He's like that', with derogatory overtones. It is also increasingly becoming a synonym for *rakkam* 'sort, type', referring to both inanimate and animate entities, as in *ī dānā dusrā jāt he* 'this is a different type of grain'. Although generalised meanings of *jāt(i)* are not ruled out in the languages of India, with glosses like 'caste', 'community', 'race', 'sect', 'genus', 'type', 'kind', 'breed' all being possible (Chaturvedi and Tiwari:1978), it is doubtful whether the primary meaning of *caste* is superseded by secondary meanings like 'type'.

4.5 *LEXICAL LOSS*

In 4.2 a vast array of loanwords, mainly from Eng, which had become an intrinsic part of SB were described. While some of these merely replaced older B words, others – especially late loans – filled a growing need for terminology dealing with the elements of a new technology, and new social situations. This process was accompanied by the gradual loss of a large number of lexical items that were once intrinsic to the domestic life of rural north-east India, but of diminished importance in the new environment, including a large number of technical terms associated with an agrarian economy. In this section I give an inkling of this jettisoning of once-essential vocabulary by examining three different areas: agriculture, caste and domestic terminology.

4.5.1 *Agricultural terms*

B is a language of an agricultural community *par excellence*, capable of expressing subtle distinctions necessary in dealing with a rural way of life. Grierson's *Bihar Peasant Life* (1885) gives hundreds of terms for categorising soils, for example. He classifies soil-names according to (i) distance from the village site, (ii) their constitutive elements, and (iii) the crops for which they are prepared or which they usually produce. While this is probably too technical a register to discuss here, we can fruitfully gauge the amount of semantic loss in SB by considering the sphere of ploughing: in IB the word for 'to plough' is *har jot* or *khet jot-*, or *hal-*. There are separate words (though morphologically related in part) for the first ploughing of the season (*pahil cā̃s* or *pharni*), the second ploughing (*dokhār* or *somrā*), the third ploughing (*tekhār*), the fourth (*chaukhār*), the fifth (*pā̃cas*), and so forth. There are special terms for the ploughing of millet when it is a foot high (*bidāh*); for the process of flooding a rice field and then ploughing it for the purpose of killing weeds (*leo*); and for lightly reploughing a field after rice cultivation (*unah* or *samār*). There are terms for cross ploughing (*āra*); ploughing in diminishing circles (*cauketḥā*); ploughing of a crookedly-shaped field (*ūna dyorhi jōt*); ploughing diagonally (*koniyā jot*); ploughing a rectangular field along its length or breadth (*sojhauā jot*); and for ploughing crosswise (*phāni* or *phāṭkī*). A small piece of land which the plough has not been able to touch is known as *pais* or *dahina*; while a centre-plot in the middle of a field round which the bullocks have no room to turn goes by a different name, *badhar*. In present day SB all but the two basic terms *har* 'a plough' and *jot* 'to plough' are unknown.

Terms like *khet* 'field', *ḍāra* 'boundary', *harāi* 'furrow', *harwā* 'ploughman', *majūra* 'agricultural servant', and *nokar* 'paid labourer' have remained in SB, but many more have become obsolete. The following terms are unknown to second- and third-generation speakers (both of rural and urban background), reflecting the superfluity of some of the more arcane terms, as well as the path of obsolescence on which the language is travelling: *kiyārī* 'a bed made in a field to facilitate irrigation'; *jhorā* 'a large bed for seedlings'; *ār* 'a low ridge around a bed'; *sā̃njh le jot* 'as much land as can be ploughed in one day'; *dophariyā* 'an area that can be ploughed in half a day'; *āntar* 'portion of land included in a plough circuit'; *harwar* or *bharasaliyā* 'ploughman who is engaged for the whole day'; *dupahariyā* or *paharwār* 'ploughman who is engaged for half a day'; *agwar jan* or *laguā jan* 'one who works on advance payments'; *angwār* 'one who receives the use of a plough for one day in three, instead of wages in cash or kind', and so on.

Equally compendious lists could be given for activities like reaping, planting of rice, preparation of cane, and for pests and diseases affecting agriculture, which have no counterpart in SB. I will conclude this section, however, by taking a look at miscellaneous terms concerned with animal husbandry – a less technical sphere than ploughing, since rearing and caring for cattle is the concern of the entire family, and since animals are kept even in towns in north-east India. The following names for animals are well known in SB: *chauā* 'cattle'; *sā̃ṛh* 'bull'; *bakkarā* 'goat'; *gāī̃* 'cow'; *bacchā* or *bacchrū* 'calf'; *bhẽṛā* 'sheep'; *bhãis* 'buffalo'; *baradh* 'bullock'; *suar* 'pig'; *gadahā* 'donkey'; *ghoṛā* 'horse'. Other terms connected with animal husbandry that are still known by older SB speakers are *dudhār* 'a cow that is a good milker'; *pahiloṭh* 'a cow with one calf'; *phenus* 'milk obtained from the first milking after calving' ('colostrum'); *jhuṇḍ* 'a flock of sheep or goats'; *lẽhaṛ* 'a flock of about twenty sheep'; *bāg* 'a flock of about one hundred sheep'; *paguṛī̃* 'to chew the cud'; *jaũta* or *janerā* 'cattle fodder'; *parti* 'lands set aside for pasture'; *gherān* 'fence to keep out cattle'; *markhāh* 'a vicious bullock'.

On the other hand a great many terms well known in IB are unknown in present day SB. These include: *dāngar* 'dead cattle'; *dhākar* 'a bull unbranded with sacrificial marks'; *adār* 'an unbroken bullock'; *nankirwā* or *nāṭa* 'a stunted bullock'; *ghoncā* 'a bullock with horns projecting in front'; *saragpatālī̃* 'a bullock with one erect horn, and one pointing downward' (literally 'pointing to heaven and hell'); *gausinghī̃* 'a bullock whose horns join in the centre'; *mainā* 'a bullock with loose horns turning downwards'; *chātar* or *phaṭhāh* 'a bullock with one horn turning left, and the other right'; *muṭhāl* or *muthrā* 'a bullock with stunted horns'; *munrerā* or *bhunarwā* 'a bullock with no horns'; *eksinghā* 'a bullock with only one horn'; *basahā* or *jatahā* 'a bullock used for religious worship only'; *purahiyā* 'a cow that calves yearly or that never stops milking'; *pachāṛ* 'a cow that breeds when it is five years old'; *bahilā* or *ṭhahrā* 'a barren cow'; *conṛhī* 'a cow that gives little milk'; *lerū* 'an unweaned calf'; *kalor* 'a heifer ready for mating'; *kas* 'a spotted cow'; *bagchallā* 'a brindled cow' (literally 'tiger-skinned'); *karkanḍha* 'a cow with black shoulders'; *guldār* 'a spotted cow'; *pā̃c kaliyān* 'a cow with four white feet, and a white blaze on the forehead'; *abhelak* 'a horse with three white legs and one black one'; *aneriyā* 'cattle left to graze without a watchman'; and *bathān* 'a cattle-yard'. In addition to these, Grierson (1885:299–311) gives a few score more items for related fields like cattle fodder, pasturage, cattle diseases, grazing fees, cattle dealers, and milk and its preparations, which further illustrate lexical loss in SB, but which I shall not repeat here.

4.5.2 *Caste terminology*

There are some terms associated with caste-names and caste-occupations extant in present day SB, despite the decline of the caste system. Nowadays vaguely defined 'high' castes are recognised (often with the surname *Maharaj* and *Singh*), who would prefer to marry within their own groups, though exogamous matches are often accepted. Extremely 'low' castes are also identified with whom other groups discourage (but do not forbid) marriage. The following terms are well known in SB, but are anachronisms in so far as they refer to ancestral occupations/affiliations, which do not have contemporary relevance: *telī* 'oil-pressers, oil-sellers'; *ahīr* cow-herds'; *camār* 'workers in leather'; *nau* 'barber'; *lohāṛ* 'blacksmith'; *baṛhāī* 'carpenters'; *dhobī* 'washermen'; *halwāī* 'confectioners'; and *baniyā* 'shop-keepers, merchants'. Other still-recognised terms are *kayasth* 'writers'; *musahār* 'rat-catchers'; *jolāhā* 'weavers'; *dusādh* 'corpse bearers'; *ḍom* 'scavengers'; *ṭhaṭherā* 'braziers'; *kahār* 'fishermen, water-bearers, domestic servants'; and *kurmī* 'cultivators', though the precise meaning of the last five terms is not clear to most third-generation SB speakers. The caste names *maharāj* 'priest', *sonār* 'goldsmith, jeweller', and *singh* (formerly a ruling caste, now a surname), on the other hand, are widely used in SB.

A few principles are discernible here. Terms best known in

SB today refer to extremes of the caste hierarchy: the Brahman at the top, outcastes at the bottom. Another set comprises caste-occupations or services that became well known within a colonial context: the shopkeeper, washerman, barber and goldsmith. Terms partially known in SB (that is, familiar to some families but not to others) include words denoting the caste(s) of grandparents who had migrated from India. In some instances families could supply the caste name of their ancestors, but were not certain of the occupational significance of the term.

Terms lost are, apart from a large number denoting agriculturalists, generally those denoting skills that were of little value in the plantation economy of Natal: rope-makers, toddy-tappers, jesters and singers would have had to survive by other means. Many such castes were considered unsatisfactory as potential emigrants, as the instructions issued by the Government Agent for Natal to surgeons examining potential migrants at Calcutta (1889) indicate:[5]

> The hands should have horns on the palmer base of the fingers showing that the emigrant is accustomed to hard work. Fakeers, Brahmins, Kyeths [*sic*], Baniahs, Mahomedans, Shop-keepers, Barbers, Toddy drawers, Bangle makers, Beggars and Weavers &c. should be rejected.

That many belonging to these castes did enter Natal and other colonies can be ascribed to the practices of recruiters, which often fell short of the ideal (see Tinker 1974:122–30).

In present-day SB the following terms have become opaque, archaic, even lost altogether: *bhuīhar* 'landowners'; *bāgdī* 'field labourers'; *baurī* 'field workers'; *bhangī* 'sweepers and scavengers'; *bhār* 'low caste tribals' (in Bihar and Uttar Pradesh); *bharbūja* 'grain-parchers'; *bhāṭ* 'bards, genealogists, heralds'; *bhumī* 'cultivators of the soil'; *gayawāl* 'mendicant Brahmans (who maintain themselves on the offerings of pilgrims in the city of Gaya); *ghāsiyā* 'musicians, fishermen, and artificers in brass'; *hārī* 'scavengers'; *hīrā* 'a sub-caste of the *caṇḍāl*'; *kalwār* 'distillers and liquor-sellers'; *kaserā* 'brass-founders and coppersmiths'; *kewaṭ* 'fishermen and cultivators'; *khaṭīk* 'labourers, butchers, vegetables sellers'; *kumhār* 'potters'; *pāsī* 'toddy-tappers'; *prabhū* 'writers'; *rājbansi* 'a caste of the Kocch tribe'; *rājput* 'aristocratic rulers/warriors'; *sākaldwipī* (a Brahman caste); *sarak* 'cultivators and weavers'; *sombattā* (a sub-caste of rope makers); *sūtar* 'carpenters'; *yādavā* 'cattle-grazers', etc.[6]

4.5.3 *Domestic terminology*

In this domain there is much retention of the original vocabulary of IB and Awadhi. A list of such lexical items is given in 5.7.3, in characterising language retention amongst semi-speakers and passive bilinguals. In this section I shall concentrate on those terms which did not survive into third-generation SB. A common pattern can be discerned here: basic terms denoting household effects, clothing, and ornaments remain; but several synonyms, near-synonyms and words denoting slight differences from more basic items have not survived.

Thus the words, *sūp* 'winnowing sieve' and *calnī* 'a woven sieve' are widely used, but more specialised types like *āngī* 'cloth-bottomed sieve for sifting fine flour' and *chilaun* 'sieve for catching fish or (in some places) for straining sugar-cane juice' are either unknown or have no special term in SB. The term *jā̃tā* is used locally for a hand-grinding mill, used to grind grains, but IB terms for a smaller type used for grinding pulses and worked by one person (*cakrī*) and medium-sized ones (*cakulā*) were not recognised even by older speakers.

The basic word for stool, *piṛhā* and a more specialised term *maciyā* 'stool or table with a woven twine top (used to keep pots etc.) survive; but words like *mō̃ṛhā* 'a large bamboo or reed stool', *mō̃ṛhiyā* 'a small bamboo or reed stool', and *tipāī* 'a three-legged stool' were not recognised by third-generation speakers interviewed. Similarly the words for 'bed' (*khaṭiā*) has survived, but special terms like *pāwā* 'legs' (of a bed or other item of furniture), *pātī* 'side pieces of a bed', and *gū̃tharī* 'foot of a bed' were unknown.

The term for a weighing scale in SB is *rātal*, but no finer distinctions with respect to size exist, whereas in IB *rātal* is reserved for a large scale, and *tarāju* for a smaller one. Specialised terms like *tannī/jotī* 'strings of a scale'; *dandī* or *nittī* 'beams of a scale'; *palrā* 'pan of a scale'; *batkharā/bat* 'weights'; and *pasanghā* 'the special weight put in at the end to balance things' were unknown to most interviewees.

The term *lāṭhī* for an ordinary long stick is widely used in SB, as is *ḍaṇḍā* for a shorter knobbed stout stick and *suṭkun* for a slender whipping stick. The term *sõṭā* 'a short stout stick', though rarely used, is understood by many older speakers. IB words that have become obsolete are: *hurrā* 'the butt end of a stick'; *chaṛī* 'a thin stick'; *besākhī* 'a crutch'; *ḍāṅg* or *labdā* 'a thick walking stick'; and *ṭhenghunī* 'walking stick used by lame people'.

Ḍibbā denotes a small container (or jewel box) in SB, while *chunauṭī* is a word infrequently used today for 'a small container used to carry lime or betel-juice'. IB terms no longer extant are: *pānbattā* 'box for holding *pān; nalā* or *telbhāṛā*, container for carrying oil'; *sandūkh* 'container/box'; *kantor* 'small box'; and *petāṛha* 'a light portable clothes-box'.

As far as vessels for cooking or eating are concerned, there is a very high degree of retention of the vocabulary used in the B of Bihar and Uttar Pradesh. We can cite the following in this regard: *taslā* 'round vessel for boiling rice', and *taslī* for a smaller equivalent; *haṇḍā* 'large pot for boiling rice' and a smaller equivalent *haṇḍī*; *kaṛāhī* 'large, broad shallow pan with handles for preparing vegetables and frying'; *dekcā* 'cooking pot' (used at weddings), *dekcī* (a smaller equivalent); *tāwā* 'iron griddle plate'; *thārī* or *thariyā* 'flat pan/plate for eating food'; *kalchūl* 'large spoon for serving out of a pot'; *loṭā* 'brass, globe-shaped drinking-vessel'; and *cimṭā* 'small tongs for arranging firewood'. The following terms mentioned by Grierson in his *Bihar Peasant Life*, used in B-speaking villages, do not exist in South Africa: *baṭṭu/baṭṭua* 'vessel made of alloy, used for cooking rice' (it is taller and narrower than a *taslī*); *baṭulī* (a smaller equivalent of a *baṭṭu*); *parāt* 'large, flat pan with curving sides'; *ḍabbū* 'large brass or iron spoon used at weddings for deep and broad bowls'; *ḍol/kūnaṛ* 'iron vessel for drawing water from a well'; *lonhrī* 'a small iron pan for drawing water from a well'; *sorāhī* 'a pot for preserving water'; *lūṇḍa* 'a handful of straw used for cleaning metal vessels'; as well as the following variations on the *loṭā*: *tamha/jhāri* 'a medium-sized drinking vessel, shaped like a globe'; *geṛua/hathar/sobarna* 'a *loṭā* with a spout'; and *abkhorā/amkhorā* 'a *loṭā* with a broad mouth'.

Of the many terms for earthen vessels in IB, only the following survive locally: *jhārī* 'water-vessel with a spout'; *kalsā* 'vessel used at festive occasions, ornamented with lime or dyes'; *gagrī* 'vessel used for drawing water'; *diyā* 'small saucer-shaped vessel used as lamp'; and *patilā* 'earthen cooking-vessel'. A large number of terms for earthen vessels have been lost without trace, no doubt on account of the relative scarcity of these in Natal: *athrā* 'a pan for baking dough'; *adhkar* 'a vessel used in distilling'; *kāṭiyā/jhabbī* 'a little vessel with a long neck into which cows are milked'; *karnā* 'an earthen vessel in which milk is boiled'; *kastarā* 'a saucer for holding curds'; *kuṛhiyā* 'a small vessel that is used to hold milk'; *kohā* 'small, round, wide-mouthed vessel for holding curds or for cooking'; *khalcī* 'a small platter'; *gamlā* 'a flower pot'; *gurkī* 'a drinking vessel'; *ghariyā/cukrī* 'a drinking vessel'; *ghailā* 'a vessel for holding water'; *ceruā* 'earthen dish used for cooking or for holding grains'; *jālā* 'a water jar'; *ṭariyā* 'a small oil-pot'; *tarkaṭṭī* 'a vessel in which palm-juice is collected at the foot of the tree'; *lād* 'large basin used as feeding trough'; *parāī* 'saucer used to cover other vessels'; and *rikābī* 'saucer'.

For men's and women's clothing similar patterns prevail. The following terms persist for men's wear, even though not all are worn today: *pagṛī* 'turban'; *ṭopī* 'hat'; *ghõghī* 'wide hat made of sacking or leaves for rainy weather, a balaclava-like head-cover'; *dhotī* 'loin-cloth'; *langoṭī* 'small loin-cloth for boys'; *bisṭī* or *bicuṭī* 'scant loin-cloth worn by poor boys'; *phannā* 'knot in a loin-cloth for holding money'; and *pajāmā* 'drawers'. The following less basic terms are not known locally: phẽṭā 'inner part of a smart turban for the well-to-do'; *cīrā* 'a checked turban'; *dhāṭhā* 'a cloth that is wound under the chin and over the head'; *dopaliyā* ' long cap made of two pieces'; *caugosiyā* 'a round cap made of four pieces'; *kacchā* 'a loin-cloth worn by wrestlers'; *curidār* 'tight pants'; *mohridār* 'pants which are loose at the ankles'; *kalidār* 'loose pants with pieces let in along the thigh'; and *janghiyā* 'tight-fitting short drawers used by wrestlers'.

For women's wear the proportion of obsolete terms is smaller, and the following terms, denoting items of clothing still worn by women, are extant: *sārī*, *lãhgā* 'underskirt, petticoat'; *oṛhnī* 'veil or cloth worn over the head'; *jhulā* 'blouse' (rare); *colī* 'short blouse'; and *acrā* 'hem of a sari'. The following terms were recognised by older speakers, though they could not provide accurate glosses for them: *ghanghrī* 'type of petticoat'; *jhimkī/cundrī* 'a head-cloth with a dyed border', while the term *phuphurī* 'that part of a sari which is gathered up and tied in front' is unknown locally.

To continue in this way for other semantic fields like ornaments, parts of the house, kinds of food, wild animals, birds, etc. would be repetitive. The loss of a great deal of native vocabulary, though symptomatic of a language in decline, need not necessarily signal a traumatic end in sight; indeed much of the vocabulary lost was something in the nature of excess baggage in the new land, where a new technical vocabulary had to be adopted, in the form of Eng loanwords adapted to the B pattern. The history of Eng shows how a language may rely heavily on a foreign source (Norman French in the eleventh and twelfth centuries) for new terminology, or new words which merely replace native items, and still thrive. If we are to specify reasons for the obsolescence of SB we must look to factors involving the numbers of speakers, their distribution, economic position, and attitude to the language, rather than shortcomings in the language itself – which had shown that it had the capacity to adapt and survive, given favourable external circumstances.

4.6 *MORPHO-SYNTACTIC CHANGE*

In this section I examine the morphological treatment of loanwords, as well as the major morpho-syntactic innovations in SB.

4.6.1 *The morphology of borrowed words*

Loanwords used by older, non-Eng-speaking individuals show a lack of knowledge of the grammatical and lexical system of the source language. Such speakers borrowed phrases and compounds, without analysing (or being able to analyse) them into their sub-components, for example, *ceikhan* (a noun based on the Eng phrase 'shake hands'). The sentence *Ose ceikhen karlak*, literally translated is 'With him he shake-hand did' ('he shook hands with him'). Similarly we can cite *rauneraun* from 'round and round'; *raiṭhen* 'right hand'; *lefṭhen* 'left hand'; *āfkaran* 'half-a-crown'; *śotpans* 'short pants'; *stāfnes* 'staff nurse'; and *laswān* 'last one' (last-born child').

English plural suffixes are sometimes treated as if they were singular (see 4.2.5): for example, *ṭamāṭīs* 'tomato', *pīcīs* 'peach', *sākīs* 'sock', *binīs* 'bean' and many others all retain the Eng plural [s] even in the singular; thus *ek sākīs* 'one sock', *ek pīcīs* 'one peach' etc. Most loans, however, are borrowed in their English singular form, which remains invariant in SB. Thus *ek kāraṭ* 'one carrot', but also *dher kārat* 'a lot of carrots'; *ek skūl* 'one school', and *pā̃c skūl* 'five schools'. If a loanword has to be marked as being plural, the pluralizers *sabh* (non-human) and *lõg* (human) are used. The plural affix *-an* (Appendix A.4.3) does not occur directly after a loanword. Thus *ṭīcar* 'teacher' (singular), *ṭīcar lõg* 'teachers'; *pūlis* 'policeman', *pulis lõg* 'policemen' (as a group). Most borrowings do not participate in productive morphological processes of SB: for example, loans do not generally undergo derivational processes; nouns borrowed do not have diminutive or equivalent femine forms in *-ī*; verbs borrowed from Eng do not take on B endings. There are a few exceptions however:

(a) Most loanwords do take the particle *-wā*, denoting definiteness or anaphora (see A.4.1). Thus *pleṭ* 'plate', but *pleṭwā* 'the plate'; *moṭar* 'vehicle', but *moṭarwā* 'the vehicle', and so on. The phonologically conditioned alternate *-yā* occurs when loanwords end in front vowels, for example, *kofī* 'coffee', *kofiyā* 'the coffee'. As noted above, the plural suffix *-an* does not occur immediately after loanwords, but frequently occurs when the loanword has been marked as 'definite' by the prior addition of *-wā*. Thus *geṭ* 'gate', *geṭwā* 'the gate', **geṭan* 'the gates', *getwan* 'the gates'; *botal* 'bottle', *botalwā* 'the bottle', *botalan* 'the bottles', *botalwan* 'the bottles'. A similar pattern occurs with MB nouns borrowed from Creole (Baker and Ramnah 1985:219). There have been very few adjectives borrowed into SB (for example, *lejī* 'lazy', *sīk* 'sick'): these do not take the definite suffix *-kā* for adjectives.

(b) The agentive relative suffix *-wālā* 'one who' is added to some nouns borrowed from Eng, for example, *penśenwālā* 'one who receives a pension'; *puliswālā* 'one who is a policeman'; *mainwālā* 'miner', and so on.

(c) The suffix *-ain* denoting 'female' or 'wife of' may be added to some loans: thus *ṭīcar* 'teacher', *ṭīcarain* 'female teacher' (or less commonly 'wife of a teacher'); *dokṭe* 'doctor', *dokṭerain* 'woman-doctor' or 'wife of a doctor'; and the slang term *loferain* 'female loafer'.

(d) Early loans do participate in the echo-construction, often preserving the vowel correspondences outlined in A.2.3. Thus *ṭī* 'tea', versus *ṭī-ū* 'tea and things' (for example, 'tea and cakes'); *breṭ* 'bread', as against *breṭ-oṭ* 'bread and things' (for example, bread, butter, and biscuits'); *khār* 'car', as against *khār-or* 'cars and things' (for example, 'cars, vans and lorries'); *bol* 'football', as against *bol-ol* 'football and the like'.

(e) The commonly used loan-adjective *sīk* 'sick' may also function as a noun, and even take verbal endings. The basic function of *sīk* is adjectival, as in *bahut sīk he* 'she is very sick', but it functions as a noun in sentences like 4.

4. ek bahīn, bicārī, sīk se cal
one sister poor-thing sick ABL go

geil.
'go' 3sg.past

'One sister, the poor thing, died (literally 'went away') through illness.'

In this sentence the postposition *se* clearly marks *sīk* as being a noun. From the root *sīk* is derived a verb form *sikā-* 'to be sick', which admits participial endings only, and is used with an auxiliary.

5. ham kā karnā? sab dehī
I what do.FUT.IMP all body

sik-āt he.
sick-PP be.3sg.pres

'What must I do? My entire body is becoming infirm.'

6.

okar	beṭā	bahut	sīk-ā
he. GEN	son	much	sick-CAUS

geil.
'go' 3sg. past

'His son became very ill.'

(f) Nouns borrowed by SB from Eng can be converted into phrasal verbs by the addition of the verb *kar-* 'to do'. Doublets like the following are quite common in SB:

NOUN	VERBAL EQUIVALENT
fon 'a telephone'	*fon kar* 'to telephone'
airan 'an iron'	*airan kar* 'to iron'
ḍivos 'a divorce'	*ḍivos kar* 'to divorce'
reṇṭ 'rent'	*reṇṭ kar* 'to rent/be a tenant'

This is a regular way of deriving verbs from nouns in B, even with native vocabulary, for example, *kām* 'work' (noun), as against *kām kar* 'to work'. The addition of *kar-* applies in SB, even when the borrowed item is a verb: *śain kar-* 'to shine'; *miks kar-* 'to mix'; *laik kar-* 'to like'; *weiṭ kar-* 'to wait'; *sṭāṭ kar-* 'to start'; *poliś kar-* 'to polish', and so on. This is a very convenient method of adoption, since the Eng loan-form remains invariant while the B verb *kar-* carries all the inflections.

7.

ham	sab	kapṛā	aiṛan	karab.
I	all	clothes	iron	do.1sg.fut

'I will iron the clothes.'

8.

braṇḍā	acchā	nei	poliś	karat
veranda	well	not	polish	do.PP

he
be.3sg.pres

'She isn't polishing the veranda very well.'

The use of *kar* in this function is not, of course, limited to SB. It occurs in most Indic languages, including IB and transplanted varieties of B (Bhatia 1982:144; Baker and Ramnah 1985:224; Siegel 1987:154–5). Kachru (1983:196) shows how this operator can be used with semantically similar loans from different sources in distinct styles of contemporary Hindi:

ENGLISHISED HINDI	PERSIANISED HINDI	SANSKRITISED HINDI
anger kar-	*gussā kar-*	*krodh kar-* 'to be angry'
marriage kar-	*śādī kar-*	*vivāh kar-* 'to get married'
worry kar-	*phikir kar-*	*cintā kar-* 'to worry'

Haugen's (1953:398) observation that verbs in American Norwegian were almost always given a native grammatical form when borrowed from Eng, while nouns and adjectives were not, thus holds good for SB as well.

Occasionally other verb forms may also be used in converting Eng nouns into SB verbs: thus alternate ways of expressing 'he passed his examinations', using the Eng loanwoard *pass* (noun) are: *pās bheil* (literally 'a pass happened'); *pās milal* ('he obtained a pass'), and the usual *pās kailas* ('he did a pass').

4.6.2 *Loan-blends*

A small number of new lexical items have been formed by combining a native morpheme with an Eng borrowing. These are invariably compounds, with the Eng element coming second: *pān-siling* 'five-shillings' (from B *pā̃c* 'five' and Eng *shilling*); *ālu-binis* 'potatoes and beans' (prepared together in a curry), literally 'potato-beans'; *tīn-kōṭe* 'three-quarters' (where *tin* is the B for 'three' and *koṭe* derived from Eng quarter); *sāṛī-blaus* 'a sari and a blouse'; *colī-blaus* 'a short blouse' (where *colī* 'a short blouse' would suffice in IB); *juttā-sākīs* 'shoes and socks' (literally 'shoe-socks'); *sutnā-pens* 'pants for sleeping in' (literally 'sleeping-pants'); and *ek-karan* 'one-crown'. A more interesting set of compounds whilst having *both* elements from Eng, nevertheless has a characteristically B syntax: *ṭī-breṭ* 'tea and bread' (literally 'tea-bread'); *jūn-julai* 'June and July'; *baṭe-breṭ* 'bread and butter (literally 'butter-bread'); and more recent ones not fully incorporated in the language, like *laiṭ-wāṭe* 'water and lights' (usually in the context of domestic bills); and *waśing-ain* 'washing and ironing'.

4.6.3 *Loan translations*

Loan translations or calques are neologisms in a language formed by conscious or subconscious translation of a word or phrase found in another language: examples are Eng *spirit of the times* modelled on the German *Zeitgeist*; and *superman*, calqued on German *Übermensch*. Whereas Eng had given rise to a number of such calques in the colloquial Hn of British India (for example, *be-tār* 'wireless' (literally 'without wire'), *garmī-nāp* 'thermometer' (literally 'heat-measurer'), *māl-mōṭar* 'goods-lorry' (Chatterji 1960:217, there is very little of this in the case of SB, despite the tremendous influence of Eng. Weinreich (1968:109) suggested that it is typical of dominated obsolescing languages that, although extensive borrowing occurs, there is virtually no calque-formation. Among the few instances of loan-translations in SB are *cinnī* 'sugar diabetes' (a common ailment), which is a literal equivalent of SAIE 'sugar', though the loanword *cūge/śūge* is of equal frequency. The phrases *sīk parlī* 'I fell sick', and *hamke sardī pakarlas* literally 'the cold caught me' might contain verbs calqued on Eng *fall* and *caught*. SB, especially of the third generation, has rarely used existing native materials to express new concepts, resorting to loanwords instead.

4.6.4 *Code-switching*

There is a great deal of code-switching between Eng and B in the present day – that is to say, shifts from one language to the other are discernible within the same speech situation. However, this is not to suggest that a new variety comprising a blend of both languages occurs; rather that in any one situation one of the languages predominates, depending on topic and speaker and context, with occasional switches to the other tongue. As Poplack (1980:615) asserts, code-switching is not a defect arising from insufficient knowledge of one language or the other, but a linguistic skill requiring a large degree of competence in more than one language. This switch can be *metaphorical* (Gumperz and Blom 1972), that is, it is motivated by factors like role relationships, prestige or solidarity between speaker and addressee (as when an Eng–SB bilingual might alternate between these two languages with a doctor who is also conversant in them, to strike up a better patient-doctor relationship). But it could also be *situational*, when one is forced to change code to incorporate young people who do not fully understand B into a speech-event, or to accommodate older speakers whose command of Eng might be inadequate, or even to switch from Eng to B with the intention of concealment of what is being said from non-B-speaking outsiders or children.

With respect to metaphorical code-switching, in my observation two third-generation women speaking SB do throw in more Eng phrases than they would in speaking to elders, to (unconsciously) promote intimacy between two who are slightly more 'modern', 'knowledgeable', and 'progressive' than their first- and second-generation counterparts. Overlapping with such a 'social' explanation of code-switching is a linguistic one, which points to frequency of certain *trigger-words* in enhancing code switches. Certainly in the case of SB, as some of the examples below will show, the presence of loanwords or other words with ambivalent status between the two languages does often provoke a switch from one language to the other. There is also a thin dividing line between some instances of code-switching involving the use of individual Eng words, and the phenomenon of borrowing (see 4.2.11); indeed many recent loans seem to have started out as original instances of code-switching, but their frequency of usage led to their social integration into the SB matrix. Many of the new loans cited in 4.2.11 are probably best regarded as examples of code-switching. A sampling of intra-sentential switching follows:

9. okar nanad bollas etnā
she.GEN sister-in-law say.3sg.past so

thaṇḍā, *whole day* *bed* se
cold ABL

nei utrā delas.
not wake.CAUS 'give'3sg.past

'Her sister-in-law said that it was so cold, and did not allow her to get out of bed for the whole day.'

Sentence 9 has two Eng items (*whole day* and *bed*) which are moulded to a B pattern by taking the postposition *se*, and by following a B word order (temporals before locatives). The switch was probably triggered by the occurrence of *bed*, which passes in this sentence as both a SB (loan) word and an Eng word, the phonological form being similar in both instances.

10.	ham	*nine son*	ke	*mother*	haĩ.
	I		GEN		be.1sg.pres

'I am the mother of nine sons.'

Once again two Eng phrases have been incorporated into the B sentence pattern, the first by use of a postposition *ke*, the second as complement of the copula *he*. Both phrases have been Bhojpuri-ised by the lack of plural marker on *son*, after the numeral, and by the lack of the Eng article *the*. This mixed sentence thus shows a B syntax whilst having all three content morphemes from Eng. To account for this particular instance of code-switching one would probably have to invoke social rather than purely syntactic causes. The speaker was, quite surprisingly, a one-hundred-and-twenty-year-old woman who had been born in India, and who had only a (good) passive knowledge of Eng. She was probably prompted to switch to Eng phrases for two subconscious reasons:

(i) that she judged that a more appropriate and prestigious language for the journalistic type of interview being conducted was Eng, despite the interviewer's request that she speak B only; and used occasional Eng phraseology to achieve that end;
(ii) her sporadic use of Eng could be for the benefit of the (young) interviewer obviously more fluent in Eng than B.

In Sentence 11 code-switching is prompted by solidarity between the two third-generation participants, both proficient in Eng and SB; but an additional reason must be that the colloquial phrase *too good* ('to love to, to revel in' in colloquial SAIE) is both fashionable (in SAIE) and carries greater emphasis than a more conventional B phraseology.

11. laṛāī khatin *too good* he
fight PURP be.3sg.pres

'She revels in quarrelling'.

Sometimes code-switching involves repetition of the same phrase in the other language for purposes of dramatic emphasis:

12. hā̃, līkh de, līkh de,
yes write 'give'IMP write 'give'.IMP

write it, Roshni, in the book.

'Yes, Roshni, write it down in the book.'

The repetition of the phrase, first in SB, then in Eng causes the sentence, begun in B, to trail off into Eng.

Sentence 13 is an example of a mixed sentence begun in Eng by an Eng-dominant bilingual.

13. *You want bhindī* ke *bī*yā?
GEN seed

'Do you want *bhindi* seeds?'

Here the word *bhindi* 'okra' which is a B word, also used widely in SAIE, triggers the switch from Eng to B. Examples of extra-sentential switching involving longer pieces of discourse are given in the Appendix.

It is beyond the scope of this section to consider what syntactic constraints operate on SB–Eng switching. There are certainly some constraints, for switching cannot occur purely at random; but whether these correspond with what Poplack (1980) calls the 'equivalence constraint' (that is, that switches at points where juxtaposition of elements from the different languages would violate the syntax of the dominant language are blocked) is a subject for future investigation.

Despite widespread bilingualism in the case of the third generation especially, which results in occasional code-switching, the syntactic influence of Eng is not very great, certainly not as great as its lexical influence. In support of this assertion a comparison with the syntactic influence of Eng on

Std Hn of India is revealing. Kachru cites the following as instances of the 'Englishisation' of Hn syntax (1983:204–5):

(a) The use of indirect speech
(b) The use of impersonal constructions
(c) The passive construction with agent overtly stated
(d) Increase in the use of SVO order
(e) The use of parenthetical clauses

With the exception of (d) (see 4.6.5), SB is devoid of these influences, which are mainly of a learnèd nature. One might enquire, for example, whether third-generation fluent SB–Eng bilinguals do not approximate towards the Eng pattern of indirect speech after verbs of 'saying' and 'thinking'. (In B deictic elements like tense, temporals and pronouns remain unchanged – see A.6.4.) However, of the first thirty-two sentences containing the verb *bol-* 'to tell, say' used spontaneously by third-generation bilinguals in my data-base, there were no examples of Eng-like indirect speech. The question of syntactic convergence is dealt with in 4.6.8. In the following sections some syntactic innovations in SB, which are partly a result of contact with other South African languages, are discussed.

4.6.5 *Word-order changes*
Although it is still very much a verb-final language, SB has become more tolerant of constructions in which complements follow rather than precede the verb. This is particularly true of the third-generation speakers, who are familiar with two VO languages of Natal – Eng and F. The slightly freer word order is enhanced by two factors:

(i) These speakers make greater use of right dislocation – a stylistic option in which the subject or indirect object is placed last for emphasis. Thus:

14. bahut bhārī freṇḍ rahal,
much great friend be.3pl.past

ū ādmiyan.
they man. PL

'They were very great friends, those men.'

15. sob ro ro ke dekhī̃, ū
all cry cry CONJ see.3 pl.fut they
logan.
people. PL

'They will all cry and watch, those people.'

16. bahut dī̃n ke admī̃, ham.
many day GEN person I

'A person of many years, I am.'

(ii) Secondly there is fairly high use made by third-generation speakers of what Hyman has called 'afterthought material'. His comments (1975:120–1) are particularly apt for present day SB:

> I should like to claim that no language requires a speaker to start the whole sentence over again in order to put forgotten information into the correct pre-verbal slot. Instead the afterthought material can be tacked on at the end (in defiance of the 'verb at the end syntax'), with the pause and intonation signalling in effect that a speaker is aware that he 'shouldn't' be doing this – at least from a syntactic point of view.

Sentences 17 to 20 all show afterthought structures in SB.

17. okar sasūr ke phī̃n,
she.GEN father-in-law DAT also
opreiśen bheil . . . *Good*
operation happen.3sg.past
Friday ke haptā me.
GEN week LOC

'Her father-in-law too had an operation . . . on Good Friday week.'

18. ū lõg . . . nei lagī̃ . . . jeise
they PL not feel.3pl.fut as
Mandrājī̃ lõg.
Madras people

'They would not seem (to you) . . . to be Tamil-speaking.'

19.

okar	māī	geil . . .	hwā	aspatāl.
she.GEN	mother	go.3sg.past	there	hospital

'Her mother went to that hospital.'

20.

ū	ṭem	ham	dekhlī . . .	Sarojni	ke.
that	time	I	see.1sg.past	ACC	

'I saw Sarojni at that time.'

Hyman conjectures that such afterthought structure may become grammaticalised, eventually leading to a change from OV to VO sentence patterns. In SB the process of grammaticalisation has not (yet) occurred.

Purpose clauses and complements of the copula *hai/rah* also admit a very Eng-like order. In Sentences 21 to 23, the complementary purposive clauses follow the main verb in paratactic constructions, instead of being embedded in the more usual IB way (see A.6.4, especially 57 and 58):

21.

calī-jā	ham . . .	bagaśa	kare.
go.SUBJ-1pl	we	visit	do.INF

'Let us go visiting.'

22.

tor	ṭhen	he . . .	kapṛā
you.GEN	turn	be.3 sg.pres	clothes
dhowe	ke		
wash.INF	DAT.		

'It's your turn to wash the clothes.'

23.

ham	jaib . . .	dekhe . . .	oke.
I	go.1sg.fut	see.INF	he.ACC

'I will go to see him.'

In these examples, taken from the data for third-generation fluent speakers, the word order is very similar to that of Eng (even though these were not translation exercises, but free conversation among mainly female speakers for whom SB was either the dominant or equal-first language). Sentences 24 and 25, elicited under similar circumstances, show the occasional postposing of complements of the copula *hai* (present), and *rah-* (past).

24.

jo	rahat	barkā	moṭar,
if	be.CF.3sg.past.	big.DEF	car

ham	lõg	mar	jātī.
we	PL	die	'go'CF.1pl. past

'If it had been the big car, we would have died.'

25.

tū	rahanā	nānī	ke
you	stay.FUT IMP	granny	DAT

sanghe...	ham	jaib.
COM.	I	go.1sg.fut

'You must stay with your granny; I will go.'

4.6.6 *Changes in the use of modals*

Replacement of *cāh-* 'to wish' by *honā* has already been mentioned in 2.9.8. In addition, the modal *pā-* 'to manage' has become obsolete, except for some instances in the speech of a few members of the second generation. For the majority of speakers the subtle (and not always clearly defined) distinction between *pā-* 'to manage' and *sak-* 'to be able' (see A.5.5), which obtains in IB and other Indic languages, has collapsed, with *sak-* being used in both senses.

Another modal-like verb, *cuk-* 'to finish' has become obsolete, being replaced by an invariant form *khalās*, plus some form of verb *kar-* 'to do', or the copula *he-/rah-/bheil* (see 2.9.9 for the origins of *khalās* and examples of its use). *Cuk* has not fared well in other overseas B (see 2.9.9).

Finally, the incorporation of the Eng modal *must* in SB in the form of a modal-like construction raises the question of why the modals should be so receptive to change. SB uses the phrase *mas kar ke*, based on English *must*, and the B *kar*, which is the same *kar* 'to do' that occurs after borrowed (full) verbs (see 4.6.1f). In this instance it is not inflected for tense, person or number. The third element of this construction is the B conjunctive particle 'having'. This is basically an 'internal compulsion' construction used in an habitual sense. The main verb that follows *mas kar ke* has an invariant ending in *-nā*. This ending is usually associated with the future imperative (see 2.9.6), but here seems to signify habitual action. Thus the sentence *Ham mas kar ke jānā* means 'I must go (because I want to)', or 'I always go (because I love to)'. It does not mean 'I must be on my way (because I have to)', for which the usual IB construction of 'external compulsion' involving use of the copula *he/rah* or the modal *paṛ* 'to fall' (or less literally 'to have to') prevails (*Hamke jāi ke paṛī*).

The construction makes no literal sense at all: *ham mas kar ke jānā*, for example, literally states 'I-must-do-having-must go'. It is a more recent innovation in SB than the other borrowings dealt with above, started by third-generation Eng–B bilinguals.

The impetus for this construction comes from colloquial SAIE, which, in addition to the usual Eng uses of the modal *must*, has a (non-standard) construction in which stressed *must* denotes habitual aspect, internal compulsion or both. With stressed *must* a sentence like *That fellow must go to the races* suggests that the subject is an inveterate race-goer; with unstressed *must* the usual Std Eng sense of external compulsion applies.

One or two recent instances of its use suggest that the construction is being generalised semantically in SB to include the more usual Eng sense of external compulsion. Sentence 26, uttered by an eighty-year-old speaker, was unusual in omitting the *kar ke* part of the formula, and in not having internal obligation as a primary meaning. Sentence 27, in having the Eng sense of 'I think you should go because you will find it fascinating', (not 'I compel you to go'), is also a deviation from the usual SB semantics ('You love going to the shop').

26.	baccan	mas	Hindī	bāt	karnā.
	child.PL	must		speech	do.FUT IMP.

'Children must speak Hindi.'

27.

tū	mas	kar	ke	dukān	jānā
you	must	do	CONJ	shop	go. FUT IMP

'You (simply) must go to the shop.'

It is again worthy of note that at least one other transplanted variety has borrowed *mas*. Mohan (1978:183) reports the use of *mas* as adverbial in TB (from Creole *mas*, ultimately Eng *must*).

4.6.7 *Deletion of the copula/aux he*

There is an optional rule in SB, even as used by the oldest speakers, of deleting the copula *he*:

28.

bahut	dīn	ke	admī,	ham.
many	day	GEN	person	I

'I am a person of many days.'

29.

baṛā	chokrī	hamār	bhāī
big	girl	me. GEN	brother

ke	beṭī.
GEN	daughter

'The big girl is my brother's daughter.'

30.

bhittar	jāī	ke	nei	hukkum.
inside	go. INF	DAT	not	permission

'Going inside is not allowed.'

In each instance it would be more usual to include the copula in sentence final position (except under right dislocation, in which case the copula precedes the dislocated NP). The past (suppletive) form of the copula – *rahā* – is, however, never deleted (that is, a deleted copula is always understood to have present signification). Sentence 31 shows that *he* may also be deleted if it is an auxiliary:

31.

ū	hamke	ām	dele.
he	me.DAT	mango	give.3 sg.past

'He has given me mangoes.'

In this sentence the aux *he*, denoting perfective aspect, has been deleted from its final position. Non-perfective aspect, without the auxiliary *he* would require a different verbal ending *-las*/*-lak*, not *-le*. (Some speakers, however, seem to use *-las* and *-le* interchangeably as endings for the third person, past transitive. Although perfective aspect in their speech is usually expressed by the *-le* ending + *he*, it is sometimes difficult to determine whether sentences like 31 above express perfective aspect (with copula deletion), or non-perfective aspect.)

Sentence 32 shows that *he* may be deleted (again optionally) even when it is used in the present habitual sense:

32.	Deban	ke	phal	ham	lõg	nei	boe.
	Durban	GEN	fruit	we	PL	not	plant

'We do not plant the fruits you get in Durban.'

In this sentence the auxiliary *he* in final position is understood. An intermediary stage, for some speakers, between the presence of the copula/auxiliary *he* is found in its phonological reduction to [ə], or in the devoicing of the entire word, making it a whisper, so faint as to be often inaudible or just perceivable as a trace of aspiration on the last syllable of the previous word. Some (infrequent) examples are:

33.	ū	kām	karat	[ə]
	he	work	do.PP	is

'He is working.'

34.	ī	hamār	bahin	ke	cokrā	[h].
	this	me.GEN	sister	GEN	son	is.

'This is my sister's son.'

4.6.8 *Syntactic convergence*

In view of the great influence exerted upon the SB lexicon by Eng, it is not out of place to enquire to what extent the two languages have converged syntactically. Studies of communities in which there is a long-standing tradition of stable bilingualism (for example, Gumperz and Wilson 1971;

Pandit 1972; Scollon and Scollon 1979) suggest that the languages involved show convergence towards a common code. In their classic study of Urdu–Kannada–Marathi trilingualism in the village of Kupwar, Maharashtra, Gumperz and Wilson (1971) demonstrate that these three languages which have co-existed there for over three centuries show a decided trend towards word-for-word inter-translatability, not characteristic of these languages in regions where they do not co-exist. Speakers in the village seem to have not three distinct syntaxes, but rather a single common core 'Kupwar syntax', illustrated by sets like the following:

35. a.	KU:	pala	jəra	kaṭ	ke	le	ke	a - ø- ya.
b.	KM:	pala	jəra	kap	un	ghe	un	a - l- o.
c.	KK:	tapla	jəra	khod	i	təgond	i	b - ø- yn.
		greens	a-little	cut	CONJ	take	CONJ	come.I.sg.past

'I cut some greens and brought them.'

KEY: KU — Kupwar Urdu
KM — Kupwar Marathi
KK — Kupwar Kannada

Gumperz and Wilson show further that linguistic change/convergence in Kupwar is generally towards Kannada and (less frequently) Marathi.

I have shown some areas of Eng influence on SB with respect to syntax. The other side of the coin is, however, much more revealing, since the Eng of third-generation Indian South Africans – the first to attain fluency in it – owes a great deal to B and Tamil. Sentences like 36–40 support my contention that if there is convergence in the grammars of third-generation SB–Eng bilinguals, it is in the direction of SB rather than Eng.

36. Just now we drank.

37. Must come!

38. Which one I put in the jar, that one is tasty.
39. Summertime, it's too hot.
40. She was watching video.

In these sentences, recorded in spontaneous, informal settings involving B dominant bilinguals, the syntax shows some convergence towards B sentences. 36 and 39 show the preposing of temporal complements before the main verb, often resulting in verb-final sentences in those instances where there is no direct object. Sentence 37 shows the deletion of pronouns (usually, but not only, second person pronouns) when context makes the referent clear, parallel with B usage. Sentence 38 shows one type of relative clause characteristic of older speakers (the correlative), which is similar to B usage (see A.6.2) and restricted to OV languages (see Mesthrie 1987). Finally, 40 shows that article-deletion may occur in a wider range of contexts than in Std Eng, thereby approximating B which has no indefinite article.[7]

But it cannot be claimed that the two languages proceed from the same grammar, or have the same (or very similar) surface structures. I present two examples which show the lack of a simple mapping between the two languages, as used by fluent bilinguals:

41.

toke	mālum	Niria	dīdī,	ham
you.DAT	known		sister	I

ghare	rahalī,	dukān	mē	becat
home.LOC	be.1sg.past	shop	LOC	sell.PP

rahalī,	*tea-room*	rahal,	barkā
be.2sg.past		be.3sg.past	big.DEF

dukān	rahal,	sob	cīj
shop	be.3sg.past	all	thing

rahal,	ham	lõg	ke.
be.3sg.past	we	PL	DAT

'You know, sister Niria, I used to stay at home; I used to sell in the shop; we had a tea-room – a big one; we had a lot of things (in there).'

The differences between 41 and its SAIE equivalent are not restricted to verb positions only. The SB sentence begins with an impersonal dative (where SAIE has a nominative 'you know'), and ends in a dative of possession (unknown in SAIE). In addition, whereas 41 consistently deletes pronouns under anaphora, an SAIE equivalent need not.

42.

ham	to	phajire	kapṛā-wapṛā
I	then	morning.LOC	clothes-ECHO

dhowe	ke	dāl	delī;	hamār
wash.INF	DAT	put	'give'1sg.past	my

chokarī,	bicharī,	hamke
daughter	poor-thing.	I.DAT

sab	dho	ke	ain
all	wash	CONJ	iron

kar	ke	delas.
'do'	CONJ	give.3sg.past

'I put the clothes in for washing; my daughter washed all of them, ironed them and gave them to me – poor thing.'

In 42 the differences between the SB and the SAIE structures are equally great. The use of the three embedded clauses – one purposive (*dhōwē ke* 'for washing'), and two conjunctives (*dhō ke, ain kar ke* 'having washed, having ironed') as well as the use of compound verbs (*dāl dēlī* 'put away' and *ain kar* 'iron'), are unparalleled in the SAIE equivalent.

Gumperz and Wilson's study dealt with three typologically similar languages in contact over a long period of time. In South Africa, within a shorter time span, with typologically dissimilar languages, and under conditions of unstable bilingualism, there is a trend towards convergence, but the Kupwar model is not replicated. Within one generation there has been a swing from fluent bilingualism to Eng dominance. For younger speakers the trend towards convergence of grammars has been halted, and one grammar has become obsolescent.

4.7 *ORAL TRADITION*

Despite a fledgling literary output, IB is still very much a 'folk' language, rich in oral tradition, abounding in stock phrases, idioms, proverbs, and short didactic poems to suit most occasions of daily living. In addition, the speech community places a high premium on aesthetic play with language, including the use of onomatopoeia, echoes, riddles, and ritualised forms of abuse. In this section I attempt to compare such functions of language with current-day practice in SB.

4.7.1 *Forms of greeting*

In Bihar and Uttar Pradesh, as in much of India, patterns of greeting differ according to the caste of the persons involved. Generally one does not greet a person of lower caste, but waits for him to pay respects before replying. According to Misra (1980) a man of middle or low caste greets a Brahman as follows: *Bābajī pāwlāgī* 'Sir, Grandfather, I touch your feet'; or *Mahārājjī gor lāgat hai* 'Sir, great king, I touch your feet'; or *Gurujī dandawat* 'Honourable teacher, I fall flat at your feet'. To these the Brahman might reply less formally, *Jiyā rah* 'May you live long', or some such phrase. One Brahman greets another formally with *pranām* or *namaskār*, whereas members of other castes are less formal to each other, using terms like *Rām Rām bhāī* 'Greetings in the name of Ram, brother'. To non-Brahman high castes (for example, *Kayasths, Kshatriyas*) a Brahman uses Sanskritic formalisms like *Āyusmān āyusmān* 'May you live a long life'.

In formally greeting an elderly woman or one of higher caste, a woman has to lift the corner of the other's sari and respectfully touch her own forehead with it five times. She must then grasp the other's foot and touch her own forehead with it. The woman being greeted replies *Ehwāt banal raho* 'May your husband live long', or *Beṭā hokho* 'May a son be born to you'.

Misra (1980:165) provides the following scale of respect in decreasing order of deference, current in the contemporary B of the state of Uttar Pradesh:

GESTURE OF GREETING	VERBAL EQUIVALENT
prostration	*pāu lāgī*
bowing, bending	*praṛā̃m/pranām*
touching the feet	*namaskār*
folding hands	*namaste*
handshake	*rām-rām*
raising hands	*jay siyārām*

In SB most of these formalities have become outmoded, with the usual form of greeting being *namaste*, accompanied with the palms of one's hands placed flat together in front of one's chest, as if in prayer. This is the form of greeting irrespective of caste, seniority or gender.

To denote particular respect for a priest (who is often, but not always, of Brahman extraction) one adds the suffix of respect *jī* to his title (thus *namaste panḍijjī*). First-generation migrants and some of their immediate descendants did retain most of the forms of greetings cited above. Older women today speak in awe of the strictness of mothers-in-law who used to expect their daughters-in-law to touch their feet in obeisance each time they left the house or re-entered it from an outside visit. The phrase *pāu lāgī* (*palegī* in SB) has become purely ritualised devoid of its etymological sense 'I touch your feet'. This can be seen by younger mothers encouraging their children to greet their grandparents thus, with the, literally incongruous, gesture of folding the palms together in respect.

4.7.2 *Proverbs*

The rich store of B proverbs did not adapt well under the changed social and economic circumstances in South Africa, since they had their original inspiration from objects and situations essentially characteristic of Indian villages. Many of the proverbs are witty observations based on animal-lore, caste-lore, and initimate knowledge of the climate and environment, which, in time, became of remote relevance to life in South Africa. I present a few proverbs current in Bihar at the time of migrations (from the stock of proverbs and other observations scattered throughout Grierson's *Bihar Peasant Life*, 1885), which must have been known by some of the incoming migrants, but which are no longer extant in SB:

43. *cālani ṭūsal sūp kē janika sahasar goṭ ched.* (p. 117)

    'The sieve which had a thousand holes, sneered at the winnowing basket' (cf. Eng 'Pot calling the kettle black').

44. *nai dhobiniyā̃ ailī̃, lugriye sābun lailī̃.* (p. 147)

    'The new washerwoman has come and applied soap, even when washing rags' (cf. Eng 'New brooms sweep clean').

45. *koṛhi barad kē phephaṛi bahut.* (p. 288)

    'It's the lazy bullock that puffs and snorts' (cf. Eng 'Empty vessels make the most sound').

46. *taslā tor ki mor?*

    'Is this pot yours or mine?' (cf. Eng 'Heads I win, tails you lose').

There is a delightful story regarding the origin of 46, cited by Grierson (1885:129):

> Once upon a time all the people of Bhojpur, in Shahabad, were robbers. When a traveller passed through one of these villages, they used to seize his cooking-pot, saying *taslā tor ki mor* 'Is this pot mine or yours?' If the traveller replied *mor* 'mine', they would set upon him, and beat him and rob him of the vessel by force. If he said *tor* 'yours', they used on his own admission, to take it from him and let him go peaceably. Thus, in any way, they plundered him. Hence the saying *taslā tor ki mor* has passed into a proverb, of which the application is easy to see.

The citing of proverbs is a lost art in SB, in the course of ordinary conversation. The following is a selection of the small store of proverbs that have survived in South Africa. They are used, if at all, by older speakers among themselves only.

47. *dudharī gāī ke dū lāto bhalā*

'Even two kicks from a good milking cow are to be valued' (often used in the context of maltreatment by employers: don't complain as long as you get what you need).

48. *calani me gāī dūhe*
bole karam ke dos.

'The cow being milked into a sieve says, "Such is my fate" or "It must be a fault of my previous life"' (a comment on the wastefulness of its owner).

49. *khet khāi gadahā*
māral jāi jolahā

'The donkey feeds in someone else's field, but its owner receives the punishment' (it's the innocent who suffer).

50. *nācce ke dhang nei*
anganwā ṭeṛh

'He who can't dance says it's the ground that's uneven' (a bad workman always blames his tools).

51. *khalerī chuṭ jāī*
damrī nei chuṭe

'He might leave his skin behind, but never his money' (a comment on a miser).

52. *goṛe ail baryāt*
samdhī ke lage hagās

'The bridegroom's party have arrived at the door, and the host decides that he wants to go to the toilet' (a comment on a laggard, or one who is ill-prepared).

4.7.3 *Didactic poems*

Related to the proverbs of the previous section is the existence in IB of a large corpus of short formulaic didactic poems, whose function is to store and hand down in a readily assimilable form short pieces of wisdom concerning agriculture, the seasons and so on. They are usually rhyming couplets of equal measure, a selection of which (from Grierson 1885) is given below:

53. *mirgsirā tabay rohini labay aradrā jay budbudāy*
kahai ḍāk sanu bhillari, kuttā bhāt na khāi
(p. 275)

'If *Mirgsira* (= May/June) is hot, *Rohini* (= June/July) rains, and *Aradra* (= July/August) gives a few drops, Dak says "Hear, O Bhillari, even dogs will turn up their noses at rice"' (because it will be so plentiful).

54. *hathiyā barse tīn hot bā, ṣakkar, sāli, mās,*
hathiyā barse tīn jāt bā, tīl, kodo, kapās (p. 281)

'If it rains in *Hathiya* (= September) three things are produced: sugar-cane, rice and pulse; if it rains in *Hathiya* three things are destroyed: sesame, *kodo*, and cotton.'

Many poems eulogise tobacco as their subject, while a great many like the following teach one how to recognise the end of the rainy seasons:

55. *bolī lukḥrī, phule kās*
ab nahī barkha ke ās (p. 283)

'The barking of the fox and the flowering of the grass (say that) the rain will no longer come.'

Such didactic poems are unknown in contemporary SB, not suprisingly, since the conditions they describe no longer obtain. However, rhyming verse, mostly humorous, does linger on to a diminished extent. I present two macaronic jingles and a folksong composed in Natal:

56. *June-July*
Kē bhulai

'June and July
Who can forget.'
(Composed, it is said, by the original migrants, in response to – what was to them – Natal's severe winter.)

57. *mālik mālik*
ginger-garlic

(A meaningless jingle, revelling in mixing codes, with *malik* 'lord', and the anti-climactic *ginger-garlic*, set to the Indic *dvandva pattern*.)

58. *kūlī nām dharāyā* *kūlī nām dharāyā*
Naṭalwā me āi ke *bhajan karo bhayā*
hāṭh me cambu *kandh me kudāri*
pardesiyā ghare jāī

'They've given you the name "coolie", they've given you the name "coolie"
You've come to Natal, give thanks in song, brother.
With a *cambu* in your hand, and a hoe on your shoulder,
Let the foreigners go home.'

This is one version of a song reportedly composed in the earliest days, conveying the hardships of the times, but also revelling in new words learnt locally – *Natāl, kūlī*, and *cambu* 'a can, container' (from Tamil).

4.7.4 *Ritual abuse*
As noted in 3.2, IB is sterotyped as a 'rough language' or 'rough person's language' by outsiders familiar with it. It is a swear-language *par excellence*, providing a large slice of the Indian army's repertoire of swear words and slang. Misra (1980:167) claims that 'disputes of one kind or other among people in the Bhojpuri-speaking villages are the order of the day. They lead to quarrels of various types which provide scope for the register of slang, abuse, swearing and cursing.'

To abuse someone with invective language is to offer a sharp and short condemnation of him, elevated almost to the stature of a game involving great artistry, especially amongst the lower classes. The term of abuse might take one of the following forms:

(a) An animal name is applied to the person being vilified: *gadahā* 'ass'; *sā̃p* 'snake'; *kuttī* 'bitch'; *sūar* 'pig'; *banar* 'monkey'; *ghoṛā* 'horse'; *ullū* 'owl' (known for stupidity, not the wisdom of its western counterpart) etc.

(b) An epithet suggesting the immoral behaviour of the accused is employed: *coṭṭā* 'thief'; *lālcī* 'glutton'; *besaram* 'shameless'; *pāpī* 'criminal'; *doglā* 'bastard son', etc.

(c) A piece of character assassination by phrases describing sexual abuse of the accused or his mother, sister or daughter: Misra provides the following examples: *tore mai ke būr codo* 'May I rape your mother'; *rupayā ke badle ā̃ri deb unhe* 'I'll give him testicles instead of money'.

Grierson (1885:298) notes that cultivators have many terms of abuse for their cattle, a favourite one being *jāh kasaiyā khū̃ṭa* 'May you go to the butcher (or the sacrificial stake)'.

Misra adds further that 'in all castes, women are more abusive than men'. It should be emphasised that such ritual abuse is accepted for what it is – a safety-valve for releasing pent-up frustrations, rather than to antagonise someone for life.

In SB this is one register that has remained more or less intact, with animal names, and epithets concerning immoral behaviour retaining their full potency. There have been, in addition, some English borrowings, for example, *sanwagan* 'son-of-a-gun'; *ḍemeṭ* 'good-for-nothing' (from *damn it*). For the third generation some terms, though widely used, have lost much of their original force because their precise meaning is not always understood. Such generalised terms of abuse include *thē̃tar* 'obstinate, stubborn'; *kulakchan* 'signifier of ill-omen'; *besaram* 'shameless'; *haramī* 'illegitimate person, bastard'. These are understood as terms of insult, but are devoid of some of the subtler overtones which differentiate them in IB.

4.7.5 *Onomatopoeia*

Finally onomatopoeia, another form of word-play which occurs extensively in IB (see A.2.3c), deserves brief mention here. This playful use of language, with most items being considered 'informal', or (−R) continues in SB to a lesser degree. The following are some instances of onomatopoeia in local use, mostly from IB, though one or two might be innovations by SB speakers: *cul-bul* 'noisiness, naughtiness'; *khur-bhur* 'irritating scraping noises'; *krang-brung* 'irritating loud noises'; *ṭhin-ṭhinā* 'to complain whiningly'; *par-parā* 'to speak incessantly'; *phus-phusā* 'to whisper'; *cup-cāp* 'quietude', etc.

CHAPTER FIVE

LANGUAGE OBSOLESCENCE

5.1 *INTRODUCTION*

Although most textbooks of historical linguistics mention the extinction of such languages as Gothic, Hittite, and Etruscan, not many descriptions of the actual processes of language obsolescence were undertaken until the 1970s. Prior to that there were isolated observations by Bloomfield (1927), and Swadesh (1948), motivated primarily by the extinction of many Amerindian languages, as well as a monograph by Coteanu (1957).[1]

It is the work of Nancy Dorian in numerous articles published in the 1970s, culminating in her book *Language Death – The Life Cycle of a Scottish Gaelic Dialect*, that has drawn most attention to this linguistic and sociolinguistic phenomenon in recent times. There exists today a fairly large corpus of articles in various journals dealing with aspects of dying languages, often bearing melodramatic titles: Campbell and Canger (1978) 'Chicomuceltec's last throes'; Denison (1977) 'Language death or language suicide'; Dressler (1972) 'On the phonology of language death'; Haas (1968) 'The last words of Biloxi'; Hill and Hill (1977) 'Language death and relexification in Tlaxcalan Nahuatl'; Miller (1971) 'The death of language or serendipity among the Shoshoni', and many others.[2]

Even though the socio-historic setting for the loss of languages on their native soil is obviously different from that of the demise of ethnic, migrant languages, very similar linguistic processes are operative in both cases (for example, reduction of certain structures, generalisation of some rules, restriction of vocabulary, etc.). It is therefore not out of place to consider the obsolescence of SB in the context of the research mentioned above. I shall accordingly outline a few such case histories before proceeding to characterise SB as a dying language.

5.2 *EXTERNAL HISTORIES*

We can differentiate between precipitate language death that occurs when native speakers of a particular language die, leaving no offspring, and a more gradual form that involves the abandonment of one language by a whole community in favour of another. The former case, where a language dies without being replaced by another, is exemplified by the fate of some Amerindian languages and of Tasmanian (Swadesh 1948). Before the arrival of British settlers in 1803 there were about five thousand Tasmanians. Within just thirty-two years that population was reduced to 203, after conflict between settlers and natives. The surviving Tasmanians were then moved to another island, where in twelve years their population decreased to 44. After being removed to a second island the rest of the population died from grief or disease, with the last survivor, a woman called Truganini living till 1876, a mere seventy-three years after the first European settlement. She died with her own language intact, and with no knowledge of the foreigner's language – Eng – save for a few loanwords.

Swadesh also draws attention to the extinction of Yahi, an Amerindian language of northern California, whose last speaker, Ishi (the last survivor of the tribe), spoke 'faultless' Yahi, learning to make himself understood in Eng only in the last years, after being taken to the University of California in 1911.

Case histories of the second type of language death – or language shift – suggest that the external circumstances are very similar: languages on their way to extinction are first used in a near-diglossic situation with the dominant language to which they eventually lose out. The dominant language is one of wider currency, necessary for communication within a larger society than that represented by the dominated language; or is one which is recognised (tacitly or overtly) as the medium for upward mobility. The functions fulfilled by the dominated language become progressively fewer, with the home being the last domain in which it persists. Children, however, begin using the new language first among themselves, and then to their parents or grandparents as soon as the linguistic competence of their elders permits it.

Reduction in usage is usually accompanied by attenuation of linguistic structures, on account of the pervasive influence of the dominant language. This is mirrored in many instances by the diminution of the prestige of the dying language in the judgement of its own speakers. This factor, in turn, only precipitates the end of the language.

Dorian uses the term 'semi-speaker' for those who have had insufficient exposure to the home language, and who, despite being far more competent in the dominant language, continue using the home language in an imperfect way. Dorian (1981:107) characterises the semi-speakers of the Gaelic of East Sutherland in northern Scotland as follows:

> Unlike the older Gaelic-dominant bilinguals, the semi-speakers are not fully proficient in Gaelic. They speak it with varying degrees of less than full fluency, and their grammar (and usually also their phonology), is markedly aberrant in terms of the fluent-speaker norm. Semi-speakers may be distinguished from fully fluent speakers of any age by the presence of deviations in their Gaelic which are explicitly labelled 'mistakes' by the fully fluent speakers. That is, the speech community is aware of many (though not all) of the deficiencies in semi-speaker speech performance. Most semi-speakers are also relatively halting in delivery or speak Gaelic in rather short bursts, or both; but it is not manner of delivery which distinguishes them, since semi-speakers of comparable grammatical ability may speak with different degrees of confidence and 'fluency'. At the lower end of speaker skill, semi-speakers are distinguished from near-passive bilinguals by their ability to manipulate words in sentences. Near-passive bilinguals often know a good many words and phrases, but cannot build sentences with them or alter them productively. Semi-speakers can, although the resultant sentences

> may be morphologically or syntactically askew to a greater or lesser extent.

As implied here, not every young speaker of a community undergoing a gradual process of language shift is automatically a semi-speaker. Dorian attributes the desire of some young speakers to continue with an imperfect variety where possible to the following factors:

(a) Late birth-order in a large relatively language-loyal family. In such a family the eldest might emerge as a fluent speaker, whereas the last two or three children will emerge as semi-speakers, because, although their parents might continue using Gaelic to them, the influence of elder siblings who bring back Eng from school is stronger.
(b) A second possible cause is strong attachment to one's grandparents, who usually use far more Gaelic than one's parents; though occasionally it is the influence of aunts and parents that also counts.
(c) Temporary (or sometimes permanent) exile often fosters a re-awakening of active loyalty to the dominated language, especially if there are fellow-exiles who share those feelings.
(d) An 'inordinately inquisitive and gregarious personality' (Dorian 1981:109) might also be a factor that causes some young people to participate in conversations with elders in Gaelic.

It seems, however, that not every instance of language shift produces such semi-speakers: J. Hill (quoted by Dorian 1981:115) says of the obsolescent languages of California, Luiseño and Cupeño, 'You either speak fairly well or not at all'.

5.3 *THE MICRO-LINGUISTIC SITUATION*

Turning now to the actual effects of incomplete acquisition histories on linguistic performance, we find equal diversity in case studies. Dying languages, as spoken by semi-speakers, and pidgins have many features in common, as several writers note (Dorian 1981; Dressler and Wodak-Leodolter 1977). In both, vocabulary is relatively restricted, inflections are generalised or simplified, and some transformations are lost. However, pidgins may become creolised by entering 'into the primary socialisation of children . . . whereas dying languages cease to be utilised for primary socialisation . . .' (Dressler and Wodak-Leodolter 1977:8).

Dorian points out some significant differences between pidgins and dying languages. In the 'semi-speech' of East Sutherland Gaelic allomorphic variety does not undergo substantial change, word-order is unchanged, embedding handled with ease, and certain categories which have marginal or indirect semantic significance persist. None of these is suggestive of a process of pidginisation.

Dressler (1972) suggests that languages die on account of rule loss, rule simplification, and the like. His hypothesis is rejected by Denison (1977) who claims, instead, that languages become obsolete when speakers no longer deem it worthy to communicate with children in a low-prestige variety, and children are no longer motivated to acquire an active competence in that language. Rule loss, and other simplificatory processes do follow in such cases, but as far as Denison is concerned the 'language suicide' has already occurred. He provides evidence (from German of Sauris in north-east Italy, under the influence of Friulian and Standard Italian) to show that dying languages may even gain rules from languages they come in contact with. The two views seem to be but different sides of the same coin.

Mohan and Zador's (1986) views concur with those of Denison, except on the connotations of the word 'suicide'. Discussing the case of TB, Mohan and Zador place a question mark over when exactly a language may be said to be dead. They claim that the speech of semi-speakers (or, in their terms, 'post-native speakers') is not the prelude to death, but the visible sign of an event that has already come to pass. The biological metaphor of death is thus apt in that it implies a state, not an ongoing process; a language, as a well-generated system, dies intact and well before suggested by earlier writers.

> . . . Dorian chooses to regard ESG [=East Sutherland Gaelic] as still alive for its rare 'semi-speakers' (who can hardly even converse in it), since the forms of the language are still to some extent retrievable, even if

> only via translation; she speaks hopefully of the rule violations elicited from the 'semi-speakers' as changes in the language. The present study, however, regards TBh [=TB] as dead after the last native speaker, and makes no attempt to rationalize formal deviation by post-native speakers as being within the life-cycle of the language. (Mohan and Zador 1986:316)

At a purely theoretical level, their position seems quite correct, but in so far as semi-speakers do participate in linguistic interactions, however limited, there is something to be gained from studying their speech and attitudes, even though theirs is not L1 competence.

Irrespective of whether we view semi-speaker speech as the residue of an already dead language, or as part of the process of obsolescence, it is of interest to examine whether certain parts of the grammar of a language are most affected by this partial competence, and whether other parts are more resistant to change. Breatnach (1964) characterising Irish dialects on their way to extinction claims that the effects of disuse are evident at all stages mainly in the vocabulary, and secondarily the morphological, phonological, and syntactic patterns, while the purely phonetic character of the language resists influence to the end. However, Dressler's (1972) and Dorian's (1981) work based on similarly structured languages, cognate with Irish (Breton and Scots Gaelic respectively), suggests that morphological patterning (for example, initial mutation of consonants as a signal of a change of word-class, and as inflectional marker) is as significantly affected as vocabulary in these obsolescent languages.

On the other hand, Mithun and Henry (1979) studying obsolescence of a very different type of language – Oklahoma Iroquois – find few neologisms in the vocabulary. They suggest that the lexicon does shrink, with specific terms (for example, 'moose', 'beaver', 'weasel') being lost before more general terms. The breakdown of morphology is first felt, not in the loss of particular productive morphemes, but in an avoidance of their combination – with lexical replacements occurring instead of polysynthesis of morphemes. Phonological simplification involves reduction of the length of words, starting with the initial syllable, though the phonetic system seems generally unaffected.

5.4 *SB AS AN OBSOLESCENT LANGUAGE*

In 3.6 the main reasons for the decline of SB were outlined, as well as current (obsolescent) patterns of speaking between different generations. The degree of acculturation to Western ideals, and the low prestige value of SB as outlined there have ensured that the number of semi-speakers is quite negligible. The term 'semi-speaker' is in fact not entirely pertinent; in Dorian's sense it refers to young people who make a conscious effort to use Gaelic with their elders, even when the addressees are known to have a reasonable command of Eng as second language. In addition, some semi-speakers of Gaelic try to use it in conversation with each other, under special conditions. As Dorian puts it, 'It seems perverse that a group of people whose control of ESG is imperfect, and whose agemates have for the most part opted for Eng only, should continue to use a stigmatised language of strictly local currency when they are fully proficient speakers of a language of wider currency' (1981:107).

Although there are a number of young speakers who converse in SB in a halting, imperfect manner, on account of incomplete acquisition at an early age or because of lack of practice, they make no special effort to cultivate the use of the language. By and large they use it only when they are forced to, usually in speaking to those few elders who lack a command of Eng. Where the older person understands Eng, but is unable to speak it, most young speakers prefer a dual-medium conversation, replying in Eng to the other's SB. Furthermore, young speakers do not converse with each other in SB; it would be inappropriate to do so, going against the very strong local linguistic-pragmatic currents. That is to say, there is no community of semi-speakers – their semi-speech arises for the nonce – pidgin-like – and then disappears till the next time.

A prominent feature of semi-speaker discourse in SB is the diminished size of the network (in the sense of Milroy 1980) it is operative in. That is, a semi-speaker has a specific group of elders – a very small one – with whom he or she uses the dying language, and avoids using it as much as possible in all other instances. One of the reasons for this must be that whereas semi-speakers feel fairly comfortable speaking an imperfect variety to elders they are close to, they become self-conscious about their ability when forced to converse with outsiders.

I will use the term 'semi-speaker' in this study to denote a person with a limited communicative competence in SB, who can and does use it to communicate with some elders some of the time. It does not necessarily follow from this definition, but happens to be the case, that these speakers do not use SB among themselves, and hardly ever to bilinguals fluent in SB and Eng. That is to say, the 'perversity' in the sense of the quotation from Dorian does not exist: the use of SB by semi-speakers is functional, hardly ever 'symbolic'.

Dorian's criteria for the genesis of semi-speakers in East Sutherland Gaelic do not apply *en bloc* in the case of SB. In South Africa the most important factor is undoubtedly the existence of at least one grandparent, whose lack of proficiency in Eng ensured that a young child had direct access to B from day to day. The continued presence of a home-bound grandmother, in particular, was often the cause of a high degree of fluency in early childhood. This was often counteracted by negative factors in later years, chiefly the influence of the Eng school. Most semi-speakers who were interviewed claimed some use of B with grandparents in their earliest years. Even more striking was the fact that in many instances they had lost their last grandparent by the age of six or so. This left little subsequent need to use B actively. In a home in which there were no grandparents, and parents did not use B directly to their children in early years, it was more likely that the children grew up to be passive bilinguals, not semi-speakers.

It seems that if one or more grandparent were alive for a longer period into the grandchild's teens, and continually spoke in B, then that grandchild developed into a young fluent speaker, rather than a semi-speaker. A 'young fluent speaker' is Dorian's term for an individual who, while speaking a fluent, versatile and idiomatic Gaelic, shows some departures from the conservative norms of older fluent speakers. Such speakers do exist among users of SB, though I have not had the opportunity to study the speech of more than three of them. Where parents spoke to children in B (and little or no Eng), this ensured a young fluent speaker (YFS);

but if it was the grandparental generation alone that was responsible for the active transmission of B, then a semi-speaker (henceforth SS) was more likely to result.

Although Dorian's next factor – late birth order in a very language-loyal family – does produce SSs, it is the converse – early birth order in an ordinary family (that is, one which is not particularly solicitous about ensuring the transmission of B to children) – that is more likely to give rise to the semi-speaking SB individual. In a family whose first child was born in the 1950s a common pattern is: first child – YFS or SS; second child – YFS or SS; third child – SS; fourth child and subsequent children – passive bilingual. Families in which children under twenty-five have a fluent command of SB tend to be poor rural ones who have missed the march towards 'progress' and modernisation. These families generally consist of parents with no education in Eng, and elder children with little schooling. The women in these households are generally home-bound, while the elder men do not hold white-collar jobs, which might have furnished incentives for greater integration into a larger society, requiring greater loyalty to the dominant language. In these impoverished families, language-loyal more by chance than desire, the eldest children tend to be fluent speakers, while the youngest usually are SSs (sometimes YFS) on account of the stimuli of B from parents and grandparents, and Eng from elder brothers and sisters.

Temporary or permanent exile from home does seem to have the effect of re-kindling diminishing loyalties to one's language and culture, but the number of people affected in this way is negligible. Any inspiration occasioned by prolonged absence from one's community would, in any case, prompt one to enquire about one's cultural and religious foundations – a path that leads to India, Sanskrit, and Std Hn, and away from SB. Furthermore, the test of loyalty as an Indian South African, after a prolonged stay abroad or in another province, is whether one returns still speaking SAIE (and not general SAE, or an accent or dialect one might have acquired abroad), rather than whether one continues with an obsolescent vernacular language of India.

An active, enquiring, sociable personality, which Dorian found to produce the occasional semi-speaker, does not generally promote the use of SB. To be 'gregarious' in the larger Indian South African society would imply shedding one's ethnic language, and using SAIE (as opposed to general SAE). It is the religious-minded young person who undertakes to cultivate the ancestral language (or one interested in his own sub-ethnic affiliation as belonging to a Tamil-speaking or 'Hindi-speaking' sub-group of Indian South Africans), rather than the outward-looking gregarious type. Even for these religiously-minded individuals the allure of prestigious Std Hn neutralises any attempts at the positive cultivation of SB.

These things suggest that there are virtually no SSs who use SB by conscious choice, and that for most imperfect speakers failure breeds failure – those who understand the language perfectly, and can string phrases and sentences together with less than natural fluency, prefer not to use the language at all.

5.5 *GATHERING OF DATA*

It is extremely difficult to observe semi-speakers in a natural speech setting, as the presence of outsiders often inhibits the insecure speaker's use of B, reducing it to a few monosyllabic phrases, or one-word replies. I was, in two instances, able to acquire valuable spontaneous discourse which included young speakers in a natural setting. The first involved a young student who had assisted in gathering data relating to the speech of the oldest section of the population under study, by tape-recording two half-hour sessions of spontaneous discourse in her home. Among the unwitting participants were her paternal grandmother, an aunt, and elderly neighbours; while her mother, who was privy to the job at hand, assisted in ensuring that conversation flowed smoothly. Of relevance to this chapter is the B used on tape by the student – imperfect by her own admission – who had not realised that her own speech could be equally worthy of study to that of her elders.[3] Her speech shows the familiar semi-speaker pattern of switching between fluent Eng (to her mother and aunt), and a simplified, virtually pidginised form of B (to her grandmother and an aged neighbour).

I gathered a second set of valuable spontaneous SS speech patterns by noting down privately the occasional B of young relatives in their interactions with elders, both in my home and theirs. In this way the inhibition that many SSs show if they are aware of their speech being scrutinised by others, was avoided.

In addition, a short questionnaire was administered to sixteen individuals, all but one of whom were under the age of thirty, and who were known to have spoken at least some B at some stage of their lives (including, possibly, the present). This was by no means a random sample, as it included many who were especially chosen because they fitted the bill. These included a few young relatives whose backgrounds were well known to me, and young people from neighbourhoods familiar to me – one or two who had been singled out by other informants as being able to speak quite well. In addition, I contacted young people from different parts of the province whom I had observed in earlier interviews with elderly fluent speakers as possessing more than average fluency for their age.

With two exceptions these were people with no education in Hn, and who could neither read nor write it. The questionnaire comprised recall of basic vocabulary items, often containing phonemes whose pronunciation by younger speakers was of interest, and translation exercises, ranging from short clauses, testing morphology, to larger complex sentences (see Appendix D). Each interviewee was finally asked to narrate a short story of his own choice in 'Hindi' (= B). This last exercise proved highly artificial in that none of the interviewees, except one who had been to Hn school for two years, could recall ever narrating stories in B. It was nevertheless retained on the questionnaire, as it was a more accurate way of assessing competence in the language than simple translation, with its major pitfall of encouraging Eng-like utterances. Some who had performed quite well in the translation exercises – much better than they, or I, had expected – performed completely differently in the narrative section, being barely able to produce connected discourse longer than two sentences at a time.

Care had to be exercised not to make the interview too stressful to these occasional users of an imperfect variety of B. The number of recall items and sentences to be translated was kept to a minimum, and no attempts were made to force them when they hesitated. Many came to look upon the interview as a special challenge, and returned on their own to items they had unsuccessfully attempted earlier on. Prompting by the interviewer was a temptation that was generally avoided, except for an occasional lexical item which helped put the speaker at ease, and helped him avoid switching to Eng or giving up altogether.

5.6 *THE PROFICIENCY CONTINUUM*

Four of the speakers interviewed were excluded from the analysis: two because they turned out to be YFSs, with a command of the language that showed little qualitative difference from that of second- and third-generation native speakers; while the other two turned out to have only passive knowledge of the language, and had never used it actively, even in childhood, despite being pointed out to me by others as having some proficiency. The skills of the other twelve ranged from a little active B with threadbare syntax and vocabulary, to some active use showing a high degree of fluency, without reproducing the phonology and idiom of the language perfectly. However, all were united in having great passive competence, being able to follow conversations quite easily, even those directed at a fast pace to other people, and to follow humorous and religious tales, especially those in a colloquial non-Brahmanical style. But there are limits to the competence of SSs: it does not extend to the decipherment of whispers, or the decoding of B speech under high-noise conditions – both of which are easily handled by these speakers for the first language, Eng. Nor does the semi-speaker display the same intuitive understanding of folk songs (especially those employing an archaic diction), and of the morphological forms of other dialect areas of Natal, or indeed of the occasional IB that reaches Natal via film and song.

A brief characterisation of some of the interviewees, giving some idea of the factors leading to the genesis of the SS, follows:

SS_4 is a fourteen-year-old primary schoolboy, the last born of three children, living in poor conditions on a farm. He is not doing well at school, his Eng in particular – a non-standard variety – seems to hold him back. Although his family claimed that he 'knew Hindi', he is far from fluent, replying to his mother's B in short staccato sentences that mask his imperfect command of verb morphology and syntactic patterns, and he uses Eng for longer discourse. His two elder sisters are much more fluent, and easily qualify as YFSs.

SS_{11} is a withdrawn fourteen-year-old schoolgirl, living in very poor conditions in the rural Midlands. She is exceptionally fluent in B for her age, with her parents (both uneducated) using it among themselves and to her, even though they have some command of Eng as second language (or, possibly, third to F). Uncharacteristically for a teenager, she uses as much B as Eng to them, though the variety she uses differs slightly from YFS speech in its greater analogical levelling of verb endings, and lesser use of characteristically B idiom.

SS_5 lived on a farm in a household that had included her grandmother, who died when this particular grandchild was six years old. She claims to have communicated with her grandmother in B, but to have ceased active use of the language after her grandmother's death, and especially after moving to the city subsequently. Her hesitancy and aberrant morphology and idiom suggest that her command of B has declined drastically with non-use (which is not unusual for many speakers), or that she might have got by as a child with conversing with her grandmother in a highly simplified B.

SS_8 is a twenty-one-year-old who has always lived in the city, and is the most fluent speaker without formal instruction in Hn, under the age of twenty-four, that I have encountered. His active command of B is due to his having lived next door to his grandmother who understood no Eng. What is rare about him is that he continued speaking some B after the age of six, when she died, to a narrow network of old relatives. However, he has never spoken to his parents in B. Even today there are old uncles whom he addresses in B, out of respect rather than total necessity, since they have a rudimentary command of Eng. Although his SB is quite fluent, and displays a wide range of mostly correct morphological forms, syntactic and phonological peculiarities mark off his speech as being that of a SS rather than a YFS.

5.7 *LEXICAL AND SEMANTIC CHARACTERISTICS*

The restriction of SB to the family domain, with mainly parents and grandparents using it to each other has had many consequences for semi-speakers and passive bilinguals. It has led to ignorance of a large number of terms which are not in habitual use at home, and in some instances to interesting semantic restrictions. The passive vocabulary of children in a dying language which is not taught in schools and which has no literature, depends entirely on the active vocabulary of elders. Because the contexts in which the language is used have become more and more limited in the last two decades, with mainly grandmothers and mothers addressing children directly in it, the child's lexicon is directly affected.

5.7.1 *Semantic change*

There are instances of age-graded semantic change restricted to the youngest generation, contingent upon the lack of a wide range of contexts of use from which the full sense (or varied senses) of a word can be gauged. It is worth noting that whereas semantic change among older speakers involves shifts in sense, narrowing of meaning, as well as occasional widening of meaning, semi-speaker semantic change involves only narrowing of meaning. Some examples follow:

(a) *lapeṭ kar-:* This phrasal verb has the general sense of 'to wrap, to roll (trans), to entangle', but the only meaning I could extract from SSs was 'to make a sandwich out of *roṭī* (round, flat Indian bread) and curry'. They did not think that the word could be used in any other sense, as in 'to get entangled in a fight'. This restriction of meaning is clearly due to the domestication of the language.

(b) *naksān:* This word has already been mentioned in 4.4 as undergoing semantic restriction, being used in its full IB sense by some speakers of 'wastage' (of energy, life, food, etc.), but being construed as referring almost exclusively to food by many third-generation speakers. It is not surprising that for semi-speakers the restricted meaning has become the sole one, with all interviewees not being sure whether it could refer to, say, the death toll on the roads.

(c) *bigar:* This noun has the basic meaning of 'a spoiling, spoilt', with a secondary meaning of 'quarrel, enmity'. The former meaning is by far the more common in SB, though older speakers are familiar with the second sense as well. For youngest speakers it is the first – more commonly heard – meaning which has entirely superseded the meaning of 'enmity'.

(d) *cirauri̅:* The primary meaning of this noun is 'begging, entreating'. The word most frequently occurs today in the imperative sentence employed by mothers or grandmothers to troublesome children, *Hamke cirauri nei kar* 'Don't beg me'. Its primary sense amongst SSs and passive bilinguals is accordingly the narrow one of 'being troublesome'. The sentence would be understood to mean 'Don't pester me (by begging/entreaty)'. Two of the twelve interviewed, however, knew both the original meaning and the SS interpretation.

(e) *bokalā*: Amongst the multiple meanings of the word in IB and the SB of older speakers are 'strips of the bark of a tree', 'husks of grain', 'bits of skin', etc., the first meaning being the more usual. All SSs interviewed thought the only meaning to be 'bits of wood (useful in starting a fire)'. The narrowing of meaning is again attributable to the usage of mothers and grandmothers, more interested in starting domestic fires than in husks in the field. This semantic change seems to have started with some of the third generation and to have been generalised by the youngest speakers.

(f) *mālik:* This refers to 'God' as well as 'lord' in a human sense, as for the head of an important household or for a landlord. The word may be used as an epithet as well. Of the two meanings only [+ divine] is known to SSs. Even then, it is more often conceived of as being an epithet expressing wonderment (as in Eng *O Lord!*) or reverence, rather than as a term for 'God'.

5.7.2 *Replacement of native words by loans*

Even though the speech of older third-generation speakers is interspersed with loanwords from Eng, if pressed hard enough they are often able to recall the B equivalent used by the earliest SB speakers. They may sometimes use these words in conversations with older non-Eng speakers. This suggests that their passive vocabulary contains many B words which are often replaced by loanwords in active speech. As the passive vocabulary of young SSs depends on the active output of older kinsfolk at home, the result is a further attrition of their SB vocabulary. Table 40 gives a sample of vocabulary items that vary across the divisions 'non-Eng speakers', 'Eng-B bilinguals', and 'Eng-dominant semi-speakers':

TABLE 40
USE OF LOANWORDS BY SEMI-SPEAKERS

TERMS USED BY NON-ENG SPEAKERS	TERMS USED BY BILINGUALS	TERMS USED BY SEMI-SPEAKERS
gājar 'carrot'	*gājar~kāraṭ*	*kāraṭ*
maṭṭar 'peas'	*maṭṭar~phīz*	*phīz*
nibbu 'lemon'	*nibbu~lemmen*	*lemmen*
kerā 'banana'	*kera~banānā*	*banānā*
phal 'fruit'	*phal~frūṭ*	*phal~frūṭ*
gobhi~kābij 'cabbage'	*kābij*	*kābij*
murai 'radish'	*murai~rēdiś*	*rediś*
pothi~buk 'book'	*buk*	*buk*
kamīj 'shirt'	*kamij~śet*	*śet*
sipai 'police'	*sipai~pulīs*	*pulīs*
bimār~sīk 'sick'	*sīk*	*sīk*
cā 'tea'	*cā~ṭī*	*cā~ṭī*
samay~ṭem 'time'	*ṭem*	*ṭem*
sabūr 'wait'	*sabūr~weiṭ*	*weiṭ*
ceṛhā 'photograph'	*ceṛhā*	*ceṛhā~foṭo*
chappar 'roof'	*chappar~rūf*	*rūf*
āthe haptā 'next week'	*āthe hapta~nekswīk*	*nekswīk*
talāw 'large tank'	*talāw~ṭhenk*	*ṭhenk*

5.7.3 *Vocabulary loss*

The loss of many concepts and words in the SB of even the most fluent living speakers, occasioned by the increasing Westernisation of their life-style in Natal, was recorded in 4.5. This process has been carried one step further – not surprisingly – in SS speech. Many more terms which refer to specialised concepts no longer in common colloquial use, but still a part of at least the passive knowledge of third-generation speakers, have become unknown to young speakers. Some such terms are:

ḍolā 'palanquin'; *jā̃tā* 'hand-grinding mill'; *maciyā* 'small table for holding pots etc.'; *sõṭā* 'whipping stick'; *cunauti* 'small box for carrying lime or betel-juice'; *taslā* 'round vessel for boiling rice'; *gagri* 'vessel for drawing water'; *majurā* 'agricultural servant'; *harai* 'furrow'; *har jot-* 'to plough'; *sā̃ṛ* 'bull'; *bhaĩs* 'buffalo'; *phenus* 'milk of the first milking after calving'; *jangar* 'strength'; *ṭhamak* 'to walk with a dancing gait'; *akāl* 'food shortage, famine'; *rop-* 'to cultivate'; *samhār-* 'to support'; *cāl-* 'to sift'; *jhõk-* 'to fuel a fire'; *ṭhambh-* 'to stop'; *dhas-* 'to sink'; *ḍā̃s-* 'to sting'; *dhū̃ṛh-* 'to search, rummage'; *ṭāk-* 'to stitch, sew'; *chāw-* 'to cover with thatch'; *lūṭ-* 'to rob', etc.

In addition, SS speech is characterised by a dearth of synonyms; the shoestring lexical budget on which they operate accordingly shows a high degree of polysemy:

bahut 'much, many, too much, an abundance of' is an overworked adjective in SS speech, whereas older fluent speakers use a greater variety of near-synonyms such as *ḍher* 'a lot of'; *etanā* 'so much, much' (as well as related forms *otnā* 'that much'; *ketnā* 'how much; so much'); *khub* 'very much'; *baṛī* 'a great amount of'; *jasti* 'a large quantity of'; and *ekdamme* 'excessively'. These near-synonyms are readily understood by SSs, but rarely used productively. In addition *bahut* has taken over the semantic space of *kamti* 'less, a little' for them, in combination with the negative particle *nahī̃* 'not'; thus *bahut nahī̃* 'a little, not much'.

thoṛā 'a little, few'. The same holds for this antonym of *babhut*, which is much preferred in SS speech to near synonyms such as *kamtī* 'a little'; *tannī se* 'a tiny bit of'; and *jarā se* 'a little of'.

acchā is an adjective whose denotation ranges over 'good', 'nice', 'fine', 'admirable', 'wonderful', 'pretty' and 'tasty' in semi-speaker SS discourse. Although the word is also of frequent occurrence in the B of older speakers, they have greater flexibility in the use of synonyms when finer distinctions of meaning are necessary. Thus the equivalent of the sentence *Khānā me sawād he* 'The food is tasty' (literally, 'In the food there is taste') is often in SS speech *Khānā bahut acchā he* 'The food is very nice'. The latter sentence shows the avoidance of a specific content word (*sawād* 'taste'), in favour of a general term, as well as an Eng-like syntax.

khet covers 'farm' (its basic meaning) as well as 'garden', 'orchard', 'pasture', etc. in SS speech, while synonyms like *bāg* 'garden'; *bārī* 'garden'; *bagaica* 'orchard'; and *partī* 'pasture, fallow land' are unknown to them.

dekh- 'to see' in SS speech usually supersedes semantically related verbs like *jhā̃k-* 'to peep' and *tāk-* 'to stare'.

This trend toward polysemy, part of a larger pattern of stylistic shrinkage, is evident to a lesser extent in OFS speech as well. The following words are made to bear a high functional load even among older speakers.

aurat has the multiple meanings 'wife', 'woman', 'lady', 'female-stranger', etc., even in the speech of fully fluent speakers. Certain near-synonyms like *patnī* 'wife'; *meharāru* 'wife', which may be used for stylistic variation in OFS, are generally missing in SS discourse.

admī 'man' is used as a general counterpart to the previous noun *aurat*, with meanings ranging over 'husband', 'person', 'people' (in combination with *lō̃g*), and even 'stranger' (n) for most SB speakers. The synonym *marad* is known to some SSs, but hardly ever used, while other synonyms like *mardānā* are generally lacking.

jangal is used as a general term for 'jungle' (the Eng term is the loanword – dating back to British rule in India), as well as for 'forest', 'woods', 'bush' etc., while synonyms like *ban* 'forest', are in disuse.

muṇḍī is the word for 'head' used by all SB speakers, with near-synonyms like *sir* and *kapar* infrequent in OFS speech and virtually obsolete in SS discourse. The related term *muṇḍā* 'head of a sheep or goat', however, remains in all varieties of SB.

All obsolescing languages in their final stages show loss of vocabulary, with resultant widening of meanings of remaining items, but polysemy in itself does not imply that a language is becoming obsolete. It is a symptom of language decline, not a cause.

As one might expect, in the absence of literacy in B, terms referring to objects in the immediate environment are the ones best retained. Some instances of these are:

(a) Among the many terms for 'rice' in IB, *bhāt* 'boiled rice' is best known among SSs; *caur* 'uncooked rice' is also known but may be erroneously replaced by *bhāt*, while *dhān* 'rice grown in the field, paddy' is unknown among SSs in this age of imported rice.

(b) Terms for domestic animals, are well known: *kuttā* 'dog'; *billā* 'cat'; *mūs* 'mouse'; *gāī* 'cow'; *gadahā* 'donkey'; *bakkrā* 'goat' etc., but terms for animals one does not ordinarily encounter, even in rural Natal are known only to OFSs: *bhālū* 'bear'; *ser* 'lion'; *siyar* 'jackal'; *nāki* 'alligator'; *bāgh* 'tiger', etc.

(c) Similarly the terms for domestic birds like *murgā* 'rooster'; *murgī* 'hen'; *battak* 'duck'; and the word for bird in general *ciraī* remain, but less important terms (as far as SB speakers are concerned) like *hās* 'goose'; *mor* 'peacock'; and *bakula* 'egret' are not known to SSs.

(d) Of the colour terms *ujjar* 'white'; *kariyā* 'black' and *lāl* 'red' are known to all speakers while *hariyal* 'greenish'; *līl* 'blue'; *pīlā* 'yellow'; *gehū* 'brownish' etc. were known to surprisingly few SSs.

(e) Terms like *naddī* 'river'; *samundar* 'sea'; and *nālā* 'stream' are well known to SSs, but not *talāw* 'pond' or *tal* 'lake'.

On the other hand the retention rate of lexical items relating to domestic activities is extremely high in SS speech, as well as in the occasional utterances of passive bilinguals. Almost all the basic terms, as well as many involving subtle distinctions of meaning, persist. These fall into the following categories:

(i) *Activities relating to cooking and cleaning up:*
pak- 'to cook'; *khaul-* 'to boil' (intrans); *bhūj-* 'to

roast'; *chauk-* 'to braise'; *sek-* 'to toast'; *mā̃j-* 'to cleanse lightly'; *kū̃t-* 'to crush'; *bel* 'to roll dough'; *mīs-* 'to crush by hand'; *pīs-* 'to grind'; *sān* 'to mix'; *chān-* 'to strain'; *baṭor-* 'to collect'; *khangār* 'to rinse'; *khakor-* 'to scrape'; *dho-* 'to wash'; *pasār-* 'to hang'; *bīn-* 'to gather, pick out'; and *põc* 'to wipe'.

(ii) *Household utensils and appliances:*
belnā 'rolling pin'; *haṇḍī* 'pot'; *dhapnā/dhaknā* 'lid'; *kalchūl* 'ladle'; *tāwā* 'frying pan'; *chalni* 'sieve'; *channi* 'tea-strainer'; *sūp* 'winnowing sieve'; *chūrī* 'knife'; *piyalī* 'bowl'; *cimtā* 'metal tongs'; *cūlhā* 'fireplace'; *jhārū* 'broom'; *phukni* 'blow-pipe (for fire)'; *chaukī* 'rolling board'.

(iii) *Ingredients used in cooking:*
tel 'oil'; *masālā* 'curry powder'; *nīmak* 'salt'; *hardī* 'turmeric'; *imlī* 'tamarind'; *cinnī* 'sugar'; *jīrā* 'fennel'; *ghī* 'clarified butter'; *ā̃ṭā* 'flour'.

(iv) *Names of vegetables and seasonings:*
ālū 'potato'; *baingan* 'egg-plant'; *sem* (a type of bean); *piāj* 'onion'; *lahsun* 'garlic'; *pudīna* 'mint'; *methi* 'fenugreek'; *dhaniā* 'coriander'; *saijan* 'leaves of a drum-stick tree'; *sarso* 'mustard'; *kohrā* 'pumpkin'; *phallī* 'nut'; *laukī* 'calabash'; *gwālin* 'tiny-beans'; *bhiṇḍī* 'okra'; *raharī* 'pulse'; *sauf* 'aniseed'; *masūr* 'lentils'; *mircā* 'chilli'; *cannā* 'gram'; *taroi* (type of gourd); *cansūr* (type of cress); *mū̃g* 'chick-pea'; *phoṛan* 'onion-mustard seed mix'; and *ilaicī* 'cardamon'.

(v) *Names of dishes and relishes:*
roṭī 'flat, round bread'; *pūrī* 'roti-like preparation fried in oil'; *dāl* 'split-lentil'; *dal-pūri* '*puri* made with *dāl*'; *papaṛ* (papery-thin, round preparation of flour and rice); *dal-piṭhī* (meal of *roti*-like preparation dipped in *dal*); *nān* 'pita bread'; *bhāt* 'rice'; *daria* 'mealie-rice'; *khicṛī* 'kedgeree'; *biryānī* (a dish of rice cooked with vegetables and/or meat); *bhajia* (a fried snack); *tarkārī* 'curry'; *gos* 'meat'; *macchī* 'fish'; *murgī* 'chicken'; *aṇḍā* 'egg'; *boṭhī* 'offal'; *muṇḍā* 'sheep-head'; *goṛī* 'trotters'; *cokhā* 'mashed potatoes'; *bhājī* 'herbs'; *accār* 'pickles';

khaṭāi (type of relish); *caṯnī* 'chutney'; *kocilā* 'grated mango pickle'; *ghuguri̅* 'fried grains'; *samūsa* (a triangular snack); and *veḍḍe* (a round, hot snack).

(vi) *Sweetmeats and desserts:*
jelebī (a very sweet snack); *gulgulā* 'round, small cake-like preparation'; *gulāb jāmun* (a cylindrical sweetmeat); *seo* 'thin, twisted crisps'; *polī* 'a snack made of grated coconut'; and other sweets like *barfi*, *laḍḍu* etc. Desserts whose names are well known include *sujji*, *sẽwai*, *halwā*, *saigo*, etc.

In her Dyirbal study Schmidt (1985:189) notes that islands of lexemes referring to body parts, human classification, and generic and well-known animates survive best. In SB domestic terms survive the best; terms relating to the external environment are less successful.

5.8 *MORPHOLOGICAL AND SYNTACTIC CHARACTERISTICS*

5.8.1 *An overview of one semi-speaker's performance*

It is instructive to take a brief look at the performance of one such young speaker in a non-interview situation. It emerges clearly from the recording that the young participant (SS_6) has a very good passive command of the language, and is herself able to participate spontaneously, making a little active competence go a long way. Her speech is like that of an L_2 learner, perhaps in the second semester of study. She uses mainly short statements and questions, partly fulfilling her role as stimulator of conversation, but also because she does not seem able to handle long complex sentences with ease, or to speak more than two full sentences at a time without breaking into English.

Of seventy-four sentences uttered by her intermittently throughout the two half-hour sessions, four were complex, and only one of these entirely well-formed.[4] Although the syntactic structures of the sentences were in order (one conjunctive construction, one indirect question, two indirect statements), the effort to put a complex sentence together seems to result in phonetic and morphological errors. In one sentence the verb form *geil* was wrongly used for *geilī*; in the second, the particle *ab* 'now' was wrongly substituted for its interrogative form *jab* 'when'; while in the third, two phonetic errors occur: the loss of an initial [ɦ], and the substitution of [b] for [bʱ].

The majority of the sentences, forty, were simple ones with single verbs (and no use made of 'full' (as opposed to 'local') auxiliaries). Of these, seventeen used the skeletal structure: Subject + Complement + Copula (*he/rāh*), as in *U hospital me rahāl;* 'He was in hospital' or *Nānī ke* arthritis *he* 'Granny has arthritis'. Another five of these involved the habitual construction: Subject + Complement + Verb Stem + *-e* + *he* (Aux), for example, *Oke pen̍sen mīle he* 'She receives a pension'. Eight of the simple sentences were stereotyped ones using *geil* 'went' as full verb: *tū logan* cable-cars *me geil*? 'Did you go on the cable-cars?'[5]

There were sixteen simple questions with a verb, as, for example, *Tū kab geil phūwā ke ghare*? 'When did you go to (my) aunt's house?' Another eight were simple verbless questions of the sort *Kaun moṭar, mousī*? 'Which car, aunt?' (which are not necessarily defective, since similar verb deletion does occur to a lesser extent in informal SB of older speakers). Of the rest, five were simple phrases, often comprising one, two or three words which the speaker has obvious difficulties in fleshing out: ... *spring ke pānī* ... 'spring water'; *lāl aur beige banāras* ... 'red and beige "banaras" saris'.

It is neither necessary nor possible in a short account of the SB of SSs, designed as part of the larger history of the language in South Africa, to describe all aspects of their speech performance. In this section I shall focus on selected areas of syntax and morphology that give an overview of the move towards simplification, and the fluctuations inherent in SS speech. We need to divide our sample of speakers into two distinct groups for clarity; Group 1 comprising six individuals who show the least fluency, and Group 2 comprising six individuals who are more fluent than those in Group 1, but still display the SS characteristics outlined in 5.4.

5.8.2 *Verb phrase elaboration*

(a) *The transitive/intransitive distinction.* The basic distinction between these two classes remains, with intransitive verbs taking an *-l* ending in the third person singular past, in contrast to *-las/lak* for transitives, though there are some individual fluctuations. The very commonly used full verb/auxiliary forms *geil* 'went' and *ail* 'came' and *lagal* 'felt' almost always show the correct endings. Some speakers belonging to Group 1 – the less fluent group – make occasional mistakes with less common transitive verbs: **liyailak* 'he brought' (for *liyail*) (SS_1); **girlak* 'he fell' (for *giral*) (SS_1, SS_6); **nikarlak* 'she emerged' (for *nikaral*) (SS_4); while SS_3 wavered between the correct *-l* ending and *-lak* on different occasions. Although SS_4 consistently used *geil* in the sentences he translated, he wavered between **geilak* and *geil* in the short story narration.

The more fluent Group 2 showed no such variation, except for one anomalous **girlak*, and one speaker who used the *-is* ending throughout for both transitives and intransitives, an unusual but acceptable rule for a small number of fluent speakers in some parts of the Midlands.

(b) *Verb endings.* In the future and past paradigms, where there are separate endings for each person (unlike most other paradigms), there is the greatest uncertainty of usage amongst Group 1 speakers, with a great deal of levelling. There is no group uniformity as to which ending is taken as the prototype. Table 41 lists the forms used by speakers of Group 1,

TABLE 41
FUTURE ENDINGS USED BY SEMI-SPEAKERS IN GROUP 1

OFS NORM	SS_1	SS_2	SS_3	SS_4	SS_5	SS_6	
-b	**-be*	*-b*	*-b*	*-b*	*-b*	*-b*~**-ī*	(1st person)
-be	*-be*	*-be*	*-be*	**-b*	**-ī*	**-ī*	(2nd person)
-ī	**-be*	**-b*	*-ī*	**-b*	*-ī*	*-ī*	(3rd person)

but gives a false impression of stability of usage which is not necessarily there. The same speaker might on a different occasion produce slightly different endings, or sometimes show some fluctuations within the same conversation. SS_1, for example, in elicitation form got all three future endings correct, but in full sentences levelled all three to *-be*.

The more fluent speakers (in Group 2) show no such

levelling, and handled verb endings with relative ease. The patterns of usage of past transitive endings are much the same as for the future, as Table 42 suggests:

TABLE 42
PAST TRANSITIVE ENDINGS USED BY SEMI-SPEAKERS IN GROUP 1

OFS NORM	SS_1	SS_2	SS_3	SS_4	SS_5	SS_6	
-lī	**-lak*	*-lī*	*-lī*	*-lī~*-las*	*-lī*	*-lī~*-l*	(1st person)
-le	**-lak*	**-lī*	*-le*	**-li*	*-le*	**-lī~*-e*	(2nd person)
-las/-lak	*-lak*	**-lī*	*-lak*	*-lak*	**-ī*	*-las*	(3rd person)

Once again, Group 2 speakers have no difficulty in producing the correct endings, with the single exception of SS_{11}, who used regularised *-is* endings throughout.

(c) *Aspect, modality, and causative verbs.* Progressive aspect (with participle forms in *-t* + Aux), and perfective aspect (with participle forms in *-le* + aux) are generally well handled by both groups, as are the basic local auxiliaries like *jā, le-*, and *de-*, whose meanings remain unchanged (see Appendix A.5.4). The less-commonly occurring auxiliaries in OFS speech (*dāl-, par-* and *ūṭh-*) are extremely rare in SS discourse.

SS handling of modals and modal-like verbs differs only slightly from that of OFSs – mainly because, as outlined in 4.6.6, the old inflected modals of B have undergone a marked decline in SB, and have been replaced by invariant forms from other sources. The only modal which does vary according to person and tense – *sak-* 'to be able' – poses problems for that reason, and seems to be on the decline in SS speech, judging from the fact that it is sometimes omitted when one expects it to be obligatorily used. An example of this is the sentence used by SS_4 *Ū kaprā dho delas* 'He washed the clothes', instead of his intended meaning 'He managed to wash the clothes' (*Ū kaprā dho sakal*).

It was not possible to study the use of causative verbs in detail, because the translation procedure using English lexical causatives proved confusing to interviewees. Errors made by them in free discourse, however, suggest that this is an area of particular difficulty: for example **corlak* 'he stole' (SS_1), for *corāilak* (from *cor* 'thief' + causative morpheme *-ā*); **cor ke bhāg geil* 'stole it and ran' (SS_{12}), for *corā ke bhāg geil*; and *gārī kailas* 'swore' instead of the more idiomatic *garyāilas*. It seems to me, though I am unable to quantify this here, that 'first causatives' (see Appendix A.5.1) survive in SS speech (for example, *banā de-* 'cause to make', and *turā-* 'cause to break'), though they might be often incorrectly produced. 'Second causatives', however, (in *-wa* of the type 'cause X to') are extremely rare, if not obsolete. They are often paraphrased by *bollas X ke* 'told X to', an example of the replacement of a synthetic construction by an analytic one (for more of which see 5.8.3 below).

5.8.3 *The noun phrase*

(a) Plurals with *lõg* or the suffix *-n* persist, as do the feminine-forming suffix *-īn*, and most postpositions (*me, ke, par se*), as well as postpositional adverbs (*ke lage, ke nicche* etc). In the speech of many (four from Group 1, and one from Group 2), the use of the postposition *ke* to denote animate direct objects is lacking. Instead, these speakers used sentences of the sort *ū baccā marlak* 'he hit the baby', (with *ke*, after the object *baccā*, missing). This renders them parallel to sentences with inanimate objects, for example, *ū ām turlas* 'he plucked mangoes'. Only one person (SS_{10} from Group 2), generalised the use of *ke* to (redundantly) denote both animate and inanimate objects.

(b) The reflexive pronoun *āpan* 'one's own, self', and its oblique form *apane* 'by oneself' seem to be lost in SS speech, with not one interviewee using them even though there was ample opportunity for that, as the following instances of free narration illustrate:

1.	jeise	ū	okar	mū	khollak
	just-as	he	he.GEN	mouth	open.3sg.past.

okar	haḍḍi	giral	pānī	me.
he.GEN	bone	fall.3sg.past	water	LOC

'Just as he opened his mouth, his (own) bone fell into the water.'

2. ū	okar	chāhī	dekh	ke
he	he.GEN	shadow	see	CONJ

bollak	dusrā	kuttā	āwat	he.
say.3sg.past	other	dog	come.PP	be.3sg.pres

'He saw his (own) shadow and said, "Another dog is coming".'

In both sentences **ū ōkar* is an ungrammatical collocation by fluent speaker norms – the rule for IB being that, where two pronouns are co-referential and clause-mates, the second is replaced by the reflexive pronoun *āpan* (see A.4.6).

(c) *Replacement of synthetic constructions by analytic ones.* Where this occurs, it seems to be a reflection of the 'mind-set' of Eng for young speakers, who often consciously plan their utterances on Eng models.

(i) Among the most prominent of these is the absence of the B definite marker *-wā* or *-yā* (as in *chapparwā* 'the – previously mentioned – roof' which has been almost totally abandoned by young speakers in favour of the more Eng-like *ū* (distal deictic) + noun (as in *ū chappar* 'the roof'). One of the immediately recognisable characteristics of SS speech (together with the over-use of the co-ordinating particle *aur* 'and') is the preponderance of *ū* (and sometimes *ī*, the proximal deictic) as article. In OFS speech the article is unstated, except when the noun is marked as 'definite' or 'anaphoric'. In various sentences, involving either free narration or translations from Eng, only two speakers – SS_2 and SS_9 – used the *-wā/-yā* suffix, and only once each, though once again an OFS would certainly have used more. For example, SS_8, going quite rapidly, spoke as follows:

3. . . . sob	gos	khā	lelak	aur
all	meat	eat	'take'3sg.past	and

khalli	haḍḍī	rahal.	Haḍḍī
only	bone	be.3sg.past	bone

okar	dāt	se	pakar	lelak
he.GEN	tooth	ABL	catch	'take3sg.past

aur	bhāgal
and	run.3sg.past

'He ate up all the meat, leaving only the bone. He took the bone with his teeth and ran.'

An older speaker would have used *haḍḍiyā* in the second sentence, with the suffix *-yā* being anaphoric. (He might have also used a conjunctive construction in preference over *aur* 'and' in the second sentence, and chosen the postposition *mē* instead of *se*, but that is not our concern here.)

Another reason for the rarity of *-wā* in SS speech (extending even to words in which it has become a permanent fixture, for example, *ekwā* 'the other' literally 'one-the') is its stigmatisation by some younger members of the speech community. On two separate occasions I was witness to two semi-speakers, whose competence bordered on that of passive-bilingualism, chastising their mothers for 'over-using' this particle, because – in their words – 'it sounds so crude to be using *wā-wā* all the time'. This curious value judgement, not shared by the older fluent speakers, is possibly a reflection of the prestige of Std Hn (in which *-yā* and *-wā* are not used in this way) filtering through directly via the popular Hn film, or via the opinions of some insecure third-generation speakers (see 3.5.2).[6]

(ii) The same holds for the particle *-kā*, which functions in the same way as *wā*, but is attached to adjectives only, for example, *lāl* 'red', *lalkā* 'the red (one)'. Once again this form did not turn up in a single interview, though there was some scope for its use in the short story narration. In the same interview situation three who turned out to be YFSs made ample use of *-wā/yā* with nouns, and occasional use of *-kā* with adjectives. On the other hand, two SSs showed their lack of familiarity with the function of the *-kā* suffix, by wrongly substituting the definite form *baṛkā* 'the big (one)', for the unmarked form *baṛā* 'big', treating them as equivalent lexical items, instead of the former being *baṛ-* + suffix.

(iii) The clitics *-hi* (proximal) and *-hu* (distal) for 'too, even' are rare in SS speech (in fact unattested in the corpus under study). Forms like *-ohū* 'he too' and *ehī* 'this one too', are replaced by a phrasal construction with pronoun followed by the free form *phīn* 'too, also' (literally 'again'), as in *ū phīn* 'he too'. Other synthetic forms like *oise-hi* 'like this too' (from *oise* 'like this'); *ek-hī* 'even one' (from *ek* 'one')' *kucc-hū* 'anything at all' (from *kuch* 'something'); *ek-ād* 'the other' (from *ek* 'one'); *ab-le* 'up till now' (from *ab* 'now'); *tab-le* 'since then' (from *tab* 'since') are absent in SS discourse.

(d) *Diminution of compounding, echoic, and onomatopoeic patterns.* Ss, in concentrating on the 'essential' sentence elements, often showing Eng influence, consistently disregard these characteristically B patterns. Compounding patterns of the *dvandva* type (see A.2.3) do survive, but are often replaced by Eng-based co-ordinate phrases, for example, *hāt aur gor* 'hands and feet' (instead of *hāt-gor*); *gos aur haḍḍī* 'meat and bone' (for *haḍḍī-gos*) etc. *Tatpuruśa* and *bahuvrīhī* compounds are replaced by periphrasis or by (non-compounded) synonyms.

Similarly, very little use is made of the echo construction in normal SS discourse. Young speakers might sometimes use it in isolation for comic effect, and sometimes parody it in English, as in *Ma, I'll go shop-wop and come back* (where *wop* is the echo of *shop*, thereby stretching and blurring the boundaries of the word to mean 'shop and neighbouring places'). One reason for the decline in the use of the construction by SSs is the belief that it is 'slangy-speech', devoid of any serious semantic content, as one university lecturer who had attempted to restrain her grandmother from using it in normal conversation (without success) confessed.

Other patterns like onomatopoeic play on words, partial and total reduplication (see A.2.3c) are, in view of the problems that SSs have with more basic functional items, not surprisingly, omitted altogether. It is informative to compare YFS performance in this regard: whereas compounding occurs frequently in their speech, there is a minimal amount of reduplication and echoic constructions, reflecting – perhaps – the greater functional significance of compounding.

5.8.4 *Word order*

Even in SS sentences the basic pattern remains, though it is no surprise to find SSs using a higher proportion of VO clauses than fluent speakers. For example, SS_8 used fifteen clauses with OV order, two with VO order (one SVO, the other OVS), which could pass as correct use of topicalisation, and another four in which the VO order was clearly inappropriate. SS_9 used twelve with OV order, one with topicalised VO order, and five VO sentences clearly modelled (inappropriately) on the English. A few examples of such inappropriate usage follow:

4. ū dekhlak dusrā kuttā.
   he see.3sg.past other dog

   'He saw another dog.'

5. ek dīn rahal ek ṭho kuttā.
   one day be.3sg.past one CLASS dog.

   'One day there was a dog.'

5.8.5 *Syntactic loss*

There is, without doubt, at least one construction which does not occur within the (partial) competence of SSs – namely the emphatic construction outlined in 2.9.5, involving use of the verbal noun in *-be*, followed by some form of the verb *kar-* 'to do', as in *ham dekhabe kailī* 'I did see it'. This rule, rare in OFS speech, but by no means obsolescent, is never used by SSs. They substitute the more usual, and less emphatic, simple tense forms, as in *ham dekhlī* 'I saw'.

Two other constructions which come close to being lost in SS discourse once again have more stylistic than purely functional weight. These are the historic present in narration and reporting; and the reduplication of present participles to convey intensity, duration, or frequency of action. Some examples taken from OFS conversations follow:

6. tā   āge - āge   ham   lõg   āwat
then   front -front   we   PL   come.PP

hai,   aur   picche-picche
be.ipl.pres   and   behind-behind

bahīn   āwat   he.
sister   come.PP   be.3sg.pres

'While we were (literally 'are') coming in front, my sister was (lit. 'is') following in the rear.'

7. admiyā   tākat -tākat,   tab
man.DEF   stare.PP-stare.PP   then

ail.
come.3sg.past

'The man stared intensely (and for long) and then came.'

These sentences give some idea of the pervasiveness of repetition as an emphatic device in fluent-speaker B, and also illustrate the use of the present participle (in 7) and present progressive (in 6) for dramatising past events. Indeed, Sentence 7, describing very emotionally the intrusion of a malevolent relative into a widow's home, employs both repetition and use of the present participle. Although YFSs have a reasonably good command of these rhetorical devices, SSs use them very rarely. In the SS corpus under study there were only two instances of repetition of the present participle, and one of the historical present. Besides being another example of influence attributable to Eng this is a reflection of the fact that SSs rarely command the stage in B, and have very little practice in prolonged, continuous discourse that might encourage the use of these constructions.

5.8.6 *Other syntactic features*

(a) *Use of impersonal dative constructions.* Even the more fluent SSs waver in conversation between correct use of the dative subjects with impersonal verbs like *lag-* 'to feel'; *honā-* 'to want'; *mālum he-* 'to know', etc., and an unorthodox subject-verb arrangement without the dative marker *ke* (on impersonal datives see A.6.7). For example, SS_{11} used the idiomatic *hamke coṭ lagal* 'I got hurt' (literally 'to me – hurt – it felt'), but – unexpectedly – faltered on much simpler *hamke honā* 'I want' (literally 'to me – it wants'), producing an English-like **Ham honā* 'I want'. Table 43 records the patterns of usage of such impersonal sentences among SSs, with lower figures for the first five on account of the very short narratives they produced, which contained fewer of these constructions.

TABLE 43
USE OF IMPERSONAL CONSTRUCTIONS BY SEMI-SPEAKERS IN FREE DISCOURSE

	SS_1	SS_2	SS_3	SS_4	SS_5	SS_6	SS_7	SS_8	SS_9	SS_{10}	SS_{11}	SS_{12}	TOTAL
No. of correct uses	0	2	2	1	1	5	1	2	2	2	0	2	20
No. of incorrect uses	2	0	0	2	2	2	1	4	2	1	1	0	17

(b) *The conjunctive construction.* It is unidiomatic by fluent-speaker norms in SB (and in most Indic languages) to use *aur* 'and' as sentence connector, especially if there is a causal or sequential relationship between the sentences (see A.6.3). It is more usual to use the conjunctive particle *ke* 'having' to combine the two propositions, and express the first verb in stem form. SS speech, on the other hand, is characterised by the greater use of *aur* 'and', and the use of finite verbs throughout.

8. ū cor ū admī dekhlak
the thief the man see.3sg.past

auri bhāg geil.
and run 'go'3sg.past

'The thief saw the man and ran away.'

This sentence, used by SS_1, has three signals of SS speech: over-use of *ū* as article; absence of animate accusative marker *ke* after *admī* (resulting in potential confusion between subject and object in this particular sentence); and the preference for *auri* as sentence co-ordinator, even though the two propositions are obviously causally linked.

Two exceptions are the stereotyped phrases *le ke geil* 'brought and came', or simply 'brought'; and *le ke ail* 'took and went' or simply, 'took away'. In these the conjunctive construction has become lexicalised, and each phrase is construed as a single unit. SSs do not substitute co-ordinated phrases in place of these very common items.

In Table 44, Row A lists the number of conjunctive constructions used by each speaker, Row B lists the number of times sentences were conjoined using *aur*, when the conjunctive construction would have been more appropriate. Row C gives a conservative estimate of the number of times sentences in temporal or causal relationship were strung together paratactically, when a conjunctive linkage of these might have been more idomatic.[7]

TABLE 44
USE OF THE CONJUNCTIVE CONSTRUCTION AMONG SEMI-SPEAKERS

	SS_1	SS_2	SS_3	SS_4	SS_5	SS_6	SS_7	SS_8	SS_9	SS_{10}	SS_{11}	SS_{12}	TOTAL
A Use of conjunctive	0	2	0	1	1	1	0	1	1	0	2	2	11
B Use of *aur*	2	0	2	0	1	0	0	5	4	5	0	2	21
C Parataxis	1	1	2	1	2	1	0	0	0	2	0	1	11

(c) *Other constructions.* It would be repetitive to continue in this way for other constructions of B. We note in passing that complementation constructions generally survive intact, no doubt because the transformational procedures are relatively simple (see A.6.4), as do both Yes/No and Wh- questions. Relative clauses, however, are infrequently used by SSs, and often unidiomatically. Speakers from Group 1, in particular, had great difficulty in producing appropriate relative clauses. When speakers from this group, in addition, use conditionals and temporal clauses they frequently use the wrong markers, often substituting *k*-words (for example, *kab* 'when', *kaun* 'which?') for *j*- and *t*- words (*jab, jaun, tab, taun* – see A.4.6).

If they do produce appropriate subordinate clauses, they struggle with the inflections of the main verb.

Group 2 speakers, who display a reasonable ability at translating temporals, conditionals, and (to a lesser extent) relatives, nevertheless show an inability to use them in spontaneous conversation. They rely heavily on parataxis instead, with a preponderance of 'crutches' such as *aur* 'and', and *tab* 'then', used to connect simple sentences loosely.

5.9 *PHONETIC CHARACTERISTICS*

In comparison with other facets of the grammar, SS phonetic realisations are the least affected by the overall language atrophy. Characteristically Indic features like retroflexion, aspiration, murmur, and the basic vowel and consonant system of third-generation fluent speakers remain. The kind of basic merger of retroflex and dental stops into one (alveolar) series that one finds in TB, for example, does not occur (see Mohan 1978:221).

5.9.1 *Aspiration and murmur*

The distinction between aspirated and non-aspirated consonants, and murmured and non-murmured (voiced) consonants remains in SS speech, with, however, some significant departures from OFS norms. Voiceless aspirates seem to fare better than their murmured counterparts, while both aspirates and murmured consonants are more often realised in word-initial position than elsewhere.

(a) *Aspiration.* In word-initial position all nine SSs interviewed produced initial [p^h] and [k^h] in citation forms, for example, in *phūā* 'paternal aunt'; *phaṭal* 'torn'; *khānā* 'food'; and *khub* 'a lot, much'. The dental aspirate [t̪h] was correctly produced by eight interviewees, with one fluctuating between [t̪^{h}] and [t̪]. Similarly [tʃ^h] was produced by eight SSs, with one tending to use [tʃ] in its place. Although all nine produced /ʈ^h/ as an aspirate, one produced it with alveolar articulation, with only slightly stronger aspiration than Eng initial [t^h], while another two produced an initial retroflex [ʈ] with similar weak aspiration.

In medial position there is greater fluctuation, with some words retaining medial aspirates better than others. For example, the word *acchā* 'good, fine', a word frequently used by SSs, almost always has a medial aspirate [tʃʰ]. *Picche* 'behind' shows less frequent retention of medial aspiration, and *pocchī* 'tail' hardly ever shows it. Individual speakers waver between different pronunciations on different occasions, as is witnessed by three different realisations of the word *patthar* 'stone', by the same SS during different parts of an interview: [pɑt̪t̪ɑr], [pɑt̪t̪ʰɑr], and [pʰɑt̪t̪ɑr]. Dressler (1972) calls such differential loss of a phone, surviving in some words but not others, 'lexical fading'. Like its opposite, 'lexical diffusion', it is a mechanism that operates in phonological change within non-obsolescing languages as well.

In citation forms medial [kʰ] was best retained, with all nine interviewees producing it in *ā̃khī* 'eye', *dekhlī* 'I saw', and *makkhī* 'a fly'. In connected discourse two interviewees were observed to substitute [kk] for [kʰ]. The phone [t̪ʰ] was used by seven SSs in the word *patthar* 'stone', with one replacing it by [t̪t̪], and another fluctuating between these two pronunciations. Medial [ʈʰ] was retained by four of seven SSs interviewed, in *piṭhī* 'back' (n), and *miṭṭhā* 'sweet', though three consistently turned [ʈʰ] into [ʈ]. Medial [tʃʰ] in *picche* 'behind' was retained by four of seven SSs, while three showed loss of aspiration here. In the word *pocchī* 'tail', two of seven showed use of medial [tʃʰ], the remaining five using [tʃ]; though all seven retained the aspiration on the frequently occurring word *acchā* 'fine, nice, good'. Medial [pʰ] does not occur in SS speech, having already become [ʋ̥] in the speech of most second- and third-generation members (see 4.3.1).

In word-final position, aspiration, where it does occur, is extremely weak (which is true to a lesser extent of all speakers – not just SSs). The presence of aspiration is often detectable by release of the stop or affricate, as against the non-release of other non-aspirated final stops. The use of [pʰ] and [tʃʰ] could not be tested on account of their extreme rarity in SS (and even third-generation) speech. [t̪ʰ] showed the highest rate of retention, occurring eight out of a possible nine times in the word *hāth* 'hand'. [kʰ] in *bhūkh* was used by five of eight interviewees, the rest using [k], while four of eight used [kʰ] in *līkh* 'to write', the rest again using [k]. Similarly four of eight used final [ʈʰ] in *jeṭh* 'husband's elder brother', the other four used [ʈ]. For the word *jhūṭh* 'lie', aspiration was retained by five, while three used [ʈ].

The three who used [k] in *bhūkh* 'hunger', and [ʈ] in *jeṭh* 'husband's elder brother' correctly pronounced the aspirates in related words having them in medial position – *bhukhail* 'hungry', and *jeṭhānī* 'husband's elder brother's wife'

(b) *Murmured stops.* Just as [pʰ] and [kʰ] were, in our limited corpus, the best retained voiceless aspirates in initial position, so were [bʱ] and [gʱ] the murmured consonants that were fully realised here. All nine speakers pronounced them in the words *bhēṛa* 'ram'; *bhāī* 'brother'; and *ghar* 'house'. The other murmured consonants also show a high rate of retention in initial position, with occasional variations. [d̪ʱ] in *dho-* 'to wash' occurred in all nine instances, but in *dhotī* 'loin-cloth', two speakers used a plain alveolar [d]. [dʒʱ] in *jhaṇḍa* 'flag' and *jhār* 'sweep' was used by eight of nine speakers, while one used [dʒ] instead. [ɖʱ] was retained in eight instances in *ḍhīl* 'louse' and *ḍhapna* 'lid of a pot', though one speaker used [ɖ] here.

The intensity of the murmur is much weaker than that displayed by older B-dominant speakers, for whom the murmur often extends into following vowels as well. The /dʒʱ/ of SSs is often devoiced with aspiration.

Medial [bʱ] in *abhi* 'now', was produced by only one speaker of eight, the rest substituting [bb]. Likewise four out of four SSs produced [bb] for [bʱ] in *sabhan* 'all the people, they'. This change brings [bʱ] in line with [pʰ], which also does not occur medially. Medial [d̪ʱ] was used by two of eight interviewees in *ādha* 'half'; while four showed [d̪ʱ] > [d̪d̪], and another two produced the anomalous [ɦa:d̪a]. Medial [dʒʱ] in *sanjhā* 'evening' was reduced to [dʒ] by five of eight SSs, only three retaining a weakened murmur. [gʱ] in *sugghar* 'beautiful' was similarly produced as [gg] by five of eight SSs, whilst the rest showed retention of the murmur. Medial /ɖʱ/ is discussed under [ɽʱ] below.

Murmured consonants are extremely rare in final position in SS speech, (and even in IB). It was not possible to find words known to SSs containing [ɖʱ], [dʒʱ], and [gʱ] in final position. In this position [bʱ] and [d̪ʱ] persist precariously, more often as fully released voiced stops, rather than as murmured ones. Two of eight produced [bʱ] as noticeably different from [b], but all the others produced a [b] in place of [bʱ] in the word *jībh* 'tongue'. Similarly [d̪] was the more frequent final consonant in *bāndh* 'to tie, wrap', being produced by six of eight speakers, the remaining two approximating a [d̪ʱ].

5.9.2 *The murmured sonorants*

In 4.3.3 the paucity of SB words containing the phonemes /mʱ/, /nʱ/, /ŋʱ/, /lʱ/ and /rʱ/ – a mere eight or so – was pointed out. Of these words only one has survived with the murmur intact in SS speech – the word *mhendi* ('henna'). The others all show [lʱ] > [ll]; [nʱ] > [nn]; [ŋʱ] > [ŋ], (with [rʱ] already lost in third-generation speech). Quite surprisingly, new forms have arisen in SS speech containing [lʱ], [mʱ], and [rʱ], on account of syllable re-adjustment accompanying the loss of medial /ɦ/ (discussed further in 5.9.3).

The [ɽ] and [ɽʱ] allophones of /ɖ and /ɖʱ/, which can be found in several words extant in SS discourse, have undergone some change. [ɽ] almost always occurs as [r], a weak, voiced alveolar trill. Members of Group 1, the less competent group, showed a complete absence of [ɽ], whereas members of Group 2 wavered between both pronunciations, no one speaker using one sound alone. Of eight people tested on the pronunciation of *pahāṛ* 'hill, mountain'; *baṛā* 'big'; *kaṛā* 'hard'; and *bheṛā* 'ram' there was uniformly a 25 per cent retention rate of [ɽ], and a 75 per cent change to [r], though it was not the same speakers who used [ɽ] all the time.

[ɽʱ] as in *piṛhā* 'stool', and *caṛhal* 'he climbed' is also most often changed to [r]. Seven of eight interviewees showed this change, with one speaker using [ɽ] in both instances.

In actual discourse there is greater fluctuation than suggested by these citation forms. De-aspiration and absence of murmur often occur in SS speech, on account of the influence of neighbouring sounds, or because phonetic accuracy, like morphological correctness, falters in (relatively) prolonged discourse. Thus forms like [ko:l] for [kʰo:l] 'to open'; [kɑrɑ:b] for [kʰɑrɑ:b] 'bad'; [beil] for [bʱeil] 'happened'; and [gɑr] for [gʱɑr] 'house' were recorded in spontaneous discourse, though even the least competent SSs habitually get them right in citation forms, and in short isolated sentences. The reverse process, replacement of a consonant by its aspirated or murmured counterpart also occurs in fast speech, but less commonly, as in [bʱand̪ɑr] for [bɑnd̪ɑr] 'monkey'; and [tʃʰo:r] for [tʃo:r] 'thief'.

Furthermore, in fast speech (though this is a relative term for SSs), the aspiration on consonants (and medial [ɦ], on which see 5.9.3 below), proves highly mobile. I have noted [pʰɑt̪t̪ɑr] for [pɑt̪t̪ʰɑr] 'stone'; [kɑtʰi:n] for [kʰɑti:n] 'for the sake of'; and [pʰi:ʈi:] for [pi:ʈʰi:] 'back' (n), though the original pronunciations almost always surface in citation forms. Such slips of the tongue are not noticeable in OFS speech.

Mobility of the murmur accompanying voiced consonants also occurs, in both fast speech and citation forms. *Piṛhā* 'stool' is usually pronounced as [pʰi:rɑ] by SSs even in isolation. *Ādhā* 'half' usually retains the medial [dʱ] in careful citation, but in continuous speech is almost always [ɦɑ:dɑ]. Likewise, *jaghā* 'place' is often pronounced by SSs as [dʒʱɑgɑ:].

Words having more than one aspirate or murmured consonant are rare in modern Indic languages, on account of an old Indo-European rule (Grassman's Law), that the first of two aspirates/murmured consonants in the same syllable, or in successive syllables, loses its aspiration.

5.9.3 *Medial* /ɦ/

Unlike final /ɦ/, which was lost even in third-generation fluent speech, and initial /ɦ/, which is relatively stable, medial /ɦ/ in SS discourse shows great instability. In most instances it is dropped, even in elicited forms, especially if it is part of the least stressed syllable of trisyllabic words. Most often the entire syllable is lost, with some compensation by making an initial stop into an aspirate and with some vowel lengthening. Thus *dulahā* 'bridegroom' which in OFS speech [dulaɦa:] is always reduced to two syllables by SSs: seven of eight producing [dʱulɑ:], and one producing the equally complex [dulʱɑ:] with a medial murmured consonant. Likewise *dulahin* 'bride' ([duləɦain] in OFS speech) was pronounced as [dʱulein] by six of eight SSs; [dulein] by one; and [dulʱein] by another. The word *kaṭahār* 'jack-fruit' ([kɑʈəɦɑ:r] in OFS speech) was known to only four of eight SSs interviewed: two pronounced it as [kʰɑṭɑ:r], one as [kɑʈʈɑ:r] and the other as [kɑʈʰɑ:r].

Medial [ɦ] fares slightly better in bisyllabic words. The word *bahut* 'much' showed retention of the medial [ɦ] five out of eight times in citation forms. For three SSs the only pronunciation was [bʱɑut], a monosyllabic form showing the mobility of medial [ɦ]. In another frequently occurring word, the copula *rahal* 'he was', the full pronunciation [rɑɦɑl] or [rɑɦəl] was retained by five of eight SSs. The other three alternated between [rɑ:l] and [rʱɑ:l]. The word *pahaṛ* 'mountain' was pronounced [pɑɦɑr] (the same as the OFS pronunciation except for the final consonant) by four SSs, and [pʰɑ:r] by another four.

However, some bisyllabic words (for example, *sahūr* 'ability', and *lohā* 'iron') show no such mobility of [ɦ]. The loss of unstressed medial syllables, and consequent movement of [ɦ] has resulted in unusual initial consonants in several instances: [rʱɑ:l] from [rɑɦɑl] 'he was'; [lʱɑ:ŋɑ:] from [ləɦɑ:ŋɑ:] 'woman's under-skirt'; [mʱɑ:k] from [mɑɦɑk] 'fragrance'; [rʱɑ:ri:] from [rɑɦəri:] 'oil-dal'; and [mʱɑ:ŋɑ:] from [məɦɑŋɑ] 'expensive', even though initial murmured sonorants do not occur in IB or the SB of OFSs. It must be said that these are alternatives to pronunciations containing no aspiration/murmur at all, or to occasional reproduction of OFS norms. Thus SSs who use a form like [rʱɑ:ri] 'oil-dal' are also likely to have in their repertoire the alternative forms [rɑɦəri:] and [rɑ:ri].

Such divergences from fluent speaker norms rarely cause confusion. For example, even though the change of medial [rʱ] might cause *caṛhal* 'he climbed' to become homophonous with *caral* 'he grazed', context usually makes the intended meaning clear, and older speakers are generally tolerant of SS pronunciation.

5.9.4 *Nasal vowels*

In SS speech no contrastive pairs of words involving nasality of vowels as sole distinctive feature occur, chiefly because of lexical loss. However, nasal vowels still have marginal status in their speech, persisting in some words for some speakers. The frequently occurring plural 'human' or 'human-like' marker *lõg* showed retention of the nasal vowel in the speech of seven of eleven SSs. The retention rate in other words is considerably lower: only two of nine speakers nasalised the vowel in *ā̃khī* 'eye', and only one in six in the word *bā̃ṭ* 'to distribute'. This is also suggestive of the process of lexical fading.

EPILOGUE

The topic of language death is a sad one, for inevitably it involves some (older) speakers caught between two worlds. The process of 'losing one's language' is neither simple nor voluntary. It goes hand in hand with entry into a more centralised world of capital and labour, where colonial languages dominate. I have attempted in this study to afford glimpses into this process for linguists and, secondarily, for sociologists, historians and interested laypersons – perhaps even speakers of Bhojpuri. No doubt I have failed to satisfy all of them all of the time.

One might wish to end on a positive note by considering the other side of the coin: the rise of a new variety of English in Natal in a distinctly Indian incarnation (in a sense a compensation for the loss of the old languages). But that is another story . . .

APPENDIX A

A SKELETON GRAMMAR OF INDIAN BHOJPURI

The main characteristics of contemporary IB are presented in outline here. The discussion is of necessity brief, and therefore incomplete in many respects. It is not the intention to treat B grammar exhaustively for its own sake, but to provide an overview from which the internal history of SB can best be gauged. Further details can be found in Shukla (1968, 1981), Tiwari (1960), Misra (1980), and Grierson (1903, 1883–1887), to all of whom I am indebted, and whose judgements I have attempted to corroborate by fieldwork in western Bihar.

Some of the difficulties facing a grammarian of IB are the immense regional variation, the absence of a standard form of the language, and the constant influence from closely related varieties like Awadhi in the west, Magahi and Maithili in the east, and more importantly, Std and regional Hn. Although previous writers have used such terms as 'Standard North', 'South Standard', and even 'Standard Bhojpuri' (based rather uncritically on Grierson's classification), no such single or multiple standard of speech or writing has yet evolved.

I attempt to present an overall picture of the features which are common to most sub-varieties, rather than focusing on one dialect alone. There is accordingly some variation, mainly morphological, in the data: for example, I sometimes use the copula form characteristic of EB *bā* (and its variants), while at other times I give preference to the form which is an alternative in WB *-hai*.

A.1 *PHONETICS AND PHONOLOGY*

A.1.1 *A typological overview*

From the vantage point of the phonological typology of Indic languages, B is unremarkable – having virtually no features which are not found in almost all the others. Ramanujan and Masica (1969), on the basis of certain phonological criteria, drew typological maps of the languages of India, which are useful for our purposes of placing B within the Indic family. The chief criteria are:

(a) *Retroflex consonants.* Retroflex phonemes occur in all languages of the Indian sub-continent, except in the North-East languages (for example, Assamese) and Baluchi in the north-west. B has retroflex phonemes among stops only.

(b) *Aspiration and murmur.* All the Indic languages, except Sinhalese, have a series of phonemic voiceless aspirates. In addition all, except Panjabi, Sinhalese, and the Dardic languages, have a parallel series of murmured consonants (or breathy voiced consonants). B has murmured nasals (like Rajasthani and Marathi), and murmured liquids (like Marathi and Oriya).

(c) *Nasal vowels.* All the Indic languages, except Marathi, have a phonemic contrast between nasal and oral vowels, though not necessarily for every vowel. B has a full set of long and short nasal vowels, corresponding to the oral set.

(d) */n/ versus /ɲ/.* A contrast between the dental or alveolar /n/ and a palatal /ɲ/ occurs in some of the Indic languages of the north-east, including Nepali, and Maithili, though the majority of the Indic languages (including Bengali, Panjabi, Marathi, Hindi, and Gujarati) have [ɲ] as an allophone of /n/ in (alveo)palatal environments. There is some doubt concerning the status of /ɲ/ in B. Ramanujan and Masica, following Tiwari (1960), include B in the group of languages having phonemic /ɲ/, though Shukla (1981) and Misra (1980) consider it to be purely allophonic. I shall argue that the latter position is the correct one.

(e) *Vowel Systems.* Together with Hn, Sindhi, Panjabi, Lahnda and other northern Indic languages, B has a five-vowel system, with length of vowels being phonemic. Like these languages B has a high-mid-low contrast, and for the non-low vowels a front-back contrast. In Marathi and Gujarati distinctions of length are lacking for some vowels, while further east in Bengali and Assamese only mid-vowels make a phonemic contrast of length.

A.1.2 *The consonants of Bhojpuri*

Table 45 lists the consonantal phonemes of IB, with some of their main allophones enclosed in square brackets. The retroflex flaps [ɽ] and [ɽʱ] are allophones of /ɖ/ and /ɖʱ/ respectively, occurring intervocalically and word-finally after vowels. In EB [ɽ] and [ɽʱ] are replaced in some words by the weaker alveolar flaps [ɾ] and [ɾʱ] respectively. Thus WB [gu:ɽ] 'molasses'; [gʱo:ɾɑ·] 'horse'; and [ko:ɽʱi] 'leper' have the EB equivalents [gu:ɾ]; [gʱo:ɽa:] or [gʰo:ɾɑ·]; and [ko:ɾʱi] respectively.

TABLE 45
THE CONSONANTS OF BHOJPURI

		BILABIAL	DENTAL	ALVEOLAR	RETROFLEX	PALATO-ALVEOLAR	PALATAL	VELAR	GLOTTAL
STOPS (Voiceless)	*Non-asp.*	/p/	/t̪/		/ʈ/			/k/	
	Asp.	/t̪ʰ/	/t̪ʰ/		/ʈʰ/			/kʰ/	
STOPS	*Voiced*	/b/	/d̪/		/ɖ/			/g/	
	Murmured	/bʱ/	/d̪ʱ/		/ɖʱ/			/gʰ/	
NASALS	*Voiced*	/m/		/n/	[ɳ]		[ɲ]	/ŋ/	
	Murmured	/mʱ/		/nʱ/				/ɲʱ/	
AFFRIC. (Voiceless)	*Non-asp.*					/tʃ/			
	Asp.					/tʃʰ/			
AFFRIC.	*Voiced*					/dʒ/			
	Murmured					/dʒʱ/			
FRIC. (Voiceless)	*Non-Asp.*			/s/					
FLAPS	*Voiced*			/r/	[ɽ]				
	Murmured			/rʱ/	[ɽʱ]				
APPROX.	*Voiced*	/w/		/l/			/j/		
	Murmured			/lʱ/					/ɦ/

The status of [ɲ] is, as already mentioned, in dispute. Tiwari cites the forms [niniɲ̃a:] 'sleep', and [bʰuiɲ̃a:] 'earth' in support of his claim that it is a phoneme. He also emphasises that this [ɲ], resembling nasalised [j], differs from the nasal allophone occurring in the environment of (alveo)palatal affricates. Other writers like Shukla (1981) and Misra (1980) regard [ɲ] to be an allophone of /n/, occurring with [tʃ] and /dʒ/, but remain silent on the words cited by Tiwari. It seems to me that the [ɲ] that Tiwari posits for 'sleep' and 'earth' is really [j̃], a nasalised allophone of [j], occurring between a nasalised vowel and a low back vowel.

That this is not an *ad hoc* procedure can be seen from Tiwari's (1960:12) own characterisation of it as resembling nasalised [j]. Furthermore, [w] shows similar nasalisation between a nasal vowel and *-a*, as in [dʰũ:w̃ɑ:] 'smoke'; and [dʒɑ̃:w̃ɑ] 'burnt brick'. [ɲ] in B can therefore be considerd an assimilatory allophone of /n/ adjacent to the palato-aveolar [tʃ] and [dʒ] as in [pɑɲtʃ] 'public'; [gɑɲdʒ] 'a bald person'.

/n/ has a further allophone, [ɳ] before retroflex consonants, and following a retroflex consonant plus vowel, for example, [tʰɑɳɖɑ:] 'cold' (adj); [gʰo:ɽɑɳ] 'horses'.

Although most traditional grammars of B and other Indic languages classify the voiced series (/b/, /d/, /ɖ/, /dʒ/, and /g/) as unaspirated, in contrast to a parallel group of 'voiced aspirates', I have avoided this terminology since the series (/bʱ/, /dʱ/, /ɖʱ/, /dʒʱ/, and /gʱ/) are neither truly voiced (in the sense of being produced by having the vocal cords close together and vibrating), nor aspirated (which would imply a period of voicelessness after the articulation of the stop, and before the onset of a following vowel caused by the (aperiodic) explusion of air). Instead, they are best characterised as 'murmured' (or 'breathy-voiced'), that is, produced by vibrations while the vocal cords are apart and by a high rate of (periodic) airflow through the glottis, with no ensuing period of voicelessness (see Ladefoged 1982: 47–48; 128–129).

Likewise B has phonemic murmured nasals /mʱ/, /nʱ/, and /ŋʱ/ (with contrasts like *ban* 'arrow', versus *banh* 'embankment'), though neither the [ɲ] nor the [ɳ] allophone has a murmured counterpart. [rʱ] and [lʱ] too are murmured rather than aspirated consonants, contrasting with [r] and [l] in pairs like *kolā* 'a small field' and *kolhā* 'string of a spinning wheel', and *mar* 'to beat' and *marh* (a type of grain). None of these five murmured sonorants occur in initial position, and the number of lexical items in which they occur is small.

Other consonantal allophones include fronted versions of the velar stops before front vowels. /ɖ/ and /ɖ^{ɦ}/ have medial allophones [ɽ] and [ɽ^{ɦ}] respectively.

/ɦ/ tends to become voiceless in final position.

A.1.3 *The vowel system*

There is much uncertainty in the literature concerning the vowels of B. Misra (1980) lists five short oral vowels, and three long vowels, in addition to the nasal vowels; while Shukla (1981) posits six short oral vowels, five long oral vowels, and ten nasal vowels, equally divided into long and short sub-classes. Finally Trammel (1968), describing – like Shukla – 'North Standard Bhojpuri' lists five short oral vowels, six long oral vowels and an equivalent set of nasalised vowels.

I present what seems to be a 'common core' phonemic inventory of the vowels of B based on fieldwork in the WB area, as well as on my interpretation of the above sources.

TABLE 46
THE VOWELS OF BHOJPURI

	ORAL VOWELS		
	FRONT	CENTRAL	BACK
High	/i/ /i:/		/u/ /u:/
Mid	/e/ /e:/	[ə] [ɝ̫:]	/o/ /o:/
Low			/ɑ/ /ɑ:/

	NASAL VOWELS		
	FRONT	CENTRAL	BACK
High	/ĩ/ /ĩ:/		/ũ/ /ũ:/
Mid	/ẽ/ /ẽ:/		/õ/ /õ:/
Low			/ɑ̃/ /ɑ̃:/

A few examples which establish the nasal vowels as phonemes are: *jā̃t* 'to press', versus *jāt* 'caste'; *goṛ* 'foot', versus *gõṛ* (a caste name); *sū̃ngh* 'to smell', versus *sūn* 'quiet', and so on.

The long vowels (oral and nasal) all have half-lengthened allophones at the end of words. /i/ has a lowered allophone [ɪ] usually in checked syllables, for example, [pɪlla·] 'puppy', in at least some dialects (Trammel 1971:129). Although /e:/ is phonetically always [e:], /e/ is more often realised as /ɛ/, especially in checked syllables, though there seems to be free variation between [e] and [ɛ], for example, [beləwa·] or [bɛləwa·] 'woodapple' (Trammel 1971: 129).

[o:] is considerably rounded in B, much more so than its short equivalent [o]. Although all writers mentioned above consider B [ɑ:] and [ɑ] to be low central vowels, it seems to me that [ɑ:] is most certainly a back vowel, while [ɑ] has a tendency to become centralised. In educated, Hn-influenced B, /ɑ/ tends to be pronounced as [ə], even in monosyllabic words, for example, [mər] 'to die'; [bəs] 'enough', and so on.

[ə] is a frequently occurring allophone of /ɑ/; usually in the least stressed syllable of tri-syllablic words, and usually formed by affixation: for example, [gʱo:ɽɑ:] 'horse', [gʱoɽəwɑ:] 'the horse'; [rɑɦɑl] 'she was', [rɑɦəli:] 'I was'. In these two instances [ə] is voiced, though it is more frequently devoiced (in the more usual environment of a preceding voiceless consonant, for example, [dɛkʰə̥lɑs] 'he sḁw').

EB has, in addition, two extremely shortened, voiceless vowels [i̥] and [u̥], in word final position – reflexes of final OIA *i*, *ī*, *u* or *ū* – which have been lost in most Indic dialects. Some examples are: EB [sɑ:su̥] 'mother-in-law', WB [sɑ:s]; EB [ri:ti̥] 'custom', WB [ri:t], and so on.

Another unusual feature (for Indic) is B's mid, central, rounded vowel [ɞ:], which occurs solely in verb paradigms. It is usually a marker of the second person neutral form, neither an honorific nor a (−R) form, which have an *ī* and *-e* ending respectively. It does not seem to occur in all dialects of B (and is not mentioned in Shukla's grammar of North-Eastern B) but is a striking feature of those varieties that do use it.

The presence of [æ] (or [æ:], depending on which grammarian's authority we rely) in B is rare, and, I think, characteristic of educated speakers who show the influence of Std Hn.

A significant phonological rule of B is that of the 'short antepenultimate' (Grierson 1903:24), which determines that a long root vowel is shortened if it becomes, by affixation, part of the antepenultimate syllable (or – rarely – further removed from the last syllable). Alternations of the following type are very common in B (and many other Indic languages): [si:kʰɑb] 'I will learn', as against [sikʰəbe] 'You will learn'; [ɑ:pɑn] 'oneself', as against [apəne] 'by oneself'; and [pɑ:ni:] 'water', as against [paniya] 'the water'.

A.1.4 *Syllables and stress*

The canonical pattern for B syllables is (C) V (C) (C) – that is, a syllable may consist of a single vowel (for example, *ū* 'that'); a consonant plus vowel (*bā* 'he is'); a vowel plus one or two consonants (*ek* 'one', *āṇṭ* 'end'); or a consonant plus vowel plus one or two consonants (*bandh* 'closed'). It is rare, however, to have a syllable consisting of VCC alone. When two consonants occur medially, they are usually separated by a syllable boundary (for further discussion see Shukla, 1981: 31–45). B does not permit initial clusters, with words having a cluster in other dialects showing epenthesis, for example, Hn *prān* 'spirit'; *briyānī* (a type of food); B *parān* and *biryānī*. Consonant clusters, where they do occur, may consist of geminates (for example, *ann* 'grain'), unaspirated consonants followed by their aspirated counterparts (*sukkhal* 'dry') (though these could be considered to be geminated aspirates with the aspiration fully realised at the end of the cluster), or nasal plus homorganic consonant (*gandh* 'smell').

Stress is non-phonemic in B. The following set of rules account for primary-stress patterns in the language at a surface phonetic level (for further details, including the rules for secondary stress, see Shukla, 1981:44–46).

(a) The first long vowel in a word is stressed fully. By the rule of the 'short antepenult', outlined above, long vowels are found almost exclusively in final or penultimate position.

(b) If a word has no long vowels, then either (i) the first heavy syllable – that is CVC (C) – is stressed, or (ii) if there are no heavy syllables, the penult is stressed.

In the following illustrative examples, a syllable boundary is denoted by '-': *phál* 'fruit' (monosyllabic content words are all stressed); *pā́-gal* 'mad', *dhaḍ-ḍhā́* 'languor', *pī́-yā* 'husband, lover', *bhin-sa-ha-rā́* 'dawn' (all conforming to rule (a)); *cál-al* 'he went', *ja-nám* 'birth', *lók-an-i* 'people', *la-ja-hár* 'a shy person' (all by rule (b) i); *mú-ni* 'a sage', *sa-mú-ji* 'understanding', and *ba-hí-ni* 'sister' (all by rule (b) ii).

Words like *dhaḍ-ḍhā́* and *bhin-sa-ha-rā́* show that syllables with long vowels have priority over other heavy syllables in the stress rule.

A.2 *THE BHOJPURI LEXICON*

The traditions of the Sanskrit grammarians still provide the most useful terminology and framework for the descriptions of the lexicon of any contemporary Indic language.

A.2.1 *Tatsamas, tadbhavas, and deśya words*

The term 'tadbhava' refers to words belonging to NIA languages which are traceable to Sanskrit and the Prakrits, via the Apabhraṁśas, and which show the phonetic changes characteristic of the MIA stage (notably the simplification of consonant clusters, the use of geminates, the frequent change of aspirated and murmured consonants in medial position to an *h*, the nasalisation of vowels, etc.). *Tadbhava* means 'derived from that' (that is, from Sanskrit), although we now acknowledge that Sanskrit was not necessarily the *direct* source for these words. The words of this group are fundamental ones in all the Indic languages of today, and the following *tadbhavas* of B are found in virtually the same form in the other Indic languages: *hai-* 'to be'; *kar-* 'to do'; *ā-* 'to come'; *jā-* 'to go'; *khā-* 'to eat'; *pī-* 'to drink; *mar-* 'to die'; *mār-* 'to beat'; *sūn-* 'to listen'; *dekh-* 'to see'; *tū* 'you'; *hāt* 'hand'; *nā̃k* 'nose'; *ā̃kh* 'eye'; *dā̃t* 'tooth'; *suruj* 'sun'; *tāra* 'star'; *gāi* 'cow', and many more. Many of the *tadbhavas* are, of course, of Indo-European origin, and typically show considerable changes from their Indo-European and OIA prototypes. For example, B *sā̃p* 'snake', *bhītar* 'inside', *bhīj* 'to drench', and *ī̃ṭ* 'brick' are reflexes of very different OIA forms, *sarpa, abhyantara, abhyañj,* and *iṣṭa* respectively (derivations from Tiwari 1960).

Tatsamas are borrowings from Sanskrit by Indic languages in modern times, which retain some Sanskritic phonetic combinations which had undergone change in MIA. *Tatsama* means 'same as that' (that is, as Sanskrit), though modern pronunciations of *tatsamas* do differ from the Sanskrit originals. The word *rājā* 'king' in B and many Indic languages is a tatsama, existing side by side with the *tadbhava* form *rao*, and the B honorific pronoun *rauwā*. *Tatsamas* are usually treated as borrowings in Indic languages, by not taking on inflections – for example, *rājā* in Hn does not have the usual oblique ending in *-e*.

Whereas literary languages like Hn and Bengali were at one stage characterised by a high degree of Sanskritisation, *tatsamas* in non-literary languages like B are few, and have entered the language via the influence of Hn, rather than directly from Sanskrit. Some *tatsamas* used in B by the more educated are *ānand* 'joy' (which might in less-educated speech occur as *ānan*); *rājanīti* 'politics'; *buddhi* 'intellect'; *vidyārthī* 'student'; and *prabhaw* 'influence'. Sanskritised names for deities like *Krishna* (or *Kṛṣṇa*), *Shiva*, and *Vishnu* have their counterparts in the *tadbhavas Kisūn* or *Kānhā, Siū* and *Bisūn*.

The term 'semi-tatsama' was introduced by Western grammarians for those old literary borrowings from Sanskrit in MIA, which then show subsequent changes undergone by other words in a particular vernacular. An example given for Hn by Grierson (1927:128), but which applies equally to B, is the development of Classical Sanskrit *vaṁśa* which could mean either 'family' or 'bamboo'. The *semi-tatsama* form *bans* means 'family' while the *tadbhava* form *bā̃s*, showing nasalisation of vowels upon loss of a pre-consonantal nasal, has the meaning 'bamboo'.

Deśya words are those of non-Indic origin which are to be found in MIA, and the vernaculars. These include borrowings from Dravidian and Munda sources (*deśya* = 'of the country, local'). B, like most of the modern Indic languages, has many onomatopoeic words which are probably of Dravidian origin (for example, *phū̃k* 'to blow'; *suruk* 'to inhale'; and *kanmanā* 'to murmur'). Other *deśya* words include *pagaṛī* 'turban', *khaṭṭā* 'sour', *gāṛ* 'to bury', and *ṭikkā* 'a dot on the forehead'.

Of course Sanskrit already absorbed some Dravidian and Munda loans prior to the MIA period. These were not recognised as *deśya* words by early grammarians, who also erred in sometimes categorising words of Indic origin that survived in Prakrit, but not Sanskrit, as belonging to the *deśya* category.

A.2.2 *More recent borrowings*

(a) *Perso-Arabicisms*
The conquest of India by several Muslim powers – Turks, Persians, Mughals – spanned many many centuries, culminating in the Mughal Empire in the sixteenth century; this brought several languages in India – among them Persian, Arabic, and Turkic languages. Of particular importance in the history of NIA is the influence of literary Persian (itself owing much to Arabic), cultivated by the Mughal administration, which resulted in the absorption of a high percentage of loans into Urdu/Hn, and subsequently into other neighbouring languages. Some of the B words traceable to Persian (and eventually to Arabic) in this way are: *mālik* 'lord, master'; *namāj* 'Muslim prayers'; *kāgaj* 'paper'; *gos* 'meat'; *tasbīr* 'picture'; *nagīc* 'near'; *gujar-* 'to pass away'; *badal-* 'to change (one's clothes'); *kamtī* 'a little'; *khus* 'happy'; *rumāl* 'handkerchief'; *jaldī* 'quickly' and others.

(b) *Europeanisms*
Direct borrowings in the NIA period go back to the fifteenth and sixteenth century to Portuguese, Dutch, and French contacts with India. Not many B words have a continental European origin: *mistrī* 'artisan', *branḍā* 'verandah', *kamrā* 'room', *kamīj* 'shirt', *sāya* 'skirt, petticoat' are all traceable to Portuguese.

The British rule in India led to an exchange of loanwords between Eng and many languages on the sub-continent. Although B shows little of the predilection for Anglicisms that Std Hn has, a number of Eng words are now in constant use, sometimes entering the language via Bengali or Hn. To this group belong *ṭikaṭh* 'ticket'; *dipṭī* 'deputy'; *heḍ- māhṭar* 'head-master'; *aksiḍanṭ* 'accident'; *aleksan* 'election'; *moṭar* 'car'; *aparesan* 'operation'; *laībareri* 'library'; *ṭaim* 'time'; *bank* 'bank (financial)'; *āphis* 'office'; *ḍāgḍar* 'doctor'; *ispīṭ* 'speed'; *iskūl* 'school'; *hoṭal* 'hotel'; *bel-baṭam* 'bell-bottomed trousers' etc.

(c) *Borrowings from other Indian languages*
In addition to many borrowings from Hn, the official language of both states in which B is widely spoken, which are themselves often traceable to various foreign sources, B shows the influence of other NIA languages, especially Bengali. From Bengali come such words as *rasgullā* (a round sweetmeat); *murhī* 'fried rice'; *bāsā* 'house'; *phāli* 'piece'; and a few more domestic terms (Tiwari 1960:xliv).

A.2.3 *Characteristic lexical patterns*
To conclude this brief characterisation of the B lexicon, we examine patterns of compounding and reduplication, which are quite extensive.

(a) *Compounds*
In describing compounding, the terminology of Sanskrit grammarians, once again, proves useful. The data for B is taken from Tiwari (1960).

(i) *Dvandva compounds*. These involve combinations of co-ordinate nouns, the term *dvandva* meaning 'two by two'. In the following examples the literal meaning of each compound is given, followed by a more idiomatic gloss within brackets: *māī-bāp* 'mother-father' (that is, 'mother and father' or 'parents'); *hāth-goṛ* 'hand-foot' ('limbs'); *rāt-din* 'day-night' ('night and day'); *dāl-bhāt* 'dal (or split lentil)-rice' ('a meal of *dāl* and rice').

In some instances more than two nouns may be conjoined: *hāth-goṛ-nāk-kān* 'hands-feet-nose-ears', ('bodily appendages'); *dāl-bhāt-sāg* 'dal-rice-vegetables' ('a meal of dal, rice and vegetables'), etc.

A related type of compound uses rhyming or alliterative synonyms: *kām-kāj* 'work-work'; *māth-mūṛ* 'head-head'; *ghar-bārī* 'house-house'. These may function as emphatic equivalents of single nouns ('work', 'head', etc.), or have the collective sense of 'work and such-like', 'head and other parts of the body', etc.

(ii) *Determinative compounds.* To this category belong compounds having one member (usually the first) qualifying the other. There are three main subcategories:

(a) *dwigu* (or numeral determinatives): For example, *cau-mukh* 'four-faces' ('facing four sides'), *nawa-ratan* 'nine-jewels' ('having nine jewels'), etc.

(b) *tatpurusa* (or subordinate determinative compounds): The most important examples in B are those having a noun whose (deep) case is understood to be an oblique one, even though the postposition expressive of such cases is absent, for example, *bijulī-māral* 'lightning-struck' (that is, 'struck by lightning' with the instrumental postposition *se* understood); *Gangā-jal* 'Ganges-water' ('water of the Ganges', with the genitive postposition *ke* understood); *jal-khaī* 'breakfast-eating' ('the act of eating breakfast', with the first noun understood to be accusative).

(c) A third subdivision consists of other appositional determinatives, for example, *mahā-rānī* 'great-queen', *kā̃c-kelā* 'green-plantain', etc.

(iii) *Bahuvrīhī compounds.* These are compounds which involve predications of a third party, for example, *lāl-pagaṛī* 'policeman' (literally 'red-turban' – so the compound refers to one who wears a red turban, not to a turban which is red); *rukh-caṛhawā* 'monkey' (lit. 'tree-climber'); and *ghā̃ṭ-phoṛawā* 'brahmin' (lit. 'earthern pot breaker').[1]

(b) *The echo-word construction*

This is a special type of compound occurring in many languages of India, in which a word is duplicated, with the first syllable being systematically changed. This type of compound, which conveys a sense of 'collective-ness', differs from others in that the second element (the 'echo') does not have independent status in the language. Some B examples are: *peṭ-oṭ* 'stomach and other organs' (from *peṭ* 'stomach'); *ghar-or* 'house and household effects' (from *ghar* 'house');

chūrī-ūrī 'knives and things, cutlery' (from *chūrī* 'knife'); *khīrā-ūrā* 'cucumbers and other vegetables' (from *khīrā* 'cucumber'); *ām-om* 'mangoes, etc.' (from *ām* 'mango'). The rule for deriving the echo can be economically stated as follows:

$$\#(C)V\,X \rightarrow \emptyset \qquad \begin{matrix} V \\ \begin{bmatrix} +\text{back} \\ -\text{low} \end{bmatrix} \end{matrix} \qquad X$$

The rule states that initial consonants are dropped, a front vowel is changed to a back vowel, with other features (length, nasality and height) unchanged, and the rest of the word repeated. Low back vowels are raised to mid position. All other vowels are unaffected by the rule. Further details concerning the social use of the construction, its applicability to other word-categories, and its analogues in other Indian languages can be found in Tiwary (1968).

A related construction in B is one which duplicates a masculine noun in *-ā*, but changes the masculine ending into the feminine *-ī* : for example, *lāṭhā-lāṭhī* 'fighting with sticks' (from *lāṭhā* 'stick'); *jutā-jutī* 'shoe-beating' (from *jutā* 'shoe'), and others, mostly restricted to the semantic field of 'fighting'.

(c) *Reduplication and onomatopoeia*

Another form of word-play which deserves brief mention here is the predilection for sound symbolism, especially among verbs and adverbs, most of which are of non-Sanskritic origin. These can be grouped as follows:

(i) *Onomatopoeia proper*, including verbs like *phū̃k* 'to blow'; *hā̃k* 'to cry out'; *chīk* 'to sneeze'; *hicuk* 'to belch'; and adverbs, usually in reduplicated form, like *jham-jham* 'profusely' (as in rain falling profusely); *han-han* 'swiftly' (as with the flight of a bird, or movement of a train); *ghaṭar-ghaṭar* 'a manner of drinking with speed and relish', etc.

(ii) *Quasi-onomatopoeic reduplication*: While not being strictly onomatopoiec, the following do have some similarities with the above group:

(a) reduplicated verbs like *phac-phacā* 'to be drenched'; *kac-kacā* 'to be startled'; *dhuk-dhukā* 'to rise and fall'.

(b) partially reduplicated verbs like *cul-bulā* 'to be eager to move away'; *kas-masā* 'to be ill'; and *har-barā* 'to be afraid to answer'.

(c) partially reduplicated nouns like *phaṭ-phuṭ* 'cracking and splitting', *kā̃ṭ-chā̃ṭ* 'cutting and trimming', *hā̃k-ḍāk* 'shouting and yelling'. This last set differs from echo-compounds in that both elements are free forms, and are roughly equivalent in meaning.

A.3 *BHOJPURI AS AN (S)OV LANGUAGE*

B is an SOV, postposing language, with the verb consistently in final position in unmarked sentences:

1.	ham	phal	tūrab.
	I	fruit	break.1sg.fut

'I will pluck fruit.'

Its word order patterns are almost identical to those of other members of the Indic family, the chief ones being outlined below.

A.3.1 *Noun modifiers*

In B these consistently precede the head noun:

(a) *Adjectives* precede nouns:

2.	ego	sunnar	meharāru	dekhalas.
	one	beautiful	woman	see.3sg.past

'He saw a beautiful woman.'

In sentences in which the adjective is used as predicate to a copular verb, the (subject) noun precedes it, and the sentence order remains S-Comp-V:

3.	meharāru	sunnar	bāṭī̄.
	woman	beautiful	be.3sg.pres

'The woman is beautiful.'

(b) Genitives also precede the head noun. In sentence 4 the head of the first NP *paharādār*, and of the second NP *jiu* are each preceded by a genitive:

4. rājā ke paharādār okar jiu bacaile.
king GEN guard(n) he.GEN life save.3sg.past

'The king's guard saved his life'.

(c) *Relative clauses* typically precede the main clause containing the NP of which the relative clause is an expansion (see further A.6.2):

5. je ban me raure sikār
which forest LOC you(+R) hunt

karile, te ban me
do.2sg.HAB that.CORR forest LOC

rahile.
live.2sg.HAB

'I live in that forest in which your honour hunts.'

(d) *For titles, kinship terms, and honorific particles,* the proper noun comes first: for example, *Singh-jī* 'Mr Singh' (where *-jī* expresses respect), *dharti māī* 'Mother Earth' (literally 'Earth-Mother'), *Gopī māmā* 'Uncle Gopi' (literally 'Gopi-uncle'), etc. This might seem to be a violation of the rule that qualifiers precede head-nouns, but there seems to be a good case for considering the title to be semantically more important than the personal name, as suggested by *Gānhī Mahātmā* and *Victoria Queen*, which are rustic B forms for *Mahatma Gandhī* and *Queen Victoria* respectively.[2]

A.3.2 *Verb modifiers*

In B these usually follow the main verb, though there are a few exceptions.

(a) *Auxiliary verbs* follow the main verb:

6. ū jae pāwal.
she go.INF able.3sg.past

'She was able to go.'

(b) *Interrogative verb modifiers* in yes/no questions take the form of rising intonation on the final syllable of the sentence, or the question word *ka* 'what' after the verb:

7. ū kukur dekhalas ka?
he dog see.3sg.past INTERROG
'Did he see a dog?'

There is, however, a less colloquial variation in some dialects, in which the interrogative particle occurs in sentence initial position.

(c) *Reflexives* are expressed in two ways: the reflexive pronoun *āpan* 'self' may be used for all persons in both the singular and plural, and always occurs before the noun it modifies (in the sense of 'one's own X'); while auxiliary verbs *le-* 'to take' and *de-* 'to give' are used to indicate whether the action expressed in a sentence is for the benefit of the agent or not.

8. āpan kām kailas.
REFLEX work(n.) do.3sg.past
'He did his own work.'

9. kām kar delas.
work(n.) do 'give'3sg.past
'He did the work' (not necessarily for his own benefit).

10. kām kar lelas.
work(n.) do 'take'3sg.past
'He did the work' (which was to his benefit).

The use of these 'local' auxiliaries is discussed further in A.5.2.

(d) *Negatives:* Negative particles modifying the verb, however, always precede the main verb:

11. ū laikī nahi paṛh sakelā
that girl not read able.3sg.HAB

'That girl cannot read.'

A.3.3 *Other typological features*

(a) *Adpositions*
B employs postpositions rather than prepositions:

12. bāgh jangal se nikral.
tiger jungle ABL emerge.3sg.past

'The tiger emerged from the jungle.'

There is only one exception, *binā* 'without', which may occur as either a postposition (for example, *Rām binā* 'without Ram'), or as a preposition (for example, *binā bolawale* 'without invitation').

(b) *Comparison of adjectives*
The standard of comparison always precedes the comparative adjective. In sentence 13 *laikī se* is the standard of comparison, and *choṭā* the comparative adjective:

13. laikā laikī se choṭā bāṭī.
boy girl ABL short be.3sg.pres

'The boy is shorter than the girl.'

(c) *Use of prefixes*
These are scarce in B; Tiwari (1960) lists 68 suffixes (denoting various categories like 'agent', 'causative', 'diminutive', 'feminine', etc.), as against 17 prefixes, most of which are Perso-Arabic loans (for example, *har* 'every, each'; *be* 'without'; *khus* 'happy') which have become opaque and lexicalised.

(d) *Co-ordination*
Conjoining of two or more nouns or adjectives is effected by the use of a particle *aur* or *au*, which occurs before the last of the conjoined elements, for example, *Mohan aur Sohan* 'Mohan and Sohan'. *Aur* 'and' and *baki* 'but' may also be used as sentence co-ordinators in much the same way:

14.	pānī	barsal	baki	ghās	hariar
	water	pour.3sg.past	but	grass	green

nahī	bhail.
not	become.3sg.past

'It rained, but the grass did not become green.'

Gapping (the deletion of an identical verb in conjoined sentences, as in *I went, and John too*) is rare in B, but if it does occur, the first verb is usually deleted:

15.	ham	aur	hamār	bahini	ainī.
	I	and	I.GEN	sister	come.1pl.past

'My sister and I came'

However, the more usual means of expression would be to retain the verb *ainī* in the first clause as well: *ham ainī, aur hamār bahini ainī*.

On account of these patterns, B can be said to have many of the features one expects from an OV language (after Greenberg 1966 and Lehmann 1973), though it does have quite a few atypical features. Its preposed negatives and co-ordination patterns are more commonly associated with VO languages, while its reflexives and interrogative verb modifiers have some features characteristic of OV languages, and others characteristically VO.

I now proceed to describe the major morpho-syntactic structures of B. Although not all of these are of equal importance in the text concerning language change and obsolescence, it is nevertheless useful to have an overview of IB in examining the formation of a South African variety of the language.

A.4 *THE NOUN PHRASE*

The basic order of elements is given by the formula:

$$\mathrm{NP} \rightarrow \left\{ \begin{array}{c} \mathrm{(Det)\ (Adj)\ N} \\ \mathrm{Pn} \end{array} \right\}$$

A.4.1 *Noun forms*

B nouns need not be classified into distinct declension groups, since the endings employed are the same for all nouns, irrespective of gender and stem form. A noun stem may end in a vowel, usually /a/, /i:/, /i/, and /u/, and less commonly /e/, /o/, /u:/, /ã:/, and /ī:/, or in a consonant. Some examples are:

rastā	'road'	*ā̃khi*	'eye'	*bhalū*	'bear'	*pānī*	'water'
dāg	'stain'	*bār*	'hair'	*hāth*	'hand'	*bagh*	'tiger'

There are usually two stem forms – a short form (as given above), and a long form, marked by a semi-vowel as being 'familiar', 'emphatic', 'definite', or 'contemptuous'. Which one of these categories is intended can be deciphered by both context and tone. A few examples are:

rāt	'night'	*ratwā*	'the night' (usually 'definite' or 'emphatic')
māī	'mother'	*maiyā*	'the mother' (usually 'familiar')
peṭ	'stomach'	*peṭwā*	'the stomach' (any of the above categories)

The alternation *y/w* is phonologically conditioned, [j] occurring after front vowels, and [w] elsewhere (that is, after consonants or back vowels), with a few exceptions.

A third form which Grierson and Tiwari call the 'redundant' form, exists in some dialects, and for some nouns only, in which [wa:] is added to the long form of the noun, with emphatic effect: thus, *nāu* 'barber', *nauwā* (long form), *nauwawā* (redundant form); *mālī* 'gardener', *maliyā* (long form), and *maliyawā* (redundant form).

In addition to the primary noun stems, there are a number of derived nouns:

With	*-i*:	*kheli*	'game' (from *khel-* 'to play')
With	*-rī*:	*pujārī*	'worshipper' (from *pūjā* 'prayer')
With	*-aī*:	*dekhaī*	'act of seeing' (from *dekh-* 'to see')
With	*-nī*:	*caṭnī*	'a relish' (from *cāṭ-* 'to lick')

A.4.2 *Gender*

Gender distinctions are not as regular as in Std Hn, where any noun is assigned to a grammatical gender (male or female), which determines the form of the adjective or the postpositional case-marker *ka*. In B agreement between adjective and noun is not compulsory, nor is the case marker *ke* inflected for gender (for examples see A.4.5). Certain gender patterns among nouns can, nevertheless, be discerned:

(a) *Masculine in -ā*
The -*ā* ending usually signifies masculine gender, a category which includes masculine animate beings, as well as inanimate objects, having the following sub-divisions:

(i) Referring to male animate beings, and having femine equivalent in -*ī*: for example, *beṭā* 'son', *beṭī* 'daughter'; *laikā* 'boy', *laikī* 'girl'; *murgā* 'cock', *murgī* 'hen'; *ghoṛa* 'horse', *ghoṛī* 'mare', etc.

(ii) Referring to inanimate objects, with diminutive equivalent in -*ī*: for example, *ḍolā* 'palanquin', *ḍolī* 'small palanquin'; *ghaṇṭā* 'bell', *ghaṇṭī* 'small bell'; *mircā* 'chilli', *mircī* 'small chilli', etc.

(iii) Referring to inanimate objects, and having no feminine grammatical equivalent: for example, *tāblā* 'small drum' (musical), *loṭā* (type of drinking vessel), *dānā* 'grain', *rastā* 'road', etc.

(b) *Masculine in -ī*

(i) Referring to masculine animate beings, with feminine equivalent in -*īn*: for example, *telī* 'oil-presser', *telīn* 'wife of oil-presser'; *dhobī* 'washerman', *dhobīn* 'washer-woman' or 'wife of washer-man'; *hāthī* 'elephant', *hāthīn* 'female elephant', etc.

(ii) Referring to masculine animate beings, inanimate objects, or abstract entities, and having no feminine grammatical equivalent: These I class as masculine because in the few dialects which have concord of adjective and noun, the adjective form here is the masculine. For example, *lakiṛī* 'stock', *sādī* 'wedding', *admī* 'man', *khetī* 'farming', *garmī* 'warmth', etc.

(c) *Unmarked masculine*

(i) With feminine equivalent in -*īn(i)*: for example, *sonār* 'goldsmith', *sonārīn* 'wife of a goldsmith'; *nāg* 'serpent', *naginī* 'female serpent'; *bēsaram* 'shameless man', *besarmīn* 'shameless woman', etc.

(ii) With no feminine equivalent: These I classify as masculine because only the masculine form of the adjective may qualify them. For example, *dhan* 'wealth'; *marad* 'man'; *bajār* 'market'; *dīn* 'day', etc.

(d) *Feminine nouns*
I classify as feminine those nouns which may govern the feminine form of the adjective, even though in most dialects of B (excluding eastern dialects) the masculine (unmarked) form of the adjective is more often used. Thus *laiki* 'girl' is feminine because *baṛī laikī* 'a big girl' is possible, even though *baṛā laikī* is the more common form in most varieties. By the same token *laikā* 'boy' is masculine because **baṛī laikā* (with the feminine form of the adjective) is impossible. In addition to the feminine classes corresponding to the masculine classes outlined above, there is an unmarked group (which may govern feminine adjectival forms), for example, *aurat* 'woman'; *sā̃s* 'mother-in-law'; *patoh* 'daughter-in-law', etc.

A.4.3 *Number*
Plurality for nouns is denoted by means of a suffix *-n(h)* or *-an(h)* for many nouns, or by periphrasis, with the addition of the free form *lõg* 'people' (for human or human-like nouns) or *sabh* 'all' (for inanimate objects or for pronouns). Thus *baccā* 'baby' has the plural forms *baccan, baccā lõg*, and sometimes even *baccā* when the context makes it clear that the noun is plural, especially if it is preceded by a numerical qualifier. Doubly plural forms, with both an *-n(h)* ending plus *lõg* occasionally occur.

A.4.4 *Case*
Semantic roles of 'agent', 'patient', 'beneficiary', 'instrument', etc. are signified by a system of postpositions, rather than by case marking. There are a few relic case endings in *-ẽ*, *-an*, or *-anhi* for the instrumental, restricted to a few words: *dā̃tẽ* or *dātan* 'with teeth'; *bhūkhẽ* or *bhūkhan* 'on account of hunger'. Locative endings in *-e* or *-ẽ* are more widespread: *gharẽ* 'at home'; *bajare* 'in the market', etc.

Most often there is a distinction between the unmarked nominative, and the oblique cases, which take an optional *-e* ending, plus a postposition. These postpositions are the chief carriers of role distinctions, though the difference between agent and patient is sometimes expressed by word order alone. Postpositions differ from case endings in that they are not suffixed to the nouns they qualify. This can be demonstrated by invoking the rule of the short antepenult (see A.1.3). Whereas the addition of suffixes, including case-endings, results in the shortening of long root-vowels in the antepenultimate syllable (for example, *pānī* 'water', *paniyā* 'water' (definite), *paniye* 'water' (definite, oblique)), this does not happen when a noun is followed by a postposition (for example, *pānī me*, not **pani me*).

The main postpositions are:

(a) *ke* – the oblique marker *par excellence*. It occurs with [+ human] patients (to be designated 'ACC'), with nouns whose semantic role is that of 'experiencer', 'recipient' or 'beneficiary' (all designated 'DAT'), as well as 'possessor' (or 'GEN'). Although nouns do not have separate dative and genitive postpostions, a distinction needs to be made between the two cases on account of pronominal paradigms, which do treat them differently.[3] The dative postposition remains *ke*; for the genitive *kar* (or some variant) is used instead, for example, *o-ke* 'to him, for him', etc., versus *o-kar* 'his'.

(b) *se* – covering the roles 'source', 'comitative', 'instrument' and 'force' (to be designated 'ABL').

(c) *me* – covering 'inessive', and 'temporal' (and designated 'LOC').

(d) *par* – covers 'adessive' (and designated 'AD').

There are no real surprises here, and these postpositions correspond fairly closely to the Indo-European style of inflections, maintaining a dative of possession, and having the same marker for ablatives, instrumentals, and comitatives. There is some evidence that postpositions might be on the way to being treated as suffixes. This is particularly true of pronoun plus postposition sequences, which are intuitively thought of as one unit, for example, *hamke* 'to me'; *ose* 'from him'; *eme* 'in this', etc. In addition there is the unusual sequencing of the postpositions *me* (locative) and *se* (ablative) as follows: *ākhī me se* 'from within the eye' or just 'from the eye'; *ome se* 'from inside that', etc. As these postpositions can be found in many of the example sentences, it is unnecessary to give more than a few illustrations here.

16. ham Rām ke dekhlī̃.
    I Ram ACC see.1sg.past

    'I saw Ram.'

17. baccan ām turle.
    child.PL mango cut.3pl.past

    'The children plucked mangoes.'

18. rāt me garjat rahal.
    night LOC thunder.PP be.3sg.past

    'It was thundering in the night.'

In sentence 16 the human object requires the postposition *ke*, while sentence 17 shows the non-use of *ke* with non-human objects. There are a few other postpositions like *talak* 'up to', *kane* 'near', which are not as basic as those set out above. In addition, there are many postpositional adverbs *(ke) picche* 'behind', *(ke) lage* 'near', *(ke) kināre* 'beside', *(ke) āge* 'in front of', *(ke) khatin* 'for the sake of' etc., which occur after the postpositions.

A.4.5 *Adjectives*

Adjectives resemble nouns formally in that most masculine forms have *-ā* or are unmarked, and have feminine equivalents in *-ī*. Pairs like *patrā* (m), *patrī* (f) 'thin'; *ujar* (m), *ujarī* (f) 'white'; *golā* (m), *golī* (f) 'roundish'; *lambā* (m), *lambi* (f) 'long' occur. As mentioned previously, not all dialects utilise such gender distinctions systematically: in most dialects a phrase like 'a thin man' would be rendered *patrā admī*, with a masculine adjectival ending, while 'a thin woman' would be either *patrī āurat* or *patrā āurat*.

There are some invariant adjectives in *-ī*, which are used with both masculine and feminine nouns, for example, *alsī nau* 'lazy barber' (m), *alsī laikī* 'lazy girl' (f).

Adjectives do not generally inflect for case and number, though some western dialects, under the influence of Std Hn, use *-e* as both plural and oblique adjectival form. Like the noun, most adjectives admit a long form in *-kā* (paralleling that of *-wā* for nouns), and in some dialects, a 'redundant' form in *-kawā*. The long forms carry the same connotations as the noun forms ('definite', 'emphatic', 'familiar', 'contemptuous'), and may be used in conjunction with the noun, though the noun is usually left unmarked if the adjective is already in long form. Thus *chotkā baccā* 'the small child' is both 'definite' and 'emphatic', but *chotkā baccawā* (with both adj and noun in the long form) and *chotkawā baccā* (with the adj in the 'redundant' (or extra-long) form) are more emphatic.

For a brief discussion of the comparative form of adjectives see A.3.3. The superlative form, a stylistic variant of the comparative, adds the phrase *sabh se* 'of all of':

19. ū laikā sabh se nīk hawe.
that boy all ABL good be.3sg.pres
'That is the best boy (of all).'

An adjective may be intensified by addition of *thoṛā* 'few, a little', *baṛā* 'big, great', or *bahut* 'much' or by reduplication:

20. kām baṛā acchā he.
work(n) 'big' nice be.3sg.pres
'The work is very good.'

21. kaccā-kaccā phal nīce giral
green-green fruit down fall.PAST P
he.
be.3sg.pres
'Very green fruit have fallen to the ground.'

Where a string of adjectives occur the ordering: (Quantifier – Attributive – Size – Colour) is the most common one: for example, *ek acchā baṛā lāl moṭar* 'a wonderful, big, red car'.

A.4.6 *Pronouns*

As full paradigms of IB pronouns, and patterns of simplification in South Africa are discussed in 2.11.1, we need not go into details here. The first person pronoun is *ham*, with plural forms *hamahan/hamanī* (or *ham lõg*, in some dialects, showing the same plural by periphrasis as nouns). The second person pronouns are *tū* (or *tū̃* in some dialects) which is a (−R) or 'familiar' form; *te* (or *tẽ*) which is unmarked; while in western dialects the (+R) form *rauwā̃* is used. The third-person forms are *ī* (proximal) and *ū* (distal), which are the same as the demonstratives.

Interrogatives, relatives and correlatives can be grouped together on account of their formal similarities, with the alternation /k/, /j/, /t/ in the initial consonant marking off a pronoun as belonging to one of these groups. Interrogatives begin with /k/, for example, *kaun* 'which', *ke* 'who', *kekar* 'whose'; relatives begin with /j/, for example, *jaun* 'that which', *je* 'he who', *jekar* 'he whose'; and correlatives with /t/, for example, *taun* 'which', *te* 'who', *tekar* 'he whose'.

22.	jab	hamarā	hāl	ke	sunabe
	when	I.GEN	news	DAT	listen.2sg.fut

ta(b)	ā̃khi	me	se	lor
then	eye	LOC	ABL	tears

girāwe	lagabe.
fall.CAUS.INF.	begin.2sg.fut

'When you listen to my news, then you will begin to drop tears from your eyes.'

Sentence 22 shows the use of /j/ and /t/ forms as relative and correlatives (see further A.6.2).

B has one reflexive pronoun, *āpan* (oblique *apane*) denoting 'self', or 'one's own', which may be used with all persons.

23.	ham	āpan	pothī	leb.
	I	REFLEX	book	take.1sg.pres

'I will take my book.'

To replace the reflexive here with the ordinary genitive form of the first person pronoun (*hamār* 'my') would be ungrammatical, since the nominative form of a noun or pronoun may not co-occur with an oblique pronoun with the same referent, in the same clause. Whereas *āpan* usually has a genitival/reflexive function, its oblique form *apane* denotes 'by oneself', 'alone':

24. ham pothī apanē leb.
    I book REFLEX.OBL take.1sg.pres

    'I will take my book myself.'

A.4.7 *Determiners*

The hierarchical order for determiners is given by the following formula (with the proviso that the definite particle -*wa* is attached to nouns):

$$\text{DET} \rightarrow (\text{Limiter}) \left(\begin{Bmatrix}\text{Demonstratives}\\ \text{Possessives}\\ \text{Definites/Indefinites}\end{Bmatrix}\right) \left(\begin{Bmatrix}\text{Totaliser}\\ \text{Numeral}\end{Bmatrix}\right)$$

The demonstratives are subdivided into a proximal set, with nominative forms *ī* (sg), *ihā̃ka* (pl), and oblique *e* (sg), *inhani* (pl); and a distal set, with nominative forms *ū* (sg), *huā̃ka/uhā̃ka* (pl), and oblique *o* (sg), *unhan(i)* (pl). These serve as deictic pronouns, and as demonstrative adjectives: for example, *Ī to lakiṛī he* 'This is a stick' or 'It is a stick' (deictic) and *ū admī* 'that man' (adjectival).

The 'totalisers' are *sab(h)* 'all' and *kulhi* 'all, whole', the indefinites *kaono* 'some, any', *ek* 'one, a', the limiters *khalli/kewal* 'only'. The numerals are based on a decimal system of counting, and in addition to the cardinals, consist of a host of ordinals, multiplicatives, collectives, fractionals, distributives, subtractives, proportionals, etc. (see Tiwari 1960:116–25).

A.4.8 *The classifiers*

These are bound morphemes *ṭho/ṭhe* (in WB and Awadhi), and *go* (in EB), used after numerals to denote discrete entities. The sequence numeral + classifier (+ noun) signifies 'x units of y', for example, *tīn ṭho ādmī aile* means 'three men came (individually)'. Absence of the classifier would suggest that they came as a group. A frequently used formula in stories *Ek-go ādmi rahal* 'There was a (certain) man', where the classifier serves to isolate the hero from other persons. As a final example, the absence of a classifier in the sentence *Rānī ke pā̃c caukidār hamke pakar lihalaī* 'The queen's five watchmen took hold of me' suggests that the five men acted as a collective unit, and not as individuals. Classifiers may occur with definite or indefinite numerals (an example of the latter being *bisani go* 'scores of'), and with some interrogatives (for example, *ketnā/kai ṭho* 'how many'), but not with cardinals or collective nouns.

A.5 *THE VERB PHRASE*

A.5.1 *Verb types*

In B there is no distinction between roots and stems in the classical sense of roots being abstract forms underlying all verb stems, which are derived from roots in a systematic manner. Instead, one finds a simple system of basic verb forms to which endings may be attached directly, and which may themselves occur as free forms. Formally there is nothing that distinguishes intransitive base verbs from transitives. Thus *kar-* 'to do'; *rakh-* 'to keep'; *le-* 'to take'; *dekh-* 'to see'; *pahir* 'to wear'; *pukār-* 'to call' (all transitive), are indistinguishable from the intransitive forms *kā̃p* 'to tremble'; *ro* 'to weep'; *jā-* 'to go'; *cal-* 'to move'. It is only in the endings of the past tense that the classes differ formally.

As the examples suggest, most verb stems (as I shall call them) are monosyllables. There are two important categories of derived verbs:

(i) the 'first causatives' which are formed by the addition of *-ā(w)* to the basic forms, whose function is to make transitive stems intransitive, or to turn transitive stems into causatives. Thus the first causative equivalent of *gir* 'to fall' (intrans) is *girā-* or *girāw* (depending on regional dialect) whose meaning is 'to drop' (trans); and of *dekh-* 'to see' (trans) is *dekhā(w)-* 'to show' (trans).

(ii) The 'second causatives' which are formed by the addition of *-wā(w)* to the basic stem, with the (transitive) meaning of 'cause/make X do Y'. The second causative forms for the above verbs are *girwāw-* 'cause X to drop

Y' (or 'cause X to cause Y to fall'), and *dekhwā(w)-* 'cause X to show Y' (or 'cause X to cause Y to see').

25. mistrī hamanī khatir kursī
artisan we.OBL for chair
ban-ā-ī.
make.intrans-CAUS-3sg.fut
'The artisan will make a chair for us.'

26. hamār beṭā moṭar ghum-āw
I.GEN son car move.intrans-1ST CAUS
delas.
'give'3sg.past
'My son moved the car.' (Literally 'My son caused the car to move.')

27. tū āpan beṭā se moṭar
you REFLEX son ABL car
ghum-wāw dehaliu.
move.intrans-2ND CAUS 'give'2sg.fem.past
'You (f) made your son move the car.' (Literally 'You caused your son to cause the car to move.')

A.5.2 *Tense and aspect*

(a) *Tense*
There are three distinct tenses – present, past, and future, with aspectual distinctions of 'progressive' and 'perfective'. Since these have all been maintained in South Africa, and since the paradigms show tremendous social and regional variants, we will list only the past tense forms here. Table 47 presents the masculine forms current in EB, using the verb *dekh-* 'to see'.

All B paradigms have feminine forms as well, most often in the second and third persons. Feminine forms for the first person indicate a female speaker; for the second person, a female addressee; and for the third person, a female referent different from both addresser and addressee. In the past tense the feminine forms are the same as for the masculine forms

TABLE 47
THE PAST TENSE IN PRESENT-DAY INDIAN BHOJPURI

SINGULAR	PLURAL
1. dekhalī̄	1. dekhalī̄-ja
2. dekhale (−R) dekhalā̤ dekhalī̄ (+R)	2. dekhalasa(n) (−R) dekhalā̤ dekhalī̄ (+R)
3. dekhalasi (−R) dekhala̤ni/dekhale dekhalī̄ (+R)	3. dekhalasa(n) (−R) dekhal̤ dekhalī̄ (+R)

From Tiwari (1960:172)

given above, with the following exceptions: the second person unmarked form (singular and plural) is *dekhalu*, not *dekhalá*; the second person plural (−R) form is *dekhalusa(n)* not *dekhalasa(n);* the third person unmarked form is *dekhalī* in the singular, not *dekhalani;* and the third (– R) plural form is *dekhalisa(n),* not *dekhalesa(n).*

The number of endings in all the main varieties of B (Western, North Eastern, South Eastern, Nagpuria), and all their sub-varieties are too many, and the differences too minute, to be listed here. Not only does the final vowel differ from region to region, but the *-l* characteristic of the past is in some dialects replaced by [n] or [u].

The characteristic ending for the future is /b/ plus a vowel, though most dialects have an /i:/ or /ihe/ in the third person. The present tense (usually non-progressive, and habitual) is characterised by retention of long stem-vowels, and the ending /l/ plus vowel.

(b) *Aspect*

Progressive and perfective aspect are denoted by use of the participle plus auxiliary. The present participle is formed by the addition of /at/ to the verb stem, and the past participle by /al/. The auxiliary verb that occurs is identical to the copula, with suppletive forms – *ba-* (*or haī* in some dialects) for the present; *rah-* for the past; and either form possible in the future. Thus *ham bānī* 'I am' (or in more eastern dialects *ham haī*); *ham rahab* 'I will be' or, less commonly, *ham hob* (with subjunctive *ham hoi*); and *ham rahalī̃* 'I was'. Some examples illustrating aspectual combinations follow:

28.

ū	rastā	par	dhīre	cal-at	bā.
he	road	AD	slowly	walk-PP	be.3sg.pres.

'He is walking slowly on the road.'

29.

ham	ghare	jā-t	rahab.
I	house.OBL	go-PP	be.1sg.fut

'I will be going home.'

30.

tū	khub	sut-al	bāṛe.
you	well	sleep-PAST P	be.2sg.pres

'You have slept well.'

31.

ego	gāī̃	rakh-ale	rahale.
One.CLASS	cow	keep-PAST P	be.3sg.past

'He had kept a cow.' (or 'He used to keep a cow.')

(c) *Duplication of present participles*
This is a common pattern in the modern Indic languages, a kind of non-paradigmatic aspect denoting intensity, or frequency, of action. It has analogues elsewhere in B grammar, especially in the repetition of adjectives and adverbs for stylistic effect.

32.

laikā	bhāg-at	bhāg-at	aile.
boy	run-PP	run-PP	come.3sg. past

'A boy came running (at speed).'

A.5.3 *Counter-factuals and subjunctives*
Counter-factuals usually refer to suppositions regarding past events, and are expressed by the addition of the suffix *-it* to the verb base, followed by the personal endings for the ordinary past (as given in A.5.2). The simple past and counter-factual paradigms are thus identical in all respects (including feminine forms and honorifics), except for the replacement of past tense /l/ by /t/ for the counter-factual.

33. ja ū dēkh-it, ta ūhū
if he see-3sg.CF then he.INCL

ro-it.
cry-3sg.CF

'If he had seen it, he too would have cried.'

In sentences having aspectual forms, the counter-factual ending is attached to the auxiliary, while the main verb remains in participial form:

34. ja ham unhukā dekhat rah-itī̃, ta
if I he.OBL see.PP be-1sg.CF then

māī̃ ke kahale rah-itī̃.
mother DAT say.PAST P be.1sg.CF

'If I had been seeing him, I would have told mother.'

Subjunctives, on the other hand, express possibility, volition, requests, and doubt, all with a future connotation. The subjunctive paradigm does accordingly resemble, and overlap with, the future paradigm, formally and semantically (see the third person future in -*ī*). The subjunctive ending is *ī* (or *ī̃*) for all persons and numbers.

35. oke bolāwa ki ham bāt
he.DAT call.CAUS.IMP that I speech

kar-ī.
do-SUBJ

'Call him, so that I can speak to him.'

36. ab ham thoṛā baiṭh-ī̃.
now I little sit SUBJ

'Now I will sit awhile.' (or 'Now I wish to sit awhile.')

A.5.4 *Compound verbs*

In common with the other Indic languages, B has a large number of compound verbs, made up of two verbs which may occur independently of each other as full verbs at other times. The first verb, expressed in stem form, carries the bulk of the meaning, while the second typically marks grammatical categories like 'inception', 'completion', 'chance', 'reflexiveness', 'intensity' or 'deixis'. Whereas the first could be almost any full verb, the second is drawn from a small set of verbs whose literal meanings have become grammaticalised in this construction. These 'operators' (as the second verbs are often referred to) are: *le-* 'to take'; *de-* 'to give'; *lag-* 'to feel'; *ā-* 'to come'; *jā-* 'to go'; *ḍāl-* 'to pour', 'to put in'; *par-* 'to fall'; *cal-* 'to move', and a few others which are less common.

37.	sāpwā	ke	mār	ḍallas.
	snake.DEF	ACC	kill	'pour'3sg.pat

'He killed the snake.' (or perhaps 'He butchered the snake.')

38.	pothī	uhā̃	rakh	deb.
	book	there	place	'give'2sg.fut

'I will place the book there.'

39.	tū̃	sob	pānī	pī	lelā.
	you	all	water	drink	'take'2sg.past

'You drank up all the water.'

In sentence 37 the operator *ḍal-* conveys intensity of action, the full verb *mārlas* alone would be grammatical, though less emphatic. The 'local' auxiliaries in sentences 38 and 39 signify completion of action, the first *de-* indicates that the action is not necessarily for the benefit of the agent, while the second, *le-*, which is more reflexive in function than the other operators, is used when the action expressed by the verb is to the agent's satisfaction or advantage. The semantics of these compound verbs, and restrictions on the operators is much too vast a topic to be dealt with here (see Hook 1974).

A.5.5 *Modals*

Modal auxiliaries differ from the operators defined above in that although they have a clearly defined meaning, they do not occur on their own (unless the full verb is understood to be deleted under anaphora). The modals of B are: *sak-* 'can, to be able', *pā-* 'to manage, be able'; and *cah-* 'to wish'. The inceptive *lag-* 'to begin' and the completive *cuk-* 'to finish' can be listed here on account of their formal similarities with the modals. These verbs take the same endings as other verbs, and are preceded by a full verb in either their stem or infinitive form. Unlike the 'operators', modals can be used quite idiomatically in negative sentences.

40.	bahinī	kaprā	nā	dho	sak-elā
	sister	clothes	not	wash	able-3sg.HAB

'My sister is unable to wash clothes.'

41.	ham	khā	cuk-lī
	I	eat	finish-1sg.past.

'I've eaten.'

42.	ū	abhi	bole	cāhat	bā.
	he	now	speak.INF	wish.PP	be.3sg.pres

'He wants to speak now.'

A.5.6 *Verbal noun and infinitive*

There is unfortunately little agreement in the literature concerning terminology and descriptions of these categories in various dialects of B. Each of the following have been described as infinitives and/or verbal nouns by some writer or other:

(a) *verb stem + ∅:* This form occurs in the conjunctive construction (see A.6.3), and as an imperative (see A.6.6). It seems best to characterise it as 'stem' rather than infinitive or verbal noun.

(b) *stem + -e:* This seems to me the only infinitive in B, functioning as complement of verbs such as *jā-* 'to go'; *ā-* 'to come'; *de-* 'to give'; cāh– 'to want'. Thus *ham sūte jāb* 'I will go to sleep', where the infinitive form *sūte* precedes the main verb *jāb* 'I will go'. The infinitive is also used in purposive constructions, where it is always followed by the dative postposition *ke* (see A.6.4).

(c) *stem + -ab:* This is a verbal noun (with oblique form *-be* in many dialects) which occurs as the complement of the copula, or co-occurs with adjectives, for example, *sūtab niman holā* 'Sleeping is good/It is good to sleep'. Tiwari (1960:194) notes that this ending was becoming obsolete in South Eastern dialects by 1960.

(d) *stem + -al:* This verbal noun form is noted in all dialects by Grierson but seems to be more popular in some areas, where it is used instead of the stem + *-ab* form, for example, *paṛhal karalī* 'I kept on reading' (where the combination of *kar* 'to do' and verbal noun suggests a frequentative sense).

A.6 *THE MAJOR SYNTACTIC CONSTRUCTIONS*

A.6.1 *Passives*

The passive construction is not as frequently used in B as in Eng, especially when the agent is known. It involves the switching of agent and patient (in terms of word order and case/postpositional marking), replacement of the main verb by its past participial form, and addition of the auxiliary verb (or 'operator') *jā-* 'to go', whose endings show agreement with the new subject (that is, the patient). The agent is most often deleted.

43. dūdh me bhei ke roṭī khā-il
milk LOC soak CONJ bread eat-PAST P

jālā.
'go'3sg.HAB

'Bread is eaten after having been soaked (literally 'after soaking') in milk.' (From Tiwari 1960:164)

44. okar khet hamār ghar se dekh-al
he.GEN farm I.GEN house ABL see-PAST P

jālā.
'go'3sg.HAB

'His farm can be seen from my house.'

As these sentences suggest, the passive is idiomatic in 'universal' and/or 'ability' statements lacking an agent, and is more frequently used therefore in the habitual present tense than any other. In the past tense it is more usual to use active sentences, containing verb compounds (most often having the operator *jā* 'to go' in its past form) which convey a perfective and passive sense.

45. sab kā̃ṭā nikal gail.
all thorn come-out 'go'3pl.past

'All the thorns were removed' (literally 'came out').

46. jal sẽ bhari gailẽ tāl-talāī̃
water ABL fill 'go'3pl.past lake-pond.

'The lakes and ponds are filled up with water.'
(From Tiwari 1960:164)

In Sentences 45 and 46 *nikal gail* and *bhari gaile* are compound verbs which are formally active, but convey a perfective and passive meaning.

A.6.2 *Relative clauses*
The usual construction is a correlative one, in which the relative clause (introduced by the relative pronoun *je* or *jaun*) precedes the main clause which itself is introduced by a correlative *te* or *taun*. The 'equivalent' NP in the main clause is usually deleted.

47. jaun laikā te liāile, taun
which boy you bring.2sg.past that.CORR
hamār gharrī corailas.
I.GEN watch steal.3.sg.past

'The boy you brought stole my watch.'

In some sentences the ordinary third person pronoun may replace the correlative pronoun:

48.

jaun	bānar	hamani	āj	dekhlī̃-jā
which	monkey	we.pl	today	see.1past-pl

ū	jangal	me	cale	gail.
it	jungle	LOC	move	'go'3sg.past

'The monkey which we saw today went away into the jungle.'

Sentence 49 exemplifies an ordinary (non-correlative) construction:

49.

ū	sādhu	je	bāhar	he,
that	holy-man	who	outside	be.3sg.pres

ū	kahā̃	se	ail	he?
he	where	ABL	come.PAST P	be.3sg.pres

'Where has that holy man who is outside come from?'

In some instances the relative clause is postposed. This (paratactic) order seems to apply to relatives used appositively, being added on almost as an afterthought:

50.

ū	manāī	hathiyā	dekhalani,
that	man	elephant.DEF	saw.3sg.past

jaun	per	tūrat	rahale.
which	tree	break.PP	be.3sg.past

'The man saw the elephant . . . which was tearing down the tree.'

Finally, embedded relativisation is a possible, but less common, strategy:

51.

ū	banar	jaun	hamani	āj
that	monkey	which	we	today

dekhlī-jā,	jangal	me	cale	gail
see.1past-pl	jungle	LOC	move	'go'3sg.past

'That monkey that we saw today went away into the jungle.'

A.6.3 *Co-ordination*

The particles *au(r)* and *baki(r)* ('and' and 'but' respectively) are used as clause co-ordinators, occurring before the second clause:

52.

hamār	bhāī	ailī̄,	bakir	nā
I.GEN	brother	come.3sg.past	but	not

rahalī̄.
stay.3sg.past

'My brother came, but did not stay.'

53.

rājā	kudle	gelak	aur
king	run.PAST P	'go'3sg.past	and

dekhelā	ṭhīke	bāt	he.
see.3sg.pres	true	word	be.3sg.pres

'The king went running, and saw that this was true.'

When two verbs are sequentially related, it is more usual to use an absolute construction in which the first verb occurs in stem form followed by the particle *ke* (historically related to *kar* 'to do'), and the second in the usual finite form:

54.

corwā	admī	lõg	dekh	ke	bhāg
thief.DEF	man	PL	see	CONJ	run

gaile.
'go'3sg.past

'The thief saw the men and ran.'

An alternate absolute form in some dialects is verb stem +-*ī*. Thus, *dekh ke* or *dekhi ke* 'having seen'.

A.6.4 *Complementation*

Complements may be strung on paratactically to a main clause, with no special mark except for a brief pause:

55.

ham	dekhīlā	tū̃	pothī	paṛhālā.
I	see.1sg.pres	you	book	read.2sg.pres

'I see (that) you are reading a book.'

Alternatively the particle *ki* may be used to introduce a complement, especially if it is in direct speech:

56.

tab	laikwā	soclas	ki
then	boy.DEF	think.3sg.past	COMP

ab	ham	baṛā	admī	bānī.
now	I	big	man	be.3sg.pres

'Then the boy thought that he was now a "big shot".'

As sentence 56 suggests, the use of reported or direct speech occurs more frequently in B than in Eng. Complementation after verbs like *soc-* 'to think'; *kaha-* 'to say'; *paṛh-* 'to read'; and *bol-* 'to relate' is expressed by direct speech, with verb forms, pronouns and other deictics unchanged. In complements expressive of compulsion or purpose, infinitive (stem + *-e*) clauses are most common.

57.

nauwā	rājā	ke	bār	kāṭ-e
barber.DEF	king	GEN	hair	cut-INF

gaile.
go.3sg.past

'The barber went to cut the king's hair.'

58.

ū	pānī	pī-ye	cahatā.
he	water	drink-INF	wish.3sg.pres

'He wishes to drink water.'

Compulsion constructions are characterised by infinitive + *ke* (dative postposition) + auxiliary verb:

59.

ek	jane	aur	khoj-e	ke
one	person	more	seek-INF	DAT

pari.
'fall'3sg.fut.

'I will have to look for one more person.'

60.	āj	sob	ghare	jā-e	ke
	today	all	house.LOC	go-INF	DAT

	bāī̃.
	be.3sg.pres

'He has to go to all the houses today.'

Temporal clauses are introduced by *jab* and *ta(b)* ('when' and 'then') in much the same way that correlative clauses are introduced by *jaun* and *taun*:

61.	jab	sanjhā	bhail,	ta
	when	evening	become.3sg.past	then.CORR

sādhu	gāu	se	aile.
ascetic	village	ABL	come.3sg.past

'When evening fell, an ascetic arrived from the village.'

'If-clauses' precede the result clause and are marked by *ta* 'then' in the second clause. In referring to past tense suppositions, the counter-factual endings in *-t* are used for the verbs in both clauses, as illustrated in A.5.3. In suppositions concerning the future, the verb in the first clause or both verbs are in the subjunctive mood:

62.	non	bo-i	ta	kaisan	ho-i?
	salt	plant-SUBJ	then	what	be.SUBJ

'What will happen if I plant salt?'

As indicated in A.5.3 the particle *ja* and correlative *ta* may be used to introduce the 'if' and the result clause respectively.

A.6.5 *Interrogatives*

B question particles usually begin with /k/, historically from the same source as Eng *wh-* words: *kab* 'when', *kā* 'what', *ke* 'who', *kahā̃* 'where', *kahe* 'why', etc. Yes-no questions are usually marked by a rising intonation on the final syllable of the sentence, though an alternate means is to use *kā* 'what', also with rising intonation, in sentence-final position (or, in some dialects, initial position).

63. toharā bahini āj aibi?
your sister today come.3sg.fut.

'Will your sister come today?'

64. ī tohār bacca hawẽ, kā?
this your child be.3sg.pres what

'Is this your child?'

In information questions, the *wh*-word often occupies the same position as the word it might replace in an equivalent declarative sentence:

65. ke khirkī khol delas?
who window open 'give'3sg.past

'Who opened the window? (equivalent to *Rām khirkī khōl delas* 'Ram opened the window').

66. tẽ kā kām karbe?
you what work(n) do.2sg.fut

'What work will you do?' (equivalent to *ham sab kām karab* 'I will do all the work').

A.6.6 *Imperatives*

Commands are effected by deletion of the second person pronoun (*tū/tẽ/tohani*) and use of one of the following verb forms: stem without an ending (for 'familiar' or 'contemptuous' usage); stem + *-ā* (for informal usage); and stem + -ī (for (+ R) usage in some dialects. An example of the 'familiar' imperative, used to close acquaintances, or to signal anger or disrespect, follows:

67. bhikārī ke kuchū de.
beggar DAT something give.IMP

'(Just) give the beggar something.'

A.6.7 *Impersonal constructions*

Certain verbs, like *lag-* 'to feel, to experience', *mil-* 'to get, to find', *hai* 'to be' (only in possessive constructions), and *par-*

'to fall' (as auxiliary), permit only dative subjects – that is, the 'deep' subject is always followed by the dative postposition *ke* – while the other noun governed by these verbs is unmarked.

68. oke gussā lagal.
he.DAT anger feel.3sg.past.
'He was angry' (literally 'to him – it felt – anger').

69. kisān ke auri paisā mīlī.
farmer DAT more money get.3sg.fut
'The farmer will receive more money' (literally 'to the farmer – it will get – more money').

70. Mohan ke baccan naikhī.
DAT child.PL be.neg.pres
'Mohan has no children' (literally 'to Mohan – it is not – children').

A.6.8 *Subject deletion*
In A.6.3 it was indicated that in both co-ordination and conjunctive constructions the subject occurs only once – that is, it can be considered to be deleted from one of the underlying clauses, usually the second. In addition, there is another instance of subject deletion, where the subject is optionally omitted, provided the context or verb-ending clarify any ambiguity of reference.

71. ā ke, dekhalas.
come CONJ see.3sg.past
'He/she/it came and had a look' (context making it clear who is being referred to).

72. Indar alas bāṭī. Kuchu nā karī.
lazy be.3sg.pres. anything not do.3sg.fut
'Indar is lazy. He will not do anything' (with the subject deleted in the second sentence).

APPENDIX B.1

A SAMPLE OF INDIAN BHOJPURI

The following story (from Grierson 1903:223) is an example of the B of the district of Saran in Bihar, which Grierson classifies as 'South Standard' (and which I call EB).

Ego siār rahale. Ego gāe rakhale rahale. Ṯâ unkar jāt log puchal 'e bhāī, kaise moṭāil bāṛâ?' Kahalan kī, 'ham phajire kā berā mũh dhõīle ek gāl ṙojo ā̃kar cabāīle, Gangājī ke pānī ek ciruā pīle, dā̃t bhaharā gail. Siār log kahalē ki, 'dā̃t hamār tūr dihalan. Calâ codanikaro ke mārī! Gail log. To nā bheṭāil. Okar jatiā gaie ke muā dihale.

> (There was once a jackal who kept a cow (and lived upon its milk). Then the other jackals, his caste-fellows, asked him 'O, brother, how have you got so fat?' He replied, 'Every morning I wash my face. Every day I also chew a mouthful of gravel and drink a mouthful of (holy) Ganges water. The result is that my teeth have all dropped out.' The other jackals said, 'This fellow has broken our teeth. Come let us kill the vile one.' They went (to look for him), but could not find him. So the jackals, his caste-fellows, killed the cow.)

Grierson's commentary is as follows: 'The jackal is chaffing them. His tribe is notorious for impiety. He pretends that he has got so fat, not by drinking the milk of the cow, but by pious practices. He lives upon the purest food, and as he no longer requires to eat flesh, his teeth have dropped out as useless incumbrances. The absence of his teeth he puts forth as an additional proof of his piety.'

* An English equivalent of 'this fellow has broken our teeth' is 'he is pulling our leg'.

APPENDIX B.2

A SAMPLE OF AWADHI

Grierson (1904:76) is also the source for the following specimen of Awadhi of the district of Partabgarh.

Ek ahīr ke ghare mā̃ cār manaī, larikā, sās, patoh, aur bāp, rahat rahē̃. Mulā cāryū̃ bahir rahē̃. Betaunā ek din khete mā̃ har jotat rahā au ohī orī se dui rāhī calā āwat rahē̃. Wai betaunā se guharāi kai pū̃chin ki, 'ham Rāmnagar kā jawā cāhit āhai. Kauni ḍagar se jāi?' Taū ū ahirawā jānis ki 'hamare baradhawan kā pū̃chat ahaī ki "becabya?" ' Au goharāi kai kahis ki 'baradhawan kā ham na becabai.' Yahi par rastā-girai ghuarāi kai kahin ki, 'ham ka bail na cāhī rahyā, jau jānat huā tau lakhāi dyā.' Tau ū janis ke, 'sau rupaiyā baradhawan kai lagāwat ahai,' au guhārais ki 'sau rupaiyā kā̃w; jau duyū sau detyō tabhū̃ ham āpan baradhawan tuhaī na deit.' Kachuk ber mā̃ ohkai mahatārī roṭī wahi ke bare lauī. Ruṭyā khātī-berā beṭauna bolā, 'māī ho, āj dui manaī baradhawan kai sau rupaiyā det rahē̃, mulā ham kahā ki, "dui sau kā ham na debai. Sau rupaiyā kaun cīj āṭai." ' Mahataryā bolī ki, 'hā̃, baccā, hamhū̃ jānit hai ki sāge mā̃ lon āj sewāi hui gawā ahai, mulā jaun kuch hoi tanī-tunī aisin khāilyā.' Laut kai jab ghare āi tau patohiyā se kahis ki, 'lon sāge mā̃ as sewāi kai dihe ki beṭaunā se roṭī nāhī̃ khāi gai.' Tau ū kahis ki 'bāsan dai kai maī miṭhāī kab lihyō rahā? Dādā jaun duāre par baiṭh rahat haī, calā, tin se hajurāi dēī.' Dūnau jhagarat jhagarat jau duāre par āī to patohiyā sasur se bolī ki, 'ka ho tū̃ hamaī bāsan dai kai miṭhāī let kab dekhe rahyā?' Tau sasurawā bolā ki, 'Goru carāwai tau tū̃ jā, au lāṭhī ham se pū̃chbyā?'

(In a cowherd's house there lived four persons – the son, the mother-in-law, the daughter-in-law, and the father, all of whom were deaf. While the son was one day ploughing in his field there passed that way two travellers. They called to the young fellow and said, 'We want to go to Ramnagar. What road should we take?' The cowherd thought that they were enquiring about his bullocks and wanted to know if he would sell them; so he called out to them, 'My oxen are not for sale.' To this they replied, 'We don't want your bullocks, but show us the way if you know it.' He thought that they were offering him a hundred rupees for them, so he replied, 'What are a hundred rupees? I would not give them for two hundred.' After a while his mother brought his midday meal, and while he was eating it the boy said to her, 'Two men offered me a hundred rupees for the bullocks today, but I told them that I would not sell them for two hundred, not to say one hundred.' The mother replied, 'Yes my boy, I know there is too much salt in the vegetables today, but make the best of it, and take as much as you can of it.' When she came back to the house, she said to the daughter-in-law, 'You put so much salt in the vegetables that my son could not eat his meal.' The daughter-in-law replied, 'When did I buy sweetmeats for cooking-pots? Come I shall have my words borne out by my father-in-law, who always sits in the doorway of the house.' So the two of them, scolding each other, went to the house doorway, where the daughter-in-law said, 'O father-in-law, when did you see me taking sweetmeats in exchange for cooking-pots?' He replied 'It's your business to graze the cattle, why are you asking me for the stick?')

APPENDIX B.3

SAMPLES OF SOUTH AFRICAN BHOJPURI

A. *AN OLD FLUENT FEMALE SPEAKER*

The speaker, said to be a hundred and four years old at the time of the interview, is one of the few SB speakers born in India. Her speech, however, is closer to that of other SB speakers, rather than to that of the district of her birth, Azamgarh. She came to Natal, as she explains, at the age of six or so. She has a command of F, and a passive knowledge of Eng, being able to speak but a few phrases. Hers is an example of the Midland variety of SB.

Hamar janam India me rahal, Ajamgarh me. Hamar bap kheti ke kām karat rahā . . . jate rahī, na? . . . aur sānj ke āte. Hamar bāp nahi hya āyā, . . . ū gujar gis Ajamgarh me.

Hamar māī jāt rahin, tīn aure aurat sanghe *ṭaun* ke. Nei malum, kuch lewe jāt rahin. Ham to ghare rahā. Tā ek thagwā taun ṭhagat lage, bole kauno caur *klīn* karnā, kauno dāl, aur sōb *groseri klin* kare ke, acchā darmahā-paisā milī. Tā phir kal ke aona – eise mānge. Tā ek bole hā̃, ek bole nahi, ohi me ū log apne me salah kihin. Tā bole, 'kuch nei, sanjhawā me ham log thorā kar leb, kal ke ā ke kar di, . . . acchā paisā mili.'

Tā phir, hamar māī kā karis . . . choṭā chokrā rahā . . . ghar ke lage ke. Uske dhaurais, bole jā ke chokrī ke liawe ke. Tā hamke liyail, aur ek chokrā, āpan bahin ke, nei malum, bhāī ke?

Wahā – jahā ī log cāur-or binī, hwā̃ se ab hamar māī logan bole, 'dekhā, sānj ho geil – ham jā he. Kab se ham kām karat he? Ketnā bon he? Ū admi bole abhi sabūr kare ke. Thoṛā ṭem me bas ghar me le geil, uṭhaī ke rakhe ke, ta ū admi cābī ḍāl dihis. Cābī ḍāl deilā, tab ī log ghar me cilāh he, kuarī ṭokhe, . . . ū admī lòg *answer* nei karis. Akhā rāt, ī log ohū me chapṭiail.

Bihān bhaile . . . tā ū log kẽwari khol ke ghusin he. Ī logan ke pakarle goṛ se, . . . chore nei, aur hamū log cilhāĩ, aur hamū log ke pakar leĩ. Dusar *rūm* rahe; ū *rūm* me le jā ke, ū logan ke ḍāl ke cābi ḍāl dihis. Haptā ke nagic rahal, ū rum me phin nei khole. Jetanā admī, otanā ghūse rahat . . .

Ta weise, ham lõg ke jahāj milā, baiṭhāĩ, ab ī log ke kapaṭ mare, ghare le jā he. Jahāj me baithā ke le ke geyā he . . . Ek bhāi raha – to ohi chuṭ geil . . . bāp ke sanghe rahal. Tā oke kā mālum he ke ṭhagle hamke?

Tā hya gora . . . Dacerā, ai ke ham logan ke *Greytown* le calal. Hamar māĩ okar *kicin* me hanḍi-bartan dhowis . . . das *silin* mahinā ke milat rahe, khānā milat rahe. Hamar māĩ dusre Kalkatiā log sanghe *kicin* me rahĩ . . .

> (I was born in India, in Azamgarh. My father used to do agricultural work – he would go (by morning) and return in the evening. My father didn't come to South Africa – he (must have) died in Azamgarh.
>
> My mother was going with three other women to town. They were going to buy something – I'm not sure where exactly, since I was at home at the time. Then a crook – the sort who recruited people – said to them, 'Why don't you take a job, for which you will be well-paid? Some of you can clean rice, some *dāl*, and others groceries. And you can come again tomorrow! – that's what they said. So the women debated it amongst themselves, some saying 'yes', others saying 'no'. Then they decided that they would do a little till the evening, and return the next day to do more in order to earn a good wage.
>
> Then what my mother did was to send a boy who lived near my house, telling him to go and fetch me. So he came and brought me, and another boy, his brother's or sister's son, I can't remember which.
>
> After I got there, and they had cleaned rice and things, my mother said, 'Look here, evening has come, we've been working a long time, and are now leaving. How much is our pay? Then the man said, 'Wait a bit' . . . and they swiftly took them into a building – carried them there – and locked them in. The women began screaming and banging on the doors, but those men would not answer. These people were held captive the entire night in that place. In the morning the recruiters opened the door and entered. They caught them by their feet, and wouldn't let them free.

When we screamed, they caught us too. They took them to another room and locked them in, where they had to remain for close on to a week. They would bring in more people, squeeze them in, and go away.

That's how it happened ... a ship arrived for us. And they deceived us into thinking that they were returning us to our homes. They seated us on ship and took us away. I had a brother, who was left behind. He had gone with his father – what did he know of our plight?

Then, here, a white man – a Dutchman – came and took us to Greytown. My mother used to wash dishes and so forth in his family's kitchen. She used to get ten shillings a month, plus food. She used to sit in the kitchen in her spare time, together with the other *Kalkatias*.)

B. *AN OLD FLUENT MALE SPEAKER*

This speaker was reportedly in his nineties at the time of the interview. Although he was born in Natal, his speech and life-style are those of the earliest migrants. He neither speaks nor understands Eng, but is fluent in Zulu. His speech shows a B and Awadhi base, with influences from Hn. Snatches from his reminiscences, which ranged over diverse topics, are given here.

... Hamar bāp kām karaṭ rahal, patthar mārat rahal. Ham log to *main* me sab patthar bīnat rahā ... thoṛā khet koṛī. Paṛhe-oṛhe to nei. Ham log Angrejī bāt samuj nei pai, bāt nei kar pai ... Koile-*main* me ham log eise patthar bīnī, ī sab khūn nikre. Ek mahinā – *thirty days* ke – ek *rān* det rahā. Aur khānā-caur, dāl, sob det rahā.

... Ham lōg ke ṭem bahut acchā rahal. Ham lōg ke bahut dukh uṭhayā, baki bahut acchā rahā. Ham log ke kaprā nei mālum – sāk oṛh ke sutat rahā. Ī ṭem dekho, bahut he, ... bas nei ... daliddar. Roj etanā līaw, ye honā, ū honā, khalās. Āj ke roje gos-macchī. Ham log ke mirchā rahe, dāl he, ālu thoṛa pakai deb, pet bhar ke ... gos nahi, kabhi mahinā me ek ṭem. Aj ke bacchā bīna gos nei khāī.

... Āj Gānhi sab ek banā gayā. India me sab panc baṭor ke; bole nei, ū garib admī he, sarkār khānā dena, *būk* denā sab ... sob ke paṛhaunā. Panc me kuch siddhe bāt karī ... Ū admī thoṛā rahā, ū to bhagwān rahā. *India* me, ham dēkhā nei . . . ī gore log bahut kuch kare he; oke bandh kare, acchā ghar banāī ke. Band kar diye, sab bagal se, sab baṛe-baṛe *geṭ* rahe . . . Ta Gānhi nikar ke bahar-bahar ghūmat he. Tab gorā ke hāl milal – ī to admī nei he, ī to admī ke rūp dekhā he . . . Gānhi phin āī, dekhabe – anjor ho jāī, Āj to duniyā galīj khallī, . . . kaljūg me he . . .

> (My father used to work (in the mines), he used to break rocks. We used to gather up stones too . . . and do some weeding. We were illiterate. We couldn't understand any English or speak it. We used to work with rocks on the mines till our fingers bled. For one month they would give us one rand, and food – rice, *dāl*, and other things . . .
>
> Those were good times. We had to face a lot of sorrow, but those were good times. We didn't know what was good clothing – we used to wrap sacks around ourselves and sleep. Look at things today, there is plenty, but not enough for the greedy. They want lots of everything, every day. Today everyone eats flesh. We made do with chillies, *dāl*, potatoes, and were contented with them. We hardly ate meat, perhaps once a month.
>
> . . . Gandhi made India one nation. He gathered all the people, saying, 'These are poor people, the government must provide for them, supply them with books, and educate everyone'. He used to talk sense in public . . . He wasn't a man, he was a God. In India (though I haven't been there), these white men did a lot of things to him. They built a huge building and locked him in. They closed it in on all sides with huge gates. But Gandhi came out and began walking around. Then they came to the realisation; this wasn't a man, this was the appearance of a man . . . Gandhi will come again, you'll see – there will be light again. Today's world is decadent – it is in *kaliyug* . . .)

C. *A THIRD-GENERATION SPEAKER*

The following narrative is by a sixty-year-old female speaker of the Coastal B dialect, and her speech is more typical of the SB of today than the previous two. The greater fluctuation in verb endings in this narrative is, however, quite unusual.

Pārbati aur Siwjī

Ek buḍḍhā aur buḍḍhī rahal. Oke baccā nei rahal. Tā ū lōg ke bahut *worry* me ho geil-'ham log ke baccā-occā nei he, ī ghar-or kaun lei?' Tā ū kā karis, ū ghar me sob angār ḍāl dihis. Sab jarā-urā ke aur sob cij peisā-weisā, dhan-daulat sab chor delak. Aur jai ke, jangal me geil, dūno jane. Jangal me jā ke, ū lōg baṛī roāt he. Tā jetnā pattā peṛ me rahal, sab pattā gir geil nicce.

Okar picche ab Parbati aur Siwjī rastā me āwat rahal. Baki Siwji ke mālum rahal ki sab cīj ke kā mahima he. Tā Parbati bole, 'ī rastā calna.' Tā Siwjī bole, 'Nei, ham nei jaib.' Parbati bole, 'Nei.' Tā mātā ke thōṛa ḍar rahal, nei – Siwjī ke bhī. Tā bole acchā. Jab Siwjī uha rastā geil, jāi ke pucche he 'kā tū log ke etanā dukh he, ki tū logan ek etanā roe se, sab pattā gir geil he? Kā dukh he?' Aur ī logan kuch nei bolat he. Siwjī tin ṭem puchlas. Tā bollak, 'jo ham kuch māngab, tū hamke de sake he?' Tā Siwjī bollak, 'hā, ham de sakī.' Tā bolle, 'dekho, hamare pās dhan-daulat bahut rahal, baki baccan nei he. Tā ū sabab se ham logan sab cīj jarā-orā ke, ā ke, ban me beiṭh geil he. Hamare pās baccan nei he, aur ham log ke baccan honā'.

Siwjī bolle, 'acchā.' Ab kā karnā, ū to jabān de dēle he. Tā hwā geil, Biśnu bhagwān ke lage, aur sob cīj bol delas. Biśnu bhagwān bole 'o log ke karam me baccā nei he, ham kā karnā?' Tā Siwjī bole, 'nei, Biśnu bhagwān, ab keiso bhī tū hamar bacan pūrā karnā'.

Juan Biśnu bhagwān ke baṛā kām karewālā rahal, ose bhagwān jā ke bolis ke dekh, tū cal jā hwā, jā ke janam le ke aur Siwjī ke bāt-bacan pūra kar denā. Ī admi bole, 'nei, ham nei jaib *mṛit lok* me, ham nei jaib – bahut dukh he hwā par.' Bhagwān bole, 'nei, tū jānā thoṛā din, bārā baris khallī rahanā, bārā baris ho jāī, okar picche tū hamke phīn se ā jānā.'

Siwjī ū buḍḍhā-buḍḍhī ke bollak 'acchā, tū logan āpan ghare cal jānā.' Jab pahucal, ī log ke ghar-dwār phīn se oisehī ho geil. Biśnu bhagwān, jaun baccā dewe ke rahal, ū de delak ū log ke. Keisan baccā, baṛhe, baṛhe ke dū din tā ekhī din me baṛhe. Aise hote hote, baccā ke kuch dīn, bārā baris hoi calat he. Tā ī kā karis – buḍḍhā-buḍḍhī – bahut khusiāili se, baccā ke sab cīj kar-ur ke, sādī ke bāt-ot ke, rājā kane okar sādi-ūdī, sāj-ūj kar ke, oke sādī ke bhejlak.

Bakī jaun dīn sādī hoī, ū dīn ū chokrā mar jāī. Buḍḍhā-buḍḍhī bahut khusi se bolat, 'baccā ke sādī hot he'. Barāt-urāt lē ke geil, wahā acchā se sādi-ūdi, dham-dhum se hoi geil.

Rāt bheil. Dulahā aur dulahin āpan kohabar me geil, aur dūno jane sut geil. Bakī ab etanā ṭem rahā ki ū prān cal jāī. Jab rājā sute lagal, tā ranī se bolis – dekh, koi bhī āwe *door knock* kare, to bolnā rajā sutal he, aur rānī jāgat he. Jab jamdūt a ke, *door knock* karat raha, rānī bolle, 'rājā sutal he, aur rānī jāgat he.' Jamdūt cal geil jamrāj kane, bole ke, 'dekh, ū to rājā sutal he, aur rānī jāgat he, keise ham prān lena?'

Tā phīn jamrāj bollak, 'jā līā de, nahi to abhī pahar cal jāī, to amar ho jāī. Aur ham log Biśnu bhagwān ke kā bolab?' Tā phīn jamdūt jā ke, duarī par ṭokhlas, phīn jabāb mīlal, 'rājā sutal he, rānī jagat he.' Phīn jamrāj ke lage geil; ū bole, 'dekh ek pahar aur rahi geil he, jo ī pahar cal jāī, tā ū amar ho jāī.' Phīn geil, *door knock* kare. Abhi koi nei bolle – dūno jane sut geil rahal. Ā ke, jamdūt okar parān le ke cale geil . . .

> (There was an old lady and an old man, who had no children. They were constantly depressed, saying, 'We have no children, what will happen to our house and property?' So they set fire to the house, and sent everything in it – including their wealth – up in smoke. They went into the jungle weeping profusely. And all the leaves on the trees fell to the ground in sympathy.
>
> A while later Parvati and Shiva were walking down the road; and Shiva was aware of what had happened. Parvati said, 'Let us take this road', to which Shiva replied, 'No I will not go on it.' Parvati said, 'No listen to me.' He was a little afraid of his wife – yes, even Shiva – so he said, 'All right.' So he walked on that road, went up to the couple, and asked, 'Why are you in such sorrow that you are sobbing, and causing all the leaves to fall? What is your pain?' But they said nothing, until Shiva asked them a second and then a third time. Then they said, 'If we ask for something, will you be able to grant it?' Then Shiva replied, 'Yes, I will.' So they said, 'Look, we had a great deal of wealth, but no children. On account of that we burnt all we had, and have to live in this forest. We have no children, and therefore ask for one.'
>
> Shiva said, 'Fine' – what else could he say, having already given his word? So he went to Lord Vishnu and told him what had transpired. And Lord Vishnu said, 'It is their fate

that they have no children, what can I do?' But Shiva pleaded, 'By whatever means, make my promise come true.'

So Lord Vishnu went to the one who was his closest assistant, and said, 'Look you must take a human birth and fulfil Shiva's promise.' But the assistant said, 'No I will not go to the world of mortals – there is too much sorrow there. Lord Vishnu said, 'No, go for a while; stay only twelve years, and you can return immediately afterwards.'

Shiva then told the old couple to go home. When they arrived there, they found the household to be exactly as it had been in former times. Lord Vishnu, who had given his word, bestowed a child upon them. It was a baby which grew very rapidly – in one day it grew by the equivalent of two. And so it went, until the end of the twelve years was approaching. And the old couple obliviously began arranging a match for their son. They made a proposal of marriage on his behalf to a king's daughter, and sent him off for the wedding.

His parents happily went through the wedding, not knowing that the day he was being married was also the day he was to die. The wedding went off very successfully.

When night fell, the bride and groom went to the bridal chamber, and soon fell asleep. But the time was approaching when his soul was to depart. When the groom felt sleepy, he said to his queen, 'Look, whoever comes to knock at the door, tell him that the king is asleep, but the queen is awake.' Soon death's messenger came and knocked at the door, and the queen did as she was instructed. The messenger went away and said to the lord of death, 'The man is sleeping, but his wife is awake; how could I take his spirit away?'

Then the lord of death replied, 'Go and try again, for if the hours pass he will become immortal. And what will we tell Lord Vishnu?' So the messenger went a second time, and received the same answer. After consulting again with the lord of death, and being told that only one hour was left before the groom would become immortal, he returned and knocked again. This time there was no answer, as both were fast asleep. So he entered and took his soul away . . .)

(The story continues at length – after many tribulations, the bride is finally re-united with her husband on earth.)

D. *A YOUNG FLUENT SPEAKER*

This is a story narrated by an eighteen-year-old girl whose first language is Eng, but who is fluent in B. Her speech is, however, phonetically and syntactically different from that of OFS speech illustrated above.

Kām Khojai

Ek dīn ek admī rahal, aur ek aurat rahal. Ū lōg ke pās dū betā rahal; ek barkā chokrā, aur ek choṭā chokrā. Ū admī bollas okar baṛā chokrā ke, 'tū kām jā ke khojnā. Ū baṛā chokrā ek rājā ke ghare geil. Tab ū rājā bollas, 'ham toke ek kām bataib'. Ek chūrī delas, aur ek cirei delas; bollak jangal me jai ke, ū cirai kāṭ denā, baki koi nei oke dekhnā. Ū chokrā ū chūrī le ke aur cirei le ke geil. Jangal mē jā ke, ū nei dekhlas koi ke, aur kāṭ delas cirei. Kāṭ ke rājā ke ghare geil. Ū de delas rājā ke, aur bollak rājā ke, 'halle, tor kām-om kar delī; aur hamke paisā honā – ham ghare jaib. Hamar bāp baṛā garīb he, okar paisa honā. Baki rājā bollas, 'tū nei dekhle koi ke, baki tū cirai kāṭ dele. Bhagwān toke dekhlas, aur asmān toke dekhlas'. Bollak, 'tū ghare jai ke, tor māī ke bolnā tū kā karle. Ab kām nei deb toke, aur peisā nei deb.

Ū chokrā geil. Hāt me kuch nei he. Okar māī ke bollas ī sob bheil. Aur okar bāp bollas tū baṛā kharāb kām karle; tū nei dekhle bhagwān toke dekhlas, aur asmān toke dekhlas. Kuch baṛā hawe, baki nei *think* karle. Tab bollak choṭā chokrā ke, 'ab kām jā ke khojnā'.

Ū chokrā geil. Ū phino se maharāj ke ghare geil. Maharāj bollas ham toke ī chūrī deb aur ī cirei deb. Tū jā ke jangal me kāṭ denā, koi nei dekhī baki. Chokrā chūrī le ke aur cirei le ke geil. Jangal me geil, tab ū *think* karlas ki 'uppar bhagwan he, aur asmān he. Asmān dekhlas, bhagwān dekhlas. Oke dekhī ki ū cirei kāṭī. Ū pāp ke cīj he. Ū chokrā le ke geil chūrī aur cirei, ū maharāj ke bollas, 'Dekh, maharāj, ab ī kām nei karab toke khatin. Tū hamke khussi kaun cīj tū bolbe, ham nei karab, kahike asmān dekhat he, bhagwān dekhat he, . . . ham nei karab. Tab ū maharāj bollas nei tū acchā kām karle, ki nei kaṭle. Hamke bahut khussī he. Ī cīj le ke ghare jā. Tor māi ke bolnā ham sob rāj-paṭ ham toke de deb.

Chokrā ghare geil, aur sob cīj bollas okar māī ke, baki māī

nei samjhailas. Tab ī rājā ghare geil. Rājā bollas, 'Nei tor baccā acchā kām karlas. Cirei nei kaṭlas. Tab ham oke sob de delī. Tab ū rājā cal geil. Aur ī māī-bāp auri dū baccan acchā se rahalas.

(Looking for work

One day there lived a man and his wife. They had two sons – an elder, and a young one. The man said to the elder son that he should go out and look for work. The son then went to a king's house. Then the king said, 'I will first give you something to do.' He gave him a knife and a bird, and asked to go into the jungle and slaughter the bird, without being seen. The boy took the knife and the bird with him. On entering the jungle, he could see no one, so he slew the bird. He then returned to the king's house, handed them over to him, and said, 'Here you are. I have done your bidding, so I want some money to go home. My father is very poor, and he needs some money.' But the king said, 'You didn't see anyone, and you killed the bird. But God saw you, and the heavens saw you.' The king asked him to go home, and tell his mother what he had done. And he said, 'I will give you neither work nor money.'

The boy went away empty handed. He told his mother all that had happened. And his father scolded him for doing such a terrible thing, not realising that God and the heavens were watching. 'You are so big, yet you did not stop to think.' He then sent the younger son to look for work.

The younger son set out, and he too ended up at the king's house. The king told him, 'I'll give you this bird and this knife. Take them to the jungle and slaughter the bird, but make sure no one sees you.' He went into the jungle, but realised that God and the heavens above would see him slaying the bird. He knew it was a sinful act; so he took them back to the king, saying, 'I won't do this thing. You can tell me what you like, but I will not do it.' Then the king said, 'No, you have done a good thing in not killing the bird. I am very pleased. Take these things and go home, and tell your mother that I will give you all of my kingdom.'

The boy went home and told his mother all that happened, but she did not understand. So they went back to the king, and he confirmed that her son had done a worthy deed, and that he had given him all of his kingdom.

The king then went away, and the parents, together with the two sons lived happily . . .)

E. *AN EXAMPLE OF SS DISCOURSE*

This is a version of the tale of 'The dog and the bone'. It is reproduced (as with D above) as spoken, without any of the deviations from OFS speech being corrected. The narrator is SS_8, a male of 24 years, whose background is described in 5.6.

Ek dīn rahal ek ṭho kuttā. Ū admī sāthe geil, kuttā. *Butcher* ke nagicce rahal. Tab e bahut bhūk lagal, aur bhittar geil. Ek ṭho tukrā gos coreilak aur bhāgal. Aur ū *shopowner* bahut gussā bheil, ta kuch nei kar sakal. Bhāgal bahut dūr, aur sob gos khā lelak, aur khallī haḍḍī rahal. Haḍḍī okar dā̃t se pakar lelak aur bhāgal . . . geil ghare. Bare naddī rahal. Okar chāhī paṛal hwā par. Oke nei mālum rahal okar chāhi rahal. Tab ū honā bhokke ke aur khaddere ke, . . . aur okar haḍḍī pānī me giral, aur ū kuch nei milal. Aur weise ghare geil.

(One day there was a dog. He was walking with his owner, and came near a butcher-store. He felt very hungry, and entered. He stole a piece of meat, and ran away. The shop-owner became very angry, but could do nothing. The dog ran away, and ate up the meat. He carried the bone in his mouth and ran homewards. There was a river nearby, and he was forced to cross it. Then he saw another dog in the water; it was his shadow, but he didn't know that. He planned to bark at it to frighten it away, and his bone fell into the water, and he got nothing in the end. In that manner he went home.)

F. *AN EXAMPLE OF CODE-SWITCHING*

The speaker here is a forty-eight-year-old woman, speaking to a slightly older companion. Both women habitually speak B to each other, with occasional switches to Eng, which they both have a good command of. The constant switching here is partly an attempt to include two daughters – who understand B, but rarely speak it – in the conversation. The speaker is expressing her dissatisfaction at the behaviour of some of her relatives.

. . . Harilāl ke āurat, ū baṛā baṛā *box* – tīn bhāī hē nā – tīn *box* liyā ke, tīn bhāī ke de delas. Aur ū *grand*-baccā raha, Harilāl ke *grand*-beṭī* . . . ek *box* uṭhā ke āpan ājī-wālā – ū le ke cal geil. Aur ū Billam-wālī – toke mālum – sawar eisan he, hamke bolat he, 'Bhaujī, ā ke bhaiṭ hyā, *come and sit*, jā ke *box* liāwat he, dekhe ke bhāī ka dele he . . . *and me now I'm getting so fed up, the way they're carrying on* . . . bole hamar bhāī dele hoi sonā *or sovereign*, kuch ḍāl ke bheje hoi. *And she's insisting I must open it*. Nei, nei, beiṭh, beiṭh, tū khol de bhaujī, hamke dekhe ke honā kā he ome . . . *I'm getting so embarrassed, because I know what's there. I opened it* . . . ta bollas, 'Are, ī kā he, . . . *lamp*. Kā karab ham lōg *lamp* se? Ham log ke sab *light* he, kā karī ham lōg *lamp* se? . . .

. . . Ek aur dafā . . . ham ke dekh ke jare lagal. Are. *I went by her. I made* namaste *and all. She said*, 'hā̃, le jā uppar, Roshṇi ke de de'. Ham nautā dewe ke *twenty rand* le geil rahalī. *I put it in the envelope*. Hamar beṭī ke sādi khatin *twenty-five rand* dele rahal. Okar pās aur beṭī otnā he, nā . . . Ta bollas, 'Hā, līkh de, *write it, write it Dolly, in the book*.' *And yet*, Kisūn ke aurat logan ail. Uno dūno gal me cummā le ke okar *parcel* le ke geil uppar . . .

> (. . . Harilal's wife had brought very big boxes (of gifts) – there were three brothers, so she brought three gifts. And the granddaugher – Harilal's granddaughter carried one of the boxes to her granny, who took it away (to keep it). And the lady from Verulam – you know, the dark one – says to me, 'Sister-in-law, come and sit here'. She went to fetch my box to see what her cousin (*lit.* 'brother') had sent her. And I was getting fed up at the way they were carrying on. She said, 'My cousin must have sent gold or sovereigns; he must have put some in this box and sent them.' And she insisted that I open it, saying, 'No, no. Sit down, sister-in-law, I want to see what is in it.' In the mean time I was so embarrassed, because I knew what was inside the box. Still I opened it, and she said, 'Oh, what's this – a lamp. What will we do with a lamp? We all have electricity – what on earth will we do with a lamp?'
>
> . . . One other time, she saw me and became jealous,

Lord! I went to her. I greeted her with 'namaste'. She said (brusquely), 'Yes, take it upstairs, and give it to Roshini. I had taken twenty rand to give her as a gift, which I had placed in an envelope. She had given me twenty-five rand at my daughter's wedding – but she has so many more daughters. She then said, 'Yes, write it, write it down in your book, Dolly.' . . . And yet when Kisoon's wife and others came, she accepted a kiss on each cheek from them, and took the present from them personally, and went upstairs with it . . .)

* *Note*: the hybrid forms *grand-beṭī* and *grand-bacchā* used here are exceptional – I have not encountered them elsewhere.

APPENDIX B.4

SONGS

A. The following is an invocation to the Goddesses and Gods, sung by a seventy-five-year-old female interviewee.

Debi ke pacṛā ('Song for the Goddess')

sumirao māī debī ko sumirao bhawānī
sumirao bābā dīu hār

tohare sarana bābā mai jaghā rokyo
more jagha pūrāna hoi

sumirao mātā ke sumirao pītā
sumirao bābā Hanumān

tohare sarana bābā mai jagha rokyo
more jagha pūrāna hoi

āwo debiyā maiyā baiṭho more angane
debo sāto rangiyā bichāī

ghīu boraye maiyā homiyā karaibe
dhūāna akase mararai

āwo bhawānī maiyā baiṭho more angane
debo sāto rangiyā bichāī

ghīu boraye maiyā homiyā karaibe
dhūāna akase mararai

āwo dīu hara bābā baiṭho more angane
debo sāto rangiyā bichāī

ghīu boraye bābā homiyā karaibe
dhūāna akase mararai

āwo Hanumāna bābā baiṭho more angane
dēbo sāto rangiyā bichāī

ghīu boraye bābā homiyā karaibe
dhūāna akase mararai

(I remember you Mother Goddess, I remember you God
I remember you Holy Father God
In your refuge, Father and Mother, let my place be reserved
So that my household may become pure
I remember you mother, I remember you father
I remember you Father Hanuman
In your refuge, Father and Mother, let my place be reserved
So that my household may become pure
Come Mother Goddess, sit in my yard
I will give you a mat of seven colours
I will pour *ghi*, Mother, I will offer oblations
So that the smoke will go up to the sky
Come Mother Goddess, sit in my yard
I will give you a mat of seven colours
I will pour *ghi*, Mother, I will offer oblations
So that the smoke will go up to the sky
Come Holy Father God, sit in my yard
I will give you a mat of seven colours
I will pour *ghi*, I will offer oblations
So that the smoke will go up to the sky
Come, Father Hanuman, sit in my yard
I will give you a mat of seven colours
I will pour *ghi*, I will offer oblations
So that the smoke will go up to the sky)

B. The following is a love-song sung by a young woman, who laments that she has no-one to offer her garland of flowers to (age of interviewee, fifty-eight).

bela phūle adhī rāte gajarā kekare galle ḍālo?
are gajarā kekare galle ḍālo?
ehī gajarā cāne galle dālo, suruje galle ḍālo
ū ta ūghe rāt gajarā kekare galle ḍalo?
bela phūle adhī rāte gajarā kekare galle ḍālo?
ehī gajarā Gangā galle ḍālo, Jamunā galle ḍālo
ū ta bahe dūno sāte gajarā kekare galle ḍalo?
are, gajarā kekare galle ḍalo?
bela phūle adhī rāte gajarā kekare galle ḍālo?

ehī gajarā Mahadeo galle ḍālo, ehī gajarā Mahadeo
galle ḍālo
oke sobhe mirgā-cāl, gajarā kekare galle ḍālo?
are, gajarā kekare galle ḍālo?
ehī gajarā Rāme galle ḍālo, Lacchmane galle ḍālo
unke sobhe dhanuk bana, gajarā kekare galle ḍālo?
are gajarā kekare galle ḍālo?

(This garland of flowers that bloom in the middle of the night
On whose neck shall I place it, on whose neck shall I place it?
Shall I place it on the moon's neck, and on the sun's neck?
But they are drowsy at night, on whose neck shall I place it?
This garland of flowers that bloom in the middle of the night
On whose neck shall I place it?
Shall I place it on Ganga's neck, and on Jamuna's neck?
But they flow in harmony together, on whose neck
shall I place it?
This garland of flowers that bloom in the middle of the night
On whose neck shall I place it, on whose neck shall I place it?
Shall I place it on Shiva's neck, shall I place it on Shiva's neck?
But his deer-skin suits him better, on whose neck
shall I place it?
On whose neck shall I place this garland?
Shall I place it on Ram's neck, and on Lutchman's neck?
But bows and arrows suit them better, on whose neck
shall I place it?
On whose neck shall I place this garland?)

C. Unlike the previous two, the following song was composed in South Africa. It is known to SB speakers as a *drāmā ke gīt* 'a drama-song', sung as part of a dramatic production incorporating a series of satirical sketches, mingled with more serious pieces. In this version of a popular song, the wife and husband bemoan each other's faults, especially new habits picked up in Natal. The first two verses are spoken by the male, while the wife has her say in the last three.

tū̃ te buṛhiyā se banle jawān
e rānī kaheke?
oṭhwa tū lāl kariho
barwā ke *curly* dallo
e rānī kaheke?

tū̃ cal ja pagaḍaṇḍī
apane se dhob haṇḍī
mū̃ me ḍālo *powder*
pahire ulṭā sārī
tū chor diye kulawā ke cāl

ye he *latest* hamar singhār
merā pahiral phuṭal tore ā̃kh
e rājā kaheke?
phaṭal ho Rām sasurariyā se jiārā

ādhī rāt ke saīya āwelā
kamāri ṭhūk ṭhukāwelā
jaun pahirin nīn se uthe
sab akhiyā camkāwelā
phaṭal ho Rām, sasurariyā se jiārā

gānjā pī ke saīyā āwe
jhagharā macchāwelā
jab ham kucchū bole
ta hamke ākhiyā camkāwelā
phaṭal ho Rām sasurariyā se jiārā

(From an old lady, you've become young
Why, O wife?
You've painted your lips red
and made your hair curly
Why, O wife?

You go out walking down the roads
I shall do the dishes myself
You dab powder on your face
and wear your sari back to front
You've abandoned family traditions

This is my latest style
My dressing shatters your eyes
Why, O husband?
My heart has become disenchanted

My husband comes home at dead of night
knocking at the door
The clothes I wear in my sleep
cause his eyes to glitter
My heart has become disenchanted

My husband comes home high with dagga
and raises havoc
Should I say something
then he makes eyes at me
My heart has become disenchanted)

APPENDIX B.5

Riddles (Bujhaunī)

1. lāl charī maidān kharī
   sās se patoh baṛhī

   'A red stalk standing in a field
   the daughter-in-law will grow taller than her mother-in-law.'

2. ek sup lāwā khet me citrāwā
   bīnat bīnat koi nei pāwā

   'A trayful of popcorn scattered in a field
   everyone tries to gather them, but none succeed.'

3. dekh le barkhaṇḍī bābā
   kaun janāwar jāt bā
   be hāt se be gōṛ se

   'Take a look, Father Barkhandi
   which animal is going past
   without hands, and without feet.'

4. ḍekhe ke lāl lāl
   khāi ta hai hai

   'Very red to look at
   but after eating one says "wow".'

5. ek ciraiyā laṭ okar dūno phakanā paṭ
   okar khalerī ujār okar mās majedār

   'A bird with tangled hair, its two wings flopping downward
   its skin white, its meat very tasty.'

6. cār kabbuttar cār rang
darbā ke bhittar ek rang

'Four pigeons with four different colours
but inside the cage they've only one colour.'

Answers: 1. *makei* 'mealie plant' (whose seeds will outgrow the plant); 2. *patthar* 'hailstones'; 3. *dhūwā̃* 'smoke'; 4. *mircā* 'chillie'; 5. *ganna* 'sugar-cane'; 6. *pān-supāri* 'betel-leaf, betel-nut, lime, and catechu, which when chewed together merge into one colour in the mouth (or cage).

APPENDIX C

Questionnaire I. Administered informally and orally in Eng (often SAIE dialect), to people proficient to varying degrees in SB and Eng:

A. *Personal Details*

Name
Age
Place of residence
Place of birth/childhood
Mother's birthplace
Father's birthplace
Grandparents' birthplace
District of origin in India of ancestors (if known)
English-educated?
Hindi-educated?
No. of years of Hindi education.
Occupation
Spouse's occupation
With whom do you use 'Hindi' at home?
With whom do you use 'Hindi' outside the home?
Do your children speak 'Hindi'; and if so to whom?
If not, do they understand it?

B. *Vocabulary*

What 'Hindi' word do you usually use when speaking at home for each of the following?

door; window; pot; lid of a pot; fire; a buck; book; to run; boy; girl; to stand up; sun; stars; moon; lightning; Tuesday; Thursday; to drown; to swim; sea; to buy.

C. *Verb Endings*

How do you say the following in 'Hindi':

I saw (the film); You saw (the film); She saw (the film);

We saw (the film); etc.
I will (see the film just now); You will (see the film just now); etc.
I am seeing (a film; don't disturb me); You are seeing (a film); etc.
I went (to the sea-side); You went (to the sea-side); etc.
I go (to work every day); You go (to work every day); etc.
I will go (to Durban tomorrow); You will go (to Durban tomorrow); etc.
I am going (just now); You are going (just now); etc.

D. *Sentences*

How do you say these sentences in 'Hindi'?

1. I live in X, but my family live in Y. (X and Y depend on place of interview.)
2. We came to visit them, but they had already gone by car.
3. I'll tell you something, but you musn't laugh.
4. As the snake came out from the hole, the baby saw it and cried.
5. The bigger girl is my daughter.
6. The baby is very beautiful.
7. Where did those people sleep last night?
8. You are a lazy child; you must go to school tomorrow.
9. Shanta wants to go to town tomorrow.
10. It might be raining in Durban now.
11. When will you do the job for me?
12. My (paternal) granny came from India.
13. If I'm still sick I'll go to the doctor.
14. I've given the books to the boy (already).
15. She doesn't like washing dishes.
16. You must be thinking about your mother.
17. The boys are grazing cows on that hill.
18. The policeman had caught the rogues last week.
19. How many children do you have?
20. The baby ate up all the food.
21. He made the boys pluck mangoes for us.
22. We saw a house which is built like an aeroplane.

23. The baby was beaten by his father.
24. We saw a house with a very big roof.
25. Tomorrow I will buy a new broom.
26. If I tell you where I've been, will you promise not to get angry?
27. The girl who used to go to school with me is getting married soon.
28. I don't think it's going to rain tonight.
29. My granny still loves to go visiting, even though she's so old.
30. Opening an umbrella indoors brings bad luck.

Questionnaire II (for semi-speakers)

A. As A. above. Add: To whom did you speak 'Hindi' as a child?; To whom do you currently speak in 'Hindi'?

B. *Vocabulary*
As for B above. *Add:* hand; bad; knife; food; together with; six; seven; eight; to wash; loin-cloth; to sweep; a flag; a stool; cold; daughter; hill; hard (not soft); bone; leg; big; to catch; to call; eyes; to distribute; we; a bridegroom; bride; iron; much; jack-fruit; a cart; bad; good; torn; to distribute; tail; one's back; behind; front; a stone; a lie; aunt; husband's elder brother; husband's elder brother's wife; louse; a male sheep; now; half; evening; morning; beautiful; to tie; expensive; cheap; fragrance; a house; a building; tongue; a thief; to open; a woman's under-skirt; hungry; oil-dāl.

C. *Morphology*
As above.

D. *Sentences*
1 to 20 as above; for those experiencing difficulty, substitute the following sentences for the ones causing problems:

1. She fell down.
2. He climbed up the hill.
3. She got hurt on her leg.
4. I shall place the book on the table.

5. I drank all the water.
6. My mother is in the room.
7. The boy ate his food and slept away.
8. She was able to wash the clothes.
9. The thief saw us and ran away.
10. The monkey which we saw yesterday ran away.

E. *Narrative*

Narrate a brief story of your own choice in 'Hindi'.

NOTES

CHAPTER 1

1. The term 'Hindustani', generally avoided in this study, is used in at least three different senses by writers:
   (i) In British India the term was interchangeable with 'Hindi' – denoting the regional language of parts of North India (Uttar Pradesh, Madhya Pradesh), as well as the language used in larger cities like Bombay.
   (ii) 'Hindustani' is used by others to denote the colloquial variety (devoid of learned Sanskritic borrowings) associated with the less educated. The term is used to distinguish it from formal Hindi.
   (iii) It is sometimes used as a cover term for both Hindi and Urdu which are seen as two variations of a common-core language, the latter having a heavily Persianised lexicon, while the former leans more towards Sanskrit in its lexicon.
2. Meer (1980:314) cites a figure of 2 004 Indians returning to India after the expiry of their contracts, in the period 1860–1866 (of a total of 11 438).
3. Kuper (1960:7) gives the following figures: 'Among 3 200 indentured coming on 8 boatloads selected at random, approximately 2 per cent were Brahmin, 9 per cent Kshatriya, 21 per cent Vaishya, 31 per cent Sudra, 27 per cent scheduled castes. Of the remaining groups 3 per cent were Christian, 4 per cent Muslim and 3 per cent unclassifiable.' We still need to determine the extent to which these figures correlate with villages of India.
4. These totals are based on figures in *India – A Reference Annual 1973*, and reflect the language groupings of the 1961 census.
5. Note that Emeneau (1956) specifically excludes the Tibeto-Burmese family from this characterisation of the 'Indian linguistic area', since it does not share a large core of common features with the other three groups.
6. The exposition is based primarily on Grierson (1927), though additional discussions by Chatterji (1960), Burrow (1955), Zograph (1982) and Shapiro and Schiffman (1981) have been useful.
7. The 1911 census figures are given as follows:

TOTAL INDIAN POPULATION	149 791		
SOUTH AFRICAN-BORN	63 776		
REMAINDER (PLACE OF BIRTH)			
Assam	31	East Bengal	3
Bengal	16 165	Madras	41 314
Bombay	10 883	Punjab	342
Burma	33	U.P. (Agra and Oudh)	265
Central Provinces and Bihar	49	Other & unspecified	15 921
		Other countries	1 009

These figures are incorrect. The number given for immigrants from Bihar is much too low, while figures for Bengal are too high. It seems that respondents reported port of embarkation (Calcutta, which is in Bengal), rather than birthplace.

8. The census records do not list separate figures for Urdu for 1970.

CHAPTER 2

1. The fieldwork on which the discussion in the rest of this chapter is based was carried out in the whole of Natal, excluding KwaZulu. Because of restrictions on time (and money) it was not possible to study the small and scattered B-speaking communities in the Cape, Transvaal, and KwaZulu. A brief interview with two women who had lived most of their lives in the Transvaal, and a man who had spent all but the last five years in KwaZulu suggests that the SB of these areas resembles Coastal B. The influence of Afrikaans on B in areas outside Natal is a topic that needs to be researched.
2. Languages whose dialects show far greater morphological than phonetic diversity are rare. Grierson's *LSI*, and other grammars of Bihari and E. Hn. suggest that phonetically the differences between the sub-varieties of these languages is minimal, compared to the morphological diversity.
3. Features 39 and 40 are not really part of the koine-forming process. Except for words associated with the experience of indentureship, and some Zulu/Fanagalo loans, the bulk of the loanwords are part of the process of language change discussed in detail in Chapter 4. They have been included here to indicate how SB differs from other Indic languages.
4. GB is an exception here, having second person form in *-iho*, from E. and W. Hn.
5. In this table a (+) signifies that a form has been recorded by Grierson in the *LSI* for more than one sub-variety of the language/dialect under question. If a word occurs in only one sub-dialect, and is probably a form influenced by a neighbouring group of dialects, a (−) is recorded. For example, the word *kharāb* 'bad' occurs in only one of eight varieties of E. Hn given by Grierson, and seems to be a borrowing from Std Hn in the one dialect. If a word differs only slightly from the SB equivalent, it is taken as being the same: for example, W. Hn *sār*, SB *sā̃r* 'bull'.
6. These four words posed problems for third-generation speakers interviewed. In general, none could recall exact terms for these, and used near-synonyms (for example, *nōkar* 'worker' for 'slave') or loanwords (for example, *sādel* for 'saddle'). R. Sitaram (personal communication, March 1984) informs me that amongst older speakers the terms *garēṛi* 'shepherd', *khetihar~kisān* 'cultivator', and *gulām* 'slave' were once frequently used. For 'saddle' the Indic terms were not widely used.
7. *Khassi* is occasionally used, however, in SB to refer to a goat to be sacrificed.
8. The forms *dūi* and *kukkur* are not included in Table 28, since they are far less frequent in SB than their equivalents *dū* 'two' and *kuttā* 'dog'.
9. For many SB speakers [ei] is replacing [ai] in these words – see 4.3.4.

10. The infinitive is expressed by an *-e* ending in SB (for example, *ham sut-e jaib* 'I will go to sleep'), and may be accompanied by the dative postposition *ke* in purposive constructions. The verbal noun has only one ending (*-be*) and co-occurs solely with *kar-* 'to do' (for example, *sut-be karī* 'he will do sleeping'). Other forms current in IB (see A.5.6) do not occur in South Africa.
11. The following paradigm for the masculine past is a typical example of this (from Shukla 1981:107): 1st (sg and pl) *dekhalī*; 2nd (sg and pl) *dekhalā̃*; 3rd sg *dekhal*; 3rd pl *dekhalæ̃*.
12. The use of *naikhe* is, however, reported in a few WB districts in the *LSI* (Grierson 1903).
13. *ho* 'to be, become' is a defective verb in SB, used mainly in a subjunctive sense, and having the following realisations: *hōt* 'if he/she/it be/become' (counter-factual), and *hōi* 'if he/she/it be/become' (subjunctive). Forms like **hoil* (past) and **hōb* (future) are ungrammatical, while present habitual *hoila* is archaic. The indicative sense of 'to become' is supplied by *ho-* plus local auxiliary *jā-* 'to go', the latter carrying the inflections: for example, *ho geil* 'it became/happened', *ho jaibe* 'you will become' etc.
14. As the usual sense of the local auxiliaries might also prevail here (for example, *rakh le* 'keep it (for yourself)'), it might be more accurate to consider this to be the unmarked form, and the stem form to be marked as $(-R_1)$.
15. Although this is probably a later borrowing from Std Hn, and not part of the original koine-forming process, it is described here under 'respect' for the sake of completeness.
16. This could be increased to four, if the form *maṭṭī* 'sand' (Baker and Ramnah 1985:231) is symptomatic of the doubling of consonants. More data from MB is required, however.

CHAPTER 3

1. There is a growing trend toward giving prominence to one's mother tongue in many parts of India, even if it is not an official state language. This attitude has promoted a growing literature, and an increasing number of popular films in B.
2. Such 'formal' B is discussed in Misra (1980).
3. Indian Immigration Papers (I.I. 1211/1880), Natal Archives, Pietermaritzburg.
4. Misra's tacit assumption that on account of such differences H is superior to L is questionable. H seems to be a hybrid of Std Hn and B.
5. There have been some ethnic newspapers using Indian languages prior to 1960, the most successful of which was the *Indian Opinion*, founded by Gandhi in 1903, carrying articles in Gujarati and Eng, and for a brief period in Hn and Tamil as well. A Hn-medium newspaper, *Hindi*, run by Bhawani Dayal Sannyasi, was in circulation between 1922 and 1924.
6. SB speakers in the Transvaal and Cape Province also use Afrikaans for official purposes, and at work. I have excluded them from the discussion on account of their very small numbers.

7. These figures hold for *c.* 1980, the time of my initial research. The age limits have advanced by ten years in the interim.

CHAPTER 4

1. By way of parallel, Mauritius came to be known as *Miric* or *Miric Deś*, and Trinidad *Cinitat* (Tinker 1974:120). These words superficially resemble those for 'chillies' and 'sugar' respectively. Whether these meanings had any validity to the migrants is hard to say.
2. Branford (1987:235) derives SAE *naartjie* from Afrikaans *naartjie*, which she relates to Tamil *nartei*. The form derives ultimately from Perso-Arabic *naranj*, a form that also gives Spanish *naranja*, English *orange*, and Hn *aranji*. SB has *nacis* and *aranji* etymologically from the same source, but with different meanings.
3. However, according to the *OED*, *varaṇḍa* of Hn is itself an adoption of Portuguese *varanda*. In SB such is the insecurity, that the B form is automatically assumed to be based on the Eng: one speaker professing that she had always considered B *branḍa* to be 'a very crude word'.
4. The form *kandh* is, however, attested in *karkandhā* 'a cow with black shoulders' (Grierson 1885:297), raising the possibility that the other SB forms are also of dialectal occurrence in India.
5. This document may be found in the Natal Archives, Pietermaritzburg, Indian Immigration File (I. I, 1/48, 1389/89).
6. *Kewat* 'fishermen' and *mālī* 'gardeners' are known to a few SB speakers, however, on account of the influence of Indian films.
7. Although these examples are drawn from the speech of B–Eng bilinguals, the influence of other South African Indian substrates cannot be ruled out – especially the influence of Tamil on SAIE. Note, too, that these examples are taken from intimate/informal speech; in more formal styles SAIE approximates more towards SAE.

CHAPTER 5

1. Cited by Dressler and Wodak-Leodolter (1977).
2. Several issues of the *International Journal of the Sociology of Language* have been devoted to this topic: No 12 of 1977, which I refer to several times in this chapter, bears the title 'Language Death'; No 25 of 1980 has "Language Maintenance and Language Shift" as its special theme; as do Vol 68 (1987) and Vol 69 (1988).
3. Regarding fieldwork ethics: permission was sought from all the participants involved. The student semi-speaker was obviously concerned about her own inability to converse at length, but gave her permission to use the material.
4. These 4 complex sentences were: (i) *ham le ke geil ... vet* 'I took it and went to the vet', (ii) *ketnā baris ho geil ab tū logan geil?* 'How many years have passed since you last went?', (iii) *Amke khalli mālum he ek accident hyā beil*

'I only know that an accident occurred here – near the sea', (iv) *bollas accha ho jai* 'She said that he would recuperate'. Only (iv) is error-free.

5. In this sentence as well as the next, the verb form is incorrect – the second person past form being *geile*.
6. Another reason is that in some contexts *-wā/-yā* is used in a 'familiar', 'playful', even 'contemptuous' way. This is particularly true of vocatives – for example, *bhaiyā* 'brother', *maiyā* 'mother', and *Mirwā* 'Meera' (a proper name) all carry greater informality and, depending on context, either jocularity or anger. SSs confuse this usage with the more commonly occurring 'definite' or 'anaphoric' function.
7. No data are available for SS_7 here.

APPENDIX A

1. *Dvandva* means 'two by two', *tatpuruśa* 'that man' (illustrative of the type of compound it names), while *bahuvrīhī* 'much rice' refers to a third person who has much rice, that is, 'a rich man' (again illustrative of the compound it names).
2. However, some titles like *paṅdit* 'priest', *rājā* 'king', and *ṭhākur* 'chief' often precede the proper name.
3. Shukla (1981) gives separate postpositions for North-east Bhojpuri: *kae* for the genitive, and *ke* for the dative.

BIBLIOGRAPHY

Archival Material

Natal Archives, Pietermaritzburg
Indian Immigration II 1/1 – 1/191, Minute papers 1875–1916.
Killie Campbell Collection, University of Natal, Durban
The James Stuart Papers.

Published Documentary Material

Indian Immigration: *Report of the Protector of Indian Immigrants*, 1876–1909.

Indian Immigrant School Board: *Indian School Report*, 1881–93.

Indian Immigration Trust Board: *Annual Report* 1887–1904.

Union of South Africa: *Census and Statistics: Population Census*. 1911:UG 32; 1936:UG 44/1938; 1951:UG 00/1959; 1960:Vol 7, No 1; 1970: Report No 02-02-09.

Books and Unpublished Theses

Andronov, M.S. 1964. On the typological similarity of New Indo-Aryan and Dravidian. *Indian Linguistics* 25:119–26.

Apte, M.L. 1974. Pidginization of a lingua franca: A linguistic analysis of Hindi-Urdu spoken in Bombay. *International Journal of Dravidian Linguistics* 3:21–41.

Baker, P. and Ramnah, A. 1985. Mauritian Bhojpuri: An Indo-Aryan language in a predominantly Creolophone society. *Papers in Pidgin and Creole Linguistics* 4: 215–38 (Pacific Linguistics A-72).

Barz, R.K. 1980. The cultural significance of Hindi in Mauritius. *Journal of South Asian Studies* New Series 3:1–14.

Barz, R.K. and Diller, A.V.N. 1985. Classifiers and Standardisation: Some South and South-East Asian

Comparisons. In D. Bradley (ed.), *Papers in South-East Asian Linguistics* No. 9: Language Policy, Language Planning and Sociolinguistics in South-East Asia, pp. 155–84 (Pacific Linguistics A-67).

Barz, R.K. and Siegel, J. (eds). 1988. *Language Transplanted: The Development of Overseas Hindi.* Wiesbaden: Otto Harrassowitz.

Beames, J. 1970. *A Comparative Grammar of the Modern Aryan Languages of India.* New Delhi: Munshiram Manoharlal. (Reprint of the original three volumes of 1872, 1875 and 1879)

Bhana, S. and Brain, J. 1984. *The Movements of Indians in South Africa* Vol 1. Unpublished report presented to the Human Sciences Research Council. Durban.

Bhatia, T.K. 1982. Transplanted South Asian languages: An overview. *Studies in the Linguistic Sciences* 11:129–34.

Bloomfield, L. 1927. Literate and illiterate speech. *American Speech* 2:432–39.

Bold, J.D. 1974. *Fanagalo Phrase-Book Grammar and Dictionary.* 9 edn. Johannesburg: Hugh Keartland.

Branford, J. 1987. *A Dictionary of South African English.* 3 edn. Cape Town: Oxford University Press.

Breatnach, R.B. 1964. Characteristics of Irish Dialects in Process of Extinction. In *Communications et rapports du premier congres de dialectologie générale*, pp. 141–45. Louvain: Centre international de dialectologie générale.

Bughwan, D. 1970. An Investigation into the Use of English by the Indians in South Africa, with special reference to Natal. Ph.D. Thesis, University of South Africa.

——— 1979. Language Practices. In Pachai (ed.) 1979:464–518.

Burrow, T. 1955. *The Sanskrit Language.* London: Faber and Faber.

Campbell, L. and Canger, U. 1978. Chicomuceltec's last throes. *International Journal of American Linguistics* 44: 228–30.

Chambers, J. and Trudgill, P. 1980. *Dialectology.* Cambridge: Cambridge University Press.

Chatterji, S.K. 1926. *The Origin and Development of the Bengali Language.* Calcutta: Calcutta University Press. (Repr. George Allen and Unwin 1970, 3 Vols)

——— 1960. *Indo-Aryan and Hindi*. 2 edn. Calcutta: Firma K.L. Mukhopadhyay.

——— 1972. Calcutta Hindustani: A Study of a Jargon Dialect. In S.K. Chatterji, *Select Papers* Vol. 1. New Delhi: People's Publishing House, pp. 204–56. (Reprint of 1931 original)

Chaturvedi, M. and Tiwari, B.N. 1978. *A Practical Hindi–English Dictionary*. New Delhi: National Publishing House.

Cole, D.T. 1953. Fanagalo and the Bantu languages of South Africa. *African Studies* 12:1–9. (Repr. in Hymes (ed.) 1964:547–54)

Coteanu, I. 1957. *Cum dispare o limba*? (How does a language die?) Bucharest. (Cited in Dressler and Wodak-Leodolter 1977:6)

Damsteegt, T. 1988. Sarnami: A Living Language. In Barz and Siegel (eds) 1988.

Damsteegt, T. and Narain, J. 1987. *Ká Hál*. The Hague: Nederlands Biblioteek en Lektuur Centrum.

Denison, N. 1977. Language death or language suicide? *International Journal of the Sociology of Language* 12:13–22.

Distribution of Languages in India in States and Union Territories. 1973. Mysore: Central Institute of Indian Languages.

Doke, C.M. and Vilakazi, B.W. 1972. *Zulu–English Dictionary*. Johannesburg: Witwatersrand University Press.

Domingue, N.C. 1971. Bhojpuri and Creole in Mauritius: A Study of Linguistic Interference and its Consequences in regard to Synchronic Variation and Language Change. Ph.D. Thesis, University of Texas.

——— 1981. Internal change in a transplanted variety. *Studies in the Linguistic Sciences* 4:151–59.

Dorian, N. 1973. Grammatical change in a dying dialect. *Language* 49:414–38.

——— 1981. *Language Death: The Life Cycle of a Scottish Gaelic Dialect*. Philadelphia: University of Pennsylvania Press.

Dressler, W. 1972. On the phonology of language death. *Papers from the Eighth Regional Meeting of the Chicago*

Linguistic Society, pp. 448–57.
Dressler, W. and Wodak-Leodolter, R. 1977. Introduction. *International Journal of the Sociology of Language* 12:5–11.
Dunning, A.R. 1901. *A Vocabulary of Hindi, Tamil, and Telugu (in Roman characters)*. Durban.
Emeaneau, M.B. 1956. India as a linguistic area. *Language* 32:3–16. (Repr. in Emeaneau 1980:105–25.)
——— 1980. *Language and Linguistic Area*. Essays edited by A.S. Dil. Stanford: Stanford University Press.
Ferguson, C.A. 1959a. Diglossia. *Word* 15:325–40.
——— 1959b. The Arabic Koine. *Language* 35:616–30.
Ferguson, C.A. and Heath, S.B. 1981. *Language in the USA*. Cambridge: Cambridge University Press.
Fishman, J. (ed.). 1966. *Language Loyalty in the United States*. The Hague: Mouton.
French, A.J. 1908. Indian Missions in Natal. *The Mission Field* 53:150–51.
Gal, S. 1979. *Language Shift*. New York: Academic Press.
Gambhir, S. 1981. The East Indian Speech Community in Guyana: A Sociolinguistic Study with special reference to Koiné-formation. Ph.D. Thesis, University of Pennsylvania.
Gandhi, M.K. 1928. *Satyagraha in South Africa*. Ahmedabed: Navajivan Publishing House.
Ginwala, F.N. 1974. Class, Consciousness and Control: Indian South Africans, 1860–1946. PhD Thesis, University of Oxford.
Greenberg, J. (ed.). 1966. *Universals of Language*. Cambridge, Mass: MIT Press.
Grierson, George, A. 1883–1887. *Seven Grammars of the Dialects and Sub-dialects of the Bihari Language*. Calcutta: Bengal Secretariat Press.
——— 1885. *Bihar Peasant Life*. (Repr. New Delhi: Cosmo Publications 1975)
——— 1903–1928. *Linguistic Survey of India (LSI)*. Calcutta: Government of India; repr. Delhi: Motilal Banarsidass 1967 (11 vols):
1927 Vol. I Part 1 *Introductory*.
1903 Vol. V Part 2 *Bihari and Oriya Languages*.
1904 Vol. VI *Eastern Hindi*.

1916 Vol. IX Part 1 *Western Hindi and Panjabi.*

Gumperz, J.J. 1958. Dialect differences and social stratification in a North Indian village. *American Anthropologist* 60:668–81. (Repr. in Gumperz 1971:25–47)

——— 1971. *Language in Social Groups. Essays edited by A.S. Dil.* Stanford: Stanford University Press.

Gumperz, J.J. and Blom, J. 1972. Social Meaning in Linguistic Structure: Code-Switching in Norway. In Gumperz 1971:274–310.

Gumperz, J.J. and Naim, C.M. 1960. Formal and informal standards in Hindi regional language area. *International Journal of American Linguistics* 26:3. (Repr. in Gumperz 1971:48–76)

Gumperz, J.J. and Wilson, R. 1971. Convergence and Creolization: A Case from the Indo-Aryan Border. In Hymes (ed.) 1971:151–67.

Haas, M. 1968. The last words of Biloxi. *International Journal of American Linguistics* 34:77–84.

Hartshorne, K.B. 1987. Language Policy in African Education in South Africa 1910–1985, with particular reference to the Issue of Medium of Instruction. In D. Young (ed.), *Language: Planning and Medium in Education.* Papers presented at the Fifth Annual Conference of the Southern African Applied Linguistics Association. Cape Town: University of Cape Town.

Hattersley, A.F. 1950. *The British Settlement of Natal.* Cambridge: Cambridge University Press.

Haugen, E. 1953. *The Norwegian Language in American: A Study in Bilingual Behavior.* Philadelphia: University of Pennsylvania Press.

——— 1973. Language Contact and Immigrant Languages in the United States: A Research Report 1956–1970. In Sebeok (ed.) 1973:505–91.

Hill, J. and Hill, K. 1977. Language death and relexification in Tlaxcalan Nahuatl. *International Journal of the Sociology of Language* 12:55–69.

Hoernle, A.F. 1880. *Gaudian Languages with special reference to Eastern Hindi.* London: Trübner and Co.

Hook, P.E. 1974. *The Compound Verb in Hindi.* Ann Arbor, Michigan: Centre for South and Southeast Asian Studies, University of Michigan.

Hudson, R.A. 1980. *Sociolinguistics*. Cambridge: Cambridge University Press.

Huiskamp, A.B. 1978. *Languages of the Guianas*. Vol II. Paramaribo: Summer Institute of Linguistics.

Hutton, J.H. 1963. *Caste in India*. 4 edn. Oxford: Oxford Universty Press.

Hyman, L.M. 1975. On the Change from SOV to SVO: Evidence from Niger-Congo. In Li, C.N. (ed.), *Word Order and Word Order Change*. Austin: University of Texas Press.

Hymes, D. (ed.). 1964. *Language in Culture and Society*. New York: Harper and Row.

——— (ed.) 1971. *Pidginization and Creolization of Languages*. Cambridge: Cambridge University Press.

India. 1973. A Reference Annual. New Delhi: Government of India.

Kachru, B.B. 1983. *The Indianization of English – The English Language in India*. Oxford: Oxford University Press.

Kannemeyer, H.D. 1943. *A Critical Survey of Indian Education in Natal*, 1860–1937. M.Ed. Dissertation, University of the Witwatersrand.

Kellogg, S.H. 1875. *A Grammar of the Hindi Language*. London: Routledge and Kegan Paul.

Kichlu, K.P. 1928. *Memorandum on Indian Education in Natal*. Presented to the Natal Indian Education Inquiry Commission, Pietermaritzburg, 17 April 1928. Pietermaritzburg: Natal Witness.

Kishna, S. 1984. Language and Language Use of the Hindustani in Surinam. Paper presented at the Third Conference on East Indians in the Caribbean. St Augustine: University of the West Indies.

Kloss, H. German–American Language Maintenance Efforts, in Fishman (ed.) 1966:206–52.

Kuper, H. 1960. *Indian People in Natal*. Pietermaritzburg: University of Natal.

Kuppusami, C. 1946. Indian Education in Natal, 1860–1946. M.Ed. Dissertation, University of South Africa.

Labov, W. 1972. *Sociolinguistic Patterns*. Philadelphia: University of Pennsylvania Press.

Ladefoged, P. 1982. *A Course in Phonetics*. 2 edn. New

York: Harcourt, Brace, Jovanovich.
Lanham, L.W. 1978. South African English. In Lanham and Prinsloo (eds) 1978:138–65.
Lanham, L.W. and Prinsloo, K.P. (eds). 1978. *Language and Communication Studies in South Africa*. Cape Town: Oxford University Press.
Lehmann, W.P. 1973. A structural principle of language and its implications. *Language* 49:47–66.
Lister, W. *c.* 1905. Recollections of a Natal Colonist. Unpublished Manuscript. Killie Campbell Collection, University of Natal, Durban.
Macgregor, R.S. 1972. *Outline of Hindi Grammar*. Oxford: Oxford University Press.
Meer, Y.S. 1980. *Documents of Indentured Labour. Natal 1851–1917*. Durban: Institute of Black Research.
Mesthrie, R. 1987. From OV to VO in language shift: South African Indian English and its OV substrates. *English World Wide* 8:263–76.
——— 1988. Toward a lexicon of South African Indian English. *World Englishes*. 7:5–14.
——— 1989. The origins of Fanagalo. *Journal of Pidgin and Creole Languages* 4, 2:211–40.
Miller, W. 1971. The death of language or serendipity among the Shoshoni. *Anthropological Linguistics* 13:114–20.
Milroy, L. 1980. *Language and Social Networks*. Oxford: Basil Blackwell.
——— 1987. *Observing and Analysing Natural Language*. Oxford: Basil Blackwell.
Misra, R.B. 1980. The Social Stratification and Linguistic Diversity in the Bhojpuri Speech Community. PhD Thesis, University of Poona.
Mithun, M. and Henry, R. 1979. Notes on Moribundity: Incipient Obsolescence of Oklahoma Iroquois. Paper presented at the Forty-third International Congress of Americanists. Vancouver, British Columbia.
Moag, R. 1977. *Fiji Hindi: A Basic Course and Reference Grammar*. Canberra: Australian National University Press.
——— 1979. Linguistic Adaptations of the Fiji Indians. In V. Misra (ed.), *Rama's Banishment*. London: Heinemann Educational.

Mohan, P. 1978. Trinidad Bhojpuri: A Morphological Study. PhD Thesis, University of Michigan.
Mohan, P. and Zador, P. 1986. Discontinuity in a life cycle: The death of Trinidad Bhojpuri. *Language*. 62:291–319.
Mühlhäusler, P. 1974. *Pidginization and Simplification of Language*. Pacific Linguistics, Series B, No. 26. Canberra: Australian National University Press.
Nida, E.A. and Fehderau, H.W. 1970. Indigenous Pidgins and Koinés. *International Journal of American Linguistics* 36:146–55.
Nowbath, R.S., Chotai, S., and Lalla, B.D. (eds). 1960. *The Hindu Heritage in South Africa*. Durban: South African Hindu Maha Sabha.
Pachai, B. (ed.). 1979. *South Africa's Indians: The Evolution of a Minority*. Washington: University Press of America.
Palmer, M. 1957. *The History of Indians in Natal*. Vol. X of Natal Regional Survey. Oxford: Oxford University Press.
Pandit, P.B. 1972. Bilingual's Grammar: Tamil-Saurashtri Grammatical Convergence. In P.B. Pandit, *India as a Sociolinguistic Area*. Gaveshkind: University of Poona.
Poplack, S. 1980. Sometimes I'll start a sentence in English Y TERMINO EN ESPAÑOL: Toward a typology of code-switching. *Linguistics* 18:581–618.
Ramanujan, A.K. and Masica, C. 1969. Towards a Phonological Typology of the Indian Linguistic Area. In Sebeok (ed.) 1969: 543–77.
Rambiritch, B. 1960. The History of Mother Tongue Education. In Nowbath *et al.* (eds) 1960:67–73.
Saha, P. 1970. *Emigration of Indian Labour (1834–1900)*. Delhi: People's Publishing House.
Saksena, B.R. 1971. *The Evolution of Awadhi*. 2 edn; repr. of 1931 edn. Delhi: Motilal Banarsidass.
Samarin, W.J. 1971. Salient and Substantive Pidginization. In Hymes (ed.) 1971:117–40.
Sankoff, G. 1979. The Genesis of a Language. In K.C. Hill (ed.), *The Genesis of Language*. Ann Arbor, Michigan: Karoma, pp. 23–47.
Sannyasi, B.D. and Chaturvedi, B. 1931. *Report on Emigrants Repatriated to India under the Assisted Emigration Scheme from South Africa*. Pravasi Bhawan, Bihar: The Authors.

Schmidt, A. 1985. *Young People's Dyirbal – An Example of Language Death from Australia.* Cambridge: Cambridge University Press.
Schmidt, R.L. 1981. *Dakhini Urdu – History and Structure.* New Delhi: Bahri Publications.
Scollon, R. and Scollon, S.B.K. 1979. *Linguistic Convergence: An Ethnography of Speaking at Fort Chipewyan, Alberta.* New York: Academic Press.
Sebeok, T.A. (ed.). 1969. *Current Trends in Linguistics.* Vol V. The Hague: Mouton.
——— (ed.). 1973. *Current Trends in Linguistics.* Vol X. The Hague: Mouton.
Shapiro, M.C. and Schiffman, H.F. 1981. *Language and Society in South Asia.* Delhi: Motilal Banarsidass.
Shukla, S. 1968. Bhojpuri Syntax. PhD Thesis, Cornell University.
——— 1981. *Bhojpuri Grammar.* Washington: Georgetown University Press.
Siegel, J. 1985. Koines and Koineization. *Language in Society* 14:357–78.
——— 1987. *Language Contact in a Plantation Environment – A Sociolinguistic History of Fiji.* Cambridge: Cambridge University Press.
Southworth, F.C. 1971. Detecting Prior Creolization: An Analysis of the Historical Origins of Marathi. In Hymes (ed.). 1971:255–73.
Srivastava, R.N. 1978. *Evaluating Communicability in Village Settings.* New Delhi: Unicef.
Swadesh, M. 1948. Sociologic notes on obsolescent languages. *International Journal of American Linguistics* 14:226–35.
Swan, M. 1985. *Gandhi: The South African Experience.* Johannesburg: Ravan Press.
Thompson, L.M. 1952. *Indian Immigration into Natal (1860–1872).* Archives Yearbook for South African History, Vol 2. Cape Town: Government Printer.
Tinker, H. 1974. *A New System of Slavery: The Export of Indian Labour Overseas, 1830–1920.* Oxford: Oxford University Press.
Tiwari, U.N. 1960. *The Origin and Development of Bhojpuri.* Monograph Series Vol X. Calcutta: The Asiatic

Society.
Tiwary, K.M. 1968. The echo-word construction in Bhojpuri. *Anthropological Linguistics* 10:32–38.
Trammell, R.L. 1971. The phonology of the Northern Standard dialect of Bhojpuri. *Anthropological Linguistics* 13:126–41.
Trapp, O. 1908. Die Isikula-Sprache in Natal, Südafrika. *Anthropos* 3:508–11.
Trudgill, P. 1980. *Sociolinguistics*. Harmondsworth: Penguin.
——— 1983. *On Dialect*. Oxford: Basil Blackwell.
——— 1986. *Dialects in Contact*. Oxford: Basil Blackwell.
Turner, R.L. 1966. *A Comparative Dictionary of the Indo-Aryan Languages*. Oxford: Oxford University Press.
Weinreich, U. 1968. *Languages in Contact*. The Hague: Mouton.
Woolner, A.C. 1975. *An Introduction to Prakrit*. Delhi: Motilal Banarsidass.
Zograph, G.A. 1982. *Languages of South Asia*, trans. G.L. Campbell. London: Routledge and Kegan Paul.

INDEX

abuse, terms of 198–9
adjectives 254, 257, 261
Afrikaans 17, 34, 109, 128–9
'afterthought' syntax 184–5
agricultural terms 167–9
aili-gaili 135–6
Andrews, Revd 3
Apabhraṁśa 13
Arabic 10, 19, 56, 142
Ardha-Māgadhī 13, 15
aspect 224, 269
aspiration 233, 242; see also murmur
Aṣṭādhyāyī 11
auxiliaries 91–3, 98–9; see also modals
Awadhi 14, 15, 24–31, 57, 94–7, 103–104, 116

bahuvrīhi compounds 252
Belvedere 3
Bhawani Dayal Sannyasi 4, 32, 138
Bhojpuri
  Eastern 104–105
  of India 26, 28–32, 57–61, 80–82, 96–105, 241–81
  subdialects in India 57
  Western 104–105
Bihar 20, 72, 106–107, 151
Bihari dialects 24–31, 57–62, 65–7
Bombay Bazaar Hindi 92, 93
borrowings — see loan words
British Guyana — see Guyana
Buddhism 13
Bundeli 107

Calcutta Bazaar Hindi 58, 73, 77–9, 93
calques 179
Cape Indians 32–3
case marking 261
caste 8, 114, 169, 308
causative verbs 224
classifiers 73, 75
clothing terms 152–4, 173–4
code-switching 121–2, 179–82, 294–6
complementation 277–8
compound verbs 271–2
compounds 228, 251–2
conjunctive construction 231
consonants 243–5
co-ordination 257–8, 277
copula 99–100, 188
counter-factuals 270–71
currency units 151–2

Dakhini Urdu 92, 113; see also Urdu
deletion of subject 281
desiderative construction (*honā*) 91–2
deśya words 249
determinative compounds 252
determiners 266
Devanāgarī 30
diglossia 106, 118–9, 121–2
domestic terms 154–6, 171–4
Dravidian languages 10, 11, 15
Dutch 1, 142
dvandva compounds 251

echo words 228, 252
education 17, 18, 38–40
  Indian language education 18, 32, 129–32, 134–5, 138–9
emphatic construction in *-be* 87–8
English 1, 17, 18, 109–14, 117–28
ergative construction 86
Europeans in Natal 2–3, 111

Fanagalo 17, 34, 91, 109–11, 116–7, 128, 144
field methods 36–40
Fiji 2, 3, 72, 131
  Fiji Hindi 27, 72–3, 91, 130, 133, 136

films (language of) 135
food terms 81, 219

Gaelic 201, 203–208
Gandhi 3, 7, 143
gender
  nouns 259–61
  verbs 94
greetings 193–4
Grierson's classifications 14–15, 24–5, 31, 57, 79–81
Gujarati 1, 15, 17, 18, 23, 113, 118, 129, 139, 147
Guyana 2, 72, 130
  Guyanese Bhojpuri 26, 63, 73–6, 130, 133

/h/ 158, 237–8; see also murmur
Hindi
  Eastern Hindi 25–30, 58–61, 80–89
  in India 23, 106–109, 183
  in South Africa 16, 24–36, 111, 132–9
  Std Hindi 36–7, 58–61, 72, 80–9, 102, 106–109, 117, 129, 182
  Western Hindi 25–30, 58–61, 80–89
Hindustani 1, 111, 308

illiteracy 1
imperatives 88, 101
impersonal datives 230, 281
indenture 2–6, 141–3
indentured workers (origins) 5–6
India — ties with 7, 37
Indian Immigration School Board 7
Indic language family 10–15
infinitive 273
interpreters 112
interrogatives 279–80
Irish 206
Iroquois 206

Jainism 13
Jamaica 3
jingles 197–8

Kaithi 30
Kalkatiyā bāt 26, 141
kinship terms 81
koine formation 55–62, 113–7
Konkani 16

language death Ch. 5
language shift Ch. 4
  external histories 202–204
  reasons for 130–39
lexical retention 219–22
lexis
  lexical loss 166–74
  lexical variation 52–5
  of IB 248–54
  of SB 79–83
linguistic insecurity 132–7
Linguistic Survey of India 23, 79–80
loanwords
  and indenture 141–3
  and semi-speakers 215–6
  blends 178
  European loans 250–51
  from Fanagalo 143–5
  from Perso-Arabic 250
  from Tamil 146–7
  in India 140–57
  morphological form 174–8
  recent loans 156–7
  translations 179

macaronics 197–8
Māgadhī 13
Magahi 24–5, 28–31, 63, 66, 81
Mahābhārata 11, 30
Maithili 24–5, 28–31, 66, 81
Malayalam 15
matrimonial terms 82
Mauritius 2, 3, 6, 7, 72, 131, 133
  Franco-Mauritians 111
  Indo-Mauritians 7, 26
  Mauritian Creole 153
  Mauritian Bhojpuri 26, 73, 130–31, 133, 153
Meman 15, 147
missionaries 1, 117
modals 186, 224, 272–3
morphological change 174–8
Munda languages 10, 11, 15
murmur 160–61, 233, 242

nasal vowels 238, 242
nasal consonants 242
negatives 256–7
Norwegian (in America) 133, 178
noun modifiers 86, 225
noun phrase 258–67
number (nouns) 261

obligative construction 86–7
onomatopoeia 200, 253–4
oral traditions 193–200

Pāli 13
Panjabi 10, 15, 24, 57
passenger Indians 6–7
passives 274–5
Pennsylvania German 130
Persian 14, 178
Perso-Arabicisms 250
phonetic selection 84–5
phonological change 157–62
phonological features of
  Bhojpuri 83–5, 241–8
pidginisation 56, 204–5; see also
  Fanagalo
place names 147–8
plantations 2–4, 111
plant names 148–51
polysemy 217–9
Population Census 6, 16, 19–20
postpositions 257, 262–3
Prakrits 10, 13, 15
prefixes 257
prestige, lack of 132–7, 139
priests (language of) 134, 138
pronoun system 96–8, 265–6
Protector of Emigrants 2, 7, 17,
  110, 143
proverbs 194–6

Rāmāyana 11, 14, 30
recruitment patterns 72
reduplication 103, 253–4, 270
reflexives 225, 256
relative clauses 255, 275–6
repatriation 7, 8, 308
'respect' feature 100–102
retroflex consonants 10–11, 242,
  243

Sanskrit 10–13, 109, 117, 178
Sarnami (Hindi) 63, 72–5, 130, 133
Śauraseni (Prakrit) 13, 15
semantic change 162–6, 214–5
semi-speaker
  definition 203–204
  lexical characteristics 214–21
  morphology and syntax 221–33
  of SB 208–39
  phonetics 233–9
  social characteristics 204–13
sickness and disease terms 154
simplification 94–105
socio-economic value (of
  Bhojpuri) 137–9
stress 247–8
style-shifting 107–108, 136
subject deletion 281
subjunctives 270, 271
Suriname 2, 63, 72; see Sarnami
  Hindi
syllables 247–8
syntactic features 85–93
  syntactic change 183–9
  syntactic convergence 189–92
syntactic loss 229–30

tadbhavas 248–9
Tamil 1, 10, 16–18, 36, 112–3,
  117–8, 129, 131, 138
Tasmanian 202
tatsamas 248–9
Telugu 1, 10, 16, 36, 112, 118, 129
temporal terms 82
tense 268–9
Texas German 130
Tibeto-Burman languages 10, 15,
  308
Transvaal Indians 32
Trinidad 2, 72
  Trinidad Bhojpuri 26, 63, 73–6,
    130, 133, 205, 233
Truro 3

Urdu 1, 16–17, 19, 113, 129, 139;
  see Dakhini Urdu
Uttar Pradesh 20, 30, 106–107, 151

verb morphology 41–55, 62–75,
  88–93, 94–6, 222–5
verbal noun 273–4
vocabulary — see lexis
vowel systems 245–7

word-order change 183–6, 229

Yahi 202

Zograph's classification 15, 16, 31
Zulu 17, 34, 117, 128, 142, 145–6

For Product Safety Concerns and Information please contact our EU representative GPSR@taylorandfrancis.com
Taylor & Francis Verlag GmbH, Kaufingerstraße 24, 80331 München, Germany

www.ingramcontent.com/pod-product-compliance
Lightning Source LLC
Chambersburg PA
CBHW052031300426
44116CB00024B/1147
* 9 7 8 1 1 3 8 3 5 2 8 9 6 *